A Pictorial Record of

GREAT WESTERN ARCHITECTURE

by A. Vaughan

Overleaf
The Board Room of the Great Western Railway at Paddington.

British Rail

A Pictorial Record of

GREAT WESTERN ARCHITECTURE

by A. Vaughan

Oxford Publishing Co.

DEDICATION

To my friend Paul Dye,
A book for pleasure,
Not a sales catalogue.

ISBN 0–902888-22-6

Photo reproduction by:
Oxford Litho Plates Ltd.

Printed in Great Britain by:
Biddles Ltd., Guildford, Surrey.

Published by:
Oxford Publishing Company
Link House
West Street
POOLE
Dorset

Acknowledgements

My grateful thanks are due to all those who helped me write this book. Mr. MacDonald and his staff in the Photographic Section of the Chief Civil Engineer's office, who printed dozens of photographs for me when they were inundated with their real work. The Chief Public Relations Officer, Mr. Hodson and his lieutenants Mr. Montague and Mr. Gallagher who were collecting material for the project before it was handed to me. Mr. P.S.A. Berridge travelled up from Teignmouth to Bath to give me a crash course in bridges and to explain the mysteries of those at Chepstow and Saltash. He also allowed me to quote from his excellent book, 'The Girder Bridge'. As a result of this meeting I met Mr. Creed who is second in command of civil engineering on Western Region and in charge of the steel work section of the drawing office at Paddington. He patiently gave me his time and explained steel bridges. From his office it is a short step to the Plans Room of the same department where Mr. L. Szczyrba is in charge. He has made a study of Brunel's works through the original plans which he lovingly tends and is gradually rehabilitating from their decayed state. Without his attention dozens of original drawings by Brunel would have been lost forever. Sean Bolan who gave a lot of helpful suggestions concerning Brunel stations and loaned me his collection of photographs for reference. Through this I contacted Mr. Maggs and Mr. Toop who sent photographs at a moment's notice when the book was almost complete. Mr. Roberts, Works Manager of British Rail Engineering (Swindon) Ltd., found me trespassing, unwittingly, and forgave me, writing out a valid permit on a piece of paper torn from his notebook. Mr. E.J. Nutty of Swindon talked to me about the 'new town' of Swindon and was courteous and helpful as always. Messrs. Siviter-Smith of Birmingham took special pains to get the best possible photographs from the ancient working drawings Colin Judge sent them, courtesy of Chief Civil Engineer and Public Relations Office. There was a great deal of friendly co-operation on all sides. Paul Dye kept a constant interest in the book, supplied mysterious details of Campanology and let me see old surveys which often cleared up a contentious point. Mr. T. Renshaw re-drew my pencil sketches of cottages and bridge parts and Mr. John Morris, Hon. Sec. of the Signalling Record Society, drove from Warminster to Carmarthen and back to photograph a mile post for me. Everyone was kind and helpful, and not least my wife, Susan, who had to put up with my moods when the going was heavy.

Contents

Author's Preface

In this book I have tried to cover a wide range of buildings seen on the Great Western Railway, from the beautiful stations designed by Isambard Kingdom Brunel to the standardised, corrugated iron huts of the early 20th century and the steel framed office blocks of the 1930's. I have tried to show the development on the Great Western Railway, of bridges and viaducts, from those of Brunel to the mid-20th century. There are sections showing the main types of footbridge, signal box, and engine shed that one would find on the Great Western Railway and an appendix containing a miscellaneous collection of pictures from lamp posts to lavatories.

The enormous genius of Brunel illuminated the early scene on the Great Western Railway. Brunel influenced other people's designs for railway buildings and built railways for Companies other than the Great Western, so it will be found, on reading the book, that items have been included which, strictly speaking, did not belong to the Great Western Railway but were designed by Brunel or very strongly influenced by him. To have adhered to the strict title of the book would have meant omitting several interesting features. In the early part of the section on stations I have denied Brunel the credit for the design of some minor stations. This was to set in order what I regard as the true record, hair-splitting some may call it, whatever it may be, it is not an attempt to denigrate the 19th century's greatest engineer and one of the modern world's most remarkable men.

I have no qualifications to write this book other than a lifelong admiration for all the works of the old Company and a wish to communicate this admiration to others. One lesson I had to learn was the architectural names for the various parts of buildings, here's hoping that I learnt the lesson well and have not made any awful blunders! There is, I believe, a great deal of information in the book which I hope is accurate, some of it took a lot of worrying over before I felt confident enough of its accuracy to put it in the text. I hope you enjoy the book as much as I did writing it.

Glossary of Terms

DENTILS	Row of rectangular or square mouldings or bricks which alternately project and recess to form a regular pattern, usually just below the eaves of a building.
FASCES	Originally the Roman symbol of authority. A bundle of rods bound around an axe. Used for architectural decoration in stylised form.
GROIN	Corners of the bricks around a window opening or of the brick columns dividing a window.
HIPS, HIP ROOF	Gables fall back to form small triangular area of sloping roof.
LANTERN LIGHT	Raised, glazed portion above general level of roof.
LOUVRE	Sloping, overlapping strips to exclude rain but allow passage of air, steam or smoke.
PEDIMENT	Triangular shape formed at gables. Originates from Classical Greece.
PILASTER	Rectangular pillar set close against a wall.
PLINTH	Lower part of wall.
SOFFIT	Lower edge of arch or beam.

Bibliography

"History of the Great Western Railway." Vols. 1 & 2. E.T. MacDermot.

"Isambard Kingdom Brunel." L.T.C. Rolt.

"Economic and Social History of England." Briggs and Jordan.

"Historical Survey of Great Western Engine Sheds." E. Lyons.

"The Girder Bridge." P.S.A. Berridge.

The original drawings of stations and bridges held at Paddington.

Documents held at the Public Record Office (B.T.C. Archives) 66 Porchester Road, Paddington.

Great Western Railway Magazine, P.R.O. ref. PER 20 et seq.

Report of Staff Housing. 1918. P.R.O. ref. GW. 18.

Statement of Station Master's houses 1890. GW. 18.

Great Western Railway standard stations. Railway Engineer. 1904. PER 4.

Report on distortion in the old and new roofs at Paddington. 1915. GW 18.

Introduction

Bristol, mediaeval city, maritime, mercantile, magnificent. Home of the Merchant Adventurers, whose deft dealing, slave trading (black and white, no prejudice), shrewd speculation, hard bargaining and flair for daring enterprise made the city second only to London in a Kingdom clashing and clanking with the noise of ten thousand fortunes being made in a score of cities. Bristol, the city where ships' masts stood like forest trees in a clearing of the labyrinth of timber tiered houses. The merchants, alert to the changing winds of trade, as to the variations of the trade winds at sea, proposed to build a railway, for freight only, from Bristol to Brentford Docks a year before George Stephenson had completed his Stockton and Darlington Railway, the first in the land. The proposed 'Bristol and London Rail Road' of 1824 was received enthusiastically and died the death reserved for all objects of sudden, unthinking, public adulation. The dead proposal had included a plan for a turnpike road to be built alongside the railway to enter the towns that the railway 'would of necessity be forced to avoid'. It had also planned to use mobile, self-contained steam engines to haul the trains, a wildly speculative notion in 1824. The Cotswold ridge had been dismissed by the engineer as mere undulations in the surface of the ground. The bold merchants of the city eagerly took up the shares but later discretion took the better part of valour and when payment for shares was called in, the hard cash was not forthcoming. No-one was surprised, nor tried to resuscitate the ill-considered plan when it died of cash starvation.

Eight years later, reform was in the wind, sensitive and thoughtful men were being heard, and, more important, understood. The year 1832 saw the reform of the voting laws and the first meeting of four Bristol men who were to found the Great Western Railway. George Jones and John Harford, of the recently completed Bristol and Gloucestershire Railway, Thomas Guppy, a merchant, and William Tothill, also a merchant and a member of Bristol Chamber of Commerce, met quietly with no publicity in a small office, determined to build a railway from Bristol to London. They decided to organise the venture under two committees, one sitting at Bristol the other in London, and on the 21st January 1833 the first meeting of the 'Bristol and London Rail Road' took place at Bristol. It was the year of the Abolition of Slavery Act becoming law. At the first meeting the committee had to choose an Engineer from among twenty-three applicants. Their choice fell upon the twenty-seven year old, comparatively unknown, Isambard Kingdom Brunel. Within eight months of his appointment he had changed the title of the undertaking from the matter of fact 'Bristol and London' to the romantically evocative, 'Great Western Railway'. Continuing with imagination unabated, he struggled against opposition from men and the elements, with only elementary manual aids for his assistance, to construct his railway. He proceeded with such skill and energy that he created not only a railway but an immortal legend. The construction was to be he said, 'the finest work in England'. And it was.

Isambard's father, Marc, was a successful engineer who lived among what was then called 'good society'. He had fled from the terror of the French Revolution and eventually settled in England, bringing with him the secret art of three dimensional drawing for constructional plans and an inventor's brain. The former was a French military secret and a great advance on the usual sketches that craftsmen had to work from, so one would have thought that he would have been received with open arms by the British government, but he was treated with suspicion. He invented a process for the manufacture of ships' blocks, the machinery for which was manufactured by the great firm of Maudslay Son and Field but this venture only led him into bankruptcy when the government wriggled out of its monetary promises to him. Lodged in the King's Bench prison for debtors, the 'Marshalsea' of Charles Dickens 'Little Dorrit', the Czar of Russia offered to pay his debts if he would go to Russia and set up his factory there. At this the Duke of Wellington arrived with the sum of £5,000 and Marc was released to join society. The period was rarely mentioned in the family and when it was they called it 'The Misfortune'.

Marc Brunel was released from prison in 1821 when his son had recently returned from France. During the father's unjust incarceration he had managed to ensure his son's education, first in England and later, between the age of fourteen and sixteen in Paris. Here Isambard had attended the Lycee Henri-Quatre, famous for its mathematics teachers, and for a while had worked under the greatest watch, clock and instrument maker in Europe, Louis Bréguet. Returning at sixteen he entered his father's office and worked there on the everyday items in an engineering drawing office. He also spent a lot of time in the works of Henry Maudslay and so learned at first hand the problems of the engineering of the time. After two years of this 'apprenticeship' he was plunged into the first great work of his life: boring a tunnel beneath the Thames between Rotherhithe and Wapping. It was with this background of accomplished craftsmanship and practical experience that Isambard Kingdom Brunel began to construct the Great Western Railway. Very little he left to others, almost every detail was the result of his imagination, certainly every problem was overcome with his ingenuity. It is not surprising therefore that the railway should have been so well constructed both in practical and aesthetic terms.

In drawing up his designs Brunel had to contend with two masters, the London and Bristol Committees under whose jurisdiction the line was divided. These bodies had differing opinions as to the amount of money it was permissible to spend on fine stations and embellishments generally, the Bristol men being more generous than their London based colleagues. This, in part explains why the stations at the eastern end of the line were so lacking in style. There were other reasons: the country traversed by the Bristol section was hilly and therefore lent itself to fine cuttings, bridges and tunnels, there were a great number of wealthy landowners in the area which gave further incentive to elegant design and construction, and last but not least, there was a plentiful supply of best quality building stone with which to construct the stations and tunnel portals and to form the elegant cornices, balusters and other embellishments with which Brunel decorated his work.

The Great Western Railway Act received Royal Assent on 31st August 1835. The science of railway building was in its infancy, indeed, one might say that it had yet to be born with Brunel, the chief midwife. George Stephenson, 'Father of Railways', used crude methods without much thought behind them. For instance, his permanent way was formed of cast iron rails on massive stone blocks. There were no sleepers, the inertia of the blocks being considered enough to keep the rails to gauge. Stephenson's road could not be 'packed' so that uneven alignment due to traffic movement over it could not be rectified except at great expense. Brunel brought his keen, unorthodox mind to bear on this and other problems which other engineers seemed to accept and had not tried to improve. Today there are a variety of engineers and architects, practitioners in soil mechanics, and a number of other specialists whose advice can be sought before an undertaking is begun. The early railway engineers were all these experts rolled into one, Brunel in particular. He thought of the constructional idea, saw the problems that would arise and how to overcome them. Relatively vast works were undertaken, affecting the lives and safety of all who have used them over the past 149 years, the responsibility for their well-being falling upon the man who made the plans and his vision in forestalling weaknesses in construction. This Brunel and the others did with little or no past experience to refer to, relying instead on their own, usually unfailing genius. A list of what they did not have to assist them would be nearly as long as the 140 years that separates our times, suffice to say that with a pencil and paper they drew their plans, with 'O' level arithmetic they made their calculations, and with the aid of horse, spade and wheelbarrow they brought their great works to life.

Brunel had few assistants to help him and those he had were often more of a hindrance (see 'Isambard Kingdom Brunel', by L.T.C. Rolt, p.107) and he had to train them as he designed the railway. This railway, which had taken shape in his head and which he was now causing to materialise, grew unorthodox and splendid. It was to be part of a line of communication from London to New York, an entire transport system of hotels, road and rail vehicles, ships and harbours. The track was unique in its gauge of 7′ 0¼″ and in the method of laying it on the ground. Nothing was done out of slavish following of precedent but all was the result of Brunel's imagination. With the exception of a few details, like the goods shed at Wallingford Road station (disused since 1892) which was designed by his assistant J.H. Bertram, Brunel designed the entire railway, 118 miles from Paddington to Bristol, the cuttings, stations, embankments, bridges and even the lamp standards on the station platforms. Brunel would not have produced all the drawings necessary to build the line, for each bridge needed half a dozen plans, but he made sketches, sometimes in pencil, of every item on the line with the dimensions he required and handed these to one of a number of draughtsmen who would eventually produce a set of water-colour tinted drawings to be used at the site of construction. Besides these working drawings there had also to be made contract drawings which were included with each legal document drawn up detailing the agreement between the Company and the contractor carrying out the work. There were also Parliamentary plans to be made for the information of the various committees of the House which were investigating the claims of rival concerns to the Great Western, or perhaps a lawsuit. The outline of the figure, a tunnel portal or a bridge or station was drawn to scale complete with measurements, in indian ink on cartridge paper, and was then shaded with colour wash in various tints to show light and shade thereby giving a three dimensional appearance to the plan; each nut, bolt and rivet had its highlight and shadow to give 'roundness' to what would otherwise have been a flat octagon or circle on the paper. His early plans were made very handsome, almost works of art, by this technique. Brunel was a clever worker in watercolours as his 'artist's impression' of his proposed suspension bridge over the Avon at Clifton shows, (see L.T.C. Rolt 'Isambard Kingdom Brunel'), he was also a very quick and dextrous worker to produce so many fine plans so perfectly. When the drawings—or paintings—were complete Brunel passed them for use by marking them with his elegant, rapidly done, signature. Most, if not all, of the drawings for the Great Western Railway between 1835 and 1841 bear his signature but then, as the volume of work increased when new railways were contemplated, his assistants, now well trained, drew and signed the plans for routine work leaving Brunel to concentrate of heavier matters.

A train stopping at all stations from Paddington to Bristol in 1845 would have called at a succession of pretty country stations, each one differing from the last yet all of them bearing the 'family likeness' and all sympathetic to the mood of the area. There were yellow brick stations in the London area, red brick between Slough and Reading, gradually giving way to timber or flint and limestone as the line curved up the Thames Valley and into the remote Vale of the White Horse, to run parallel to the high chalk ridge of the Berkshire Downs. West of Swindon, creamy Bath stone was Brunel's building material. One could have judged, roughly, how far along the route one had progressed by the substance used to build a station's walls. The town stations were not always as well made as those in the country, Slough and Reading had stations as ugly as Box and Pangbourne were pretty but apart from this there was an overall continuity of design and a completeness about the Great Western Railway which we today can only guess at. The succession of neat stations between Paddington and Slough were swept away during the quadruplings of the 1870's and the rest, as far as Didcot, were demolished during the 1890's; practically all the survivors were destroyed between 1965 and 1975 when British Rail withdrew stopping train facilities. Not only was the Great Western Railway and British Rail ruthless in the removal of the buildings, but the former destroyed many of the old plans and during the 1939-45 war fire destroyed many more. So we can never know what all the original stations looked like. In the following pages, before we come to my selection of photographs, I will trace what I can of the architectural styles of Brunel and mention a little of the history of some stations.

As there are so few wayside stations surviving which were built by Brunel, it is difficult to make a survey of his architectural styles for this sort of station and come to a definite conclusion. For instance, between Paddington, Swindon and Oxford, a distance of nearly eighty miles, only the Hotel buildings of the old Moulsford station, Culham, Steventon, Challow and Shrivenham were standing in 1967. Today, 1976, only the Moulsford buildings and Culham remain. Photographs are a help in the search for styles in station architecture but many stations were rebuilt before they could be photographed. It is not possible to say, therefore that Brunel built x types of wayside station. It seems likely that he built at least four basic styles, but even this classification does not embrace all known styles, there is one awkward customer which does not fit into the classification – Box station. One could say, however, that this station was so elaborate that, although it may have been considered as a wayside station in 1950, Brunel regarded it as being of greater importance and built accordingly. *Figure 1* shows what I imagine to be the four basic styles for wayside stations by Brunel.

Roofs and awnings formed the most distinctive feature of these buildings. In style 'A' one has the steep pitched roof with an awning supported on beams which lie across the building from wall to wall and project beyond the walls to support the canopy. Type 'B' has an awning constructed in the same manner as 'A' but with a low pitched roof. Type 'C' has a steep pitched roof which spreads wide enough at the eaves to form the platform canopy, and type 'D' has a low pitched roof which forms the canopy over the platform. I think that buildings constructed to the general outline of type 'A' are the most handsome of the four styles. If such a building was in red brick it often had a limestone string course in the gable, underlining, so to speak, the coping stones lining the outer edge of the roof. Brunel was an artist as well as an engineer and varied basic design slightly so that the succession of stations along the line did not appear monotonously the same. He used diamond shaped chimneys as shown in type 'A', or a stack carrying stone slabs as in type 'C'. The former is usually associated with type 'A' but the diamond shaped chimney could be used on any of the styles. Brunel built his chimneys in limestone but sulphur and rainwater corroded the stone and the Company had to rebuild most of the old chimneys in brick. Windows and doors could be 'square headed' or have slightly pointed arches, though in the case of type 'C', I believe Brunel favoured an Italian, semicircular arch. Where windows were 'square headed' the panes of glass were fixed in mullions, the other types of window having simple wooden frames. Further diversity could be attained, whilst retaining the standard outline, by varying the building material. Brunel built his stations in brick, flint stone, limestone, timber or a combination of stone and brick. Steventon and Challow were built in the general outline of type 'B', in timber, Shrivenham was also type 'B' but constructed in flint with limestone quoins. That Steventon station should have been built in timber is surprising because the station was built to serve Oxford, and the guides and gazetteers of the time referred to it as 'a station of the first class'. Brunel had built here, for the Company's Officers, two fine stone houses and a row of eleven terraced cottages in brick after the Tudor style. The terrace was of single storey and built parallel to the down main line between the station and the first level crossing, Stocks Lane. Brunel designed them with four gables, two at either end, one facing east and one facing north, while at the western end one faced west and the other north. Brunel had designed the terrace with an inlay of geometrical patterns using two colours of brick but in recent times the inlay had become obscured by dirt. All doors and windows, which had leaded, diamond shaped panes, were finished off with Tudor cap or hood over their lintels. The terrace was destroyed about 1968. But to return to my description of Brunel's wayside stations. The awning which he designed for types 'A' and 'B' had four distinctive features, it extended all round the building, it had no valance board, it appeared to have no slope to run off rain water, and

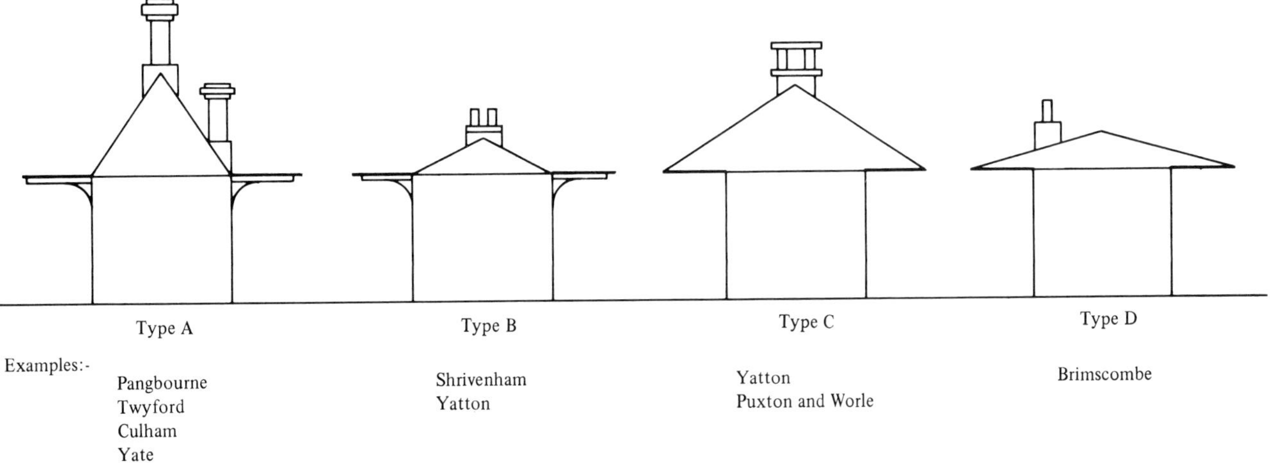

Figure 1

the method of weather-proofing the upper surface produced an instantly recognisable style. This weather-proofing was sheet lead fixed to the canopy with flat sided, round topped battens over which the lead was rolled. The effect was a shiny, ribbed surface which was decorative in a peculiar way.

Brunel's designs for principal stations can be categorised as those of the 'one-sided' type and those of conventional layout, the latter being subdivided into those with and those without an overall roof. The 'one-sided' station was one of Brunel's less successful ideas. He arranged that the up and down main lines should pass clear of the platforms which were ranged along one side of the tracks, each platform a separate station with its own offices for tickets and parcels. The two platforms were not connected so that one had to walk out of one station, along the street and into the other if one was changing from an up to a down train. This type of track layout involved up and down trains crossing running lines, which might have been dangerous in the early days before signalling was effective, but no more so than at any other junction. In later years, when traffic had in-

Figure 2

Charfield Station, on the Bristol and Gloucester Railway, was designed by Brunel and opened in 1844. Except for the lack of a bay window at the further end of the building, beneath what is left of the awning, the station is identical to that erected at Twyford in 1838. The waiting shed on the opposite platform is also by Brunel and has the typical pointed arch over the doorway.

Colin Maggs 11.5.61

Figure 3 Chippenham Station around 1841.
British Rail

creased, the arrangement was a nuisance because safety regulations over the crossings caused a great deal of delay to trains trying to get into the station. But that was in the future. Brunel has said of this type of station, 'Nothing but experience will determine whether the one-sided station is more safe or more dangerous than an ordinary station but it is a very convenient arrangement, it gives great accommodation to the passengers'. Certainly there were no stairs for passengers to climb. There were four of these stations, at Exeter, Taunton, Reading and Slough, the last to be replaced was that at Reading in 1897/98.

Of the six principal stations between Paddington and Bristol which Brunel constructed in a two-sided layout, four had overall roofs; Paddington, Didcot, Bath and Bristol. That at Didcot (see MacDermot, vol. 1 p.100) was probably the most peculiar building, perhaps one ought to say the *only* peculiar building which Brunel designed. Swindon and Chippenham were built without overall roofs, the latter being more in the nature of a wayside than market town station. It was in the general style of type 'D' in my catalogue of wayside stations in *figure 1.* Two of its chimneys were in the same style as those at Box while the third was disguised as an Italian campanile. Below the eaves the window and door arches were semi-circular, again in the Italian style. *Figure 3* illustrates the building and Brunel's marvellous 'Egyptian' goods shed opposite the station which makes a lovely contrast of rectangles against circles and triangles. From such a design as this did Brunel's assistants derive the imitations that were erected on the Berks and Hants line and elsewhere. There do not appear to have been many stations of intermediate size. Stroud and Chippenham, which one might have expected to possess a station at least as fine as Cirencester's, had little, low buildings like a wayside station. Keynsham, which was merely a village near Bath, was blessed with a tall gabled station office on the lines of Steventon's houses for Officers. If one wanted to point to Brunel's medium size station building one would make an example of Cirencester and Keynsham.

The line from Paddington to Bristol was opened in sections between 1838 and 1841, the last section being that from Chippenham to Bath, through the Box Tunnel, which was opened on 30th June, 1841. Brunel was then thirty-five. The task had taken six years during which time his daring and original ideas had made him internationally famous, but perhaps more important to him, he had collected a team of well-trained assistants who knew his business and made it their own. Several names survive in the pages of catalogues of drawings; J. Geddes, J. Nolloth, J.R. Hannaford, Mr. Prinsit and W.G. Owen, the latter to become Chief Engineer in time. Two about whom a little more is known were R.P. Brereton, who supervised the launching and lifting of the Devon span of the Royal Albert Bridge, Brunel being very ill at the time, and J.H. Bertram, who was Chief Engineer in all but name from August 1857 until eight months after Brunel's death in September 1859. Therefore, it is safe to say that Brunel personally designed the stations and nearly all the other constructions on the Great Western Railway between Paddington and Bristol. These designs were also carried onto the Bristol & Exeter Railway, the Bristol & Gloucester Railway, and even on to the Taff Vale, the Oxford Railway and the Cheltenham & Great Western Union Railway, all these being under construction between 1835 and 1844. However, one cannot be so sure about the other routes of which he was engineer which gained Parliamentary and Royal Assent after 1845. These other routes included those of the Oxford, Worcester & Wolverhampton Railway, the Oxford & Rugby Railway and also those of the Berks & Hants, the Wilts, Somerset & Weymouth, and the South Wales Railway. With a team of trusted assistants he could leave details like stations to them and concentrate on more important engineering matters. There was a large pool of experience for the assistants to draw from, dozens of stations having been built, and they well knew what Brunel would like.

The stations on the Berks & Hants line were very 'Brunelian' but there is no proof that Brunel personally designed them. The one at Aldermaston was probably a derivation of earlier designs used at Yatton or Puxton & Worle, and Midgham could well be the work of an assistant in a vaguely Brunelian theme. The Berks & Hants line was opened in December 1847 and ten months later the first part of the Wilts, Somerset & Weymouth, from Thingley to Westbury, was opened. By this time, there had been drawn up, at Paddington or at Brunel's office in Duke Street, plans for what were termed 'standard stations' in two distinct styles and sizes. One could choose between large and small size Italianate or Gothic. None of these drawings were signed by Brunel but by J. Geddes and I. Nolloth. As it has been established that Brunel never signed anything that was not his work it is reasonable to suppose that these new standard plans were not the work of the Master but solely that of the assistants, though the former's influence is very strong. Unfortunately none of these drawings for standard stations have survived to be compared with actual buildings, so we cannot say for certain which stations were erected to these standard designs, we only know of the drawings through ancient catalogues which have been preserved. Melksham and Trowbridge, both opened in 1848, were built to the Geddes/Nolloth plan and stations on the Salisbury line, with the exception of Warminster, were the work of R.P. Brereton who also designed the stations between Frome and Dorchester. In the case of the Salisbury line stations, Brereton's design was approved so highly by Brunel that he included them in a book he wrote on the construction of railways. The stations west of Frome – Witham (see *figure 4*), Bruton, Castle Cary, Sparkford, Marston Magna, Yetminster and Maiden Newton, were all of very similar design, larger or smaller, and built in a variety of materials, brick, stone or flint. Evershot was the odd man out, being constructed in timber to a design which was used extensively between Oxford and Birmingham except that the latter were constructed in stone. Both lines were constructed at about the same time.

On the South Wales Railway not one drawing in a hundred was signed by Brunel who appears to have reserved his time for great works like the Wye Bridge, the S.S. Great Eastern, and a portable 1500 bed hospital for the Crimean War. All the usual names appear in the catalogues of South Wales Railway drawings, Hannaford who designed many

Figure 4

Waiting room on the downside at Witham. The design is by R.P. Brereton but see how the chimney follows closely the example set by Brunel. The rafters have been used very cleverly to form a dentil-like pattern by allowing them to project beneath the eaves.

R.E. Toop 20.6.59

around Cardiff, Lancaster Owen who designed Chepstow station, Neath and Newport, and R.P. Brereton's name appears, responsible for bridges and embankments. The same tale can be repeated for the Oxford & Birmingham line. One curious detail regarding stations erected during 1846-56 is the representation in cast iron of a lion's head, which was placed at three or four feet intervals along the edge of the platform awning. Where the woodwork was not deep enough to accommodate the casting a special plaque was fitted. These decorations were to be seen all over the system, from Clynderwen, in West Wales, to Mutley at Plymouth and Kidlington near Oxford. One was fixed to the front of the Gloucester Junction Signal Cabin at Swindon in 1873 and survived until the end of manual signalling there in 1968.

Concerning the famous overall roofs of the Great Western Railway, it can be said that Brunel built the most beautiful of these, and his designs formed the pattern for all future designs, none of which came up to his own standard of workmanship. The Great Western Railway traversed an area full of wealthy people and had a unique traffic of private carriages to be conveyed between intermediate stations. It was considered essential that these passengers had ample shelter while they were on the platforms and ample rooms in which they might wait for their trains. Hence the large number of stations fully enclosed from the elements. After 1845 it is unlikely that Brunel designed any of these overall roofs. We know that the station at Westbury, (*figure 5*) which had enclosed platforms, was designed by J. Geddes, who also drew the roof for Basingstoke, both stations being very crude and not at all like the elegant Geddes stations at Melksham and elsewhere. The roof at Warminster station was very similar to that at Frome, the former being the work of J.H. Bertram, and the latter of J.R. Hannaford. Hannaford was also responsible for the goods and engine sheds at Frome but the timber viaduct over the Frome river on the Westbury side of the station was designed by Brereton. J.H. Bertram made some five overall roofs, two of them being at Merthyr and Weymouth. At Merthyr each rafter had a curved soffit but at Weymouth only the outer rafter had this shape, the rest being the usual triangular shape. Brunel built the roofs at Bristol, Bath, Didcot, Reading, Windsor, Slough, Paddington and Exeter but all others were scaled down versions of

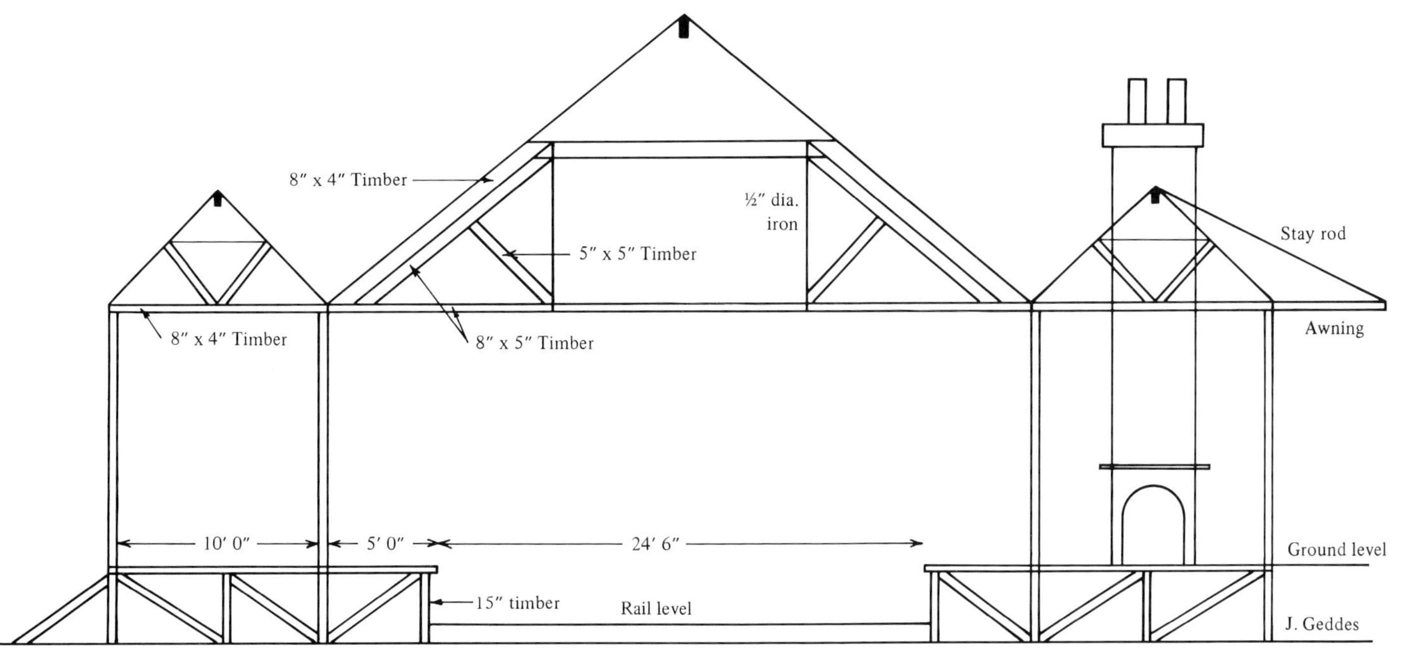

Figure 5

A cross section of the original timber station erected at Westbury (Wilts) during 1847-48. An additional platform was probably added between the existing platforms during 1852-1855. The building was demolished during 1898-99. Diagram made from the 1847 plans.

Figure 6

The downside exterior at Taunton station about 1905. The overall roof of the station was erected after Brunel's one-sided layout had been removed but one of the old station booking offices was retained for use at the new station. There is a similarity between this building and that built for the one-sided station at Reading, see *plate 64* in Chapter One.

British Rail

Brunel's conception carried out by his assistants. This is not to say that the great man lost his influence over the work in this and all the other fields of building on the Great Western Railway, but simply that as he became more famous he became more concerned with great works – his portable hospital for the Crimean War for instance – and therefore left the lesser problems to the men he had trained. His influence continued to be felt, and seen, in the stations built after his death in 1859, until 1870.

Brunel signed his last report, as Engineer, to the Great Western Railway Board of Directors in August 1857. He spent most of the next two years in Egypt and Switzerland and was generally in very poor health, so that he was no more than Consulting Engineer to the Company, (an office that he detested and had, on more than one occasion, refused), the day to day work being undertaken by Brunel's assistant J.H. Bertram. After Brunel's death in September 1859, Bertram was given the title of Chief Engineer and he held this post until Michael Lane succeeded him eight months later. Lane had been a bricklayer under Brunel's father during the driving of the Thames tunnel at Rotherhithe between 1824 and 1829. For eight years this bricklayer, who had risen to be one of Brunel's closest assistants, carried out the duties of Engineer until they were taken over by W.G. Owen in 1868. Owen retired in 1885, the office falling to his son, W. Lancaster Owen. The latter had been assistant to J.W. Armstrong, the Hereford Divisional Engineer in 1866. In 1872 W.L. Owen was Engineer of the Gloucester Division, therefore he received the post of Chief Engineer over the head of his former chief, Armstrong, and possibly some other senior engineers too. However, he was never given the title that went with the job but remained 'New Works' Engineer. After six years he resigned and the job went to a London and North Western Railway man, Louis Trench. He only held it for a year when it passed to a Great Western man, James Inglis. Such a curious sequence of events hints at a 'story' behind the scenes. Inglis remained as Engineer until 1903 when he became General Manager of the Great Western Railway, the vacant post being taken up by W.W. Grierson with W. Armstrong as New Works Engineer. The latter retired in 1916 and his function was merged with that of Chief Engineer which continued to be undertaken by Grierson.

From the death of Brunel until 1870 any new stations that were built retained the characteristics of the 'Brunelian' era. The stations on the Berks & Hants Extension are an illustration of this. After 1870 it seems that a new feeling overcame the Chief Engineer's drawing office and red brick wayside stations were constructed in a quite standardised and uncompromising manner. By 'uncompromising' I mean that they were not disguised as lodge gates houses, or medieval monasteries, but were merely railway stations and were not afraid to appear as such. Marlow and Mells Road stations, (*figure 7*) although separated by scores of miles and in a totally different geographical area, were identical. A new type of station appeared during the 1870's, the suburban, as opposed to the rural, wayside station. Between Paddington and Maidenhead, and more particularly between Paddington and Slough, new concentrations of red brick villas were being erected in the green fields, housing a growing population which largely wanted to work in London. At the same time as these new stations were erected, the traditional up and down main lines were supplemented by new, up and down

Figure 7
Mells Road Station from the East.

slow lines. The quadrupling of the tracks was carried out in sections, westwards from Paddington. The first was from Portobello Junction to Southall, opened in October 1877. The four tracks reached West Drayton in November 1878, and to Slough in June 1879. The Wharncliffe Viaduct had prevented quadrupling from extending westwards until it had been widened and the river bridge at Maidenhead too prevented any further westward extension until it had been widened, so the four tracks stopped just east of the bridge from 1879 till 1893 when Maidenhead was reached. It was in 1880 that the title 'Fast' and 'Slow' lines was abolished in favour of 'Main' and 'Relief' lines. During this progressive widening most of the Brunel stations were demolished. Hanwell & Elthorne remains, heavily rebuilt. The new stations have a certain family resemblance in so far as the brickwork and ornamentation are concerned. A great deal is made of various colours of brick, white, yellow, red, with smooth sides or bearing some impression, a flower device or 'dog tooth' ornament. The shape of the buildings varies enormously. Langley (1878, Lancaster Owen) has twin tower-like roofs with a low linking roof between. These towers are very similar to the 'spire' that was erected within the pinnacles of the clock tower at Bristol 'Joint' station and are crowned with the inevitable railings of spiky iron. The result is somewhat French, or 'chateau-like' in appearance. At West Drayton the offices and entrance to the station are below rail level. The roof rises, nearly to a point from all sides, and there is a short, straight ridge crowned with the railings mentioned earlier. In outline, the roof has the appearance of the circus 'Big Top' crowned with many flags on opening night. Taplow, the best of all the stations between Maidenhead and Paddington, in my opinion, is quite different. Here the station office is at rail level even though these are on an embankment so that a tall facade could have been erected from the foot of the bank. The office is long, low and heavy, with a simple roof unadorned by any railings. Among all these stations, Maidenhead, Taplow, Langley, Southall, Hayes and Harlington, etc., there is minimal repetition of design as regards outline shape, but a family resemblance has been maintained by the use of similar ornaments and ornamental procedures. They were designed by two, maybe more architects but J.E. Danks and W. Lancaster Owen are the names positively known in this respect. Slough station was also rebuilt during the widenings but a very special design, which does not come into the same category as the rest of the stations, was drawn up by J.E. Danks in 1886. One can only assume that this is when the station was rebuilt, but the date on the drawings is not really a guide, as Taplow station was redesigned on paper in September 1871 and not actually rebuilt until 1884.

After 1894 the Great Western Railway entered a period which the late Mr. E.T. MacDermot has called 'The Great Awakening'. The Company planned new railways to give shorter routes and faster train services. The building of new lines required new stations, most of them rural, and to this end several designs were created. The first of these may be said to have been erected at Ross on Wye in 1892, two years before the start of the stipulated period. This station was a curious place in that it appeared to have 'standard' features below the eaves of the roof and the traditional '1870' type roof towers above. That the plans were drawn up by J.E. Danks goes some way to explaining this strange marriage of the old and the new. After Ross, there was a new station built at Westbury in connection with the opening of the line from Patney and Chirton. The 'Westbury' style was also used at Newbury, and on the 'New Line' from Princes Risborough to Aynho in 1910. Bicester station, on the latter route, was given a rather more ornate treatment than the others but even the smallest, Aynho Park Platform, had a frontage as large as that at Westbury, and as ornate. Between the building of Westbury and Newbury stations, a period of 10 years, a great number of new routes were opened. The first of the important lines was the Wootton Bassett to Patchway, opened in 1902. In 1904 parts of the Cheltenham to Stratford line were brought into use, in 1906 from Castle Cary to Cogload, and the Birmingham and North Warwickshire in 1907. On all these the style of standard station is quite different to those of 'Westbury' standard pattern. The line from Wootton Bassett to Patchway, known officially as the Bristol & South Wales Direct Railway, and unofficially as the "Badminton line", had seven stations in two styles which were to be used to the exclusion of all others during the period 1902-1917 for rural premises. They all had four tracks between an up and down platform, the latter being served by loops, thus leaving the two centre tracks for express trains to pass clear of stopping trains. The Great Central Railway had a cheaper method of building rural stations before the first world war. They used an island platform with the result that the express trains had to take the outer track when passing stations, thus being forced to negotiate a curve where the rails swerved around the shape of the platforms. The Great Western Railway's method was more expensive to construct but produced a better layout. The stations at Little Somerford, Badminton and Chipping Sodbury were larger and had a different type of building than the other four stations, Brinkworth, Hullavington, Coalpit Heath and Winterbourne, but both types[1] were utterly standard in their particular way. At Chipping Sodbury the platforms were 450 feet long paved with a mixture of Hippsholme (York) stone and Groby (Leicestershire) patent stone. The platforms fell slightly towards the rails and the awnings completely covered the platforms. The buildings were constructed in pressed red brick with groins and plinths in Staffordshire blues, window sills, heads, and also chimney caps were in Forest of Dean 'Bluestone'. The roof was hipped, with lantern lights on the hips, and slated with Bangor slate. The awning was supported by steelwork attached to the wall of the building. The other design was similar below awning level but the roof was formed by the platform awning which extended from the rear wall of the building to the rail edge of the platform. All the 'Badminton line' stations had covered footbridges and waiting rooms equipped with the latest slow burning stoves.

One feature which made a station recognizably 'Great Western' was the platform awning, or canopy. It appears to me that after 1880 the Company began to use more wrought iron and steel and less timber in station construction. Once metal came into regular use it was only a matter

[1] See *plates 231/241* for the larger type and *plates 232/233* for the smaller type.

of time before the first standard designs appeared. First in the progression was an awning or canopy with a ridge-shaped roof supported by rafters on a double row of cast iron columns. The eaves of the roof butted against the wall of the station building on the one hand and followed the line of the platform edge on the other. The rafters were in iron or timber with some sort of ornament within the apex angle. The roof they supported could have been wholly of timber boards, weatherproofed with lead sheet or it may have been wholly or partially glazed. Various motifs embellished the cast iron columns, a twining ribbon, stylised flowers or fluting. This type of construction can be seen at Worcester and Slough. The next period used a pylon shaped column to support a variety of roofs. The pylon was built up of steel angles connected with flat pieces of steel, latticework fashion. The lower parts of such a column were covered in by sheets of steel riveted to the angle pieces. Examples of this type of column, in use between 1890 and 1900, can be seen at Yatton, Bath and Reading, in each instance supporting a different type of roof, see *figure 8*. In 1899 a new, simpler form of roof column had been drawn up at Paddington. One of its earliest applications was at the rebuilt Westbury station, opened in 1900 (see *figure 9*). Here a channel-shaped column was built up out of angle steel with wide webs riveted to flat steel uprights. Across the top of the column was a steel beam extending from eave to eave of the awning, and within the angle formed between the upright and the crosspiece an ornate bracket was fixed. Ten years later at Newbury the same basic design was employed but all ornateness had been dispensed with and a protective plinth had been built around the base of the column. This design was then used throughout the Great Western Railway for many years, see *plate 227* – Chapter One.

The ends of Great Western Railway platform canopies were usually a solid triangle of timber boards. Earlier canopies had a decorative fringe at the gable end, often the fringe was curved as at Didcot and Radley. Later the curved end was abandoned for a straight line though the decorative fringe was retained. Very often, in these cases the triangular outline of the gable end was emphasised by a second triangle, drawn, so to speak, in wooden moulding within the main outline. The standard stations of 1902 design had a fringe along the platform edge of the canopy only, though

Figure 8
Bath up platform in 1897, soon after removal of Brunel's famous roof. Note the 'pylon' type columns, typical of the 1890-1900 period.
British Rail

Figure 9
1899 pattern column at Westbury.
Author

their gable ends sometimes had the emphasis just mentioned.

Having now developed a design for a small station, the Great Western Railway turned its attention to the large stations that needed rebuilding. The first and greatest of these was Birmingham Snow Hill, reconstruction taking about three years between 1909 and 1912. The result was a vast steel, brick and glass station that would have been suitable for any of the London termini and a decided improvement on some in the southern parts of London. Exeter St. David's was also rebuilt during this period. At Paddington work had started in 1906 to widen the approaches to the station and provide accommodation for the constantly increasing traffic. The engine sheds at Westbourne Park were removed to new buildings at Old Oak Common in this year and in 1909 the various brick arch bridges that had cramped the layout since 1838 began to be replaced with the present structures. Having provided a wider track bed, the Engineer now turned his attention to the terminus itself. More platform accommodation was needed and so a fourth span, similar to the original three, was erected on the north side in 1916 using steel instead of wrought iron for the arching ribs of the roof, and steel instead of cast iron for the supporting columns. These steel columns were hexagonal whereas the originals had been cylindrical. The Engineer who was concerned about the brittle qualities of cast iron under the impact of a runaway locomotive, sought and obtained permission to replace all the cast iron columns with the steel constructions with which we are all familiar today. Only a few were replaced, before the War forced the abandonment of the operation. It is interesting to note that the replacement of these columns was only a first step, as far as the Engineer was concerned, towards the eventual replacement of the whole of Brunel's roof. Work was resumed at Paddington in 1924 and continued until 1934 by which time power signalling, longer platforms and better facilities for passengers, among other things, had been provided.

Newton Abbot, Newport, Taunton, Bristol and Cardiff stations were rebuilt or added to between 1927 and 1934. A standard pattern for awnings and platform buildings was drawn up, also for subways, lavatories and signs, only the exteriors showing any marked individuality.

During the period 1927-39, the Company carried out a vast programme of station rebuilding, track layout improvements, signalling improvements, bridge strengthening and the like. Many schemes were small, involving only an additional loop line or a new building on one platform of a station, but some encompassed the entire renewal of a station. Challow station was renewed as a single storey brick construction, and a very poor thing it was too. Stoke Canon was rebuilt very nicely, also in brick, at the same time and for the same reason as Challow, due to quadrupling of the tracks between 1932/34. Wellington (Som.) was a large version of the station at Challow, though not quite so harsh as the latter, while the new station at Bourton on the Water was a delightful place in Cotswold stone. The last station which the Great Western Railway rebuilt before yet another war began was that at Leamington. They had intended to rebuild Oxford, Banbury and Reading but this plan was never carried out and later fell to British Railways; Banbury in 1953, Oxford in 1972 and Reading in 1962. The proposals for Reading in 1962 were similar as those of the Great Western Railway in 1938. A down main platform loop, new offices on the downside in the form of a long concrete and glass rectangle, and a shorter rectangle perched above the first at one end, and finally, power signalling. The last item was installed in 1965. Since 1962 British Rail has modernised much of the interior of the downside at Reading, leaving the mid-nineteenth century offices intact to provide the only interesting building in the area.

Having surveyed briefly the station building history of the Great Western Railway, I should like to discuss in more detail some of the stations illustrated in this section. Let us begin with Bristol Temple Meads.

The building which Brunel designed as the western terminus of the Great Western Railway was constructed in stone and has the appearance of a 16th century university. The period of the construction of the station and the entire railway (1835-40), coincided with a change in architectural fashion, when the pediments and columns of Classical Greece gave way to the Oriels and arches of Tudor England. This was the case where domestic buildings are concerned, churches were erected in the 'Early English' style of the 13th century. Various reasons for this change have been put forward. It has been said that men like Brunel were far too individualistic to build in the anonymous style of the Athenian Acropolis. Better for him to make his presence known by erecting buildings which could be instantly recognised as his work. Ramifications of towers, turrets, chimneys, archways and beautiful windows can far more easily be made to bear the mark of one's personality than columns and pediments, however beautifully proportioned. In a more general sense, the country was confident and trade was brisk. The United Kingdom was probably the most powerful country in the world owing to its early industrialisation. There had been no major war since 1815, recent reform of the franchise laws and the abolition of slavery made the country feel as if it were entering on a new era of peace, prosperity, industry and justice. There was an air of confident nationalism in the country so it was not surprising that architecture should turn to the styles of the most glorious period (according to contemporary thought) in English history, the Reformation, when nationalism asserted itself, threw off the slavery of Rome and laid the way open to the present, Victorian, era of peace and justice. The novels of Sir Walter Scott were enormously popular during this period, and had done a great deal to romanticise the terrible, bloody events of the religious and political revolutions of the Tudor and Stuart periods. Brunel, more confident and progressive than most at that time, epitomised the spirit of the times and built the Bristol station with a marvellous Tudor flourish.

The station exterior at Bristol is very similar to that which Brunel saw built one hundred and thirty-five years ago. The right hand gateway has been demolished and a small rectangular block has been built on the right hand side of the roof. Minor details of embellishment were altered even before the building was erected, but basically the

Figure 10

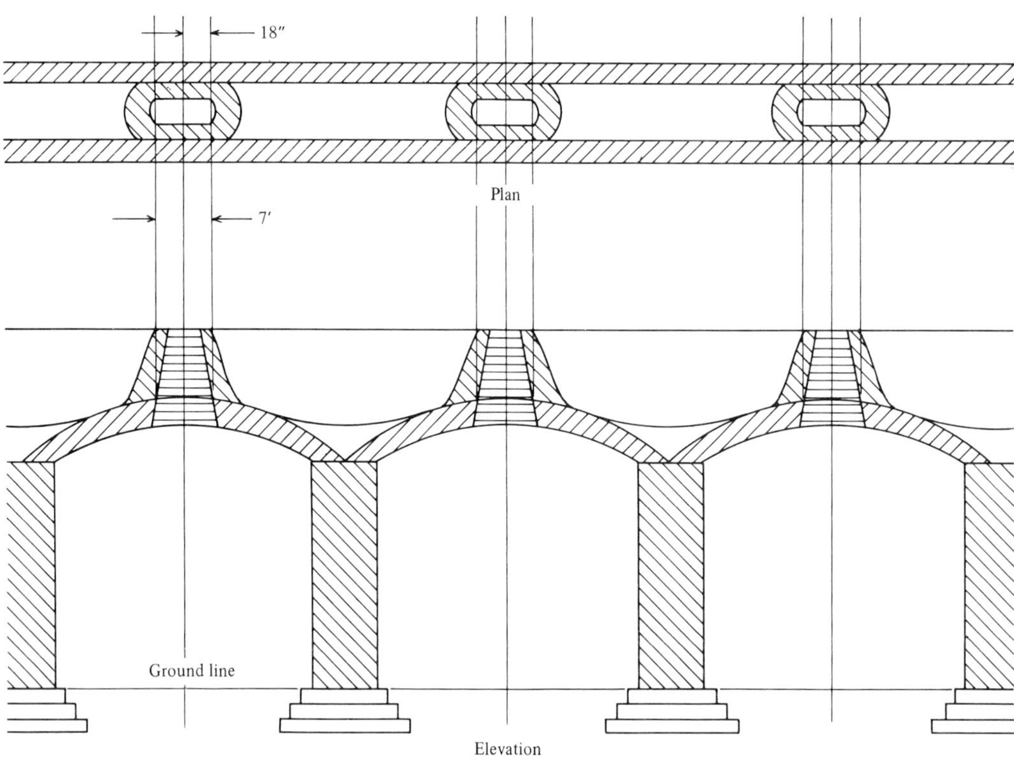

Arches beneath the old station at Bristol Temple Meads
Copied from I.K. Brunel drawings

station front is unchanged. The archways, one on each side of the central block, gave access to the booking office on the upside, and passengers coming from the trains walked out through the downside, or right hand archway. In the central block were various offices dealing with the operation of the railway including the Boardroom. Brunel designed a splendid staircase, wide and well lit, to reach this most important office which had two fireplaces one at each end of the room. The surrounds to these were made in white, statuary marble, carved like a gothic arch with octagonal pillars, one at each side, to a design very similar to the newels of the great staircase. Company business was directed from this office until 1855 when the new station at Paddington was opened and the Boardroom transferred to that place. Since then the offices have had various tenants, the Goods Agent for the Bristol Division housed his staff in them for many years and now they are used for classrooms and conferences, the large rooms divided up by plywood and plaster board partitions, the marble chimney pieces covered in for their own protection.

Brunel had to carry the railway line into Bristol at such an elevation as to give mast room to sailing ships where the tracks passed over the 'Floating Harbour'. This and the manner in which the land fell away steeply to the west at the terminus site meant that the rails were 15′–20′ above ground level. Rather than build an embankment, Brunel built a series of curiously constructed arches, *figure 10,* doubtless with cellarage in mind, upon which he laid his tracks and built the magnificent overall roof. This had a span of 72 feet and a length of 220 feet, the platforms extending beyond the roof for a further 200 feet. The roof was supported by timber cantilevers, twenty-two in all, at 10 feet centres. These were supported by hammer beams and cast iron columns, the latter acting as fulcrums to the cantilever so that the walls had no out-thrusting strains to bear from the roof. This arrangement had the disadvantage that the columns were so close to the platform edge as to make entraining and detraining difficult when there were crowds of people milling around. This feature was common to most of the overall roofs designed by Brunel and later, by his assistants, but was abated somewhat when the seven feet gauge was abolished and the platforms widened. The terminus at Bristol was indeed a beautiful piece of work, the array of hammer beams, carved bosses and curving brackets gave the impression that some hall or baronial magnificence had been magically transported from the Border Marches to the nineteenth century for use as a railway station. Brunel disguised the cast iron columns as cloisters by linking them all with his style of late gothic arch and one always felt that there should be mouldering 'colours' of long defunct regiments hanging at peace between the beams, above the cloisters.

From the opening of the terminus in 1840 until 1845 the Bristol & Exeter Railway used it for all their trains. After that date they had their own station, built very close to the Great Western Terminus. A curve joined the two companies' lines, known as the 'express curve', probably because it was used mainly by express trains between Paddington and Exeter. This layout was rather awkward because trains had to back out of the terminus clear of the 'express curve' facing points, and then draw forward for the journey to the West; conversely, trains from the west had to back into the terminus. The station had five tracks and two platforms so it was fairly congested, but in June 1854 the Midland Railway were empowered to run into the station over the narrow gauge track which Parliament had allowed them to build. Now the operating problems were insuperable, only a new, larger station would solve the problem but with three separate companies the arguments over costs, especially when the 'Midland' formed one of the parties, were endless. However conditions became so bad that they were forced to act and in 1865 obtained the necessary Parliamentary permission and began to build a new 'Joint' station.

It was built along the line of the old 'express curve', the original terminus platforms being extended to 352 yards from about 140 yards. In the triangular space between the curve and the old station, all the offices for passengers were erected, the restaurant being particularly well done in brick and stone after the Tudor style. There were seven platforms, numbered from the south, one to four, number one being the longest at 286 yards, numbers two, three and four being 143 yards each. Platforms 5 and 6 were the southern face of the old station platform divided and platform seven was the northern platform. The new station was enclosed by a very fine, wrought iron roof spanning about 130 feet. Brunel's old friend and collaborator Matthew Digby-Wyatt, who had designed the ornamental ironwork at Paddington in 1854, was architectural advisor for the designs and embellishment of the new station. He preserved Brunel's gothic motif in the shape of the roof arch and the supporting stone towers at each end, this non-symmetrical arch and the sharp curve which it had to follow, must have made it a very difficult problem for the contractor who erected it. The Midland and the Bristol & Exeter Railways had running powers of the entire layout, and there were three station masters, which caused endless arguments over whose trains should have priority and whose signalman had caused the delay. When the Great Western Railway absorbed the Bristol & Exeter in 1876 the situation eased a little, but the Midland presence must have been a sore trial for the Paddington based company. As the three Companies were so jealous of their operating independence, it seems reasonable to suppose that this individuality affected the building of the station, who paid for what and who was to design what. Unfortunately the original plans do not give any clue as to what features were designed by which company, however, one thing is fairly certain, that Francis Fox of the Bristol & Exeter had a great deal to do with the design. The canopy along the outside wall of the station is very similar and the iron work supporting this is virtually identical to that used at Weston-super-Mare station which Fox is known to have designed.

The original drawings show two separate plans for the central clock tower, that is, with and without the central 'spire' (see *figure 19*). This was removed about 1925, rightly so in my opinion, for it was not in keeping with the rest of the building. Therefore, although the 'spire' is missing, the building is still in original condition because it was conceived without that appendage. Each Company had its own booking hall within the Great Hall and an identified door by which passengers entered to buy tickets of the company of their choice. The Midland Railway had the left-hand door (as one looks with one's back to Victoria St.), the Bristol & Exeter the centre, and the Great Western Railway the right hand door. Above each doorway was a scroll bearing the relevant legend.

In the 'well' at the side of the approach ramp, stands what is known as the 'Bristol & Exeter building'. This was designed by F.C. Fripp, Engineer to that Company and his initial, carved in stone, is set high on the north face of the building. The offices of the B. & E.R. were housed here until the 1876 amalgamation when it became the home of the Bristol Operating Division. On the other side of the approach ramp, in a narrow canyon between the ramp retaining walls and the precipitous walls of the old terminus was a terminus of the Bristol Corporation tram. A staff canteen now stands on the site but the old tram lines can still be seen, set in cobbles, disappearing under the prefabricated hut. In 1880 the layout was simple, just a single track from the 'main line' along Victoria Street, but by 1910 it had been enlarged into a little station in its own right (see *figures 11* and *12*).

The Joint station remained undisturbed from 1876 until 1932 when platforms 2 and 3 were demolished to make way for through lines, while the remaining platforms were extended and additional platforms were built on the south side utilising land taken from the Corporation cattle market. The platform extensions on the north side were provided with a facade designed by P.E. Culverhouse in sympathy with the existing 1876 front. The 'Old Station', the original

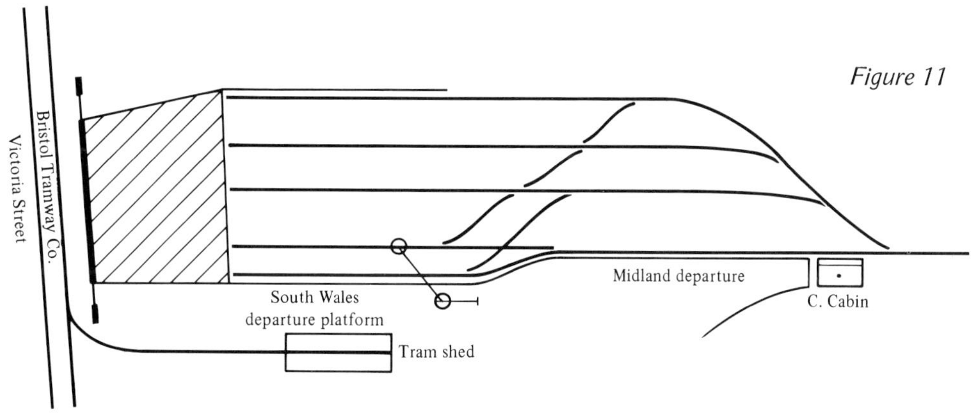

Bristol Old Station layout in 1881. Taken from a Great Western Official Survey.

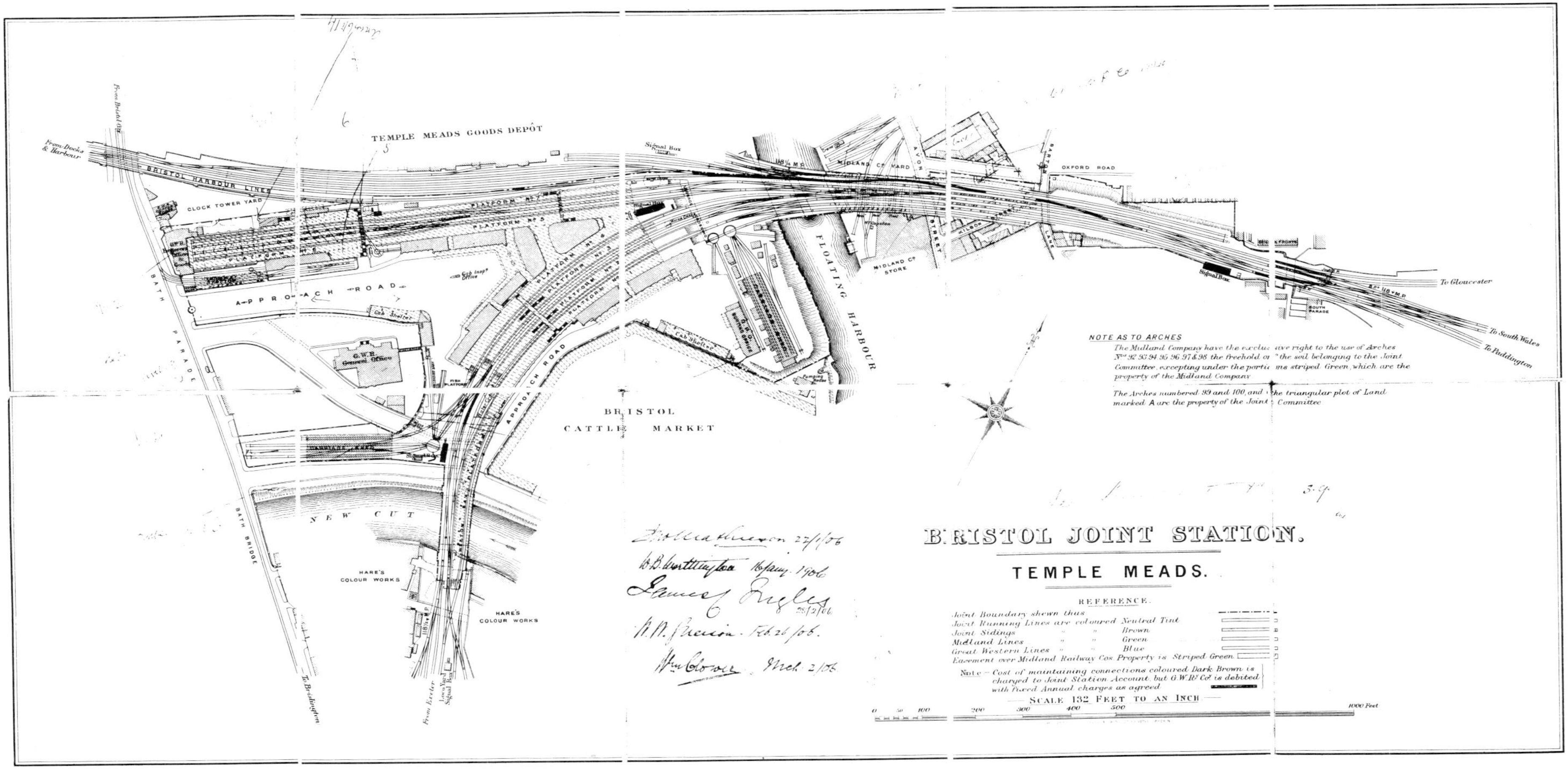

Figure 12 From a Great Western Railway Survey dated 1906.

NOTE AS TO ARCHES

The Midland Company have the exclusive right to the use of Arches Nos 92 93 94 95 96 97 & 98 the freehold of the soil belonging to the Joint Committee, excepting under the portions striped Green, which are the property of the Midland Company.

The Arches numbered 99 and 100, and the triangular plot of Land marked A are the property of the Joint Committee.

BRISTOL JOINT STATION.

TEMPLE MEADS.

REFERENCE.

Joint Boundary shewn thus

Joint Running Lines are coloured Neutral Tint

Joint Sidings " " Brown

Midland Lines " " Green

Great Western Lines " " Blue

Easement over Midland Railway Cos Property is Striped Green

Note. — Cost of maintaining connections coloured Dark Brown is charged to Joint Station Account, but G.W.Ry Co is debited with fixed Annual charges as agreed

SCALE 132 FEET TO AN INCH

terminus, continued virtually unchanged for another 40 years, until 1970 when it was shut down and turned into a car park.

Bath station (or Depot, as it was called on the original drawings) was constructed to the middle size of three plans drawn up by Brunel. He envisaged an upside building very similar to the present one but without the eastern wing, the second plan was the one actually constructed, but the third design was the largest and most imposing. There was to have been, in this design, a central block as there is today, with the same ornaments beneath the windows, but it would have been taller and proportionately wider. Instead of the three gables actually built, there was to have been a Manson roof behind a balustraded parapet. A long, eastern extension would have been built but this would have run parallel to the tracks and not curved round as is the case with the present building. Though the present upside building closely resembles its original plan there are some important differences. Most striking is the awning over the booking hall entrance. Brunel designed this as a timber structure supported by the station wall and by two timber columns at the street's edge. These columns were square in section and tapered slightly, being thicker at the top than at the base. The roof of the awning was level, probably not glazed, and sported the oddest ornament that Brunel ever designed for a station. It took the form of a chain of half-moon shapes linked by rectangles across adjacent 'horns', leaving the semi-circle open and facing upwards like a good luck horseshoe. Whether this device was actually put up I do not know, but it was shown on the original plans. As for the rest of the upside building, it appears to have lost a ball ornament over the central gable and gained a clock.

The downside facade is plain and square, the limestone wall being pierced with well-proportioned, mullioned windows. All that is constructed in limestone is original but the brick addition at the west end was probably added when the roof was removed in 1897. There was a booking hall on the downside with a hip sided awning, the latter being removed in about 1925 and a standard canopy substituted. The booking hall was closed in 1962 and the canopy removed. It is possible to reach the station from the south, over the Avon, using a bridge erected by a private firm, i.e. not the G.W.R., in 1877 to replace a suspension bridge which had collapsed in that year with some loss of life.

Opposite the Up side facade there are two identical blocks which gives the impression that they were built by the Great Western Railway as hotel accommodation. That now known as the "Berni Royal" was once the "Station Hotel" while the other was the "Railway Hotel". In 1840, when the station was opened, they would have made an impressive gateway to the City which would have been seen at the end of the long avenue through the "frame" of the two hotels. A footbridge connected the "Station Hotel" and the station but this was taken away in January 1936. Despite the close associations between the railway and the Hotels, these were never railway property.

Brunel provided a splendid overall roof at the station but little record remains of this (*figure 13*). One can look at the Bourne lithographs and read what that gentleman said of the roof on page 70 of MacDermot's "History of the Great Western" Vol. 1. It is not certain when the roof was removed, but it was intact in 1881 and probably demolished in 1897, having been replaced by the present ironwork. The awnings provided are very fine, with a ridge roof and a lantern light. The steelwork is light and dainty, and on a sunny day it is a very pleasing sight to see the sun streaming through the glazing.

Figure 14 shows the layout at Moulsford station, the surviving buildings of which are illustrated in *plates 278* and *281/282*. These buildings, out of railway service since 1892 or 1893, were opened to the public with the rest of the Reading to Steventon section on 1st June 1840 and are the sole remains of the original stations on that section. The buildings at Steventon are as old but were built for staff and not the public. There are no buildings shown on the platforms at Moulsford, probably because the hotel doubled as booking office and waiting rooms. Pangbourne, Goring, Didcot and Steventon had the usual offices on their platforms. *Figure 15* shows the layout at Pangbourne, typical of its kind. There was no footbridge at this or any of the stations between Reading and Didcot in 1873, with

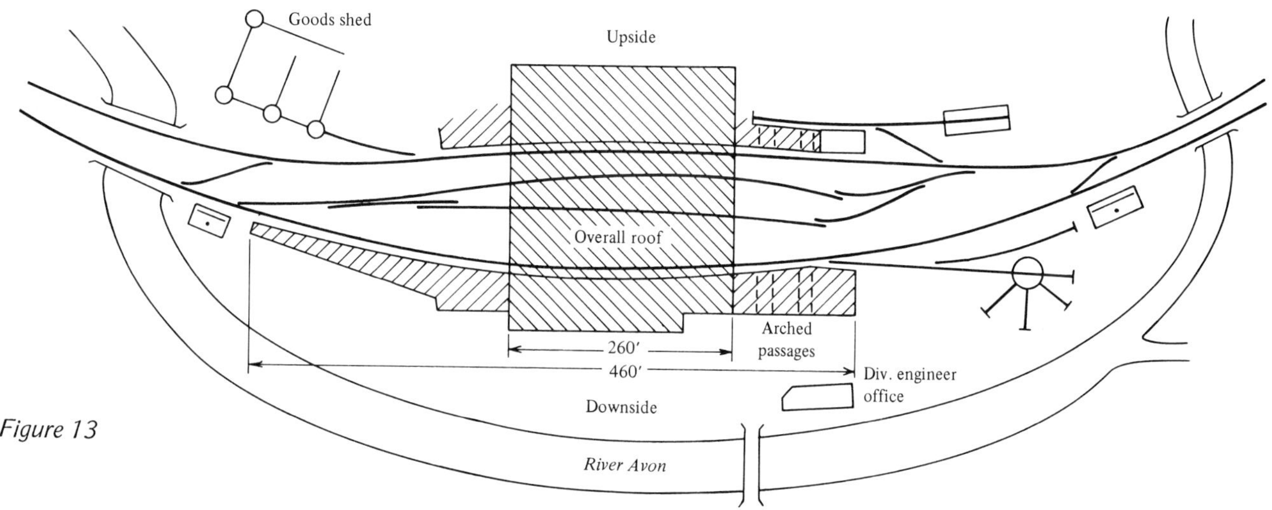

Figure 13

Drawing showing track layout and extent of the overall roof at Bath Station in 1881. Taken from a GWR Official Survey.

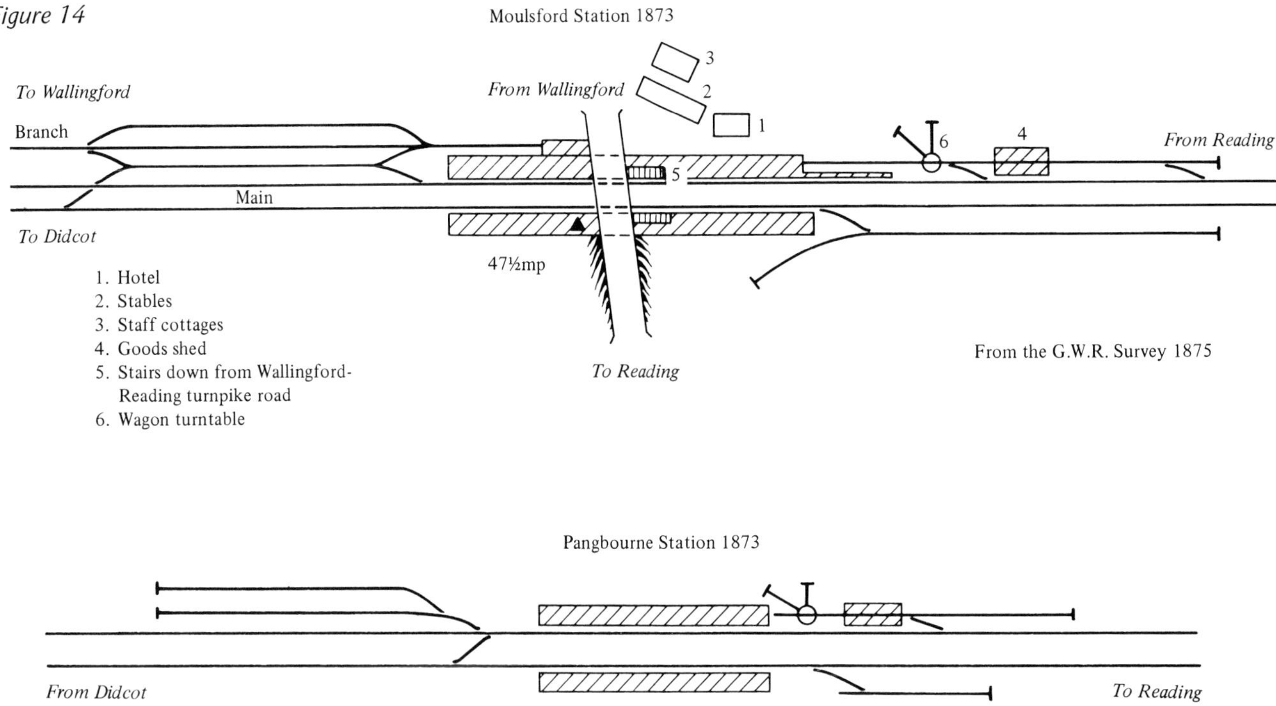

Figure 14

Figure 15
A typical layout at a wayside station. From an official survey by the Great Western Railway.

the exception of Didcot. The bridge carrying the public road over the line acted as a footbridge, or one used the barrow crossing at the foot of the platform ramp.

Had it not been for the bitterness that eventually became a kind of tradition between the Great Western and the London & Birmingham Railway (later the L. & N.W.R.), there would have been no Paddington station. No such terminus was envisaged by the Great Western Railway's Act of Incorporation of August 1835. In that Act powers were granted for the Great Western to make a junction with the L. & B. in the village of Kensal Green and run from there to a common terminus at Euston. Luckily for us, the L. & B. did everything in their power to obstruct the Great Western in this, so that in 1837 the Company sought and was granted power to construct the "Acton Extension Railway". To this day, Western Region main line bears north east between Acton and Old Oak Common, pointing across to Kensal Green, silent testimony of the Company's original intention. Trains began running from a temporary station at Paddington on the 4th August 1838.

This station consisted of a timber shed which butted against the western face of the brick arched, Bishop's Road bridge, the arches forming booking halls, waiting rooms and all the other offices necessary at a station. The Great Western Railway had once intended that all passengers should be booked on and off trains at an office in the City and had purchased premises for this purpose. People would have been conveyed to and from the terminal (which then would have been Euston) by horse-drawn omnibus. On the eastern side of the bridge at Bishop's Road the Company built a goods shed, the layout in 1838 being the opposite of the present arrangement. The ground upon which the station was built fell away from a height to the north whereupon stood the Town Hall of Paddington. To level the land and raise it sufficient for his purpose, Brunel had clay laid down to depths varying from 14 to 21 feet. One can imagine the horrible slime as scores of horses and carts trudged to and from the site, great lumps of stodgy clay being flung over the ground from the carts by shovel-armed navvies. The goods shed could not be built on this clay layer because of the weights it would eventually contain so a series of brick arches, very useful for extra storage space, were constructed and the shed built on these. The entire terminus was a temporary affair, which lasted sixteen years, and one gets the impression that it was only rebuilt when conditions became intolerable.

Brunel was very pleased when the Directors finally authorised expenditure on a new terminus at Paddington. He wrote to his friend Matthew Digby-Wyatt a letter, bursting with impatience for the "go ahead", asking him to come and decorate the new station. The letter can be read in L.T.C. Rolt's biography, Isambard Kingdom Brunel, page 232. Brunel had become friends with Digby-Wyatt when they worked together on the "Committee of Machinery" and the "Committee of Design" for the "Great Hall", otherwise known as the "Crystal Palace". Brunel had been very impressed with the latter and with Digby-Wyatt's part in the work which included a "Moorish Pavilion", so Brunel now invited his friend to come and embellish Paddington, for, as he said in the letter, "I have neither the time nor the knowledge for it."

The new Paddington consisted of three spans: 69 ft. 6 ins, 102 ft. 6 ins and 68 ft. The wrought iron ribs, or arches, which formed the backbone of the roof, were supported on cast iron, cylindrical columns and by a lattice-work girder of wrought iron which was carried the length of the platforms on the heads of the said columns. Beneath each column was a very large, pyramid-shaped block of brick and concrete through which passed bolts 1½ ins. in diameter by which means the columns were secured to the masonry. Brunel did not provide tie rods across the spans but relied on the massiveness of the foundations to keep the columns, and therefore the roof, upright. At least a third of the surface area of the roof, and all of the windscreens at the eastern and western ends were glazed, using Paxton's patent glass and glazing bars. Joseph Paxton was the leading authority of the day on the glazing of large buildings, having built railway station-sized glass-houses for the Duke of Devonshire at Chatsworth House, further hot-houses at Kew, and, of course, the Crystal Palace. The lines of the glazing bars in the windscreens were very harsh, rectangular and Digby-Wyatt relieved this by fitting swirling Moorish arabesques of wrought iron. Curving lines were the theme for the decoration applied to the plain surface of the roof ribs, the design was cast in sections and bolted onto the wrought iron. At the zenith of each span a number of drillings were made which were decorative and practical as they could accommodate scaffolding poles to enable the glass to be cleaned and the iron to be painted.

Beneath the point where a rib joins the latticework girder, Digby-Wyatt placed a wooden finial inverted, to bring the lines of the rib through the girder, so to speak, and finish it off in a round tidy manner. The importance of these inverted finials to the appearance of the ribs can be judged best at the points where they are missing!

The departure side of the station was completed in 1854 but it was another twelve months before the roof over the arrival side was ready. By the time it had been completed, the Great Western Royal Hotel was also ready for inspection and the whole complex of buildings was toured by His Royal Highness the Prince Albert, Prince Consort, and the King of Portugal, who announced themselves delighted with the lavish arrangements provided for the public. Over the years the station was one of the "sights" of London because of its bold design. Paddington station was the first public building in London to be illuminated with electricity when in November 1880 the Anglo-American Brush Electric Light Company installed a generator and supplied current for thirty-four lamps. This arrangement did not last long and in 1884 the contract to light the station passed to the Telegraph Construction and Maintenance Company of which Sir Daniel Gooch was Chairman. His company ran sixty-four lamps from a gas engine generator, the arrangement lasting until 1907 when the Great Western Railway's Park Royal generating station came into use. Primarily its function was to supply current to the Metropolitan/Great Western Joint, Hammersmith and City lines which were converted from steam to electric running in that year. Park Royal was a very large installation at the time, and still today generates current for the National Grid. When it came into use all the small generating plants on the Great Western in the London area were abolished and at Paddington the existing sixty-four lamps were replaced by one hundred and thirty-six lamps "each three times as powerful as the ones they replace."

By 1907 the various brick arches over the approaches to Paddington were strangling the layout, preventing it from expanding to meet traffic requirements, and the Company announced in that year that they would be undertaking a vast plan of reform which would entail the demolition of these bridges and their replacement by "modern steel constructions". The latter allow the track perfect freedom of movement. The old sheds for Paddington, at Westbourne Park, were removed to Old Oak Common in 1906, so once the brick arches had been demolished, the way was clear to extend the width of the track bed and lay down an improved track plan. In 1909 work commenced on Bishop's Road bridge at the end of the platform at Paddington and by 1913 an improved layout was being constructed. There are ten bridges over the line in the three miles from Old Oak Common to Paddington and before the Company could rebuild them all the Great War intervened. Work on the layout stopped from 1916 until early in 1927. Empty coaching stock and light engines to and from the terminus and Old Oak Common sidings and engine shed, had used the ordinary running lines, usually the up and down relief lines, to the great detriment of punctuality, and the Company's first priority was to build special "engine and carriage lines" for all "light" movements. To carry out this improvement the down main became an "up engine and carriage line" and Westbourne Park station, which had three platforms, one of which was an "island", was remodelled to have two "island" platforms. Out at Old Oak, a "flyover" was constructed to allow empty trains to cross the running lines into the depot without interfering with the working. These "E. & C. lines" were the first tracks in the Paddington area to be colour light signalled. When the new layout was complete, in 1928, three hundred and fifty sets of points, five hundred crossings and seven miles of plain track had been relaid, a further eight miles of track had been slewed, lifted and variously adjusted.

Work also commenced in 1913 on clearing land to the north of the station to make space for an additional span at Paddington which would accommodate platforms to be numbered 10, 11 and 12. The land to be cleared was the High Level goods yard and the old approach road to the station, which was situated between the goods yard and the terminus (see *figure 16*). The new span was constructed in the same style as the rest of the station except that steel instead of wrought iron was used in the "ribs" of the roof. It was also the largest span in the station, being 109 ft., there being good reason for this. Grierson, Chief Engineer, had investigated the old roofs and found that the smallest,

Figure 16 Paddington Station about 1910. In the foreground is Bishop's Road Station and, left, part of the extensive stables attached to the terminus. Above the stable is the High Level Goods Yard with some wagons being loaded or unloaded. The site of the new span is between the high level road and the first arch of the roof. The present arrival side exit road occupies the same position as it did in this picture, there appears to be a road, above the stable, going out to join with the Bishop's Road and the wide, cobbled road in the foreground probably leads to the low level goods yard, the latter being still in use today. The small footbridge can be seen leading from Bishop's Road station to the terminus. The arrival side signal box is half hidden by the walls of the 'underground' station, but it is still possible to see its curious wedge shape. Very obvious in this picture is the difference between the centre and left hand spans, one can imagine how the latter was pushed over by its big neighbour. There appears to be some kind of supporting strut propping the column common to these two spans. *British Rail*

northern span was being pushed over by the large, centre span, which in turn, was dragging the southern span. The columns of the northern span were 5½ ins. out of plumb in 1915! The bolts holding the columns to their foundations had elongated under the severe strains set up by the side thrust of the untied arches above. It was natural for the arches to thrust out sideways as they had not been fitted with tie bars and this tendency was aggravated by the unbalanced nature of the whole building. The new span, at 109 ft., was to act as a counter-balance to the central

102 ft. 6 ins. span. Grierson reported the fault to the Board recommending that all the cast iron columns should be replaced by steel columns as he felt that there was a grave danger that if a locomotive struck the cast iron columns there would be disastrous consequences. This should also correct the out of plumb situation which would be the first step to the eventual entire replacement of the Brunel roof which by then was getting towards the end of its days. The Directors took his point about the danger of brittle cast iron and allowed him to replace these but objected to the demolition of Brunel's roof. The first columns to be renewed were in the roadway between platforms 8 and 9. Plate steel was the new medium of construction, the plates being riveted into hexagons, 17½ ins. at their base and 15½ ins. at their heads. Owing to the unbalanced roof spans the very greatest care had to be exercised in the removal of a column, and only one was taken out at a time after suitable support had been given to the roof on each side of the column. The work was undertaken by the Cleveland Bridge Company who were so successful that not a pane of glass was cracked in all the years that it took to complete the job. They worked for a year from 1915 to 1916, when all works were suspended for the duration of the War, and from 1922 to 1924, forty-four columns being replaced during that two year period. When all was complete and the new span built, the columns were again measured and found to be a maximum of 7/8 in. out of true on the 68 ft. span. The roof was threatened with demolition ("life expired") in the 'thirties and was the subject of an attempted demolition in the 1940's but it survived for us to enjoy today.

Only the Great Western Railway could have devised "The Lawn" as the title for the area behind the buffers. Passengers awaited trains or people waited to meet friends off trains, on the Lawn. The phrase conjures up such visions of white trousered, striped blazered, languid gentlemen, reclining in deck chairs in front of a beautiful glass conservatory, while their elegantly dressed ladies played gently at tennis on the green lawn. In fact, the "Lawn" was a smoky, dirty place, full to overflowing with parcels and luggage and trundling barrows propelled by busy porters who were not too careful about whose toes got in the way of the iron wheels; many a shin must have been bruised and many a long dress soiled when passengers shared the "Lawn" with the baggage. In 1928 work commenced on a new parcels depot in order that the "Lawn" could be returned to the passengers alone. The old excursion platform, No. 1a, was the site of rail access to the new depot, and behind this a large site was cleared into Westbourne Terrace which required the demolition of a number of houses and the partial demolition of others, some being cut through diagonally. The foundations of the new buildings were 8 ft. below basement level of the surrounding houses and difficult operations had to be carried out on these houses to prevent their collapse. The area of the parcels depot was 15,951 sq.ft., the whole of which area had to be piled. There were 759 piles driven into the tough, London clay to a maximum depth of 35 ft. below finished ground level, each pile being designed to carry between thirty and sixty tons. The foundations and walls of the building were made strong enough to carry further storeys should they be needed and these were added a few years later. A roadway, 50 ft. wide, was driven from Westbourne Bridge to the depot necessitating the widening of Westbourne Bridge. Soil had to be excavated from the south side and a new abutment constructed out of steel columns backed with piles. A new subway had also to be constructed connecting the old subway between the platforms with the new parcels depot. Tunnelling was undertaken without a shield with the aid of Brunel's arches constructed in 1838 for the original goods shed. A crane was positioned on one of the old arches and "fished" down through a hole broken in the next arch. The stiff clay was excavated and lifted in a tub through the hole by the crane, which then lowered a cast iron ring, 14 ft. in diameter and 20 ins. long, into the passageway. As the tunnel extended, a 2 ft. gauge track was laid and the trucks of spoil were winched back to the crane by electric motor. The tunnel fell at a gradient of 1 in 29 in a straight line and turned north-east, under the 90 ft. high wall of the main office building, and through a vertical curve to make a junction with the existing subway. To support the office wall over the subway, two groups of piles were constructed, one on either side of the wall, carrying reinforced concrete caps on which rested the lintel girders. On these lintels were placed the main girders parallel to and clear of the wall which was then opened in short lengths for the introduction of steel "needle" girders, the whole assembly being then encased in concrete. Great care was exercised through the tunnelling work and no damage was caused to buildings owing to the settlement of the ground beneath.

Having built the new parcels depot, the Company then re-furbished the "Lawn" with a new steel and glass roof, that part nearest the Royal Hotel being glazed with coloured glass. New refreshment rooms were built at the edge of the area, and seat reservation offices, lost property, cloak rooms, and all the other paraphernalia of a passenger station were grouped conveniently around the "Lawn" in the centre of which an arrival and departure indicator was erected. "Quick snack" refreshment rooms with cosy, "intimate" decor were opened on Platform 1. These also had wide windows, all of which spoke of a change in public attitudes. The very term "Quick Snack" would have been considered vulgar twenty years before, and indeed still was considered vulgar by many. Eating in public was only to be done in a dignified manner, not quickly and certainly not in full view of the rude turmoil out on the platform. But times were changing and people wanted the convenience of a quick cheap meal and did not care so much for appearances.

The Great Western Railway had always worked in close co-operation with the General Post Office and had provided the world's first travelling sorting office train which began running from Paddington to Bristol on 1st February 1855. This had not been solely for the G.P.O. but conveyed passengers too. The first train on the Great Western Railway to convey only travelling sorting office vans ran from Paddington in 1866 and picked up and set down mail whilst passing at speed, Slough and Maidenhead. On 22nd May 1935 the first Crown Post Office to be opened on a railway station came into use at Paddington, opened by the Postmaster, Sir Kingsley Wood.

The length of passenger trains entering the terminus had been increasing since G.J. Churchward became Chief Locomotive, Carriage and Wagon Engineer and had introduced stock 70 ft. long. By the late 'twenties the need for longer platforms was urgent and the Company set about providing these. A new type of pre-cast concrete unit was designed from which the platforms could be built. These were so shaped at their edges that a concrete dowel would drop down between two units and lock them together, no mortar being needed. Paving stones were laid across the tops and these formed the platform. The units could be placed by hand, if necessary, on a bed of rammed sand or ashes, 200 ft. of completed platform being laid between, say, midnight and 6.30 a.m., the period when the station was quietest. The work took place between 1932 and 1934, during which time the station and approaches were re-signalled with a power operated colour light system, and the result of the platform extensions was that the station, including Paddington Suburban, now had a total platform length of 2.84 miles. One platform was 1,150 ft. long, another 1,090 ft., and four were 950 ft. long.

The greatest work of re-construction was in amalgamating the Bishop's Road station, of the London Passenger Transport Board, with Paddington station to become "Paddington Suburban". Bishop's Road station had been built in 1863 for the Metropolitan Railway's service to Farringdon Street. In the following year the Hammersmith and City line entered from the west, the whole becoming the joint property of the Metropolitan and Great Western Companies in 1867. The station originally had a timber overall roof and its only physical connection with the Great Western at Paddington had been a footbridge. The Company intended to provide additional platforms and a better layout of tracks. This meant that the wall of the goods shed had to be "set back" to allow for the re-alignment of the rails and the extension of the platforms. The Goods Agents Offices were also in the way of expansion and a corner of this lofty building was removed and a steel pillar inserted where before there had been an obstructive brick pier. In addition to this, the lines of the "tube" railway had to cut through the sidings in front of the goods shed, which was of course in use twenty-four hours a day, and made homeless one hundred horses used in shunting and cartage. Not only did these worthy animals have to be re-housed, but the "Goods Department Dining Club", founded in 1875, also had to find new premises. The latter is another example of the Company's use of lordly sounding titles, there was nothing plebian about the Great Western Railway, even the day and night canteen for shunters and carters in the goods shed was a "Dining Club"!

To provide additional track space in the station it was necessary to demolish part of the old "cut and cover" tunnel and substitute a network of steel girders to support the roadway above. A 5-ply, plywood shield was used to assist in dismantling the brickwork. The point of installing steel work was to give the tracks beneath plenty of room for manoeuvre and for this reason no intermediate support could be given to the backbone of the girder work, a single steel monster 133 ft. long and weighing 126 tons. When complete it supported 4,500 sq.ft. of road. The work of enlargement was completed with a short, engine lay-by tunnel and a new covered footbridge from the "Suburban" station to the terminus. The work was commenced in 1928 and finished in 1934.

Headquarters offices for the Great Western Railway, including, of course, the Boardroom, were situated along Eastbourne Terrace, on the departure side of the station. In 1907 two more storeys were added to the existing offices, the additional accommodation being considered remarkable at the time, for each possessed a main corridor nearly 300 yards long. A pneumatic system of message delivery was installed, serving all parts of the station, offices and Royal Hotel, the compressed air being supplied by a Crossley petrol engine at the end of No. 1 platform which drove a compressor. By 1930 the need for yet more office space was urgent and the Company added another storey to the existing departure side offices, purchased and demolished houses at the western end of Eastbourne Terrace so as to extend their office block. The space between the block and the Royal Hotel was filled with a new office. This was, and still is, a steel framed building faced with artificial stone at the front and London stock brick at the rear and was built to harmonise with existing buildings on the departure side. In it are housed the Medical Officer and part of the Chief Civil Engineer's staff, while in the basements are heating plants for the station, offices and Hotel, lost property offices and record stores.

In 1934, at about the same time as the new block for the Medical Officer and other staff was being constructed, using modern methods in an "old fashioned" design, there was taken in hand the construction of a new tower block on the arrival side of the station. This too was a steel framed building but was, for the time, uncompromisingly modern. Its steel skeleton contains about 500 tons of steel which was erected in five weeks.

Access to the "Great Western Railway Royal Hotel" was from the "Lawn" (of course) or from Praed Street. The building was designed by P.C. Hardwick and has the appearance of a Louis XIV chateau. The firm of Holland's constructed it, commencing in 1854 and taking only 14 months to finish the job. It was opened by Prince Albert, the Prince Consort, and the King of Portugal. Then, as now, it rivalled the finest establishments in Europe, its role undiminished with the passing years, and now houses more conferences and delegations than ever before. The Hotel is tangible evidence of Brunel's great vision of a vast transport system which was to have carried people to the New World and back, staying in hotels of Brunel's design, on railways of his design and on ships which he also designed and which amazed the world with their size and elegance.

Although physically close to the terminus, indeed, the Hotel forms the facade for the station, the Hotel was not part of the Great Western Railway. Money had been raised to build the place by a section of the Great Western board in 1854, but they formed a separated company to administer its affairs. Brunel was a Director of the Hotel company for a time and the Hotel became part of the Great Western Railway in 1896. Strange as it might seem, the Company had no catering department, hotels or refreshment rooms under its direct control until 1891. Dozens of stations had these facilities but they were all under the control of contractors whose responsibility to the Great Western Railway stopped with paying their rent. In 1876 the Great Western took leases on the "Tregenna Castle" and "St. Ives" hotels but did not own them until 1895. Then, in 1895, ten leases on rooms in the West Country fell due and, instead of renewing them, the Company took over the running and set up a headquarters for catering at Plymouth.

At the same time the lease on the notorious refreshment rooms at Swindon fell due and these too were taken over by the Company. When the Great Western Railway took over the Royal Hotel at Paddington in the following year, they transferred the headquarters of the catering department to Paddington but the organisation was not sufficiently mature to undertake the catering on the first restaurant cars which the Great Western ran in 1898. The contractors holding the Paddington station refreshment rooms, Browning and Wesley, catered for the Company. The firm of Browning and Wesley had 23 rooms all over the Great Western system, mainly in the West Midlands and north to Birkenhead.

The Hotel that the Great Western Railway took over at Paddington in 1896 was a magnificent building, magnificently furnished with a fine organisation, staff and tradition of service. Every new invention that was of use to a hotel was installed and by 1907 it had lifts, telephones, an exchange that could put a guest in touch with any part of the world, and all was illuminated by electricity. By the use of the pneumatic tube, a telegram message could be sent from one's bedside to the exchange where it could be sent to South America or anywhere else one fancied. Photographs show an Edwardian magnificence which will become increasingly magical and unbelievable as the years pass. The dining rooms with snow white damask table cloths and silver cutlery on beautifully carved mahogany tables, each table with a silver vase of sweet peas, irises or lilies of the valley. The waiter in livery, attentive, napkin on arm and that slight bend from the waist indicating deference to one's wishes, all this and the attitude of mind that went with it, was swept away in the 1934 re-furnishing.

We still benefit today from the improvements carried out by the old Company forty or more years ago but, unhappily, we suffer a nett loss. In 1950 it was possible to listen to the Great Western Railway Silver Band, (though there was a blur where the "G" of "GWR" was once painted on the board announcing the players) the band whose music had to compete with that other, more echoing music, which whooped, hissed and rang, as beautiful steam engines whistled and moved with a determined gracefulness under the Broad Gauge roof. Today there is no band, no steam, no music, and no excitement, only Brunel's roof endures, well preserved by British Rail in spite of successive attempts by Great Western Railway engineers to have it destroyed.

The station at Reading was opened to passengers on 30th March 1840 and was constructed on Brunel's "one-sided" system, all the buildings for the use of the public being on the south side of the line, nearest the town.

In effect there were two self-contained stations, one for "up" and one for "down" trains. Each station included a single line of rails passing between two platforms linked by a footbridge and sheltered by an all-over roof. Access to either station was through its booking office which, with other offices, was contained in a large, square, brick building like a town house, the awning excepted. Wantage Road station office was built to a similar, though smaller plan in 1844. (See page 339 *plate 518*.) A goods shed stood between each station so that their platforms did not meet and on the north side of the tracks, opposite the station, Brunel placed the engine shed.

Brunel was non-committal regarding the dangers of the one-sided station but there does appear to have been considerable potential danger with the very primitive signalling of those early days. Consider the method of operation at Reading. Trains calling at the station, or those requiring to pass by on the main line, were dealt with by two or maybe four points-men who had responsibility for the eastern, central and western ends of the station respectively. They walked about the layout pulling hand points according to traffic requirements, setting up routes with absolutely no interlocking to help them, and were obliged to remember what points were turned and for which direction. This they did in sun and rain, by night and by day. Very few signals were provided and these did not tell a driver over which route he was to travel but only that a way was clear. The points-man did not know in advance what train was approaching, he had a watch and a time-table so that he knew what ought to be coming but he had to recognise each train as it appeared in sight by its formation. Drivers had instructions to approach Reading carefully. The description so far could apply to any large "through" station, what made one-sided stations more dangerous than those of conventional layout was the constant crossing of running lines by trains calling at the station with no protection against a conflicting movement authorised by a forgetful, or tired, wet and cold, points-man. Only one story survives concerning a failure of the system and this involves the *Flying Dutchman,* then the fastest train in the world and one that did not call at Reading. As it approached the station a points-man "recognised" it for a "stopper" and turned the points for the platform. The "All Right" signal the driver saw did not indicate the route which had been set and the *Dutchman* went over the turn-out at 55 mph. The stability of the wide, broad gauge vehicles saved the day and the passengers and train crew received no more than a shaking. The culprit was found still grasping the point lever, standing upright in a dead faint.

The down main line passed quite close to the outside of each station's wall and to the rather insubstantial columns supporting the roofs. In 1858 a goods train became derailed and collided with these columns causing the collapse of the roofs. Thus the slow process of modernising the station began with a bang. The goods shed was removed and the up and down stations were joined together with a new length of platform sheltered by an awning. A larger depot for freight was put under construction on the north side of the line, at the front of the embankment and became known as the "Vastern Road" or "Low Level" goods yard. At station level, the engine shed was demolished about 1861 and a larger one erected on a new site, probably that occupied by the present diesel depot. There was now room to lay additional tracks and Caversham Road bridge was widened to accommodate them. Goods lines and a single track passenger line were laid. The latter were standard gauge and linked the standard gauge rails from Oxford at Reading West Junction with the South Eastern Railway, which lay on the south of the Great Western Railway and to the east of Reading Station. The new track was only a mile and a quarter long but it was a very important connection in the north west to south east rail communication.

In 1856 a third rail had been laid between the broad tracks from Oxford to Basingstoke to enable standard gauge trains to run from the north and north west to the south coast, a new loop line being built from the Reading-Didcot main line to the Berks & Hants branch. The former became known as Reading West Junction and the latter Oxford Road Junction. In 1857 the L. & S.W.R., in disguise as the "Staines, Wokingham & Reading Railway" had obtained Parliamentary powers to build a line over the Staines and Wokingham section and use the existing S.E.R. line into Reading. They had also been given permission to build a line from the S.E.R. station to Reading West Junction if the Great Western Railway had not built an equivalent line within a year. Not wanting "foreign" railways making junctions on their territory, the Great Western Railway laid the required track and put the junction on the other people's land! The new line descended the station embankment at Reading on the north side of the line at a gradient of 1 in 40 (this incline is still in use for shunting purposes) and turned sharp right into a tunnel beneath the Great Western main line, and so gained the metals of the S.E.R. Trains from Manchester to Dover used the line, but they did not call at the Great Western station until 1st October 1869 but reversed into the S.E.R. station.

The third rail was added to the broad gauge between Reading West Junction and Paddington on October 1st 1861 so that there was now a double line of rails for both broad and standard gauge trains, the old single track then being disused for passenger traffic between West Junction and the top of the incline. Yet Reading station could only accommodate broad gauge trains and it was eight years before the third rail was laid alongside its platforms. These were not the venerable broad gauge platforms but new platforms placed at each end of the earlier station. So the one-sided system was maintained and standard gauge trains had to call at separate up and down stations, using platforms that were too small for the trains, necessitating "drawing up" to get the rear coaches to the platform.

Under the one-sided system, the new platforms required their own offices but even the Directors could see that four separate booking offices at one station was too much of a good thing and tradition would have to be violated, so they built the present, Italianate facade. Construction was in yellow stock brick with a row of large well-proportioned windows above the awning. There were two styles of window, the more ornate forming a central group. Surmounting all was a clock tower and a finial in exact imitation of the type used on semaphore signals of the time, but, of course, the station's finial was much larger. The station looks grim, in my opinion, a businesslike station with no frills, well suited to a town of hard working factory hands and shop keepers. However, it was a great improvement on the wooden shanty town that the old station had become as bits were added over the years. Though the front was now respectable the inside was still a dreadful hotch-potch of tracks cobbled together from different periods of the station's development and it was to be another twenty-eight years before anything was done about this situation.

Reading station must constitute some sort of endurance record, for it endured as a blot on the Company's operating procedure even after the tracks from Reading to Didcot had been quadrupled in 1892. The shambles seems to have been tolerated because it had become a tradition, like getting lost at Crewe. At last, in 1896, a contract was signed between the Company and an "outside firm" to rebuild the station. The old platform was demolished in the following year, and the fact that it took ten new platforms to adequately accommodate the traffic previously served by one, gives a hint as to the chaos which must have prevailed at Reading over those past years.

Birmingham Snow Hill station was the first major station to be rebuilt by the Great Western Railway in the 20th century and the third station to occupy the site. The first station which was opened in 1852 and consisted of a "temporary" wooden shed, was dismantled in 1871 to make way for a permanent building. The old train shed went to Didcot on the site of the present locomotive depot of the Great Western Society. To judge from the single photograph I have seen of the old station it was eminently suited for use as a carriage or cattle shed. The 1871 station had an iron roof arching over the platforms and tracks in a single span. Only the windscreens were glazed so it must have been a dark and dismal place. Beneath the roof the layout consisted of an up and down main, and up and down platform loops with two bays at the northern end of the station. Only two tracks led to the station from the north and the south so that, by the turn of the century, traffic congestion was such that the queue stretched back in either direction for miles. A larger station was essential but the site posed a difficult problem. At the southern end of the platform was Snow Hill tunnel, a "cut and cover" construction from 1852 and now completely built over so as to make widening of the tunnel or its demolition practically impossible. To the east and west lay Snow Hill and Livery Street respectively and therefore the station could only expand northwards.

Work began on the new station in 1910. In expanding northwards the Engineer had to deal with the steep slope of Snow Hill which fell away to the north. He not only overcame this problem but turned it to advantage as will be seen. He constructed a viaduct falling to the north at 1 in 250 and so arranged the arches and gateways that all cart entrances were on the level of the destination of the inward bound carts. The cab entrance to the main booking hall was at the top of Livery Street while further down the hill the cart entrance to the docks for fish, milk, fruit and other perishables, was almost at rail level. Below this entrance was the "rolling way" for barrels to the cellars under the down-side refreshment rooms and below this again the cart entrance to a warehouse near the foot of Livery Street and

Great Charles Street. At the corner of these streets three shops were built for renting to increase the revenue earned by the site, other sites were available on the Snow Hill side. Under the viaduct were stables, garages, stores, an electricity sub-station and a parcels depot. The sub-station received current from the Corporation generator at 5,000 volts and reduced it to 110 volts for lighting and 440 volts for power for lift motors. There was also a small generator for charging batteries for the power signalling system which required, by day, 140 volts at 2 amps. Access to the parcels depot was from Snow Hill, the cart entrance being 24 ft. below rail level. The depot dealt with inwards and outwards parcels and there were electrically operated lifts to take merchandise to and from the platforms. These lifts communicated with the passenger subway and gained the platforms by means of the subway lifts. Above the parcels depot, but beneath the platforms, were living quarters for staff and kitchens for the upside refreshment rooms. At the intersection of Snow Hill with Great Charles Street the Company built a tower-like office to house the administrative staff of the station and to provide, architecturally speaking, a "full stop" to the northwards extending bulk of the great station.

The main entrance to the station was through an archway cut in the front of the Great Western Hotel which formed the facade of the station in Colmore Row. This archway gave access to the main booking hall, though one could also reach this by the cab entrance just round the corner in Livery Street or by a stairway from Snow Hill. The booking hall was a wide circulating area with the ticket windows on the right as one entered from Colmore Row and was entirely covered with a fine, steel arched roof. This could be described as being made of three hinged, lattice steel ribs of 93 ft. 9½ ins. span, a rise of 31 ft. 6 ins. from the springing point to the crown of the arch, the distance from there to the ground being 54 ft. Above the arch was a lantern light with louvred sides, 17 ft. 6 ins. across the base of the lantern. The glazing of the roof and windscreens was ¼ inch thick rough cast glass held in with 6 lb. lead. Tie rods, to check the out-thrust tendency of the ribs, were fitted and provided with adjustable screw couplings, the rods being some 2 inches in diameter. Halfway down Livery Street was the entrance to the passenger subway, 20 ft. wide, divided into a 12 ft. passage for pedestrians only and an 8 ft. passage for luggage. From the subway, stairs and electric lifts communicated with the platforms. There was also a "low level" booking hall, 18 ft. below rail level at the north end of the station on Great Charles Street.

From the main booking hall the passenger walked down a gentle slope to a footbridge 18 ft. above rail level and so to the platform of his choice by way of a wide staircase. As far as a passenger could tell the station consisted of two "island" platforms just over 1200 ft. long with a north facing bay 500 ft. long in each of these. The down bay had a "sector table" to enable a locomotive to "get out from under" its train when that engine was against the buffers. Four running lines passed between the island platforms, the up and down mains and their platform loops, while the up and down relief lines went behind their respective platforms. There were scissors crossovers half way along the main platforms to enable two trains to use one platform face at a time and to make it possible to number a platform face as two separate platforms. At the south end of the station the four lines converged into double tracks to pass through the tunnel and there were some sidings on each side of the line for fish, milk and horse traffic.

At the north end the four lines continued for some way and empty coaching stock sidings on the upside added to the appearance of a wide, vast layout. The station was signalled by electrically operated points and semaphore signals operated from two signal boxes at the north and south ends of the station respectively. The South box had 65 working levers and 15 spares and the North had 185 working and 39 spare levers, all these being miniatures, at 2 inch centres—not that our observant passenger would have known that unless he read the Great Western Railway Magazine! Our passenger could while away the time in a waiting room or in the oak panelled refreshment room where silver and porcelain gleamed against the sombre background of dark oak (see *figure 17*). All the platform buildings were rectangular in ground plan, built in brick and faced with a shiny red tile material. Over the door and window arches, which were semi-circular, segments of white tiling were inlaid, which produced a "Moorish" effect in my opinion. Each building had an ornate cornice and every arch its keystone, all of which were constructed as hollow castings with a moulded pattern to the fore. That they were hollow can be ascertained by viewing their vandalised remains—having first obtained permission to enter the premises from the resident car park attendant.

The platforms were sheltered by a very fine roof, a masterpiece of civil engineering in its time, now providing shelter for the all conquering motor-car. The station was built to a hanging level, i.e. its end walls were at right angles only to the falling gradient beneath, thus preserving a uniform clearance beneath the roof and the tracks, and this may account for the visible tendency of the now derelict building to fall to the north, down the slope. When constructed, however, no-one could have envisaged the station being deserted and left to rot and fall about. The station was light, well sheltered and ventilated by its magnificent roof, the style of which was known as "ridge and furrow" with a lantern light above each ridge. These ran at right angles to the tracks and terminated in hip gables 100 ft. above Livery Street and Snow Hill. The lantern light had steel louvred sides and open ended gables for additional ventilation while a space of 22 ft was left open above the four central tracks to allow steam and smoke to escape and "entirely remove that depressing sensation which is so frequently felt in all over roofed stations."

The area of roof was 12,000 square yards, most of which was covered with ¼ inch glass in Mellow's patent glazing bars, and it sheltered 500 lineal feet of platform beneath. Beyond this the platforms had the umbrella type of canopy found at many stations except that at Birmingham it was wider and therefore stronger than usual. Walkways were constructed on the roof to enable men to clean the glass and repair damage, the handrail at the eaves above Livery

Figure 17

Refreshment Room at Birmingham Snow Hill.

Street and Snow Hill doubling as a water main for glass cleaning. Ample consideration was given to disposal of rainwater falling on this wide area. A central eaves gutter was 20 ins. wide and 13 ins. deep made out of 3/8 inch plate steel while the gutters at the outer eaves were 21 ins. wide and 13 ins. deep, and all down pipes were 6 ins. diameter cast iron fittings.

Brick walls rose tall above the pavements of Snow Hill and Livery Street up to platform level and from there to the roof the space was filled with glass windscreens divided into sections by the great steel columns that supported the roof. These, like all load bearing columns in the station, were cased in ornamental cast iron plates having a fluted pattern rising to an egg and dart motif at the caps. The Engineer designed the columns to two parts, the lower part was in a box section of steel plate and the upper parts, about 12 ft. above the platform, were made of two rolled steel channels, 15 ins. wide and 4 ins. deep in the channel, braced together with steel plates. At the top of each column a flat steel plate was riveted in position and drilled to take rivets from the roof girder when that was mounted. The roof girders were riveted solid to their supports and there was no expansion gap or movable joint, like a roller bearing, to compensate for the contraction and expansion of the metal under extremes of temperature, though the length of finished girder would be, in some cases, 276 ft. This saving was possible owing to the construction of the supporting pillars which had enough "give" without any other compensating factor being introduced.

I think that the accuracy with which these roof support columns were sited was only a little short of miraculous, for consider the problems facing the engineers 64 years ago. About 56 columns had to be erected, four under each roof main girder, in some cases a year before the roof was ready to go on. In these cases it was because the column was sited within the brick wall of a platform building. Therefore, that building had to be marked out and built with the same tolerance of accuracy as that allowed to a rivet in its hole. Amongst the muddy turmoil of a building site the positions of the buildings, the exact points in the yet to be built wall, under a yet to be erected roof where the supporting columns were to stand, had to be plotted with the accuracy of the driven fit rivet. Across the station from Livery Street to Snow Hill one could name the supporting columns under any one girder as:— right outer, right inner, left inner, left outer. Owing to the shape of the site, the left and right outer columns followed a bulging curve around the rear of the platforms while the inner columns followed the dead straight line of the main line platform face. The distance between the right hand outer column and its inner colleague varied all along the platform as the width of the platform increased, and this applied also to those at the left hand side of the station. The distance between opposing inner columns was constant at 103 ft. across the width of the four tracks. From the centre of one row of columns to the next was an unvarying 35 ft. 10 ins. All these distances had to be pinpointed with the greatest accuracy. A tape measure was used for all measurements on one platform but there arose another problem when the engineers came to measure across the four main lines; there was so much traffic that they did not have time to stretch the measure across and make precise readings! Sitings were therefore made with a theodolite working from a base line of pegs in the down platform road. Heavy use of the track tended to alter the position of the pegs as did the packing and maintenance of the permanent way gangs but the base line was checked carefully and adjusted as required. It is said that on several occasions a surveyor only just escaped with his life, leaping clear with his heavy tripod as some train bore down on him. In spite of all these hazards the job was done, the columns erected and when the roof girders were lowered into position the holes in their flanges and those in the column cap plate were in perfect alignment.

The roof was composed of main girders running transverse to the tracks and of roof trusses parallel to the tracks. The main girders were of the parallel flange, open web type, measuring 8 ft. in depth and 15 ins. across the flange. Vertical and diagonal bracing in an "N" formation was provided by three, 3½" x 3½" x ½" angles. The vertical members were at 6 ft. 9 ins. centres except for the three central bays where they were at 7 ft. 4 ins. The central bay was double braced. Springing from every second vertical member of the main girder were the roof trusses which also carried the framework of the lantern light. These trusses were built up in angle steel, ridge-shaped at their outer edges, with an inner section of "Z" form latticework attached to an elliptical soffit. Timber valance boards were fitted to the line of these trusses along the central opening of the roof above the tracks. The valances had fretted edges and wooden mouldings and did a great deal to remove the metallic angularity of the building.

Erection of the roof was in two parts, the assembly and raising of that part of the main roof girder which was to rest over the left or right hand outer and inner columns, and the far more difficult business of lifting the 15 ton, 103 ft. long, central section of the girder 28 ft. above the platforms and carrying it to rest on the opposing inner columns so that it spanned the four central tracks. The former operation was simplified by riveting the girder work together on the platform and lifting it onto the columns with a small derrick. Girderwork for the trusses was lifted up with a pole carrying a block and tackle and riveted to the main girder by men aloft. To erect the 103 ft. section of the main roof girder, a special travelling stage was built. If the Engineer had been able to close the station for a year while he rebuilt it, each girder could have been assembled on the platform and jacked up into its final position, but in those days it seems to have been a point of honour not to interrupt the train service. Whether one was erecting a signal, dismantling or rebuilding a station or even widening a tunnel from single to double track, the trains never stopped running. In modern times we have closed a major station for a fortnight in order to renew the signalling system. At Birmingham in 1910 the traffic never ceased running by day or night, on Sundays it slackened but the work of reconstruction was never allowed to interfere with the running of revenue earning trains.

The travelling stage was made from three lattice work girders by the steel work contractors for the station, E. & C. Keay, a famous Birmingham firm. Each girder

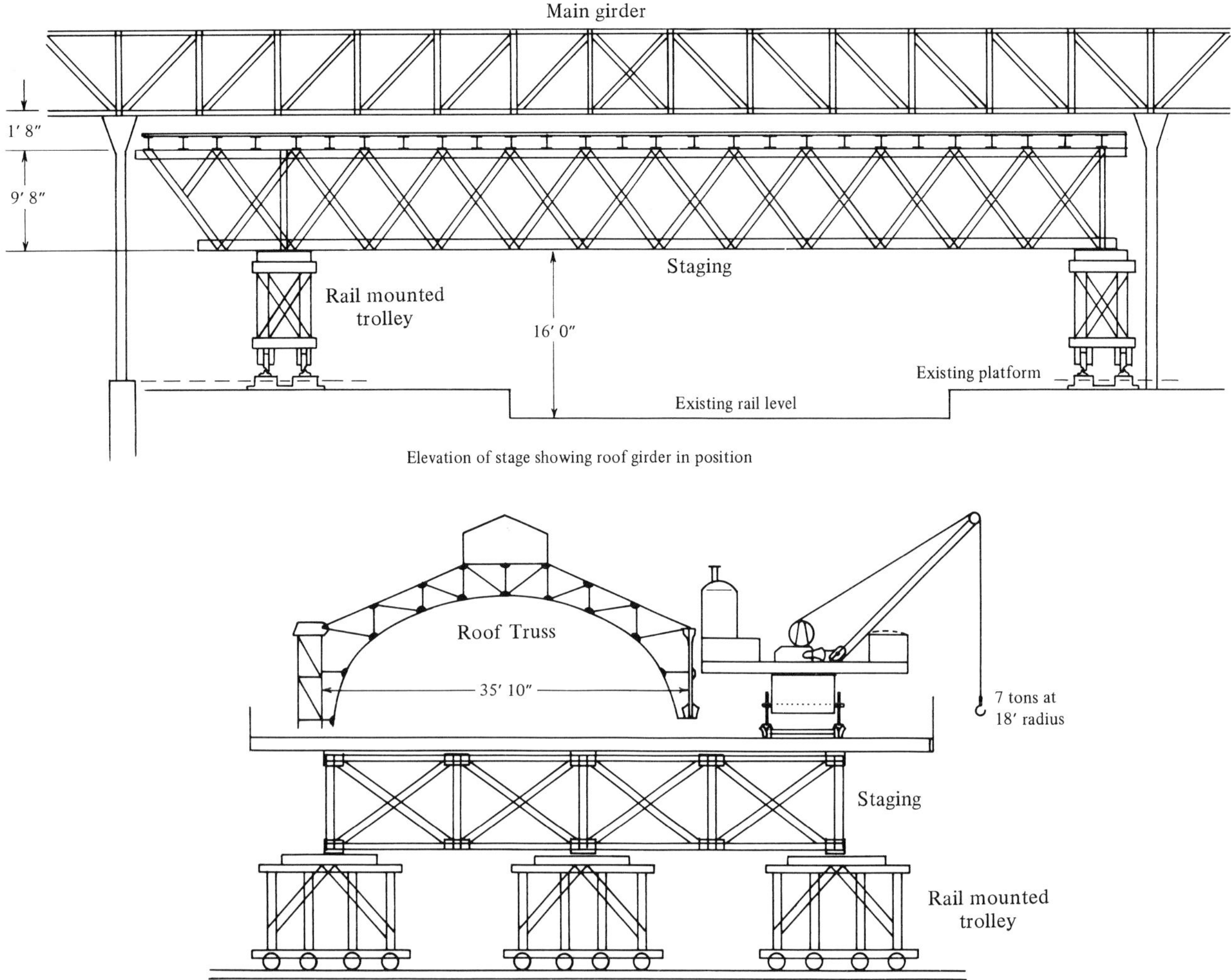

Figure 18

Temporary staging and travelling crane used to erect the roof of Birmingham Snow Hill Station in 1912.

weighed 11 tons, was 95 ft. long (80 ft. of which was to span the rails and platforms), 9 ft. 8 ins. deep and set at 25 ft. centres from its neighbour. They rested, when in use, upon trestles made of six 1 ft. square timbers, well braced together and mounted on eight wheels. One of these trestles sat on each platform on a special rail track over which the assembly moved. Keay's sent the girders piecemeal from Greenwich where they were last used and they had to raise them across the station before they could use them to lift the main roof girders. To do this they built one rail mounted trestle on each platform and on the up platform a second temporary trestle was raised. This was done at the widest part of the platform (80 ft.) and by means of a long wooden pole and a block and tackle the sections of the girders were raised up and bolted together till the entire 95 ft. rested on two trestles. The "nose" and "tail" projected 7 ft. 6 ins. over the up relief and up platform line but was high enough to be clear of the trains beneath. Early one Sunday morning the up platform, up main and down main lines were blocked for two hours, single line working being operated on the down platform line, while the girders were pulled and shoved out across the track. Having obtained the possession of these running roads, the Engineer erected temporary supports for the girders as they passed over the space beneath. When the three girders were safely at rest on the down and up platform trestles, all temporary supports were removed and the station could return to normal working. With the great steel beams in position the next move was to space them to the 25 ft. centres already mentioned and lay on a timber decking of 2 inches thick planks 96 ft. long and 76 ft. wide (see *figure 18*). This was a truly enormous piece of work, designed to take the weight of an entire centre section of the main girder if necessary and to afford complete protection for the trains and passengers below. From rail level to the soffit of the stage was 16 ft, thus clearing the loading gauge and allowing the normal business of the station to proceed unhindered, while the deck of the stage was 2 ft. 4 ins. below the level of the main roof girder when finally erected. A self-propelled steam crane was now lifted onto the stage and set to move across its length on a rail track. This crane was capable of lifting 7 tons at a radius of 18 ft. One road was now taken by the Engineer in order to stand a wagon, bearing the central section of the roof girder in three pieces, beneath the crane. The latter then lifted the section up and held them in position while the workmen, using pistol type riveters, fixed them solid to the columns. These riveting guns worked at 90 psi derived from a small oil engine driven compressor. Thus the station was completed with only the simplest of equipment, a block and tackle, some hefty timbers, winches, spanners and tape measures. The steam crane and riveting guns were the nearest thing to power tools and both of these were of modest proportions. It would have been possible to have had a hand winch on the stage and close the rivets up by hand then the methods would have all been familiar to Brunel. Lacking our specialised knowledge of metals and equipment, the mechanics of 1910 used what they had to hand and a great deal of effort and initiative. Today we would have done the job simply, using a tower crane, but even with such aids we do not build stations like Snow Hill any more.

I have gone into the construction of the station in some detail because it was a very fine example of early 20th century railway engineering and because I thought that the methods that were employed to erect it seemed primitive in comparison to what was achieved by their means. Perhaps the only mistake that was made was to build the station to a hanging level, so that now, after ten years of neglect the building is falling northwards down Snow Hill. I walked round it in June of 1974. The track space had been filled to platform level and cars stood everywhere like the foul smelling, brightly coloured fungus that grows on rotting trees. In the gloomy stillness of the arches beneath the station more cars ranged while all round was silent ugliness. The cellar walls were lined with tiles that had once been white but now were dingy, broken, yellow and covered in aerosol scrawls. The walls above the arches, in falling northwards, had torn a jagged crevasse in the bonding of the bricks, the windscreens broken or wholly removed. The station today makes a pitiful sight.

Birmingham Snow Hill station was designed by Mr W. Armstrong, New Works Engineer of the Great Western Railway. The contractor for the brick work, plumbing, timber and painting was Henry Lovatt, and the thousands of yards of glass and miles of glazing bars were supplied and erected by Mellowes & Co., Keay's, as already stated, being responsible for steel and steel work erection.

Regarding staff housing, it was always the Great Western Railway's policy to have at least one member of the staff living close at hand for then the station could always be supervised and there was little risk of passengers being left without attention due to a porter oversleeping and arriving at work late. It follows from this that the problem of housing was more acute in the country where a station was often far from any housing. The Company's Rule Book stated "Employees must reside at a place appointed by the Company." The rule was probably meant to direct staff to railway owned dwellings at their place of work but as these were always in short supply (the Company employed scores of thousands of men) the rule was always interpreted liberally. It is possible that all stations built between 1835 and 1855 had dwellings built with them, Moulsford, Culham and Steventon all had housing as old as the stations, the accommodation at Steventon being unusually extensive. Where a road crossed the railway and gates had to be erected it seems almost certain that the Company provided a house of some sort for the crossing keeper at every such place.

Against the convenience of having the staff living close to their work, the Company had to balance the expense of building and maintaining such a building. If it cost £100 to put up and that investment would earn x%, then the Company wanted x% in rent or it would be making a loss on the house, and if that sum was beyond the means of an employee to pay, then he did not get the house. So long as costs remained fairly stable it was possible to build a cheap house for the man without loss to the Company but after 1854 the profits of the line fell from the 4% of that year to 1½% in 1857 and did not reach the 4% mark again till 1871 when they stood at 4.15/4.16%. During this period of poor trading the Company could not afford to build housing and after 1875 the cost of construction was raised by an Act of Parliament laying down basic standards for working men's new houses which again made it difficult for the Directors to authorise expenditure on such buildings. New stations continued to be built because they could be expected to earn a bigger percentage for initial outlay and the larger of these stations had station master's accommodation built in but the plight of the rural station staff remained acute. The provision of Staff Housing continued in a desultory manner until 1897 when a far ranging programme was undertaken which lasted until 1914.

Of course, this was the period of the "cut-off" and "new line" construction through remote and often sparsely populated parts of the country so that it was in the Company's interest to provide a house or houses at each station to encourage men to work at "out of the way" places. But it was not only on the new lines that housing was provided, during the 1897-1914 period standard types of housing were built at older stations where no house had existed before; one can see identical and handsome houses at Athelney, Cranmore, Savernake and Challow. 80 years ago there was a housing shortage and a man who took promotion also took the risk of failing to find a house with the result that he might have to take a single room, leave his family miles away at the old job and only return to visit them as his duties allowed. In a report to the Great Western Railway Directors the General Manager in 1912 said, "In rural areas a man coming fresh to the neighbourhood is looked on as a "foreigner" and refused accommodation for this reason, because it is needed for local workers and because it is thought that this Company is big enough to build homes for its staff." The houses that the Great Western Railway built during this period were not mean or skimped but well built, dignified and substantial.

During the 1914-18 War there was no house building so that a terrible shortage existed at the cessation of hostilities. The government of the day passed the Housing Act of 1919 to assist local councils to levy rates and for the government to give these councils grants for the purpose of building houses. The Great Western Railway found it almost impossible to build houses because costs had risen four-fold in the six years between 1913 and 1919. In 1919 the General Manager had received 300 requests for houses at various stations but almost always preventing action from being taken was the price of materials, labour and money. To let a house at a realistic rent required that payment to equal 7% per annum of the capital cost of building. Most railway employees could not afford more than 3%. In reply to these applications the General Manager advised the men to "badger" the local councils "who have the statutory power to raise cheap loans for house building." On the positive side the Company did loan money against the security of a life policy and in the last resort actually did build the house and let it out at an uneconomic rent.

Figure 19
Temple Meads Station circa 1900.

Chapter One

A Selection of Great Western Station Architecture

Bristol Temple Meads

Plate 1

The noble front of the 'Joint' station built by the Great Western Railway, Midland and Bristol and Exeter Companies. It was commenced in 1865 and completed in 1876.

British Rail

Plate 2
The Victoria Street front of the original, terminal station of the Great Western Railway in Bristol, as it was in about 1900.

British Rail

Plate 3
This is a photograph of Brunel's original plan, which looked a little different to the completed building.

British Rail

Plate 4
The 'Gothic' staircase, Bristol Temple Meads, Old Station. Brunel's terminus would not look out of place in Turl Street, or the 'High' at Oxford. The medieval character of the building is no meaningless facade but is apparent throughout the building including cobbled courtyards and this staircase. The handrail, newels and balusters are made of oak and the stairs are wide, in fact wide enough for two ladies in crinoline dresses to pass one another without touching. In Brunel's pencil sketches for the staircase he gave the octagonal newels a lantern-like top and, in the sketch, there is the suggestion that a candle could have been housed therein. Although eventually constructed with these lesser ornaments, the staircase is still good enough to grace a country house and seems far too grand for a railway station.
Author 1973

Plate 5
The '15th' century ceiling, looking up from the foot of the 'Gothic' staircase. The plaster between the beams was painted deepest red throwing the 'wheel' and its pendant boss, dead white, into sharp relief.
Author 1973

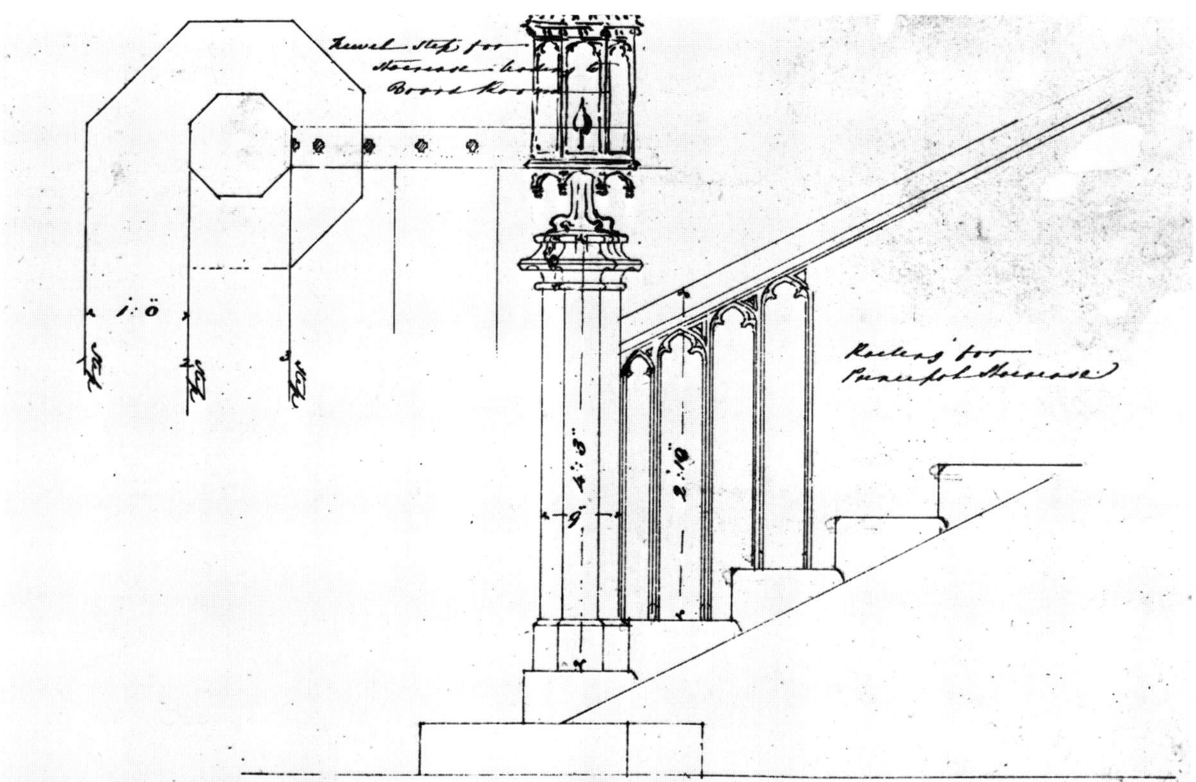

Plate 6
Working drawings prepared from Brunel's sketches for the chimney pieces in the Boardroom at Bristol and for the ceiling over the Boardroom staircase. ▼

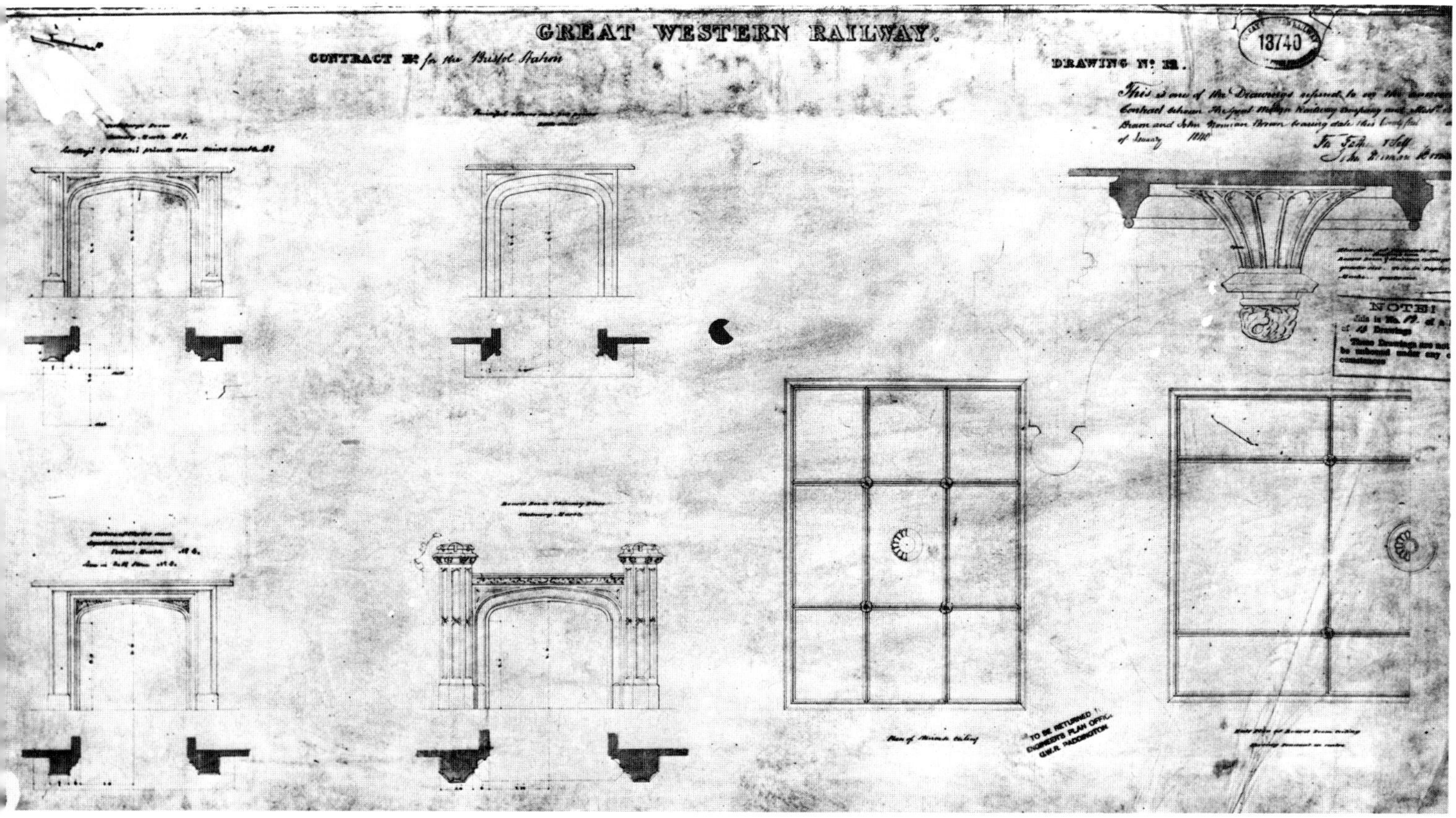

▲ *Plate 7*
This plate is made from a sketch by Brunel for the newel posts of the staircase to the Boardroom. The handwriting is Brunel's.

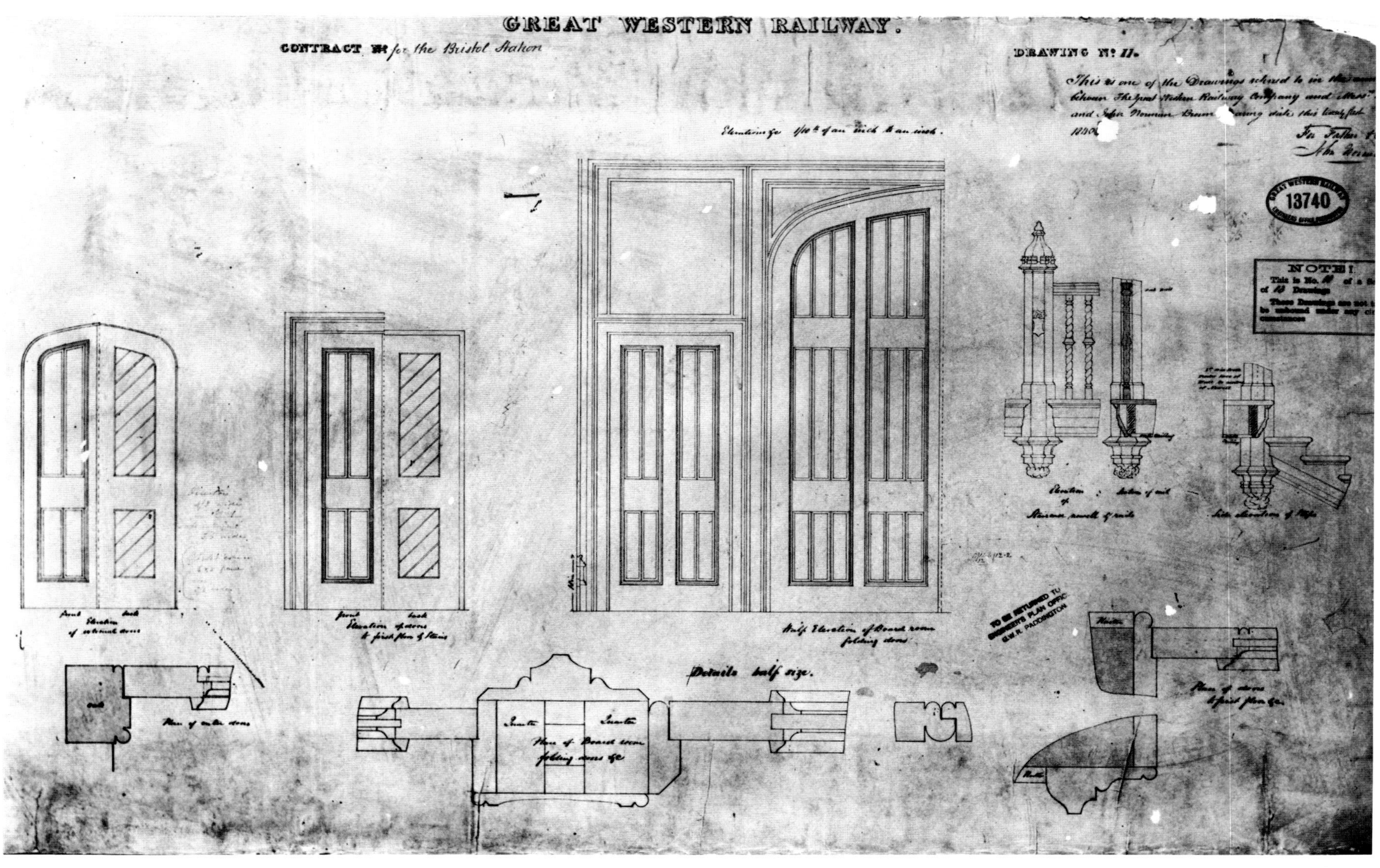

Plate 8
Detail of sliding doors for the Bristol Boardroom and for newels and balusters in the staircase to the Boardroom.

Plate 9
Detail from the head of a newel.
Author 1973

Plate 10
Interior of the original terminus at Bristol Temple Meads looking west to the buffers. The roof supports and colonnade are constructed entirely in timber perpetuating the medieval motif of Brunel's design. These timbers, now over 130 years old, continue a useful, if somewhat degraded life as the roof of a car park.
British Rail

Plate 11
Detail of the magnificent timbers forming the roof supports at Bristol Temple Meads Old Station. They form a roof as fine as that of Westminster Hall, London, Brunel having perfectly recreated the atmosphere of the 15th century in his design.

British Rail

Plate 12
Sunlight streams into the 'cloisters' at Bristol Temple Meads—just as Brunel planned.

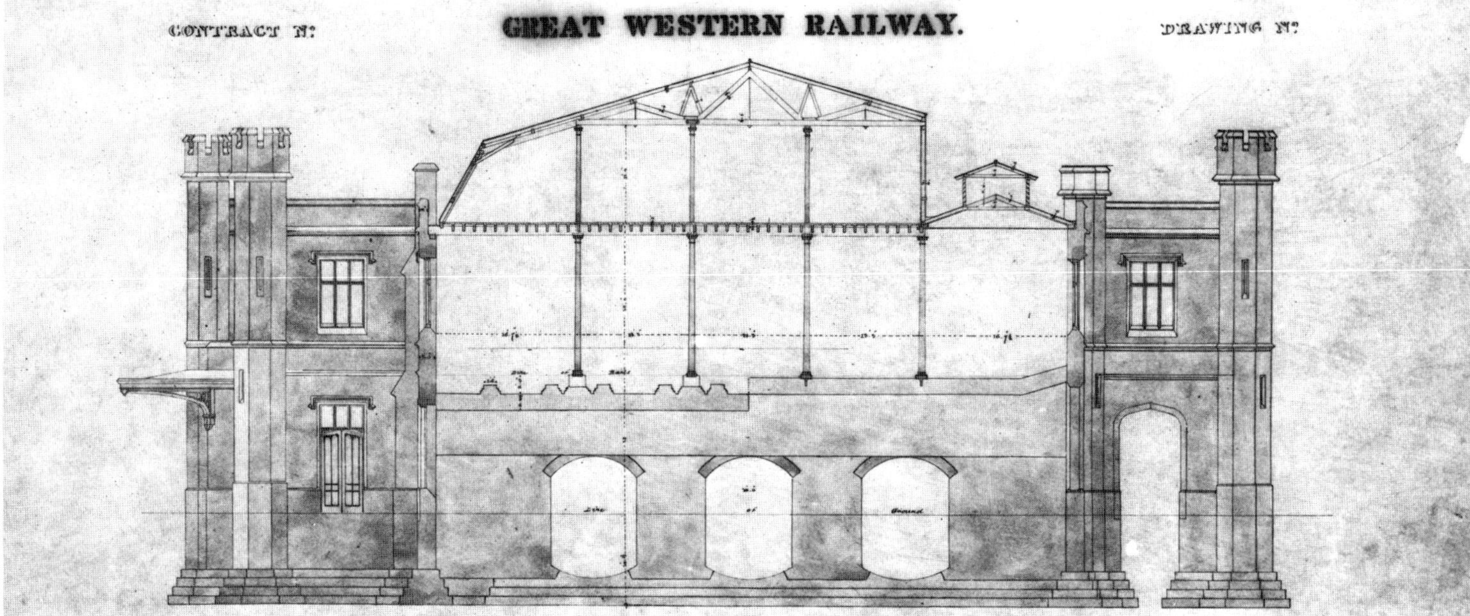

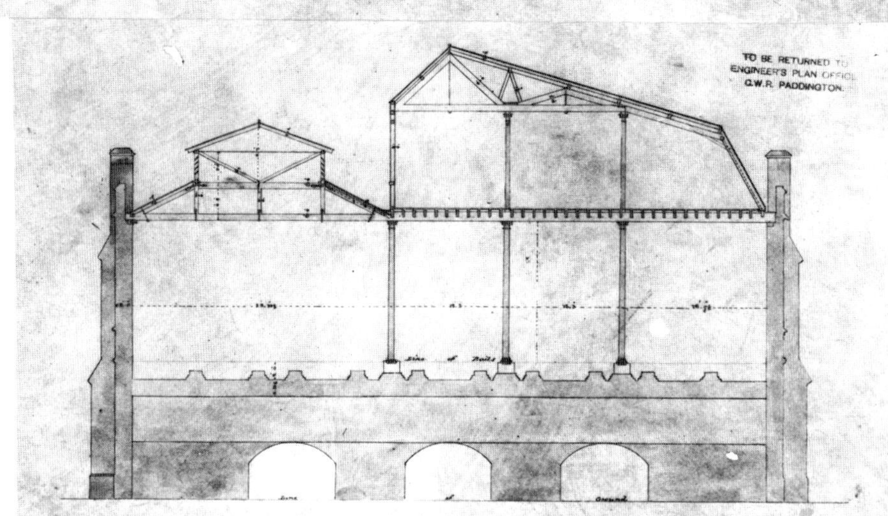

Plate 13
These are photographs of the sections and elevations for the terminus at Bristol, probably drawn by Brunel himself. The drawings from which these photographs are made are treasured by the staff of the Plans Room of the Chief Civil Engineer's Office, Paddington.
British Rail

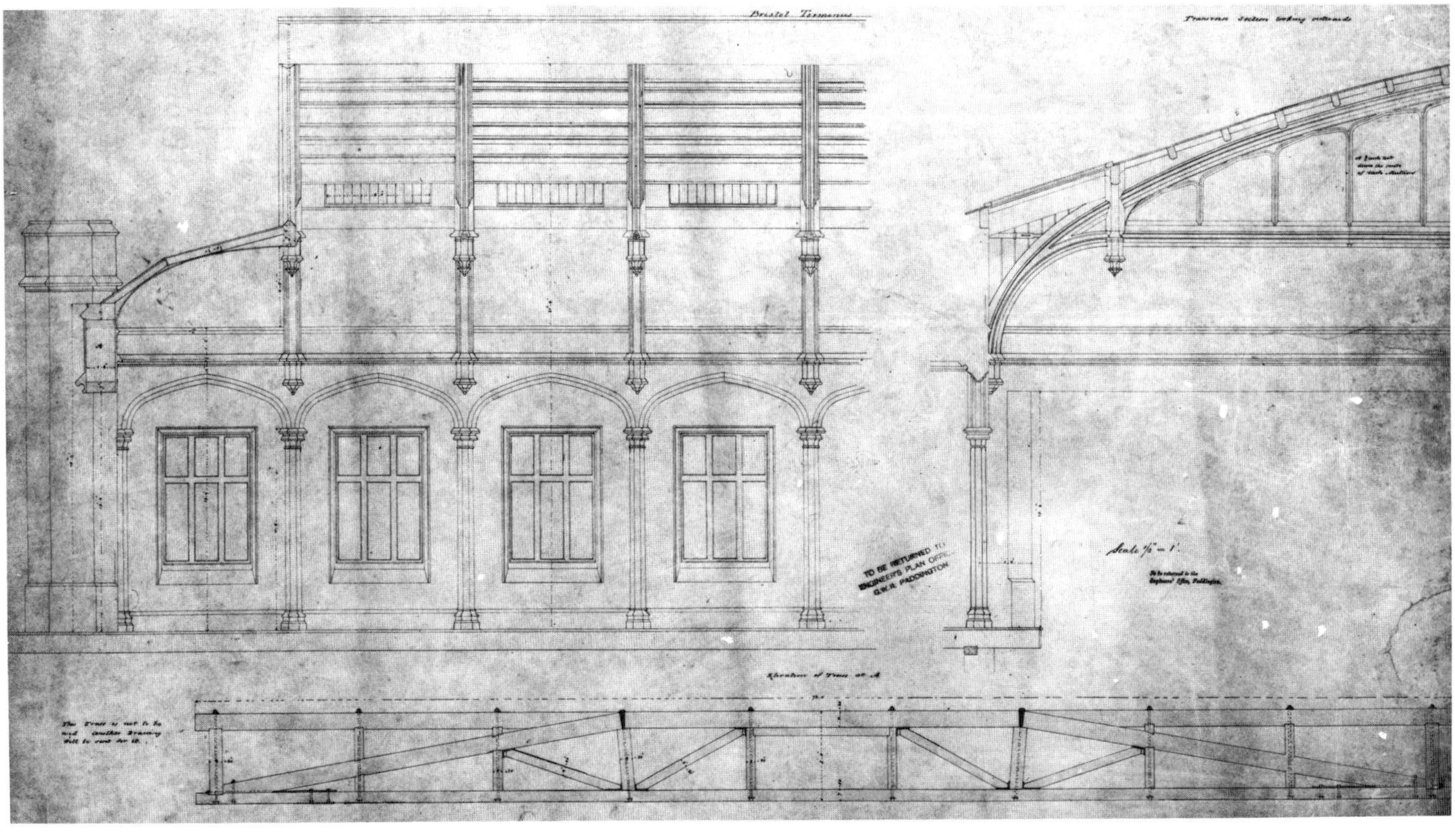

Plate 14
The cathedral-like splendour of the booking hall in the 'Joint' station, Bristol.

British Rail

Plate 15
Two plans were drawn up for the 'Joint' station, one difference between them being the spire which rises from the central tower. It was not included in one plan. Fortunately the spire has been removed. The cones over the turrets were much more ornate on both original plans and have probably lost their decorations due to the crumbling of the stone and to various cleaning operations undertaken over the years.

British Rail

Plate 16
Detail of verandah seen in the left of plate 15. The iron work is very similar to that employed at Weston-super-Mare. The latter station was designed by the Bristol and Exeter Railway Engineer, F. Fox, and as the Joint station was built in co-operation with the B. & E.R. it is very likely that Fox drew up some of the plans. In my opinion the stone work on the station front is very like the work of Fox.

British Rail

Plate 17
Head of an iron column supporting the roof near the restaurant on platform 3.

Author 1973

Plate 18

Top left. Converging rows of columns at the east end of number 3 platform, Bristol Temple Meads station. On the left are those columns supporting the roof over the old terminus when that roof was extended between 1865 and 1876. The right hand row support the roof of the 'new' station.

Bottom left. Tie rods in the 'new' roof.

Top right. Upper windows in the restaurant on platform 3.

Bottom right. Doorway at the front of the station. This illustrates well the recurring theme of quatrefoil; the oaken doors are embellished with a series of stylised Tudor roses.

Author 1973

Plate 19
Western end of the 1876 roof of Bristol Temple Meads station. By giving the span a shape closely corresponding to the stone arches elsewhere in the station, the designers have managed to construct a typically Victorian masterpiece in iron which remains in sympathy with the rest of the '15th' century station. Added to the complication of the shape of the roof arch is the fact that the line of the roof must follow a very sharp curve. To soften the harsh line of the verticals in the windscreen of the arch, ornamental ironwork has been fitted to the upper ends of the glass panels in an imitation of lancet windows.

British Rail

Plate 20
Details of parts of the windscreen in the '1876' roof. The painstaking arrangement of wrought iron strips to form lancets is well illustrated here.

British Rail

Plate 21

A view from platform 3 (numbered 9 when this photograph was taken) looking towards the new platform built during 1932/34 beyond the arcading of the 1865/76 station.

British Rail

Plate 22

A view west along No. 4 platform which became No. 9 when the work was finished and today is numbered 3.

British Rail

Plate 23

The new 1934 buildings retained some similarity to the 1876 station in that their windows were still mullioned and had the same proportions, but brick rather than stone was the building material. The various rooms and offices were faced with 'Carrara ware' except for the plinth which was in polished granite. Early period platform seats are set against the wall.

Author 1973

Plate 24

Several stations were enlarged during the 1930's including Cardiff, Newport, Taunton and Newton Abbot. This plate illustrates a standard design of awning and column used a great deal in the new stations. The columns are cylindrical, tapering slightly to the top which has fillets and a flare up to the cross girder bearing. At Cardiff these columns have recently received a very bright livery.

Author 1973

Plate 25

Two styles of sign. In the foreground is the modern 'Gentlemen', and on the wall behind, the ceramic tiles from 1934. The surround for the words of the latter and the words themselves are formed with dark reddish-brown bricks against the stone coloured glazed tiles. The pointing hand is constructed in pink ceramics, protruding from a coat cuff of the same reddish brick already mentioned. This style, an up-dated Victorian theme, seems to have been the standard for all the stations re-built at this time.

Author 1973

Plate 26

Plate 27

Plate 26

Interior of the buffet on Platform 9, numbered 3 nowadays. This appears to have been re-modelled during the 1932/34 extensions to the station layout and buildings. A modern flooring material has been laid, and there is a new counter and lighting. Here is a fine, spacious, airy room, built like the drawing room of some great house, with elegant windows and a high ceiling to allow plenty of air in to dilute the steam from tea making and sausage frying operations. Today, with an eye to providing a 'cosy' atmosphere, the fine timbered ceiling has been obscured with a scaffolding of aluminium tubing hanging from the beams to within 8 feet of the patrons' heads. This is said to have improved 'customer comfort' by relieving feelings of agoraphobia which may have been suffered in the original lofty room, a humid atmosphere being preferred. The scaffolding is also of material advantage at Christmas time when the seasonal decorations are merrily attached to the tubing.

British Rail

Plate 27

A waiting room at Bristol Temple Meads as refurbished in the taste of the 1930's. A parquet block floor, walnut veneer panelling and the ubiquitous mural of the 'Cornish Riviera' leaving 'Parson and Clerk' tunnel between Dawlish and Teignmouth.

British Rail

Plate 28

The splendid new booking hall at Bristol Temple Meads. The ceiling is fit for a country house; I wonder how many passengers looked up at it and thanked the Great Western Railway for providing fine ceilings free of charge!

British Rail

BRISTOL TEMPLE MEADS STATION

REFRESHMENT ROOMS ETC

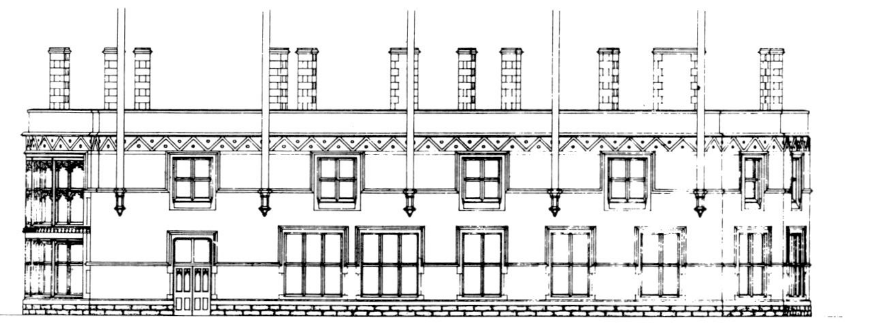

ELEVATION TO PLATFORM No 4

END ELEVATION

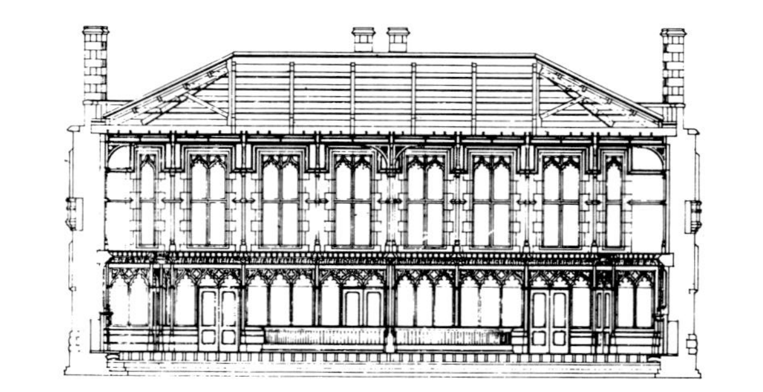

SECTION A.A.

PLAN

SCALE: 8 FEET TO 1 INCH

Entrance
2nd Class Refreshment Room
2nd Class Dining Room
Ladies' Room
Lav.
Office
Pantry
Kitchen
Passage
Scullery
Stall
Ladies' Rm
1st Class Dining Room
1st Class Refreshment Room
Entrance
Entrance
Entrance
A
A

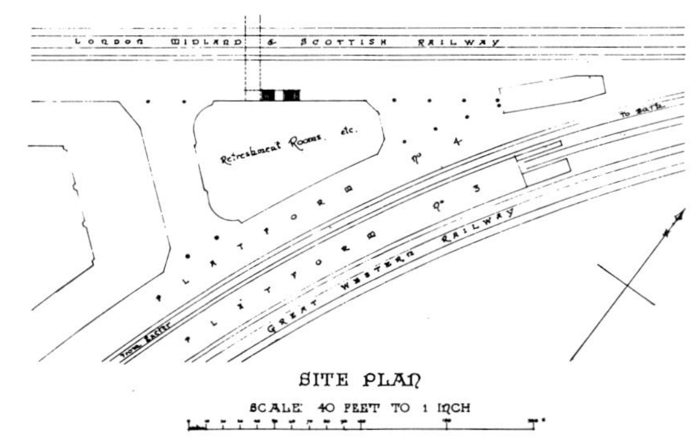

SITE PLAN

SCALE 40 FEET TO 1 INCH

Plate 29

ENGINEER'S OFFICE
PADDINGTON. W.2

Plate 30
The small post office at Temple Meads. Dated 1910.

Bath

Plate 31
The Northern, or upside, facade of Bath station. The building is constructed after the manner of the 17th century to Brunel's designs and was completed in 1841. The present building was constructed to the middle size of three plans drawn up by Brunel. The largest plan included an extension eastwards along the platform, featuring the mullioned windows employed in the station as built. The smallest plan was for a short facade only without any wing or extension. In all three cases the central portion was to have identical decorations but the largest plan showed a 'Manson' roof behind the Dutch gables. The central gable lost its pinnacle and gained a clock after 1931. The present porte-cochère dates from the 1880's or 90's, originally there was a glazed, timber awning on timber posts. On the left of the picture is a footbridge which connected the station with the 'Railway Hotel'. The bridge was demolished in January 1936.

British Rail

Plate 32
Bath Station is built on a viaduct, so it is remarkable to see how much track the engineers have managed to squeeze in. The station had an 'overall' roof which is believed to have been removed about 1895/97. The platform for passenger trains began on the far side of the ramp on the left of the picture. The track between the ramp and the left hand edge of the picture led to wagon turntables and a goods shed, the site of which is now part of the station car park.

British Rail

Plate 33
A window in the wall on the downside at Bath station. The window frame and mullions are in Bath stone and this was part of the 1841 station.
Author 1973

Plate 34
East facing wall on the downside at Bath station.
Author 1973

Plate 35
The 'Upside' facade at Bath station from the 'Berni Royal Hotel', by courtesy of the Manager.
Author 1973

Plate 36

This shows most of the original facade on the 'downside' at Bath. Not shown are five windows, also part of the 1841 building, which extend beyond the picture to the right. The window on the extreme left is one of a series set into a yellow brick wall and not part of the original building, but probably erected after 1895. The canopy over the booking office entrance, seen here as a 'standard' Great Western Railway construction was, before 1925, an iron hip-sided affair. The footbridge which spans the Avon to connect the station with Widcombe High Street was built in 1877 to replace a suspension bridge which collapsed under a heavy load of people during that year. This was a toll bridge and was built by a private company, i.e. not by the Great Western Railway. The single storey dwelling on the north end of the bridge was erected after 1860 and was for many years the offices of the Divisional Engineer. The downside booking office was closed in April 1962.

British Rail

Cirencester

Plate 37
Cirencester station was built during 1839/41 to Brunel's designs for the Cheltenham and Great Western Union Railway. This Company's line was open to the public from Swindon to Cirencester on May 31st 1841, and from Kemble (which then became the junction for Cirencester) to Cheltenham on May 12th 1845. Brunel stated in one of his early reports to the Shareholders of the Great Western Railway that he built his stations to a size and scale of magnificence as seemed in keeping with its importance, and Cirencester was an important county town. The style is reminiscent of that employed at Steventon in the Superintendent's house there, but Cirencester station was rather larger and more ornate than the Steventon house. It appears from this photograph that the station once had an overall roof and a canopy over the booking office entrance. There is also over the bay window an ornate scroll which has never been engraved.

British Rail

Plate 38
Part of Cirencester station.
British Rail

Pangbourne

Plate 39
Pangbourne station, soon after it was opened to the public in June 1840. Brunel called these little places 'roadside' stations and tried to make them blend in with their surroundings; take away that awning and you have the lodge house at the gates of a Gentleman's park. The plate is a copy of a lithograph by J.C. Bourne who has captured in his drawing the youthfulness of the Great Western Railway on an early Spring day.

British Rail

Plate 40
Shrivenham station soon after its opening in 1841. A print by an unknown artist. This style of building, personally designed by Brunel, can be termed typical. It is recognisably 'Brunelian' yet it also has a unique quality of its own. This was the art of Brunel. He drew up four or five basic designs and then, by varying the building material, or an awning, produced a building that was at once both standard and unique. He was able to create the impression that the line from Paddington to Bristol was furnished with 'one off' buildings without incurring the expense of such a policy.

British Rail

Shrivenham

Plate 41

Shrivenham station has a slightly unusual awning in that the supporting beams do not lie across the entire width of the building but spring from the wall like a bracket. Apart from this peculiarity the station appears to be a flint stone version of a 'standard' style seen at other places both in limestone or brick. The goods shed seems to me to be very old and could date from the early 1840's. The 'lean-to' type office and chimney with the stone and brick stack, are very typical of the early period on the Great Western Railway. This is as I remember the station; 'Castles' and 'Kings' eternally beating through the middle road and down the Vale of White Horse. This particular train was the 8.00 a.m. up, from Neyland.

British Rail 1960

Plate 42

Shrivenham station looking east.

British Rail 1960

Plate 43
Culham station, just north of Didcot, is probably the sole surviving example of the very early 'Pangbourne' type station. It is definitely the only example still in the public service. Culham was built to Brunel's drawings three or four years after Pangbourne, for the Oxford Railway. As far as can be ascertained from comparing the Bourne print of Pangbourne with the present Culham station the two are identical except that Bourne does not show the cast iron brackets below the awning support beams.
Author 1973

Culham

Plate 44
A view over the roof of Culham station from the footbridge. The steep pitch of the roof is accentuated by a string course in limestone and by limestone coping stones. The diamond shaped chimneys are positioned exactly as shown in the Bourne print of Pangbourne (*plate 39*). This type of awning is encountered in all but one of Brunel's roadside stations and in those stations designed by Brunel's assistants who merely copied the 'great' man's work. These awnings are parallel to the platform and extend all round the perimeter of the building. There is no valance and a minimal slope to act as a rain water run-off. Beyond this early Victorian station are the buildings of the Astro-Physics Research Establishment, Culham.
Author 1973

Plate 45

This photograph shows the close detail of the wall, cast-iron bracket and window-arch at Culham. The wall has false pointing along the actual bonding to give the impression of a better class of work than was actually carried out. Most of this has now fallen away, but the bonding was painted dull red to match the bricks and the thin lines of mortar then painstakingly applied. It is said that this was done for the benefit of Lord Harcourt who lived nearby and used the station for his family and for the conveyance of the produce from his farms. His Lordship's influence was so strong that he was able to have the exterior woodwork of the station painted green instead of cream and brown as he thought that the former colour blended better with the surroundings.

Author 1973

Plate 46

A view of Culham station from the downside yard. The footbridge has timber 'stringers' i.e. the beams that support the treads and risers of the staircase, which suggests that it is a very old bridge, but probably it was brought to Culham second-hand in 1908 and has not been here for all of its life. The bridge inspector considers this unlikely and believes that it was erected here in the late 1870's, but certain documentary evidence suggests to me that it came here in 1908. The station is still in use and one can still have the pleasure of buying a ticket at Paddington for this delightful spot in the upper Thames Valley, or better still, of going into the dark little booking office at Culham itself and purchasing your train ticket. Experience the feeling while you still have the opportunity.

Author 1973

The Dorchester-on-Thames to Abingdon road crossing the Oxford Railway on the level at Culham. The engraving shows the scene, looking east as a down train approaches the south end of the station.

CULHAM, LATE ABINGDON ROAD STATION, 1844.

Plate 47

Midgham

Plate 48
Midgham station was opened in December 1847 as part of the Berks and Hants line, though at that date the station was called Woolhampton. This name was changed in 1873 doubtless to avoid confusion with Wolverhampton. The station has the broad gauge style awning as used at Culham and other stations, but here the windows are quite plain, with no 'Gothic' pretensions. There is a low roof instead of the almost flat roof of Shrivenham and some other early stations, and is therefore an advance on the latter, as the station now has attic space. The chimneys and valance boards are later additions to the building which was probably designed by one of Brunel's assistants, R.P. Brereton, or J.H. Bertram.

British Rail

Plate 49
Castle Cary station is built in a local stone from quarries at Kineton. The ground plan is a simple rectangle, indeed, the whole building was built to the simplest design possible. It was built for the Wilts, Somerset and Weymouth Railway to designs of R.P. Brereton who designed practically all the buildings on this line from Frome to Maiden Newton. Similar stations were to be found on the Westbury to Salisbury line.

Author 1973

Castle Cary

Bradford-on-Avon

Plates 50/51/52

The station at Bradford-on-Avon was built during 1848, but the rails were not laid and the station did not commence to serve the public until 1857. The station is very handsome, with bay windows, fine gables and diamond shaped chimneys (all in Bath stone) though the latter have been rebuilt in engineer's brick. There is a similarity in this design to the stations at Melksham and Trowbridge, although this station (Bradford) is smaller, and one is tempted to say that it is an example of the 'Standard Station', the designs for which were drawn out by J. Geddes, J. Nolloth and F. Prinsit in 1848. No drawings remain of these designs, only a reference in the files. There were four designs, 'Gothic' and 'Italianate' in large and small sizes. The awning is the usual kind, parallel to the platform, extending around the station, though by the time these photographs were taken it had been dismantled except for the portion over the platform. The marks exist on the wall to show where the supporting brackets once stood. In all its one hundred and twenty years, a valance was never fitted.

Author 1973

Yatton

Plate 53
Building on up platform at Yatton. Yatton station was originally the property of the Bristol & Exeter Railway and was opened to traffic in 1841. Brunel was the engineer of the line and at this early date it seems likely that he personally designed the station. It is curious in that there are two styles of building, on the downside the buildings are very similar to those I have categorised as "Type B" in *figure 1* while on the upside stands a "Type D" building.

Plate 54
Entrance to booking office in upside buildings.

Author 1973

Plate 55
1896 style pylons support a canopy on the down platform.

Plate 56
Three hundred and fifty feet above the English Channel, amid the chalk downs north of Dorchester stands Maiden Newton station. This station is a flint version of the smaller stations at Sparkford, Castle Cary and Bruton (to name a few) which were built in limestone. All the stations from Bruton to Maiden Newton were of a similar ground plan and style of varying sizes with the exception of Evershot, which was built in timber with a bay window in the end wall. This station matched Shepton Mallet. The Yeovil to Weymouth section of the Wilts, Somerset and Weymouth Railway was opened in January 1857, the line to Shepton Mallet from Witham on the W.S.W. Rly was opened in November 1858. When nearly all the stations between Westbury to Salisbury and Westbury to Weymouth were built to a 'standard' pattern, why did one station have to be completely different? Did the designer, in this case Brereton, get someone else to design Evershot?

British Rail

Maiden Newton

Plate 57
A view of Maiden Newton from the north showing the timber overall roof of the Bridport Branch bay, which looks very similar to the small roofs at Weymouth.

British Rail

Plates 58/59

Kidlington station, opened in 1850, was constructed in a style very similar to that used at Box station ten years before. There is a low pitched roof and limestone chimney stacks which do not carry chimney pots. Beneath the awning, which has acquired a valance since it was erected, the walls are in limestone with bay windows at either end. On the valance are the mysterious lions' heads that were to be seen on many stations dating from the 1848/50 period.

British Rail

Kidlington

Charlbury

Plate 60
Charlbury station, north west of Oxford, was built during 1852/53 for the Oxford, Worcester and Wolverhampton Railway of which Brunel was Engineer. The style of roof was first used at Yatton, subsequently at Aldermaston (21.12.47) and later at Mortimer (1.11.48). These last two stations give Charlbury its style for the latter is a faithful copy, in timber, of these brick stations. Even the semi-circular brick arches over doors and windows are reproduced in wood at Charlbury. It is doubtful if Brunel personally designed this station, as he was fully engaged on heavy engineering up and down the line, besides his great steam ship adventure was just starting! Since 1835 he had been teaching and training assistants and it is probably that one of these drew up the Charlbury station's plans.

British Rail

Plate 61
General view of the station looking towards Worcester about 1952.

Chepstow

Plate 62
Chepstow station was the first station on the South Wales Railway, the section Chepstow to Swansea opening in June 1850. Brunel was Engineer of this line but the station at Chepstow was designed by Lancaster Owen. The illustration shows the usual style of building on this line with a low roof, semi-circular arched doors and windows in an Italian style. The building is strapped together with sleepers and is being jacked up by screw jacks pressing against the beams beneath the building foundations. What is behind it all can only be guess work, but I imagine that the building is being raised with the platforms, perhaps after or during the process of changing gauge in 1872.

British Rail

Plate 63
Grange Court station showing the Victorian conception of a 'bus shelter'. Note the empty spaces where once hung the lions' heads mentioned earlier. It is interesting to note the difference in the brickwork of the platform in the picture as compared with Charlbury.

British Rail

Grange Court

Plate 64
Most of Brunel's thinking was unorthodox but he rarely made a mistake. The case of his 'one-sided' stations, of which Reading is an example, may be thought of as one of these rare lapses. The up and down line had a separate platform, which, with individual up and down booking offices made in effect, separate stations. This photograph shows the down station office.

Plate 65
Reading station looking east shortly before rebuilding. The roof once spanned a single track running between two platforms linked by a timber footbridge. The track nearest the row of columns occupies the site of the outer platform. The new station was built by Pattison of Westminster for an estimated £6,000. Note the "covered way" on "new" platform which linked the up and down stations from about 1861 until 1896.

British Rail

Reading

Plate 66
Various additions were made to Reading station during the years 1840-1896 and in 1863 a goods shed was added between the up and the down stations. This is illustrated here.

British Rail 1870

READING STATION
1850

Plate 67
This is a diagram of the 1850 track layout – before the goods shed referred to in the previous picture was built. It is interesting to see that the draughtsman has labelled the platforms 'arrival' and 'departure' which cannot, surely, be correct. The left hand 'arrival' platform is in fact the 'down' and the right hand the 'up' platform.

British Rail

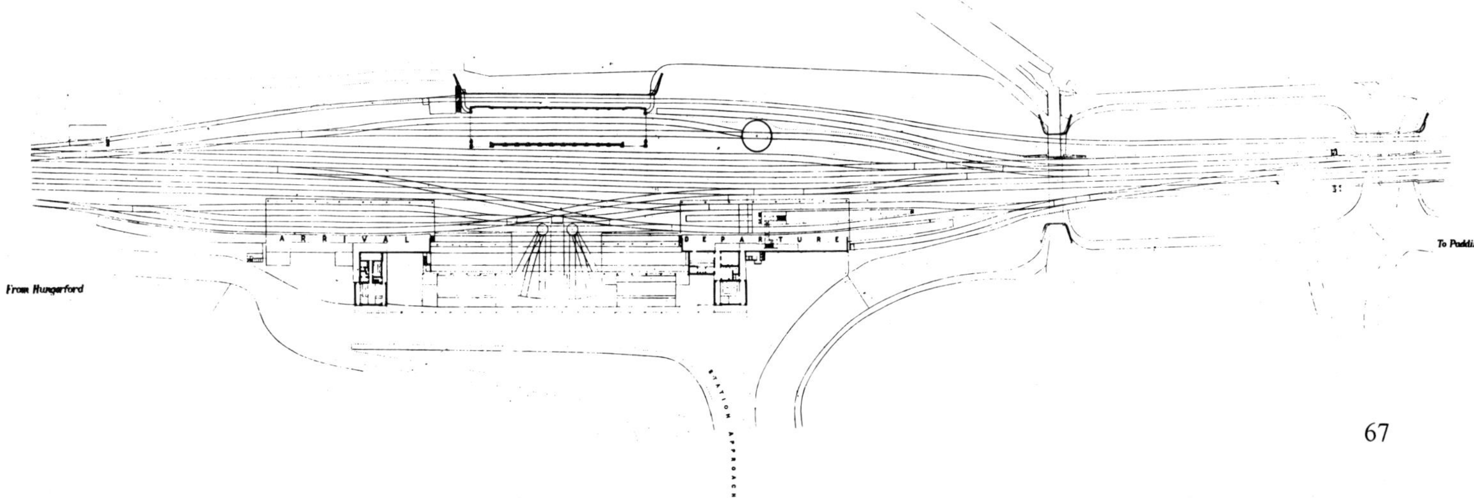

Plate 68
Reading station looking east from the top of the down main home signal. The curious part of the new layout was that there was no platform loop for the down main, as there was for the up main. Periodically a scheme to provide such a loop was put forward to avoid delays which necessarily happened in the absence of a loop but nothing ever came of them. Today the problem is to some extent overcome, by allowing down trains, not calling at the station, to travel past a train at the down main platform, by going through on the 'up' main. The latter is the central track of the three in the foreground of this plate.
British Rail

Plate 69
The 'Italianate' exterior of Reading station. This was built about 1870.
British Rail

Basingstoke

Plate 70
The Berks and Hants Railway opened from Southcote Junction, Reading, to Basingstoke in November 1848. Over the platforms at Basingstoke this sturdy, but very plain, overall roof was erected. Comparing this photograph with the working drawings of the original Westbury station overall roof (June 1848) one comes to the conclusion that they were identical.

British Rail

Banbury

Plates 71/72/73
Banbury station had an overall roof which has always been referred to as 'Brunel's design for less important stations' or some other similar description, but it is doubtful if the great man did design it. It is far more likely that Bertram or Hannaford carried out the design and got the approval of their chief afterwards. Brunel in these later years was usually involved in getting out the plans for the heavier problems involved in building any line. Be that as it may, this roof is very typical of a selection that were erected during 1850/55. Dimensions altered from place to place, and the finish of the windscreen varied but the basic proportions remained the same. The classical pediment supported on twin columns is the hall mark of this style. The station was opened in 1850 and its roof survived until 1953 by which time every express train that passed threatened to shake it down. The roof became a legend for its latter day frailty which is sad as it should have been admired for the length of service it gave.

Plate 71 Banbury station looking south. Built in 1850, the classical theme of a portico flanked by columns and surmounted by a pediment still looking handsome after 80 years wear. It survived until 1953, a legend for its frailty and was replaced by a featureless concrete building.

British Rail

Plate 72 Interior of Banbury station, up platform.

British Rail

Plate 73
Banbury station. External view of station buildings showing parcels office, booking hall, and additional offices built in 1910.
British Rail 1935

Frome

Plates 74/75
Frome station was opened in 1850 and was part of the Wilts, Somerset and Weymouth Railway of which Brunel was nominally the Engineer. The station illustrated here, together with the engine shed and goods shed was designed by J.R. Hannaford. The usual iron columns under the pediment were not used, timber being employed instead, probably due to the need for economy—the W. S. & W.R. being very short of money at the time of its construction. The station is still in use today.

Plate 74
The up platform buildings and booking office from the west.
Author 1973

Plate 75
The station from the west.
Author 1973

Salisbury

Plates 76/77

Salisbury, terminus of the Wilts, Somerset and Weymouth branch from Westbury was open in 1856. It was built between 1850 and 1855 and has a good facade consisting of three sections, a central block flanked by pavilions. The red brick is enlivened by judicious use of limestone dressings. The awning is typical, parallel to the ground with no valance, and well supplied with lions' heads. The interior is a clean, business-like design. The platform support columns are rather close to the trains, a frequent failing of this sort of station which made it difficult to move around when a well loaded train was discharging its passengers. Though embellishment is minimal the moulded caps on the timber columns and the 'X' bracing above blend with the functional tie rods to make, in the photograph at any rate, a handsome building, spacious, well lit and free from icy-draughts and rain.

British Rail

Henley-on-Thames

Plates 78/79
Henley station, opened in 1857, has an overall roof, the pediment-end of which is very similar to that at Salisbury. The brick building in front appears to date from about 1900.
P. Kelley 1966

Plate 78

Plate 79
The station from the west.

Plate 80
Henley station showing the old roof and later canopy extension dating from about 1910.

British Rail

Plate 81

Plates 81/82
The original timber columns have been sawn off (*plate 81*) above ground and broad gauge bridge rail used to replace the rotted timber. Though there is a 'family resemblance' between this and the other overall roofs there are various detail differences; panelling instead of the usual 'X' bracing, columns which are free standing on one side of the station and built into the wall on the other. Notice the slightly different mouldings to finish off the various parts of the woodwork.

Author 1973

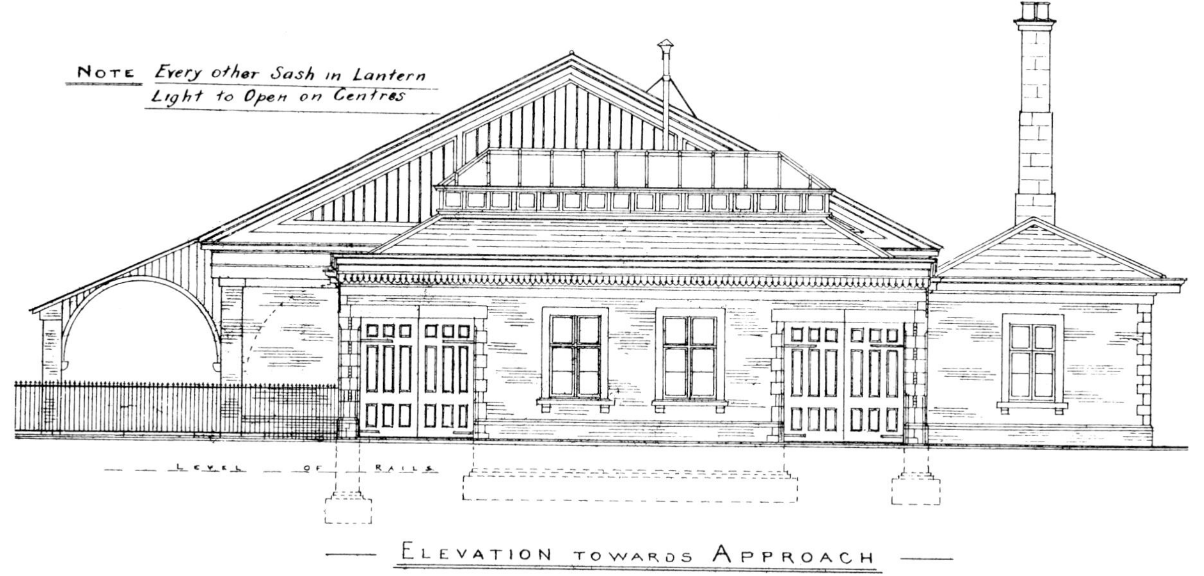

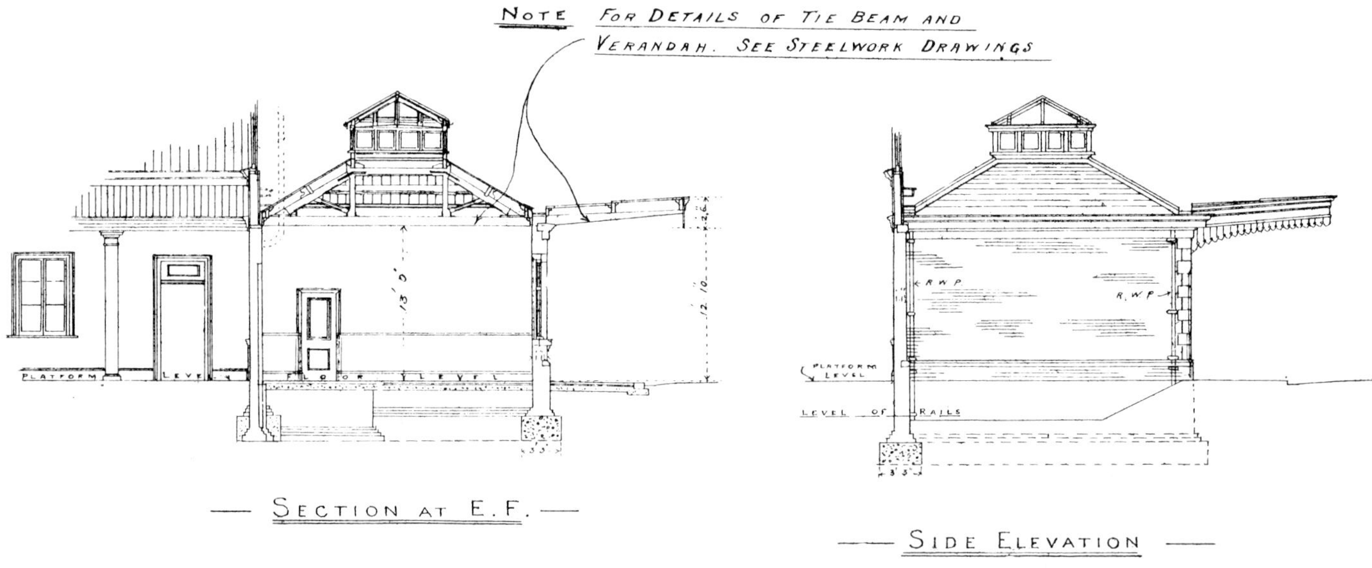

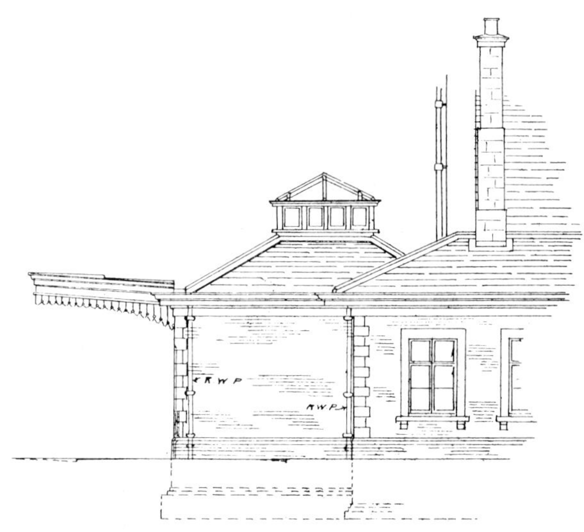

Plate 83

Official drawings of Henley station produced at the time that the new brick building was placed at the front of the old timber roof.

British Rail

Merthyr Tydfil

Plate 84

Merthyr Tydfil was the terminus of the main line of the Taff Vale Railway which Brunel engineered. Drawings for the station at Merthyr are dated 1856, though the line was opened in 1841, and they are signed by J.H. Bertram. There is a striking similarity between this station and Salisbury (1850/55) in the columns and 'X' bracing above. The roof timbers are complicated, ordinary rafters are provided but these are supported by curved cross beams. This feature is well illustrated in *plate 85.*

British Rail

Plate 85

Plate 86
The overall roof at Weymouth was constructed from working drawings signed by J.H. Bertram, one of Brunel's chief assistants and Engineer of the Great Western Railway for eight months after Brunel's death. There is a marked similarity between this roof and the one at Merthyr, but for some reason Bertram did not continue the curved main beam spanning the tracks as he did at Merthyr but only had it at the front of the station for show. Within the station, under the roof, the rafters rest on ordinary straight cross beams. The scene in this picture seems to me to be almost like fairy-land with the beautiful engines standing on the well maintained track and even the glass in the windscreen of the station polished till it flashes in the dull light. A rail-motor is on the left hand platform, perhaps for Abbotsbury and its Swannery, a 4-4-0 'Bulldog' No. 3324 is the station pilot attached to a Dean clerestory coach and a 'cell' (battery's) truck. The engine is un-named here but did receive later the magical name *Glastonbury*. On the right is one of the London and South Western Railway's 4-4-0's, nicknamed 'Greyhounds'. She would have been lined out in purple-brown, black and white on apple green to contrast strangely with the quiet, solid Brunswick green, brass and copper, black, red and orange of the Great Western engine.

British Rail

Weymouth

Plate 87
A short canopy from the right hand roof of Weymouth station and from the supporting brackets hang the pendant ball typical of this period. There is an interesting contrast here between the spaciousness of the Great Western Railway coaches and the mean looking, ex-London and South Western stock.

British Rail

Plate 88
The left hand bay roof at Weymouth with the supporting columns built into the wall as at Henley. By the way, the advertisement on the left for the Great Western Railway removal service is amusing.

British Rail

Plate 89
Exterior of the upside buildings at Weymouth. There is a distinct resemblance here to the buildings at Oxford prior to 1972. The bay window in the end of the building faithfully follows earlier and contemporary practice on the Great Western Railway, except that in this case construction is in timber rather than stone. The underside of the awning is carefully finished by some simple but effective shaping of the beams and of course the pendant ball ornament has again been included.

British Rail

Oxford

Plate 90

The Oxford Railway Company's line from Didcot terminated at this station close to the banks of the Thames just south of Folly Bridge. It was opened in June 1844 in the form illustrated here. The overall roof spanning a siding as well as the platform road was typical of this sort of building, though of course they were usually 'through' stations not termini. The light roof and frail columns resemble buildings at Slough and Reading. Hanging from the roof, on the platform line is a loading gauge. In those days luggage and servants were piled on the roof . . . . Present day Marlborough Road, which runs roughly parallel to the main Abingdon Road in south Oxford, was laid out upon the line of this, the first railway into Oxford. Old people will tell you that they remember buffer stops and a water column in the back gardens of the houses on the south side of the road. Western, and White House Roads were probably first laid down as approach roads to the terminus. Traffic began running to Banbury from this station in 1850 which meant that trains had to reverse into the place if they were coming from Banbury and reverse out if they wanted to go to Banbury. This rather "Limerick Junction" situation was not tolerated and in two years a new station was built on the site of the present day station. The old terminus remained in use as a goods station for many years but was eventually closed and the land sold in 1872. It lay derelict for some years until the present housing estate was erected in about 1885.

British Rail

Plate 91

This is how the Oxford, Worcester and Wolverhampton Railway Company's prospectus envisaged Oxford station would look if they were allowed to build their line. As anything that this company said was to be taken with a large pinch of salt it would be as well to admire the building's style and notice the licence allowed to the artist. If the Company could take such liberties with the geography and topography of the neighbourhood – not to mention the complete absence of any 'dreaming spires', they could (and did) take liberties with anything else.

British Rail

Plate 92
Having to back trains into and out of the old terminus was an intolerable state of affairs for a trunk route, and in 1852 the station illustrated here was opened on the west side of the town. An overall roof in the style of Banbury (see *plate 71*) was provided but removed by 1893. The remainder of the timber station was demolished in 1972. It had been built after Brunel's usual style. The platform buildings have a low roof sheltering timber framed walls covered horizontally with weatherboarding. Beams bridging the walls and projecting beyond support the flat awning which does not carry a valance board. Pendant spheres, which are a feature of this and other timber stations, attach to these beams. The window surrounds have timber pilasters after the style adopted in some stone built stations, and the chimneys, though built in brick, have been made to conform to the fashion of the day with stucco.

British Rail 1935

Plate 93
Further north along the upside buildings at Oxford showing the original timber brackets and pendants.
British Rail c1935

Plate 94
The south end of the upside buildings showing the low, hipped roof. Regrettably, the window surrounds at this end of the building, away from the main passenger area, are quite plain.

British Rail

Plate 95

Oxford station up platform looking south, towards Didcot, which is how a well bred station should appear! The window near the bay line buffer stops is handsomely done with coloured glass in lozenge shaped leads. The room was probably a refreshment room but seems to be used as a Catering Department store in this picture. Along the platform a machine can be seen for stamping one's name on a metal plate, 22 letters stamped for one penny.

British Rail c1935

Plate 96

Interior of 'upside' at Oxford looking north. The canopy dates from the demolition of the overall roof. The nearest column has a projection which suggests that at some time the canopy extended further.

British Rail

Plate 97
The down platform at Oxford looking north.
British Rail

Plate 98
Exterior of the downside building seen in plate 97.
British Rail 1935

Plate 99
General view of the downside buildings looking north. At the far end is a rendered building similar in style to the old station at Leamington. The lamp standard was perhaps the last piece of the old station to be removed in 1973 or 1974.

British Rail 1935

Leamington Spa

Plate 100

The downside at Leamington Spa just before re-building. The overall roof, or rather what is left of it (it had been partially dismantled) can be seen above the amazingly scruffy sign painted on the valance over the subway entrance. On the wall there are some interesting advertisements, 'The Great Western Railway regrets . . .' I've heard a similar sentiment expressed recently . . . and a monthly ticket to go anywhere for 1¾d (¾p) per mile.

British Rail

Plate 101

The downside buildings at Leamington Spa were probably built in brick, rendered over in stucco. The general style follows closely that of Weymouth and Oxford; there is the bay window, the same low pitched roof, the windows flanked with pilasters and a pavilion at the far end of the building. The station was opened in 1852 and was built on the site of a Georgian block of houses 140 yards long and four storeys high; it is not only modern developers that are guilty of vandalism. The station had an overall roof spanning 60′ supported on timber columns above ground and by massive timber piles which had been rammed into the ground so deep that they reached to below the level of the present road. In 1938 the station was rebuilt and the entrance placed at present road level which entailed considerable excavation. The new building was made of a steel frame with a brick filling but instead of concrete to face the bricks limestone was used. Within, the lower parts of the walls were lined with polished granite and the upper parts with glazed tiles. In the refreshment rooms the walls were panelled with walnut veneer and the windows surrounded with stainless steel. On the platforms, which were 650/670 feet long, a streamlined form of the traditional canopy was erected putting 360′ of the down platform and 480′ of the up platform under shelter.

British Rail

Plate 107
Interior of the old Leamington Spa station looking north. The mangled remains of the roof show that it was similar to that at Salisbury as regards the interior, with 'X' bracing over columns set rather too close to the platform edge. When the line was Broad Gauge the platform would not have been as wide as it is shown here.

British Rail 1905

Plate 103
Exterior of the new station on the downside, looking towards Banbury. One or two of the old pine trees have survived the excavations.
British Rail 1939

Aldermaston

Plate 104
Aldermaston station was built in 1846 after the style of Yatton. It is in red brick with semi-circular arches over doors and windows picked out in yellow. This type of architecture was used extensively on the Berks and Hants line.

British Rail

Plate 105
The South Wales Railway was opened from Chepstow to Swansea in June 1850. Its principal stations (with the exception of Neath) Chepstow, Cardiff, Newport, etc., appear to have been constructed in a very similar style to the station illustrated here, Port Talbot. They may have been larger or smaller, of course, but the stonework, roofing, window and door arches, were all about the same. There appears to be a certain resemblance between this station and Aldermaston shown above.

British Rail

Port Talbot

Newport

Plate 106

Plates 106/107/108
Newport station, built for the South Wales Railway during 1848/50. Between 1875/78 the station was enlarged and the original buildings on the downside were incorporated while all others were demolished. The designers, Lancaster Owen and J.E. Danks, kept the style of the old buildings which in their enlarged form have been improved immensely. *Plate 106* shows the buildings on the island platform, *plate 107* the exterior of the Goods Agents offices on the downside, and *plate 108* the downside buildings and tower at the end of the footbridge over the four tracks through the station.

Author 1973

Plate 108

Plate 107

G.W.R. NEWPORT HIGH STREET STATION. DOWN SIDE.

PUBLIC FOOTBRIDGE

G.W.R. NEWPORT STATION G.W.R.

ELEVATION TO APPROACH

SCALE EIGHT FEET TO AN INCH.

G.W.R. Chief Engineers Office July 1927 No 1310 Architectural Dept Paddington

C 6177

Plate 109

The official drawing for the new downside office building erected during 1928. It is in brick in a kind of Georgian style but too hopelessly cluttered to photograph now. The 1878 building butts against the left hand side.

British Rail

Paddington

Plate 110

The first terminus of the Great Western Railway in London was the Bishop's Road bridge. It was the facade of the station and its arches served to accommodate the necessary offices. It was a temporary expedient, built in a hurry, and continued as the terminus for 16 years from 1838 to 1854. Had it not been for the bitter relations which grew up between the London and Birmingham and Great Western Railways there would never have been a Paddington station at all. The original Act of Parliament authorising the construction of the Great Western Railway gave permission for that railway to turn north east at Acton and join the L & B 'in a certain field lying between the Paddington Canal and the Turnpike Road leading from London to Harrow on the western side of the General Cemetery in the Parish or Township of Hammersmith . . .' The London and Birmingham did not want the Great Western Railway on its property and the former's delaying tactics forced the latter to ask for a new Act, in 1837, for an extension of the line to Paddington. Brunel always intended that the terminus should occupy its present site but had to make do with the Bishop's Road site in order that the Company should have a station ready for the advertised opening date. The goods shed in the right foreground occupies approximately the position of the present station.

British Rail

Plate 111

Paddington station as built in 1855. The view is to the west. Note the cylindrical columns holding up the great roof, the absence of tie rods across the span and the Moorish Arabesques on the western windscreen.

British Rail

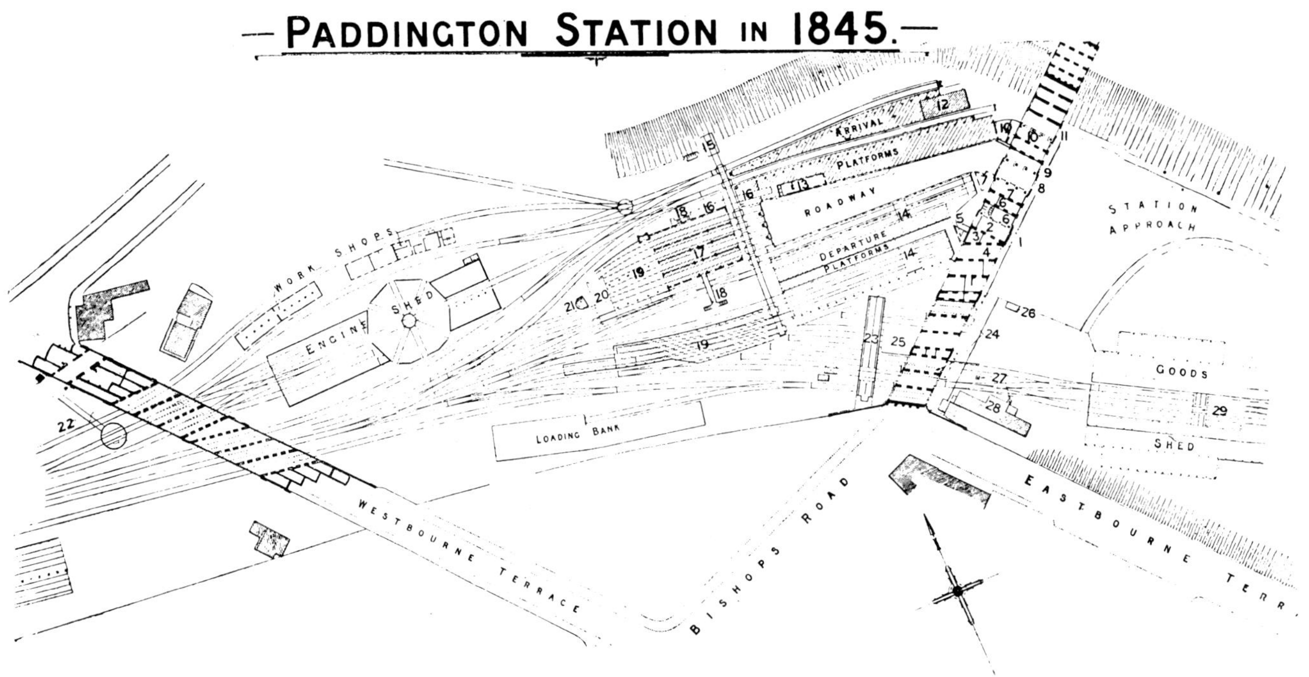

DESCRIPTION.

1. Verandah in front of booking hall.
2. Booking hall.
3. Booking office.
4. Luggage way and auxiliary booking office.
5. Station master's office.
6. Waiting rooms, &c.
7. Down parcels office.
8. Carriage entrance.
9. Carriage exit.
10. Cloak room and lost property office.
11. Arrival exit.
12. Up parcels office.
13. Arrival waiting rooms.
14. Traversers between departure platform lines and adjoining sidings, by means of which trains could be strengthened or lightened without shunting. Probably used also for forming trains on departure lines, without recourse to locomotives.
15. Examination pit.
16. Overhead gangway, connecting with offices over carriage shed. Probably used for observation purposes by Traffic officers.
17. Carriage shed with offices over. In these offices were probably housed the Manager, Secretary, and other chief officers of the Company.
18. Steps giving access to offices.
19. Carriage sheds.
20. Traverser serving carriage shed.
21. Yardmen's shelter.
22. Shear legs. Probably used for lifting engines under repair. The turntable giving access to the siding under these shear legs is of much greater diameter than the one in the engine shed, and presumably, therefore there were in existence about 1845 some engines which could not be turned in the engine shed.
23. Traverser used for goods traffic.
24. Goods sidings and platforms under bridge.
25. Carriage landing.
26. Police office.
27. Yard cranes.
28. Goods offices.
29. Traverser.

Plate 112

Paddington station track layout in 1845.

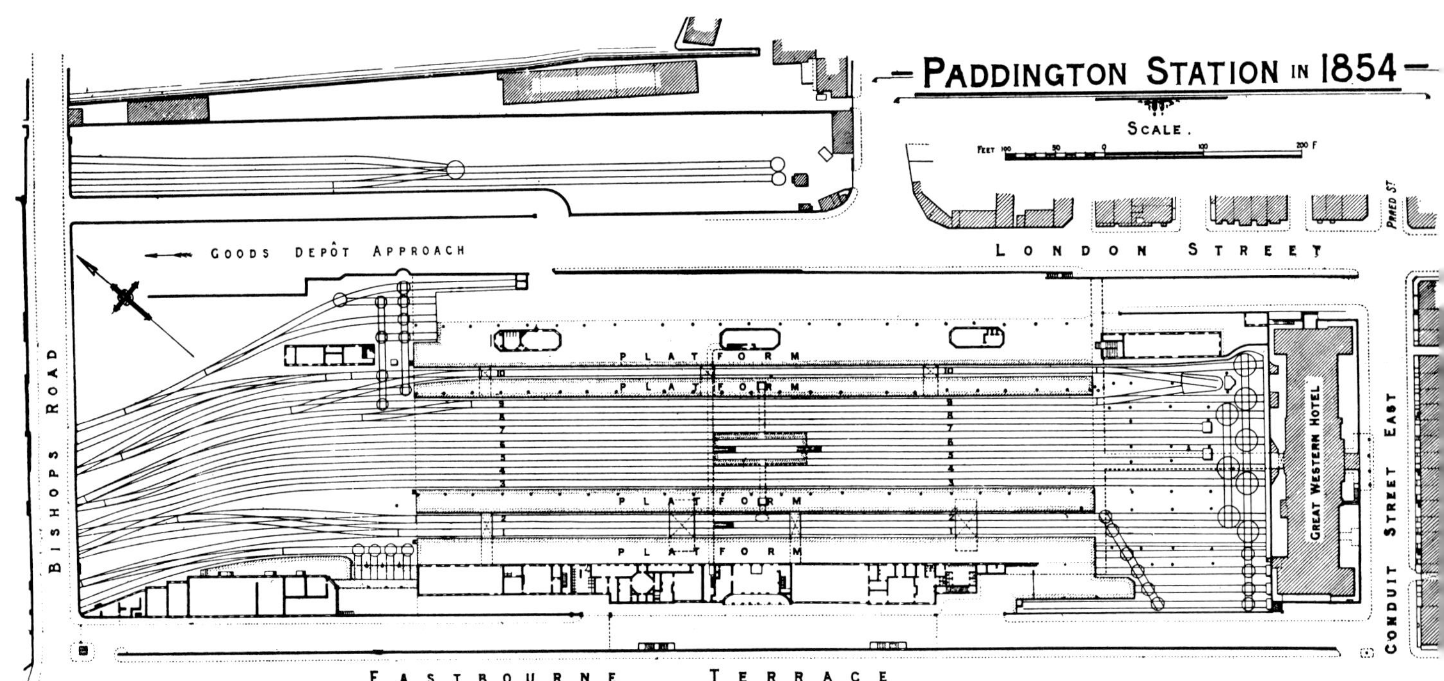

Plate 113

At the top of the plate part of the High Level goods yard can be seen. A great deal is done with wagon turntables in the station, a very useful device when carriages and wagons had short wheelbases. At the Hotel end, on the arrival side there is a sector table, the only one in the station. It may be that this was to release locomotives that were against the buffers, the ordinary turntables being too short. A great deal of room exists for empty stock between the platforms, space which accommodated extra platforms later. The sidings and wagon turntables extend to the very walls of the Royal Hotel, not an elegant arrangement.

British Rail

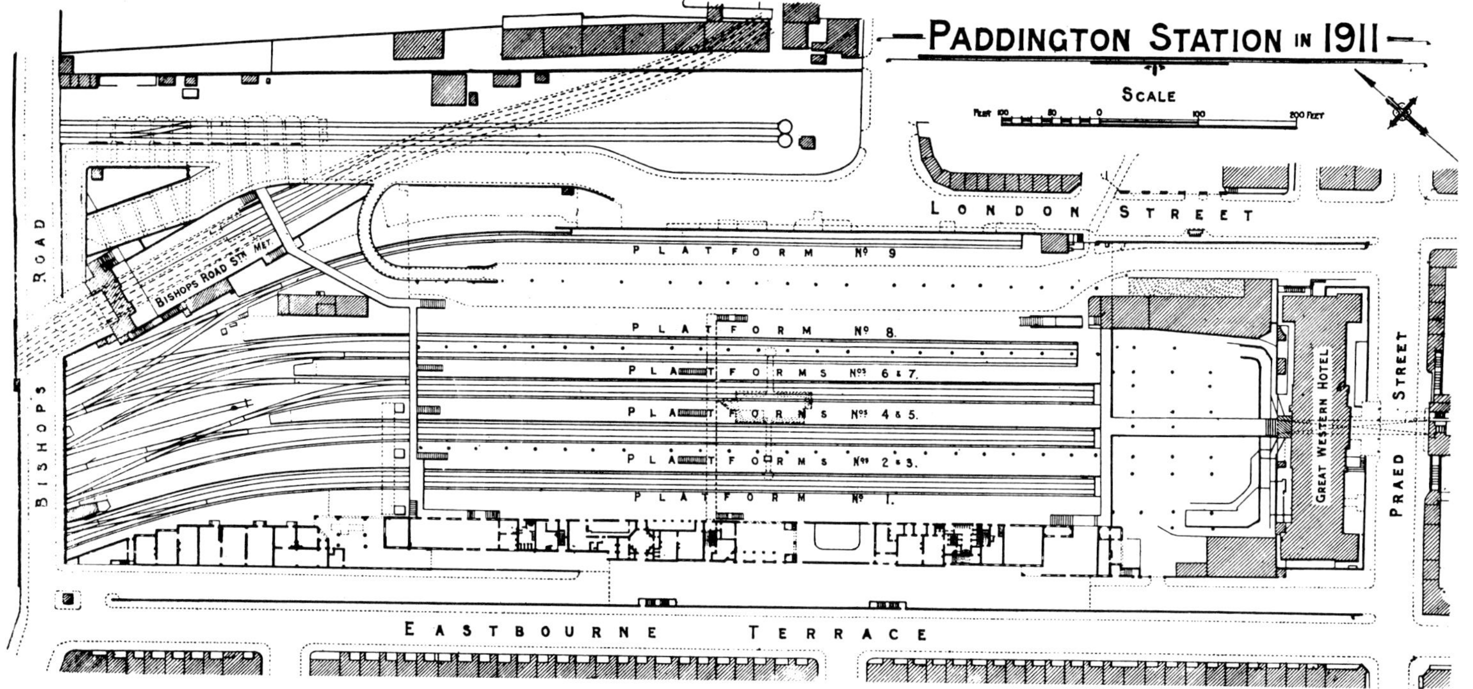

Plate 114
The siding space has been filled now; 180′ occupied by wagon turntables has been paved over to form "The Lawn". The Metropolitan Railway has its station in the north west corner and passes beneath the High Level goods yard. London Street has been raised to cross the Metropolitan and a cab road ramp now drops from London Street into the Great Western Railway station. The platforms were only originally connected by a subway, the footbridge at the west end being added about 1870.

British Rail

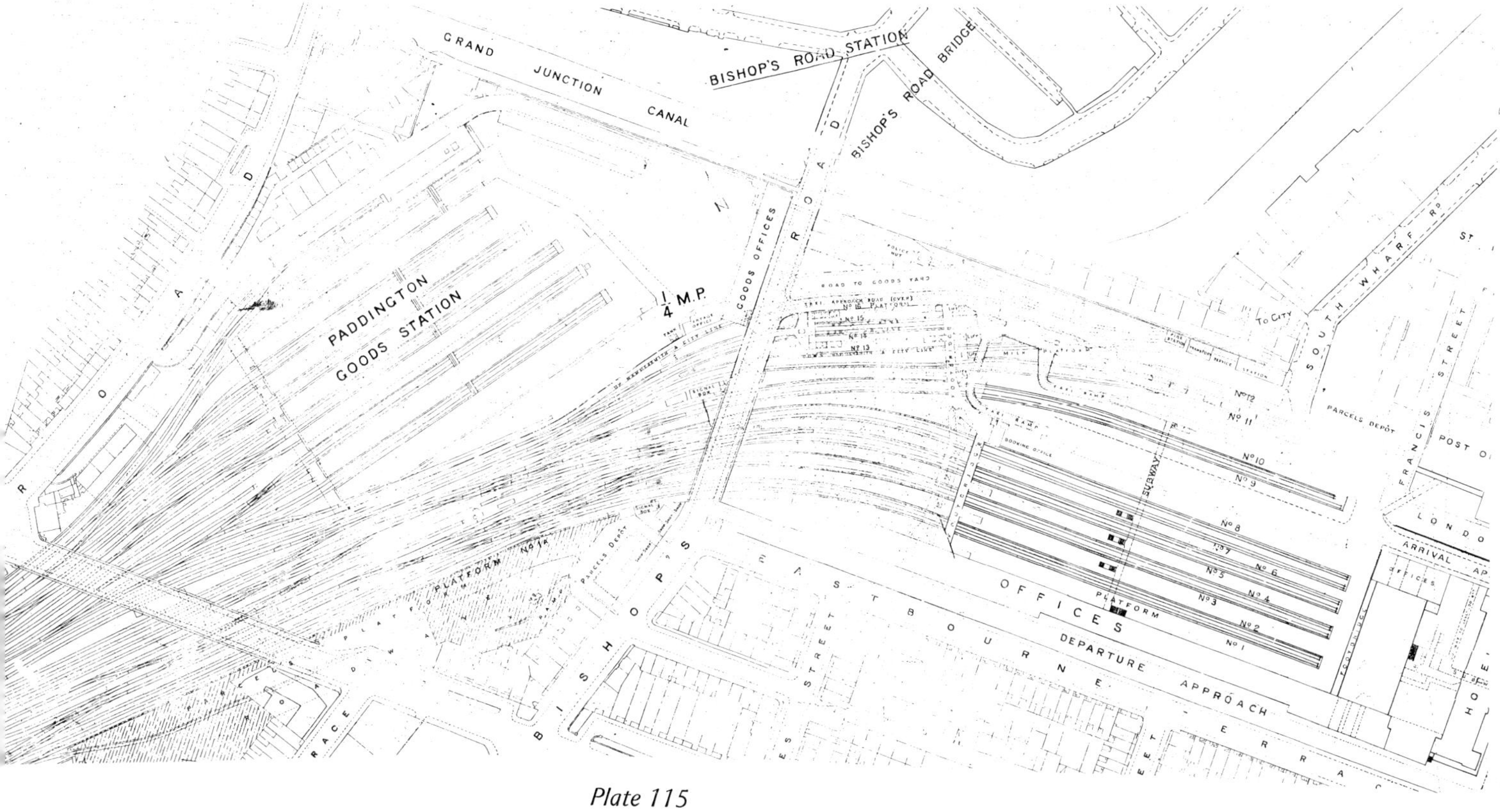

Plate 115
Paddington layout 1937.
British Rail

Plate 116

◀ The Directors Balcony at Paddington. The decorative iron work at Paddington was designed by Brunel's friend Matthew Digby-Wyatt who had been a member of the committee which drew up the designs for the 'Great Hall' of the Crystal Palace in 1851. He had conceived a 'Moorish' pavilion on that occasion and it would appear that he was still full of the idea when he accepted Brunel's invitation to embellish Paddington. The segmental arch design above the windows suggests a Spanish lady's mantilla with its lace veil hanging down on each side of her head.

British Rail

Plate 117 A view from the Directors balcony.
M.W. Earley c1950

Plate 118
View from the GWR goods offices across the whole of Paddington station. A clever panoramic picture taken in the '30s by the Company.

British Rail

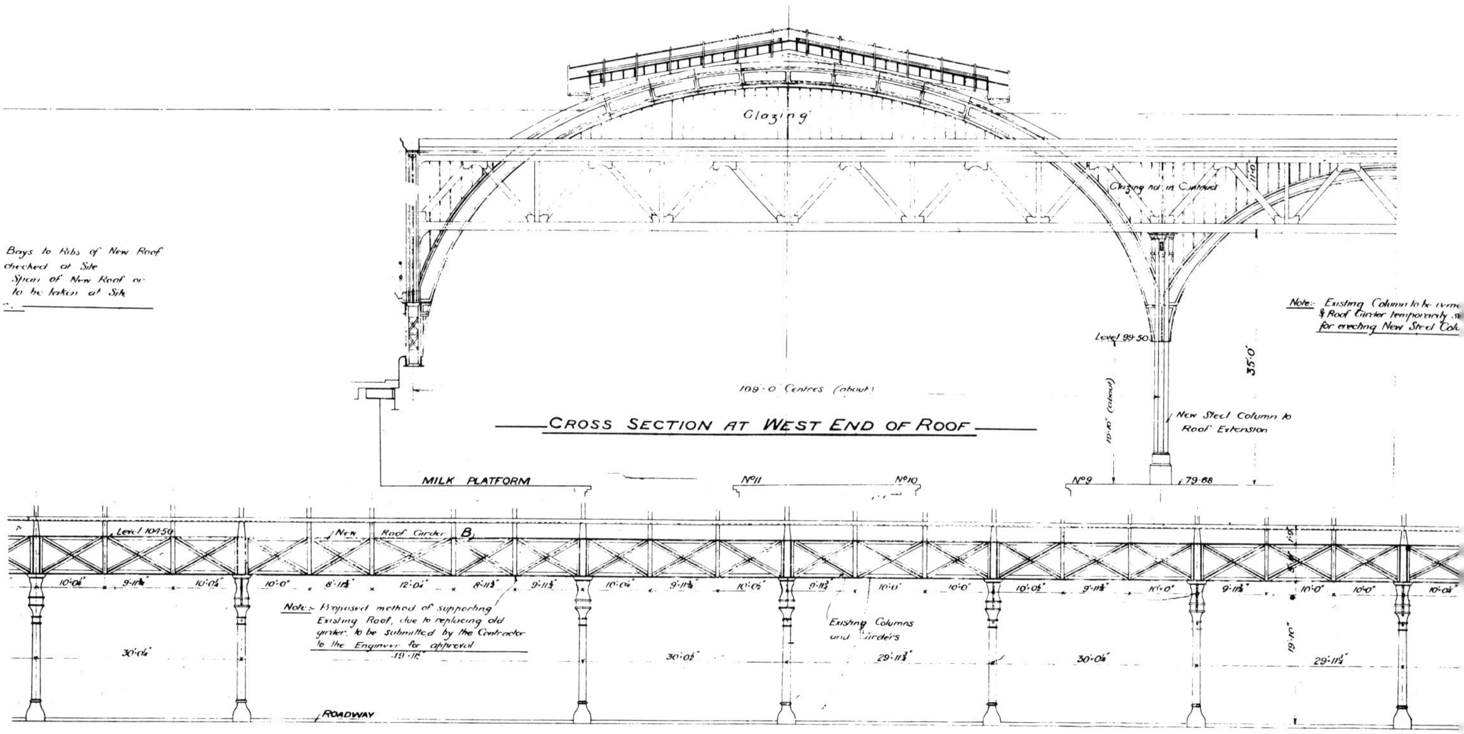

Glazing

CROSS SECTION AT WEST END OF ROOF

MILK PLATFORM

ROADWAY

Plate 119
General elevation of the 1916 span.

Plate 120
Wrought iron ribs springing from the head of a column at Paddington. Matthew Digby-Wyatt's ornamental work is in sections of cast iron bolted onto the plane surface of the ribs.

Plate 121
The Transept, Paddington.
British Rail

Plate 122
Scaffolding supported by the wrought iron arches at Paddington. This illustrates the utility of those variously shaped holes cut in the ribs. The 'blackberry' shaped ones take a scaffolding pole and prevent it rocking from side to side, the others, like a planet and its satellites would accommodate a piece of scaffolding in the 'planet' hole, while the 'satellite' holes would take bolts. The scaffolding would have a 'collar' and this would be bolted tight to the rib through the latter holes. Perhaps this was their purpose during the construction of the roof.
British Rail

Plate 123
Paddington's style is unmistakable. The roof arches are continued to the ground by plaster work columns, the arches over the doors and windows making a continuous arcade the length of the platform. Above the arcading, between the ribs there is the same sort of 'X' bracing encountered at the lesser overall roofs, i.e. Salisbury and Leamington. The scroll work around the bracing is painstakingly intricate and similar to metal grilles on the South Devon Railway at Newton Abbot.

British Rail

Plate 124
The exterior of the station, on the departure side, had rather more ornate finishes than the interior.

British Rail

Plate 125
The entrance to the Royal Waiting Rooms on the downside at Paddington.
British Rail

Plate 126
Doorway on platform 1 next to the War Memorial.
Author 1973

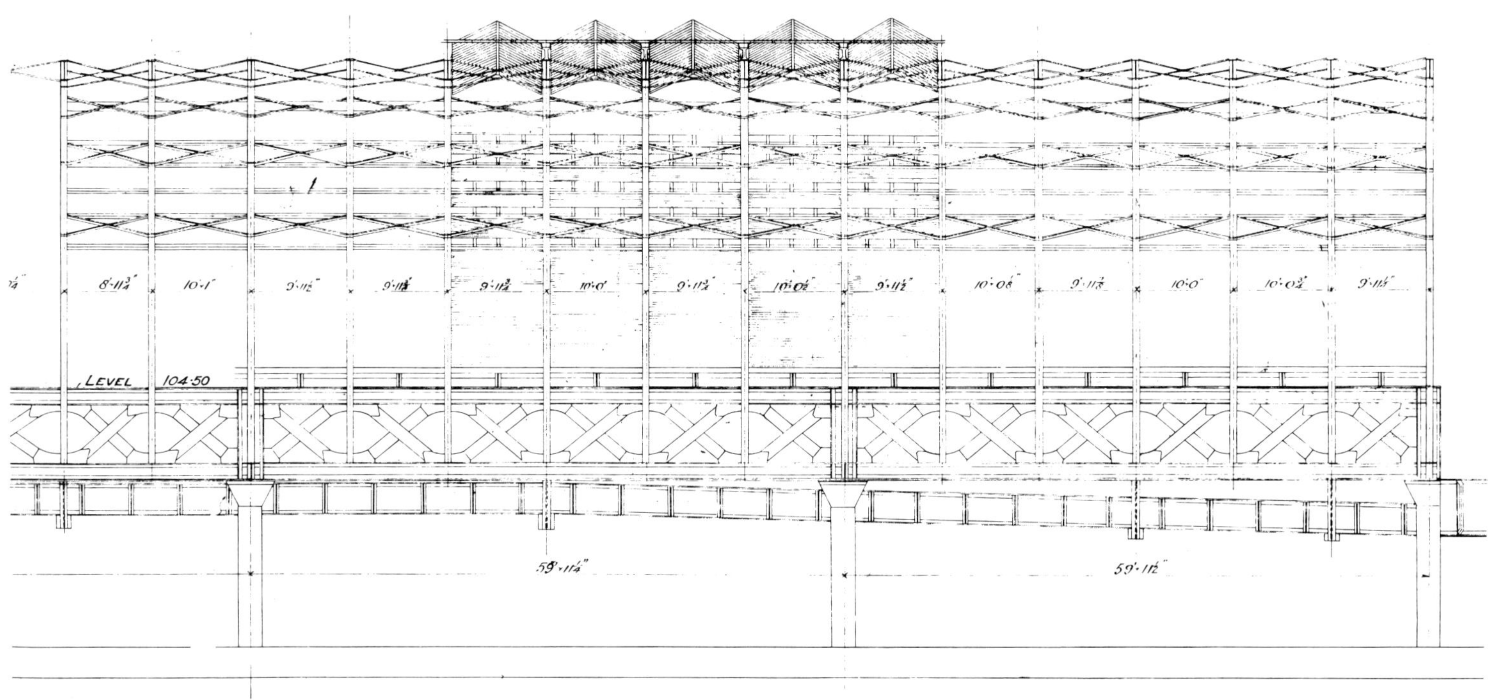

Plate 127
Official drawings of the roof at Paddington showing the cab ramp descending.

NOTE: THE CONTRACTOR TO BE RESPONSIBLE FOR THE ACCURACY OF ALL LEADING DIMENSIONS

Contract No 12

Plate 128
Official drawings of the roof at Paddington showing glazing and walkway.

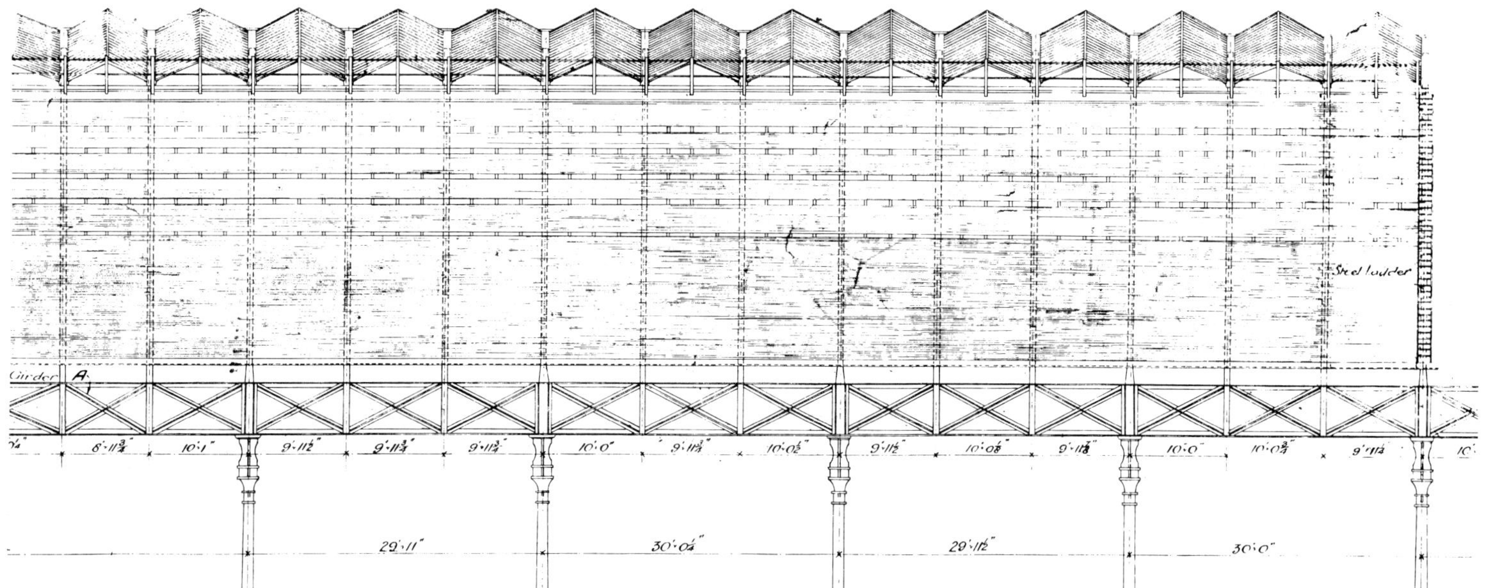

Steel ladder

Girder A

29'·11" 30'·0½" 29'·11½" 30'·0"

No 9 Level 79·68

ROADWAY

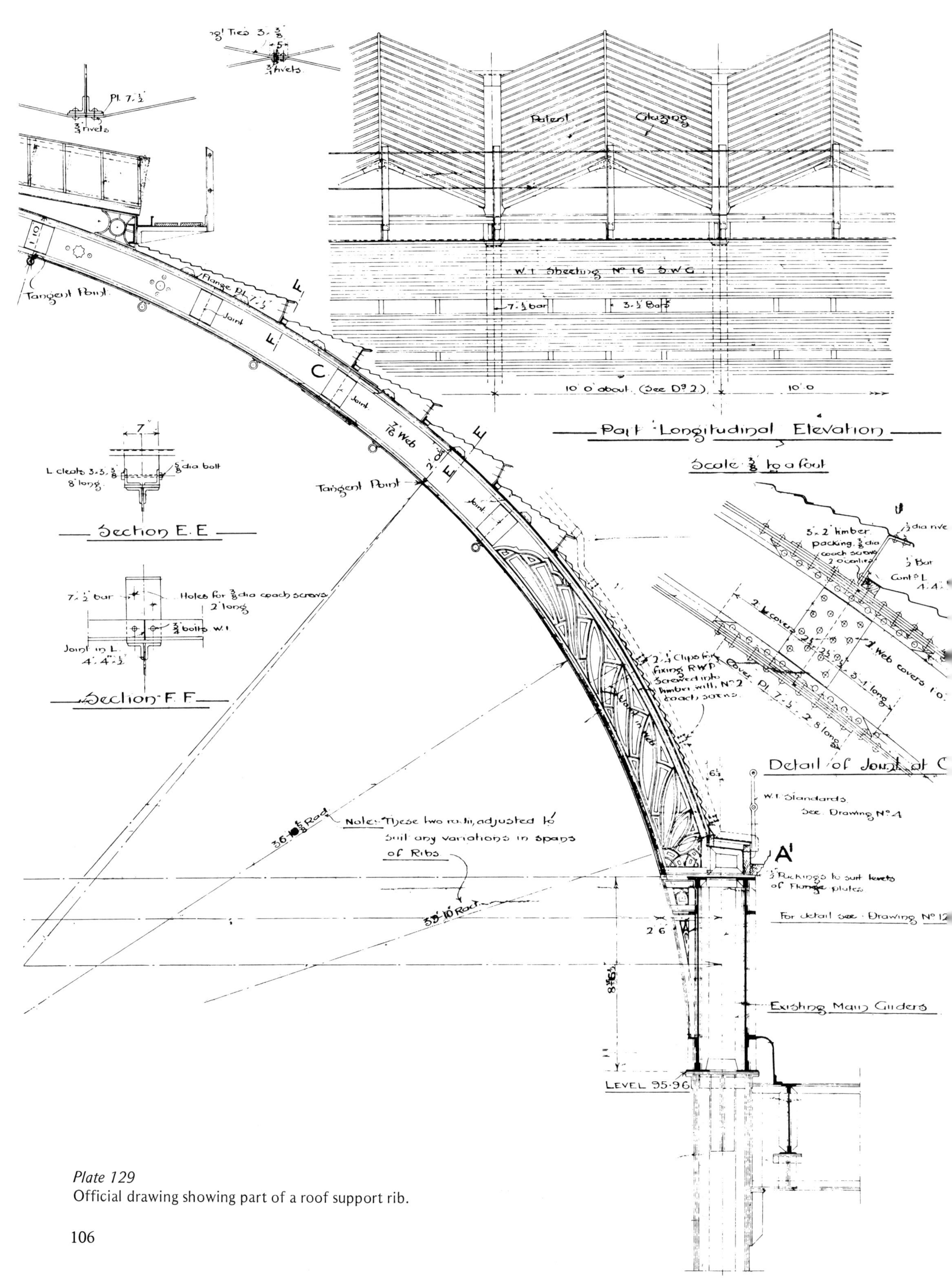

Plate 129
Official drawing showing part of a roof support rib.

Plate 130
Between 1908 and 1934 the Great Western Railway carried out an almost continuous operation of improvements at Paddington interrupted only by the Great War. This plate shows how the platforms were extended. Precast concrete sections were laid on a bed of rammed sand or ashes. These sections were constructed to be pinned together by a concrete dowel pushed down vertically to lock each piece together. In the picture it appears that this is the first platform to be extended and now awaits only the platform covering to be placed across the gap. The process was cheap and had the added advantage that the work could be carried out in between the trains.

British Rail 1932

Plate 131
The concrete sections were unloaded from open wagons and laid straight into position. In this photograph the 0-6-4 pannier tank *Steropes* is employed, the driver operating the crane. This must have been a Sunday 'occupation' for the terminus would not have stood two platform lines to be occupied on a weekday. At those times the sections could be unloaded by hand. The photograph is particularly interesting as it shows the engine actually working. Further, it shows the new Arrival box, just beyond the engine's chimney and the manually operated box it replaced. The new colour light signals are in position and their lamps are alight, but the old box still has festoons of temporary wires going to it which suggests that it is still in use for the moment.

British Rail 1932

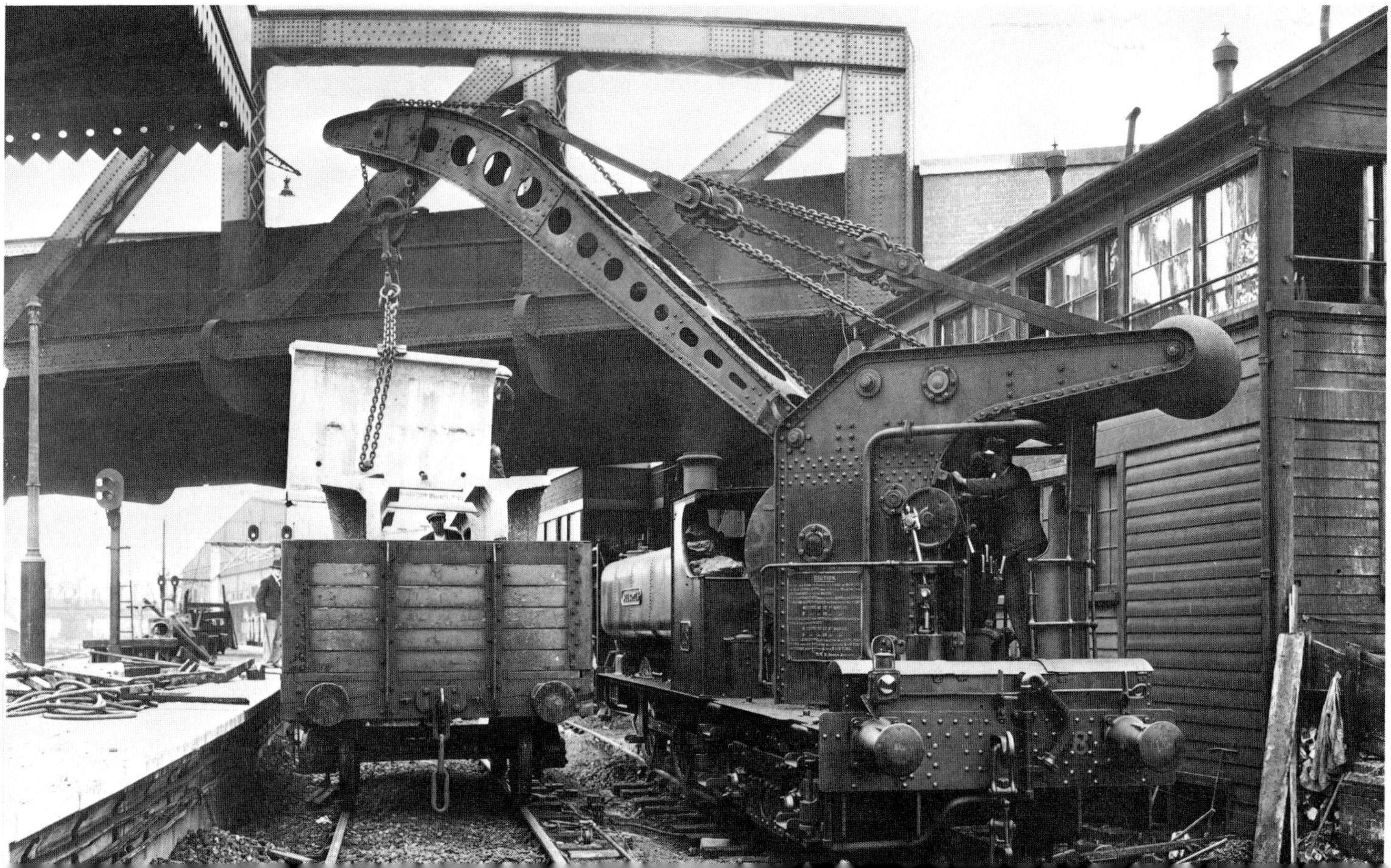

Plate 132

Plate 133

Plate 134

Plates 132/133/134
Hexagonal steel columns at Paddington. This is how most people remember the station, but these distinctive shapes are not original. The first roof support columns were cylindrical. They were replaced between 1916 and 1924, as part of a procedure to replace the entire roof. *Plates 133 and 134* show a column about to be removed, the load of the roof being taken on temporary steel-work. Note the old cap, it was a more ornate design than that which replaced it.

British Rail

Plate 135

Paddington today has four spans, the fourth being erected between 1914 and 1916. To accommodate the extension, the High Level goods yard and part of London Street had to be excavated to main line level. This photograph shows the scene on the arrival side before work started. In the left foreground are the roofs of offices of the Company demolished around 1934 to clear a site for the present Arrival Side offices. The Arrival Side arch with medallion has not yet been put up and will only arrive with the completion of the fourth span. There are two men working over the existing archway which has a valance bearing the legend, 'Great Western Railway Arrival Platform'. Over 40 horse cabs are drawn up in sight of the camera, the rest are in the station, and all appear to be very smartly turned out. The building in the right hand foreground corner still stands but the buildings beyond, the 'Mint' stables, have been demolished. Here, the Great Western Railway housed a very large number of its draught horses in a two storey building. Beyond the 'Mint' stables is the High Level goods yard. The Bishop's Road bridge is seen here in its original form. This photograph may well have been taken as a 'before' picture in what was to be a continuing series to show the building of the new span.

British Rail 1908

Plate 136
Paddington station was resignalled and the layout improved, the work of alteration being carried out between 1928 and 1932. To accommodate extra track and improve facilities at the Bishop's Road station, afterwards known as 'Paddington Suburban', the wall of the goods shed had to be set back several feet. Here the work is in progress with the old wall coming down while the roof behind is supported on girder work ready for the new wall. The new 'Arrival' signal box is also under construction with the old Bishop's Road signal box in the background.

British Rail

Plate 137
A close up view over the roofs at Paddington which shows the 'new' fourth span and the 'Arrival' side offices mentioned in the caption to *plate 135*. It is an interesting view because it shows how small was the outer span of the old arrangement. One can see how it was pushed out of plumb by the weight of the other two spans (see Introduction). This is a part of the panoramic view seen in *plate 118*. ▶

M.W. Earley 1953

Plate 138
Matthew Digby-Wyatt has provided his ornamental ironwork even on the outer face of the wrought iron ribs. Paddington sheltered some beautiful locomotives. Here, before the Great War, stands No. 111 *The Great Bear* and No. 2233, a 'County' tank engine. An interesting legend concerning the 'Great Bear' (and not in the least concerning architecture) is that the engine bears a number which ancient peoples believed had 'evil eye' powers. Churchward, who designed the engine against his better judgement, acting under instructions from the omnipotent Board, was interested in astrology, knew of this old belief and was reported to have numbered the 'white elephant' with the evil magic number to get his own back on the Board! ▶

British Rail

Plate 137

Plate 138

Plate 139

Number 1 platform, Paddington awaiting the departure of a Birkenhead express. On the right hand side of the photograph can be seen a bridle iron by which the tie rods spanning the platform from one rib base to the other were attached to those ribs. Before 1915 or 1916 there were no tie rods across the spans so that sideways thrust went sideways, instead of being taken to earth through the columns, as it now does.

British Rail

Plate 140

Paddington Clock no longer moves by "clockwork" but through the agency of electricity. Only the handsome face remains of the original instrument.

Author 1976

Plate 141
Paddington taxi-cab rank.
British Rail

Plate 142
Number 1 platform, Paddington looking west at 10.27, with the Cornish Riviera waiting to leave. This is one of a set of five photographs taken of this view between 10.25 and 10.30.
British Rail

Plate 143

A magnificent claim, the theme of the Company's centenary celebrations, '1835 - 1935' One Hundred Years of Public Service. The Great Western Railway regarded itself as an English Institution whose function was to provide profits for its shareholders and to provide a transport system for the public, subsidising uneconomic branch lines, rather than closing them. This remained Company policy to the end of its existence in the bitter, bitter winter of 1947. Since becoming a Social Institution, the railway has been reduced with the result that Society has been deprived of a large part of its entitlement.

British Rail

Plate 144

Brunel's roof standing up magnificently while some of its arches lie shattered by high explosive carried in the nose of a V1. pilotless jet plane of the 2nd World War, a hazard Brunel could hardly have foreseen.

British Rail 22.3.1944

Plate 145
The War Memorial on platform 1 at Paddington was unveiled by Lord Churchill, Chairman of the Board, before a gathering of 6,000 people, mainly relatives of dead soldiers and ex-servicemen, on Armistice Day, November 11th. Beneath the bronze figure of an infantryman is a plaque which reads, 'In Honour Of Those Who Served In The World Wars. 1914 - 1918. 1939 - 1945'. A further tablet reads, '25,479 men of the Great Western Railway joined His Majesty's Forces. 2,254 gave their lives'. The words, matter of fact, or even brisk sounding, are as moving as the bronze figure itself with the informally slung greatcoat and firmly planted feet. So many men volunteered that the Army would not accept them without a special certificate from the Company saying that the man could be spared from his work.

Author

Plate 146
Looking across at the main line station from the platforms of the 'Hammersmith & City Line', Paddington Suburban.

British Rail c1935

Plate 147

Except for the addition of tie rods the roof over number 1 platform, Paddington has not changed since it was erected in 1855. Brunel would recognise it — 120 years old having survived two world wars and at least two attempts by the Chief Civil Engineer to demolish it. The sign on platform 2, 'Subway' is 60 years old if not older, and the kiosks date from about 1920.

British Rail

Plate 148
An artist's impression of the rehabilitated "Lawn".
British Rail

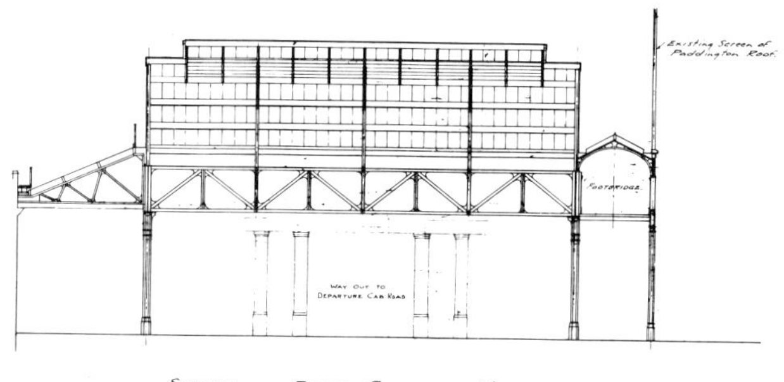

SECTION AT RIGHT ANGLES TO HOTEL

CONTRACT No 32
SHEET No 1A

G. W. R. PADDINGTON IMPROVEMENTS.
RECONSTRUCTION OF ROOFING ETC. OVER CIRCULATING AREA.
EIGTH SCALE SECTIONS.

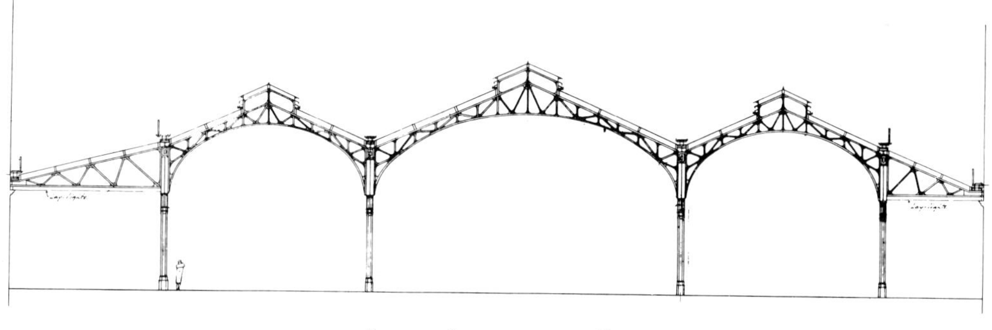

SECTION PARALLEL WITH HOTEL

C 10329

CHIEF ENGINEERS OFFICE
PADDINGTON. W.

END SCREEN TOWARDS HOTEL

Plate 149
Official drawings of the new 'Lawn' roof, Paddington.

Plate 150 Skylights in the fashion of Art Deco, in red, blue, green and translucent glass illuminate the refurbished circulating area known from time immemorial as 'The Lawn'. Polished granite encases the steel girders supporting the roof, Victorian chocolate dispensing machines flank the entrances to the 'Tube' and seat reservation office, while coniferous trees embellish the grand portals of the Great Western Royal Hotel.

Plate 151 Parcels sorting operations had gradually overtaken the 'Lawn', rendering it by 1930 anything but a passenger circulating area. The parcels were banished to the old excursion platform, 1A, and the 'Lawn' was then modernised and re-furbished. A new train departure indicator was installed which is showing the 10.30 a.m. to Penzance; 10.32 Slough; 10.45 Cheltenham; 10.59 Windsor; 11.05 Birkenhead; 11.15 Weston-super-Mare; 11.20 Oxford; 11.25 High Wycombe; 11.40 Windsor; 11.55 Milford Haven and 12.00 Kingswear departures.
British Rail

Plate 152
Late Victorian elegance in beaded mahogany and figured oak. The booking office at Paddington echoes an age of opulence which contrasts strangely with the drab 1930's style clothing of the intending lady passenger.

British Rail

Plate 153
After modernisation the booking hall looks clean cut and severe with riveted girders where once was a plastered ceiling, and cement where there had been figured oak.

British Rail

Plate 154

Wrought iron arabesques in the arch over the arrival side entrance at Paddington. The station had only this and one other side street entrance, an unusual arrangement for a great London station.

British Rail

Plate 155

The departure side arch has much in common with the arch over the roadway at Windsor and it is very probable that they were both erected in the 1890's. The 'square deal' for which the Railway was asking was more Government money to be spent on improving railway stations, signalling and installations, removal of the common carrier status of the railway which obliged it to carry uneconomic loads and to curb road competition which the railway felt was unfair.

British Rail 1935

Plate 156
Additional accommodation for office staff was built during the first half of the 1930's, this taking the form of new office blocks on the arrival side, the building of extra storeys on existing buildings along Eastbourne Terrace and the erection of entirely new blocks between Eastbourne Terrace and the Great Western Royal Hotel. This shows the gap nearly closed with a fine new building built to match the adjacent hotel's style. The last section of the new building to completely fill the gap appears to be in the course of construction low down on the right.

British Rail

Plate 157
Offices rise above the departure side awning. The view is looking west.

British Rail

GWR Hotel Paddington

The Great Western Royal Hotel was the first of its kind in the country, part of the Brunelian dream of a magnificent transportation system conveying people from London to New York on trains, ships and in hotels, horse and carriages all of the very best, and all to be supplied by the Great Western Railway Company. The Royal Hotel was built simultaneously with the 'new' station at Paddington to designs of P.C. Hardwick in the style of a Louis XIV chateau. It ranked with the finest hotels in London, Paris or Berlin, having 165 rooms equipped with the best of modern equipment, cuisine and service. In the centre of the building, framed by the splendid pediment, can be seen that favourite device of the Victorians, the allegorical sculpture. It depicts 'Peace, Plenty, Science and Industry' and is the work of 'Mr. Thomas' a famous worker of the time who was responsible for the statues and carvings in the rebuilt House of Parliament. The Hotel was completed in 14 months and was inspected and opened by Prince Albert, the Prince Consort, and His Majesty the King of Portugal on June 9th 1854.

The installation of modern equipment has been mentioned and this included electric lighting, a telephone system to connect every room with a switchboard that could connect a caller with any part of the world, and a pneumatic tube to every room so that messages could be written and sent down to the kitchens or to the telegraph office – if one wanted to send a telegram. These inventions were installed as they became available and they were all functioning in 1907.

The Hotel had been built with money raised by a section of the Great Western Railway Board of Directors but managed as an independent company. Brunel had taken a personal interest in the running of the place and had even been Chairman of the Hotel Board in spite of all his other commitments. Whenever passenger comfort was at stake one could be sure of finding Brunel setting and maintaining standards. This arrangement ensured that the Hotel gave good service to its patrons and enhanced the reputation of the Great Western Railway – even though the Hotel was a separate concern. The Great Western Royal Hotel came into the possession of the Great Western Railway in 1896 when the infant Catering Department moved its headquarters from Plymouth to Paddington and began to take over the catering duties of the line previously carried out by various contractors.

GREAT WESTERN ROYAL HOTEL.

The above new Hotel, connected with the Paddington Station, was opened for business on Friday last, the 9th instant.

These premises have been built by the Company, and are fitted up with every modern convenience for Families as well as for Single Persons, while the Terms have been fixed for every description of Hotel Business upon a very moderate Scale of Charge.

Parties are strongly recommended to order their Apartments previously, by letter, addressed to Mr. Wheeler, Manager, Great Western Royal Hotel, Paddington Station, who is authorised to enter into arrangements for the reception of Parties for a given time at a rate of charge by the Week or the Day.

Passengers by the Trains can pass between the Platforms and the Hotel at once, without trouble or expense, and proper persons will be always in attendance to receive and carry the Luggage to or from the Trains.

TARIFF.

GROUND FLOOR.—Sitting Room, per day, 6s.; Small sitting room, 4s.

LARGE APARTMENTS ON FIRST FLOOR.—Drawing Room and Two Bed Rooms (with Water Closet enclosed) *en suite*, per day, 22s. 6d ; Drawing Room and Two Bed Rooms, 20s ; Drawing Room and Bed Room, 15s.; Bed Room and Dressing Room, 10s.; Single Bed, 5s.

SECOND FLOOR.—Sitting Room, per day, 7s. 6d.; Large Bed Room, 3s. 6d.; Small Bed Room, 2s. 6d.

THIRD FLOOR.—Large Bed Room, per day, 2s. 6d.; Small Bed Room, 2s.

FOURTH FLOOR.—Large Bed Room, per day, 2s.; Small Bed Room, 1s. 6d. Except the Suites, 1s. extra will be charged when the Bed is occupied by Two Persons.

EXTRAS.—Sitting Room Fire, 1s. 6d.; Bed Room Fire 1s.; Breakfast with Eggs, 2s.; Breakfast with Cold Meat or Chop, 2s. 6d.; Breakfast with Broiled Ham and Eggs, 3s.

COFFEE ROOM DINNERS, &c.—Joint and Plain Vegetables, 2s. 6d.; Chops, 2s.; Steaks, 2s ; Cold Meat, 2s.; Basin of Soup, 1s.; Sandwich, 6d.; Cup of Tea, 6d.; Cup of Coffee, 6d. Visitors' Servants' Meals, 4s. per day; Hot Baths, 2s. 6d.; Cold Baths, 1s. 6d.

WINES.—Draught Port, per pint, 2s. 6d., per bottle, 5s.: Old Bottled Port, 3s. and 6s.; Very Old Port, 3s. 6d. and 7s.; Draught Sherry, 2s. 3d. and 4s. 6d.; Golden Sherry, 2s. 6d. and 5s.; Brown Sherry, (East India,) 3s. and 6s.; Pale Sherry, (East India,) 3s. 6d. and 7s.; Amontillado, 3s. and 6s.; Madeira, 3s. and 6s.; Old East India, 8s. per bottle; Champagne, per pint, 4s. and per bottle, 7s. 6d.; Claret, (Johnson's,) 8s. 6d. per bottle; Claret, (Johnson's,) 7s. 6d.; Chateaux Margaux, (Johnson's,) 6s.; St. Julien, (Johnson's,) 5s. 6d.; Medoc, (Johnson's,) 4s.

SPIRITS AND LIQUEURS.—Brandy, per glass, 1s.; Hollands, 1s.; Rum, 6d.; Gin, 6d.; Whiskey, 9d.; Maraschino, 1s.; Curacco, 1s.; Noyeau, 1s.; Orange Brandy, 1s.; Liqueur Brandy, 1s.; Cherry Brandy, 1s.; Eau de Vie de Danzic, 1s.

ALE AND STOUT.—Allsopp's Pale Ale, per pint 6d., per bottle 1s.; Scotch, 6d. and 1s.; Burton, 6d. and 1s.; Stout, 6d. and 1s.; Cyder, 6d. and 1s.; Soda-Water, 6d. per bottle; Brighton Seltzer, 9d.; Lemonade, 6d.; Carrara Water, 6d.

HOTEL ARRANGEMENTS.—The Servants of the Establishment are not allowed to receive any Fees or Gratuities whatever from the Visitors; but, in lieu thereof, 1s. 6d. will be charged to each Visitor for attendance for the first day, and 1s. per day afterwards. Visitors not having Apartments in the Hotel will be charged 6d. attendance for each meal. The charge for attendance includes the removal of Luggage to and from the Hotel, and for all services rendered throughout the Establishment. The Proprietors will not be responsible for any property lost in the Hotel unless given in charge of the Superintendent. Visitors may lock up their Rooms during their absence, giving the key in charge of the Superintendent.

Drawing No 3.
G. W. R.
Great Western Royal Hotel Paddington.
Elevation to Praed Street.
Scale: 8 Feet to 1 Inch
Engineers Office. Paddington W.
Z.94

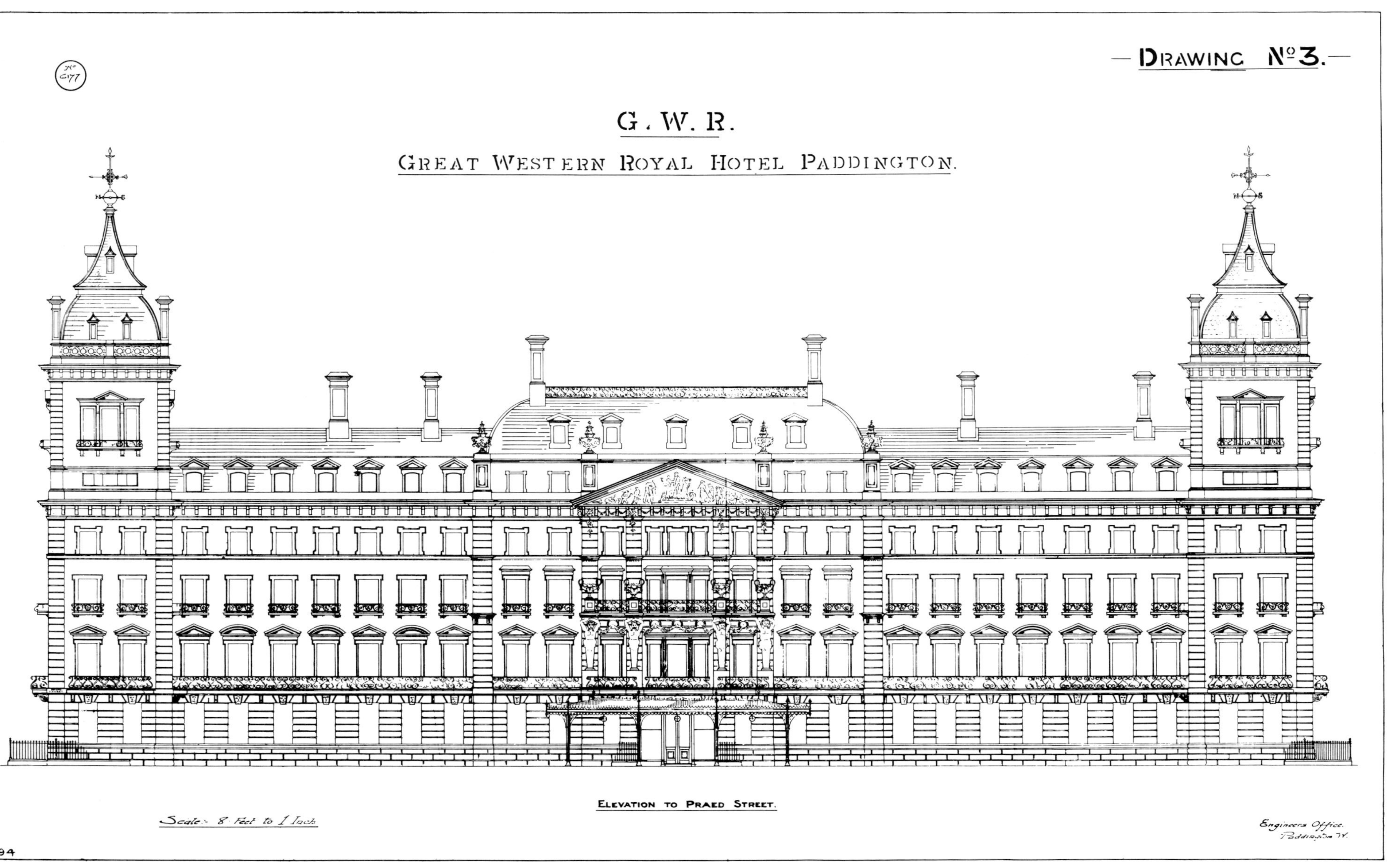

Plate 158

Plate 159
Plate 160

Plate 161

The Hotel from the south. The front of the building, grimy after 55 years exposure to London fumes, has a great deal of ornate ironwork, urns and balustraded balconies, the latter being supported by caryatid figures. The photograph is undated.

British Rail

Plate 162

The Hotel was cleaned and modernised between 1933 and 1936, losing most of its ornamentation in the process. View from the north.

▼

British Rail

Plate 159

The last gap between the offices in Eastbourne Terrace and the Hotel is now filled with a building which matches the style of the Hotel — now that the latter has lost so much of its decoration. At the corner of the new building hangs a simple sign, 'Superintendent of the Line'.

British Rail

Plate 160

This photograph was taken just before the work of stripping and modernisation of the Hotel was commenced. Iron snakes intertwine on window balconies supported by stone scrolls or, in some cases, by caryatids. Some windows have round tops within the main rectangle and there are four different styles of plaster work at the window frames. Many feet below the windows a frilly porte-cochere gives shelter to arriving and departing guests as they walk to or from their conveyances. View from the south.

British Rail

Plate 163
The Hotel Foyer as it was before rebuilding. The porte-cochère can be seen through the plate glass door held by the solemn page boy. The atmosphere is club-like, with mahogany and leather.

British Rail

Plate 164
In the foyer, the only surviving item from the above picture appears to be the ashtray on the far right.

British Rail

Plate 165
One of the original dining rooms decorated in the style which so pleased the Prince Consort. Elegant statues carrying the cups and bowls of symbolic plenty, line the walls where a wealth of pierced plaster moulding encrusts curving edges. Skilled craftsmanship can be seen everywhere, maybe too fussily done for some taste, but still very skilful nonetheless. Silver plated, monogrammed cutlery is on every table.

British Rail

Plate 166
The re-modelled staircase, with palms.

British Rail

Plate 167
False columns here support an artificial ceiling, the real work being done by ugly steel girders, well hidden. The futuristic lines of column and cupola are dramatised by skilfully concealed lighting and a false impression of size is lent to the room by the all but invisible mirror behind the wine waiter and his trolley.

British Rail

Plate 168
An un-rebuilt corridor among the bedrooms.

British Rail

Plate 169
The Art Deco. period bathroom was an unqualified improvement on the cluttered Victorian model. All surfaces can be easily cleaned and even the waste pipe is chromium plated.
British Rail

Plate 170
And so to bed.
British Rail

Swindon

Plate 171

The Brunel designed booking office on the downside at Swindon with 1872/3 extension at the further end. The earlier building has a fine pediment, with an ornamental cornice supported by small, stone scroll-like brackets at the building's corners. The effect of this decoration is to give the impression that square columns are supporting the roof. Instead of chimney pots Brunel provided those 'gravestone' type slabs. Between the nearest window and the corner of the building is a very ornate drainpipe bearing a 'twining ribbon' motif similar to that employed on platform canopy support columns.

British Rail

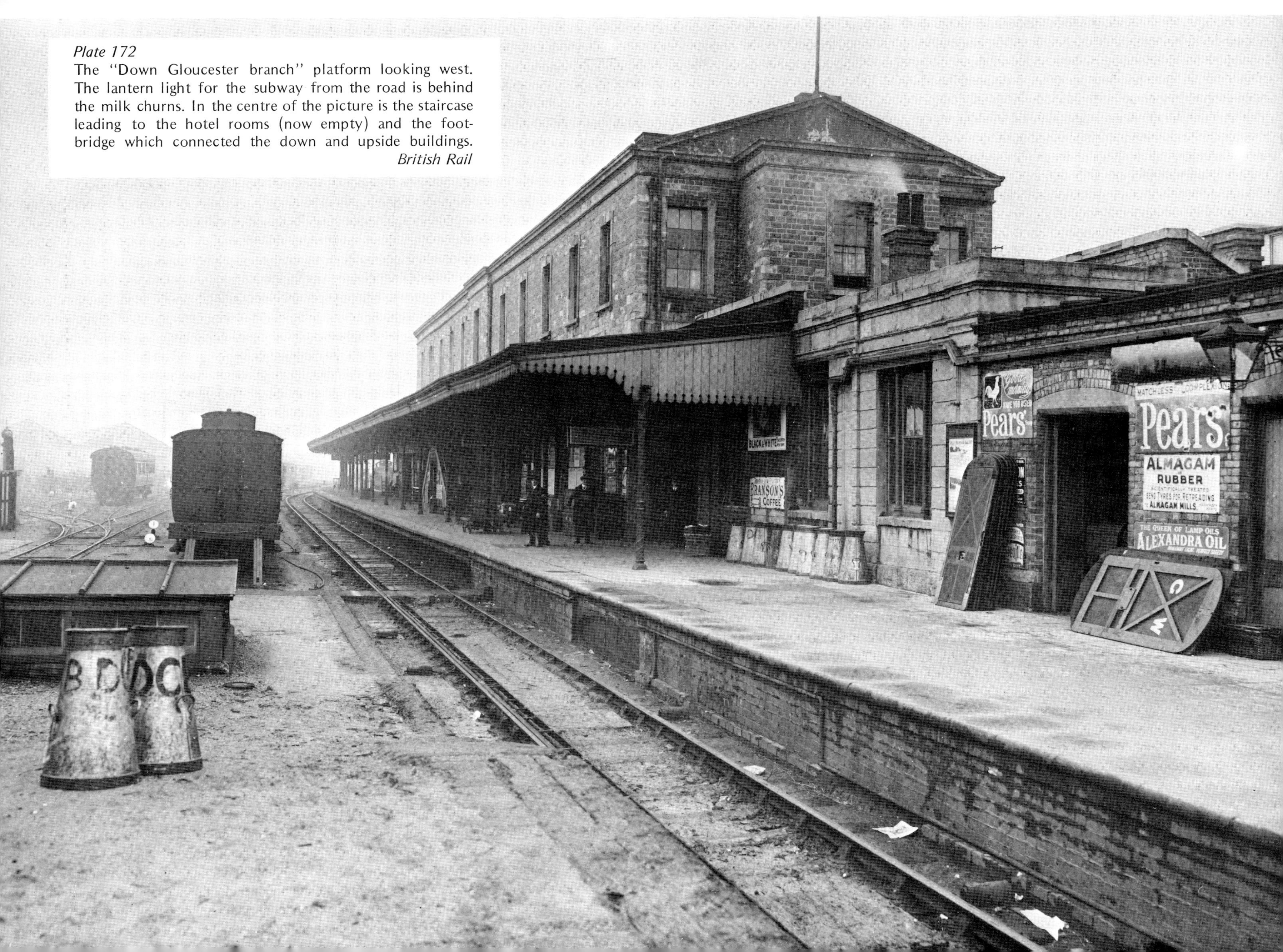

Plate 172
The "Down Gloucester branch" platform looking west. The lantern light for the subway from the road is behind the milk churns. In the centre of the picture is the staircase leading to the hotel rooms (now empty) and the footbridge which connected the down and upside buildings.
British Rail

Nailsea

Plate 174

Pewsey station, on the Berks and Hants Extension Railway, was opened to traffic with the rest of the new line from Hungerford to Devizes on November 11th 1862. The Brunelian concept of a small country station remains, if rather lower and more squat than the great man would have had this particular style. There is a total lack of platform canopy, which Brunel never omitted, but the treatment of those timbers supporting part of the roof is exactly how he would have had it, the diagonals forming 'Gothic' arches. The station building blends well with the other houses that were in the vicinity at the time it was built.

C. Maggs 1968

Plate 173

From the platform, the station at Nailsea looks deceptively small. In fact it was quite large, built on an embankment so that the front rose from the road to the roof some forty feet. Whether or not this was designed by Brunel is not known, it is possible that it was constructed in 1860, which means to say that it was not even a Great Western Railway station originally, but I include it to show the undoubted influence of Brunel on the architecture of stations.

British Rail

Pewsey

Savernake

Plate 175

Savernake station, on the Berks and Hants Extension Railway was similar to Pewsey, but it lacks the squat appearance of the latter. At Savernake ornamental brickwork has been incorporated in the end walls which resembles closely the work in the lodge houses at the home of the Marquess of Ailesbury, which was close by, when the station was built in 1862.

C. Maggs 29.9.62

Dauntsey

Plate 176

Dauntsey also followed the Brunelian idea for roadside stations. It was built during 1867/68 to the designs of George Drew, using knapped flint and limestone quoins. The waiting shed on the down platform is very much in the spirit of 1850 though the roof has a rake allowing the rain water to run off.

C. Maggs 23.5.63

Radstock

Plate 177

The line from Frome to Radstock was opened as a goods line in 1854. In 1873 the Bristol and North Somerset Railway opened to Radstock and the station illustrated was built. This would appear to be an early example of the rural station in a new style not influenced by Brunel. Several stations on the line looked similar to this one, though here use has been made of limestone for decoration, the others are of plainer brick. Marlow station, built at the same time as the North Somerset, is very similar in style.

C. Maggs

Radley

Plate 178
The working drawings for the construction of Radley station are dated 30.10.72 and signed 'H.H.'. The buildings were opened to the public in 1873. They were in the manner of a miniature country house with red brick and limestone decoration at the plinth, quoins and cornice. The ground plan is 'I' shaped, the bars of the 'I' being formed by handsome pavilions. These have low, hip roofs and add a pleasing finish to the whole building.

Plate 179
Radley station in its last extremity with a corrugated iron sheet where there had once been a proper awning.

Plate 180
A view along the island platform at Radley looking towards Didcot. The Abingdon branch is on the right. I should hazard a guess that the waiting room canopy extension on this platform was not part of the original station but added about 8 to 10 years later with the footbridge which would appear to date from 1882.

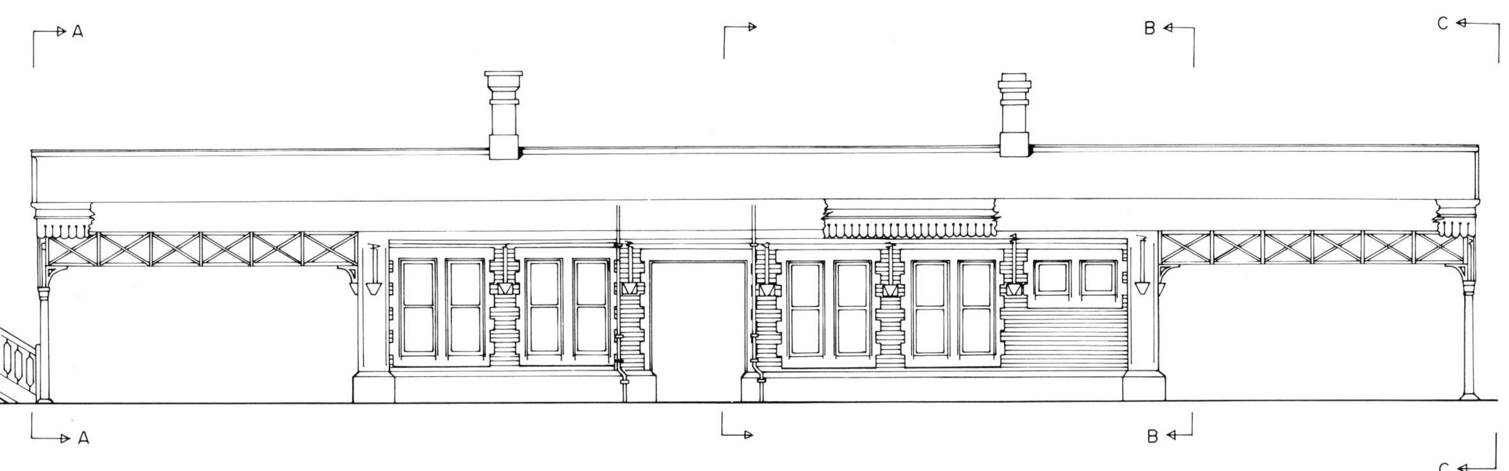

Plate 181

Unofficial drawings of Radley station.

Top Elevation of upside buildings from station approach.

Middle Elevation of upside buildings towards rails.

Bottom Elevation of island platform buildings.

C. Judge

Plate 182

Buildings on the island platform, branch line side. It is possible that the canopy extension is younger than the brick buildings, the former only being constructed when the footbridge was built.

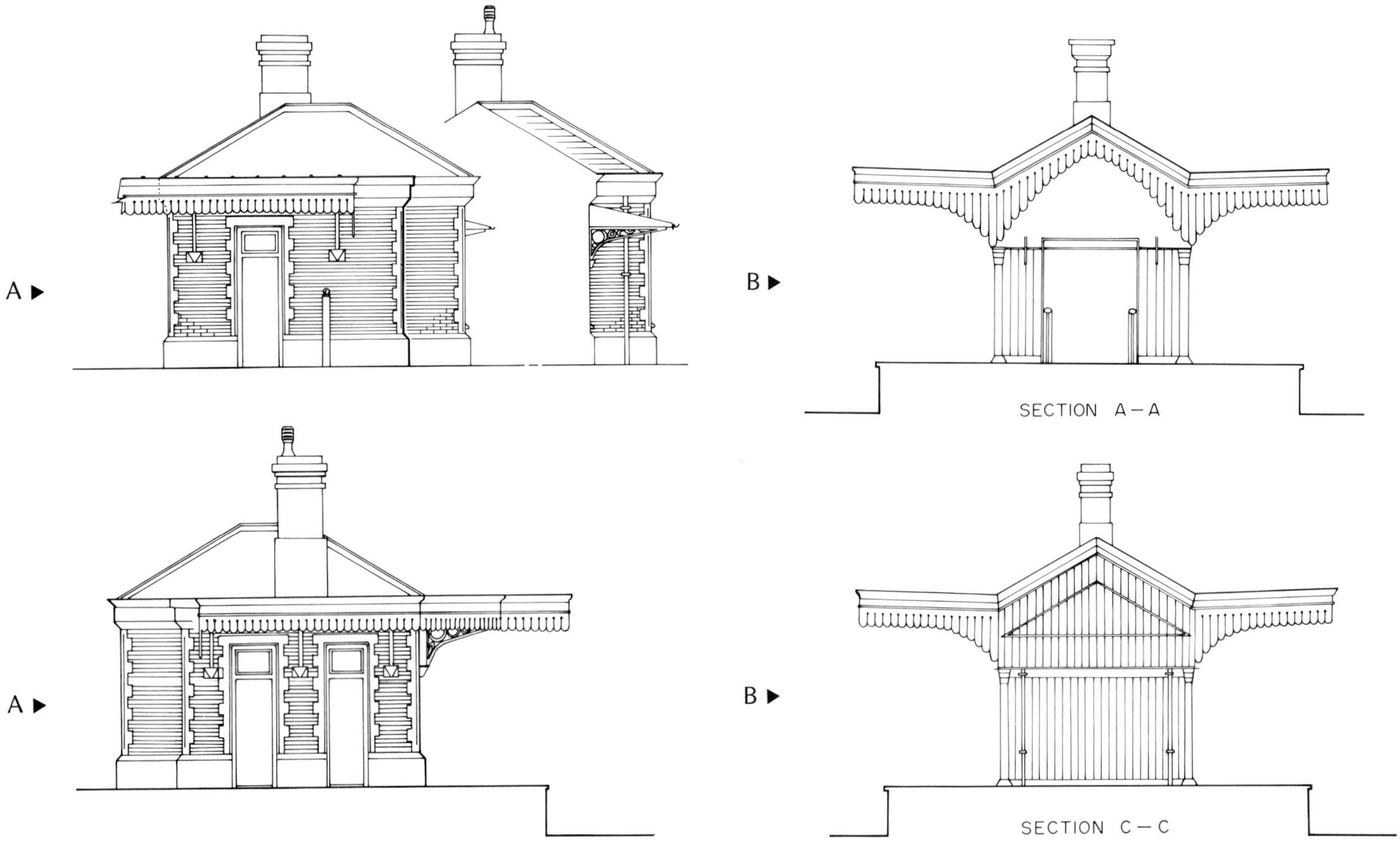

A ▶

B ▶

SECTION A – A

A ▶

B ▶

SECTION C – C

C ▶

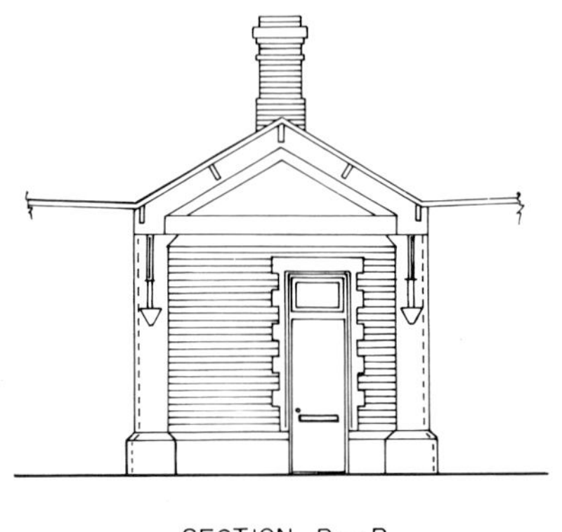

SECTION B – B

Plate 183

A. End elevation at Radley station, upside buildings.

B. End elevation at Radley station, downside buildings.

C. Section across island platform (downside) buildings.

C. Judge

Plate 184

Pavilion and hip roof, Radley station.

C. Judge

Taplow

Plate 185
The exterior of the upside buildings at Taplow showing the effect of good brickwork on an otherwise plain exterior. Simple gables are underlined by dentils beneath the coping stones and by a pediment marking string course. A blind lunette in contrasting colours of red and terra-cotta, has imitation keystones in the latter colour. The porte-cochère, once fully glazed, still retains its hip sides.

British Rail

Plate 186
The up main platform at Taplow. The station was designed in 1871 by J. E. Danks but was not built until 1883/4 when the lines through here were quadrupled. Semi-circular arches over doors and windows form an arcade interrupted by an elliptical arch over a passage-way which connects this platform with that for the relief line.

Author 1973

Plate 187
On the down relief platform, here, as elsewhere, the walls are in a mild red brick, with blue bull-nosed bricks at plinth corners. Arcading in yellow brick springs from pilaster tops which are covered with a stone coloured moulding. Adding to the variety of shape are the window arches which are recessed within the intrados of the arches. All in all a marvellous essay in the use of brick, shapes, light and colour.

Author 1973

Plate 188
The island platform buildings at Taplow, looking east. The chimney stacks are interesting with no chimney pots, a wide cornice and fillet beneath connected with small trusses.

British Rail

Plate 189
The up main platform at Taplow. Is it a coincidence that the valance over the main line platform is more ornate than that over the relief line? (see *plate 190*).

British Rail

Plate 190
Up relief line platform at Taplow.
British Rail

Plymouth North Road

Plate 191

The original station for Plymouth was in Union Street, built for the South Devon Railway and opened in April 1849. The Company was formally absorbed by the Great Western Railway in 1878 but plans by P.J. Margary, Resident Engineer of the line, for a new station for Plymouth on its present site had been drawn up by 10.2.76. The station illustrated here is the result of those plans. The distance across the station from the large gable on left and right was 150′, each gable spanning 46′ leaving the central part, never roofed over, 58′ wide. From the bottom of the windows in the gable front to the ridge of the roof was 15′ 6″. Spanning the tracks, but not visible in this photograph, was a very fine footbridge in painstakingly ornate cast iron. The building is largely made in timber except for the cast iron columns which, again, were beautifully turned out. In 1898 a complete set of drawings to enable this station to be replaced by another, this time in steel and glass, were drawn up and signed by J.C. Inglis, the Chief Civil Engineer, shortly to become General Manager of the Great Western Railway. However, they never materialised.

British Rail

Plate 192
Plymouth North Road station. Opened to the public in 1877.

British Rail

Weston-super-Mare

Plate 193
The Great Western Railway built this remarkable station in 1882 when the line which had terminated at Weston-super-Mare was continued to form a through loop, returning to the Bristol-Taunton main line at a point three miles west of the diverging point. The roofs and gables are piled up in medieval style, rough dressed stone blocks completing the antique aspect of the place. There is a striking resemblance between this station and that at Yeovil town, built by the Bristol and Exeter Railway during 1860/61. I have a suspicion that a draughtsman employed by the Great Western Railway had previously worked for the B. & E.R. and so brought his distinctive style with him to show in any further buildings he might design for his new employers. The designer of Weston-super-Mare was none other than Francis Fox, Chief Engineer of the Bristol and Exeter Railway since 1854. He drew the plans during 1875/76 (they are dated May 1876), the B. & E.R. having been absorbed by the Great Western Railway in January of that year.

John Morris 1973

Plate 194
Hip ends to the gables give what would otherwise be a functional 'ridge and furrow' roof great style and distinction. The valance board is unusually painstakingly cut out.

Author 1974

Plate 195
Exterior of the upside buildings at Weston-super-Mare. A fully glazed porte-cochère extends the full length of the frontage. It has a ridge and furrow roof and is supported by cast iron brackets very similar to those employed on the exterior of the 'Joint' station at Temple Meads station, Bristol. At intervals, tiny dormer windows illuminate the station attics, one such window can be seen to the left of the central chimney.

Author 1974

Plate 196
Beneath the canopy on the upside at Weston-super-Mare with the 3.35 p.m. to Paddington waiting to leave. This photograph shows how well the 90 year old roof illuminates and shelters the platform, few modern awnings are as effective. The cross beams of cast iron beneath the furrows of the roof have a basic 'zigzag' pattern which is enlivened by an additional rib upon the first and by tiny lobes of iron which make the open triangular spaces between the 'zigzag' into a heart shape. The whole effect is very similar to that achieved at Bristol 'Joint' station and one wonders just how much of the latter station we owe to Francis Fox of the B. & E.R. The cast iron columns here are decorated in a manner which was in common use during the 1850's.

Author 1974

Plate 197
Minehead station before the extension of platform awning and buildings. This station has now been restored by the West Somerset Railway Co.
British Rail

Plate 198
Exterior view of Minehead station.
British Rail

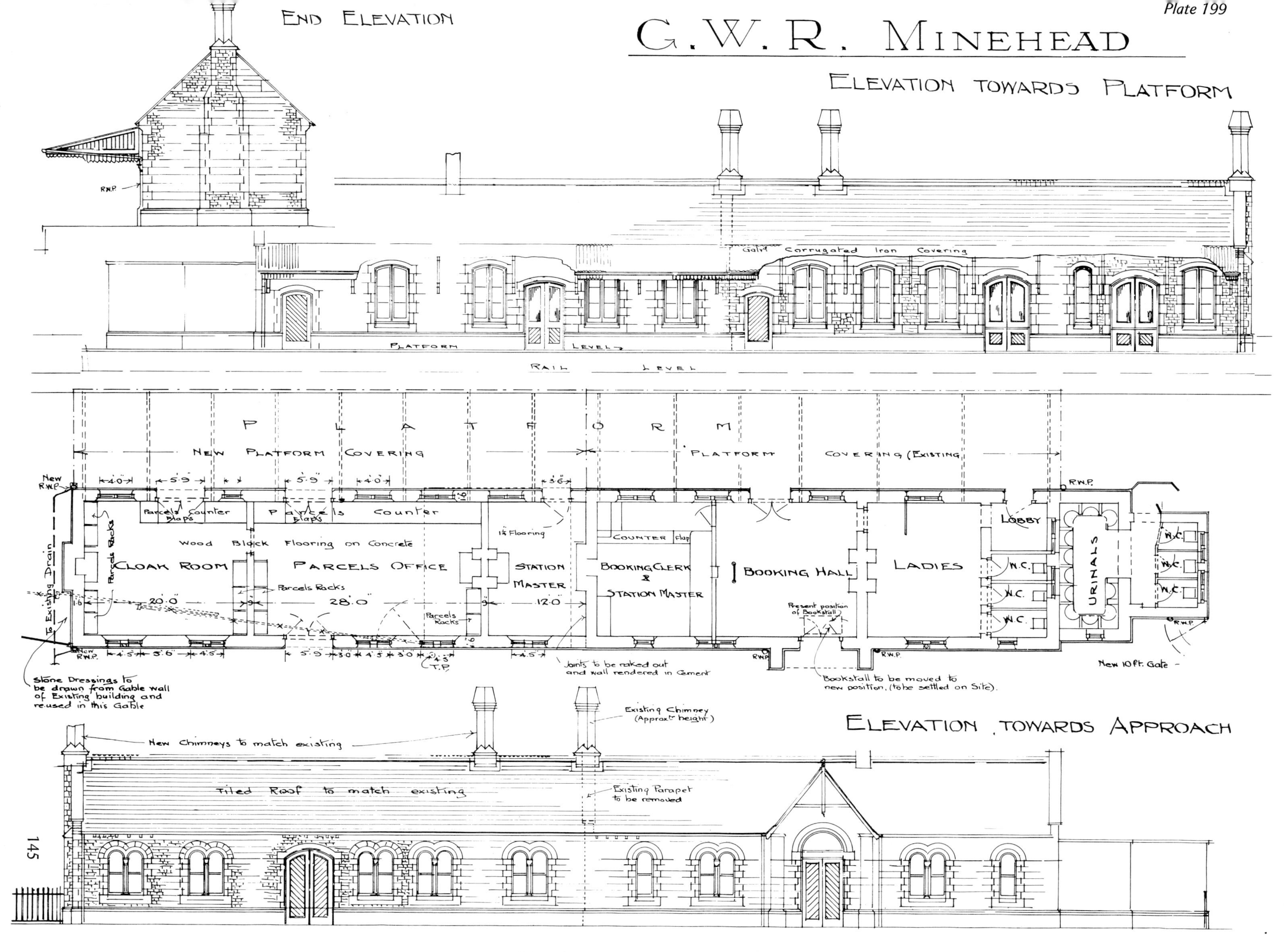
G. W. R. MINEHEAD
ELEVATION TOWARDS PLATFORM
END ELEVATION
R.W.P.
Galvd Corrugated Iron Covering
PLATFORM LEVEL
RAIL LEVEL
P L A T F O R M
NEW PLATFORM COVERING
PLATFORM COVERING (EXISTING)
New R.W.P.
Parcels Counter Flaps
Parcels Counter Flaps
1½ Flooring
Wood Block Flooring on Concrete
CLOAK ROOM
PARCELS OFFICE
STATION MASTER
BOOKING CLERK & STATION MASTER
COUNTER Flap
BOOKING HALL
LADIES
LOBBY
W.C.
URINALS
Parcels Racks
Parcels Racks
Parcels Racks
20.0
28.0
12.0
To Existing Drain
Present position of Bookstall
R.W.P.
New 10 ft. Gate
T.P.
Stone Dressings to be drawn from Gable wall of Existing building and reused in this Gable
Joints to be raked out and wall rendered in Cement
Bookstall to be moved to new position, (to be settled on Site).
ELEVATION TOWARDS APPROACH
New Chimneys to match existing
Existing Chimney (Approx. height)
Tiled Roof to match existing
Existing Parapet to be removed

Slough

Plate 200

The first station at Slough was opened to the public in June 1838. It was designed by Brunel as a 'one-sided' station and this early building is illustrated here. There were two stations, the up and the down, 50 yards apart with sidings and wagon turntables between, none of which are shown here. The up station was closest to Paddington and stood 18 miles 22 chains from that place. Opposite, on the north side of the line, between the two stations a goods shed was built, again not featured in this drawing. The fairytale type building in the background is the artist's rendering of the 'Royal Hotel' which, with the 'North Star', was probably built by the Company in 1837, on Great Western Railway land. The station would have been difficult to operate owing to the necessity of trains calling at the station being obliged to cross the running lines to reach the platforms but the arrangement lasted until 1879 at least. In that year the Great Western Railway completed its four track system as far west as Slough and may have had a temporary station between then and the erection of the new station about 1886. Alternatively the four tracks could have stopped short of the station and the antiquated system dating back to 1838 may have continued until the new station was built. The old station is absolutely typical of its type.

British Rail

Plate 201

The drawings for the new Slough station were drawn by J.E. Danks and dated November 1886. In this plate we see a close view of the 'upside' roof. At close range the wealth of decoration is rather overpowering. The windows, which can just be seen over the top of the awning are square headed with a stone lintel, the corner bricks and the lintel have a bead moulding which is similar to the style which was to be brought out later on 'standard stations' like Newbury. The station at Ross-on-Wye has windows in the same style though without the bead moulding. Over the windows is a line of dentils and a cornice. Pilasters, rising on both sides of the windows, terminate in trefoil caps and between these caps are lunettes. These are in moulded brick with an acanthus leaf at the keystone. The clock has a hood in the form of a curved pediment surmounted by a ball. As if all this was not sufficient, Mr. Danks has contrived these curious tiles for the unusually shaped roof. The 'fish scale' effect has been obtained by the use of 'tiles' of metal pressings. The metal is about $\frac{1}{16}''$ thick and has a central stiffening rib. At the corners of the hips and around the base of the railings a weather seal is effected with a metal pressing resembling a heavy rope hawser. The crowning railings, prickly as a holly bush, were a long lived fashion which appears to have come into vogue after 1865.

British Rail

Plates 202/203
The station buildings were arranged in the Palladian manner with three pavilions linked by low roofs. This plate shows the strong verticals in white patent stone and arcading over doors and windows in the same material. One almost expects to see the Imperial 'N' emblazoned on the building, so majestic it appears. The courtyard is very spacious, enough, you might well think, for a regiment of Horse Guards to be drawn up before the station, for after all, Queen Victoria used it frequently. There is also an interesting contrast shown here between the rather crude motor buses and the graceful horse cabs which they superseded.

British Rail

Plate 205

Plate 204
The roof on the downside building at Slough. Compare the chimney here with the one shown in *plate 188*. The cornice and fillet with connecting brackets of the latter, 1871 station has become reduced at Slough (1886) to insignificant proportions and a chimney pot is now provided.

Author 1974

Plate 205
An elegant, fluted, cast iron column supporting the awning on the down platform at Slough.

Author 1974

Plate 206
The canopies spring from a timber roof which is supported on the cast iron columns mentioned in *plate 205* and by the wall of the station. Iron rafters with much decorative ironwork rest on lattice girders and the brick wall of the station.

Author 1974

Didcot

Plate 207

Didcot Junction has had two stations since opening in 1844. They have both been timber constructions with the exception of the present brick entrance. Although we do not know what earlier offices stood on the site it seems likely that the entrance to the station has always been below rail level, a feature which would have been unusual in 1844. Illustrated is the present station built during 1885 to replace the original destroyed by fire in March of that year. A frame of stout timbers is enclosed by a double wall of planks, the butted joints sealed with narrow vertical strips which have the accidental virtue of adding texture to the walls. Where the main beams form a panel, the outline is picked out in dark brown in the general cream background to give a finish to the walls. Feathery valance boards extend, wing-like, over the platforms to give the place its distinctive Great Western Railway appearance. It is not certain when this style of gable-end to the platform awning came into use but it led to the style used in all free standing awning gables from 1884 until the Great War brought an end to station rebuilding. When the rebuilding programme was restarted the vast changes wrought by that War showed in the style of architecture used. Plate 207 shows the up main platform face, the camera looking west.

British Rail 1934

Plate 208

Didcot station 'up' main platform with the camera pointed eastwards towards Reading.

British Rail 1934

Tilehurst

Plate 209

Tilehurst station was not among the original stations opened by the Great Western Railway in the 1840's but was built during 1881 and opened in 1882. The buildings were designed by J.E. Danks and Lancaster Owen and are still in use today. They were not demolished to make way for the quadrupled tracks between Reading and Didcot, as was the fate of Pangbourne, Goring and Moulsford stations. The building shown here is the booking office situated by the down main line. It is built in a yellowish stone with limestone quoins. A few yards away the goods shed was built with the same material.

Author 1973

Plate 210

A view of the booking office at Tilehurst from the main road.

Author 1973

Plate 211
On the 'up' relief line platform at Tilehurst stands this waiting shed. It seems likely that this was part of the original 1882 station and was moved to this site when the extra platforms were built. To the right of the shed there used to be a gate with a lock which could be opened by inserting one penny in a slot. Thus opened it gave access to a footpath which led to the river. I have always thought that, with the growing popularity of river boating, the Great Western Railway built Tilehurst in the hope of developing a traffic to the Thames, this particular point chosen being close to some beautiful scenery in the Goring Gap where the river flows under the beech trees of the Chilterns.

Author 1973

Plate 212
When the line from Reading to Didcot was quadrupled in 1892 the three stations between Tilehurst and Didcot were demolished and rebuilt to designs of J.W. Armstrong. This gentleman also designed the waiting rooms for the island platform at Tilehurst. This plate shows the standard type building which he drew. At the end nearest the camera the awning has three sides, at the furthest end it is flat, with a curved down valance similar to that at Didcot. The building material is red brick with engineer's blues at the plinth.

Author 1973

Goring

Cholsey

Plate 213
Cholsey and Moulsford is the grandest of the four stations between Reading and Didcot. It was built in 1892 to designs by J.W. Armstrong, replacing the old station three quarters of a mile to the east. Built on an embankment, it has been given the distinction of a proper front, unlike Pangbourne, which, in an identical situation has a low, dark brick front. The ground at Pangbourne could have been excavated so as to make the station rise tall from road level but it had not the importance of Cholsey which was the junction for Wallingford. Although the facade is plain it is not ugly, its height giving some grace. The windows have concrete lintels with relieving arches in engineer's brick.
Author 1973

Plates 214/215
The stairs from the booking hall in the subway at Cholsey lead up onto the platform. They were originally made of stone but countless shoes have worn the surface away which has been replaced with cement. The iron balusters for the handrail are remarkably fine, in my opinion, quite fitting for a country mansion.
Author 1974

Plate 214

Plate 215

Ross-on-Wye

Plate 216
This station at Ross-on-Wye was built when the Great Western Railway took over the little Ross and Ledbury Railway in 1892. It has a curiously hybrid appearance. All construction below the roof has the appearance of the standard stations soon to be built at Westbury and on the new line from Princes Risborough to Aynho, while the roofs look like those erected on a number of stations in the London suburban area since the 1870's.

M. W. Earley 1960

Ealing Broadway

Plate 217
Ealing Broadway station was rebuilt with the quadrupling of the line from Paddington about 1877. Strangely, each roof is a different size from its neighbour.

British Rail

Windsor and Eton

Plate 218

An engine driver's view of the original station at Windsor. In the illustration the tracks curve into the station from the right, whereas in fact they curve in from the left, but apart from this detail the drawing is very accurate. The track is mixed gauge, showing that the picture was drawn after 1855; the branch to Windsor from Slough had been opened in 1849 on the broad gauge – before the station was completed in fact – and the third rail to allow 'narrow' gauge trains into the station was laid in 1855. The drawing shows the 'common' rail correctly as being on the near side in each direction of travel, with a narrow gauge only siding on the extreme left. The artist gives the impression that the station is made of stone but it is almost certain to have been constructed in timber. One imagines that it was the normal overall roofed station provided at so many new stations with some additions to suit it to its august surroundings. This has been done cheaply and effectively by raising the pediment above the entry arch and adding a row of windows. Doors in the front of the building divide up the blank wall and give the impression of pillars supporting the deep lintel over the portico. A very clever arrangement for the 'standard' timber roofed station.

British Rail

Plate 219 (overleaf)

Between 1895 and 1897 the station at Windsor was rebuilt with separate accommodation for the Royal family. This illustration shows the public station. The glazed roof, probably erected by Walkerdyne Co. of Derby, has a splendid 'lantern' or clerestory, suspended from which are some 150 candle power gas lamps. Dark red brick, relieved with limestone string courses, from the walls which are piered with handsome window frames. The offices are conveniently grouped and very well advertised. The walls bear some advertisements which make interesting reading. On patrol at the station, keeping a discreet eye on the photographers are a policeman and a guardsman. Though many of these delights have been swept away, the place was built well enough to look tidy and solid after 77 years and is well worth a visit today.

British Rail

LATFORM Nº 3
PLATFORM Nº 2
PLATFORM Nº 1
GENTLEMEN'S LAVATORY
WAY OUT
GREAT WESTERN RAILWAY
3RD CLASS BOOKING OFFICE
LADIES RO
1ST & 2ND CLASS BOOKING OFFICE
STATION MASTERS OFFICE
3RD CLASS WAITING ROOM
Channel Islands
LONDON
EXETER
PLYMOUTH
DINING LUNCHEON BREAKFAST CARRIAGES
DINING SALOON
BREAKFAST & LUNCHEON SALOON

Plate 219

Plate 220

In 1897, as the Company's gift to Her Majesty, Queen Victoria, to commemorate the 60th year of her reign, a new Royal station was opened adjacent to that used by the public. Pictured here is the entrance arch to both buildings. The arch looks similar to that at Paddington Departure Side though perhaps of a greater span and more ornate. The entrance is set between shops and an illusion of greater width is given by the use of strong horizontals in white limestone. The windscreen carries the legend "Great Western Railway" in ornate brass lettering which will be seen again in Chapter 8. I do not think I have ever seen the Company's Arms more nobly emblazoned than in this instance.

British Rail

Plate 221
The gates across the approach to the Royal station at Windsor. The photograph, taken about 1898 shows them superb in glossy black and gilt paint. In 1976 they are rusty, thrown back against the brick wall of the yard.

British Rail

Plate 222

That great glass roof, enormous, worthy of a London terminus, was built to shelter the Royal waiting room and mounted guards of the Royal escort. It now stands peeling and unwanted except to shelter a solitary Thames Valley bus. The Royal waiting room and its glass cupola can be seen at the left of the picture.

British Rail

Plate 223
Beneath the great roof at Windsor the Royal waiting room was built and faced with white tiles. This photograph shows the sitting room. On the floor there is an Indian carpet which appears by the fireplace to be somewhat threadbare, a mat having been laid over the worst areas. On the mantelpiece the clock is decorated in an Indian style with dome and elephants' heads to serve as handles. The decoration is restrained for the period, and very well lit by means of the fine cupola. There was one other room, a kind of luxurious entrance lobby. The suite was last used by King George VI in 1936, since then it has been a police office and is now a dump for newspapers.

British Rail

Newbury

Plate 224
Newbury station. Buildings on the upside looking west.
British Rail 1910

Plate 225
Newbury station, looking east shortly after rebuilding in 1910. The track and ballast are still rough and untidy looking. Awnings, gas lamps, station buildings and, to a certain extent, the layout of tracks, are all standardised equipment. Planned large scale expansion, such as the Great Western Railway carried out after 1896, required planned, standardised equipment; it is worth noting that this policy has not had a detrimental effect upon the appearance of the place.

British Rail

Plate 226
Buildings on the upside at Newbury.

Author 1974

Plate 227
Newbury station has first class brickwork in English bond using a smooth red brick. Over the windows and doors a limestone cap or lintel has been placed in the late Perpendicular style of the early 16th century. Bullnose bricks at the plinth prevent passengers from coming into contact with sharp edges while for the same purpose doors have a moulded bead in the corner bricks. Standing by the locker is a locomotive jack.

Author 1974

Plate 228
The canopy on the down platform at Newbury is typical of hundreds erected all over the system. Two steel channels are riveted back to back, forming the principal column upon which rests the lightly made angle iron rafters and cross beam. This triangle rests its base tips on a plate girder which extends the length of the platform. Purlins and ridge beams are deep, there are still latticework girders but the span between principal columns is quite long, so still intermediate rafters are provided.
British Rail

Plate 229
The gable at the west end of the downside buildings at Newbury. Similar designs were employed ten years earlier at Westbury (Wilts), on the 'New Line', Princes Risborough to Aynho Junction, in 1910. Even Aynho Park platform had a booking office in this style, though without the ornate gable.
Author 1974

Gerrards Cross

Plate 230
Gerrards Cross station was one of four new stations built by the Great Western Railway during 1904/5 between Northolt Junction and High Wycombe. This was part of their joint line with the Great Central Railway aimed at making a shorter route to Birmingham. The building on the right is almost identical to a style built on the 'Badminton and South Wales Direct Railway' during 1902, except that the door and window lintels are shaped in limestone.

British Rail

Calne

Plate 231
At Calne, a '1902' style standard station used on a branch line.

British Rail

Lambourn

Plate 232
The original station at Lambourn was erected by the Lambourn Railway Company independently of the Great Western. The latter company rebuilt the station in the second of their two '1902' standard patterns, this being carried out around 1910. In this design the canopy shelters the whole building and not just the platform. The advertisements are of interest, including one from the Daily Mail, 'New German Campaign of Mischief' and an *excursion* to Killaloe from Paddington. Killaloe is in County Clare in the far west of Ireland!

British Rail

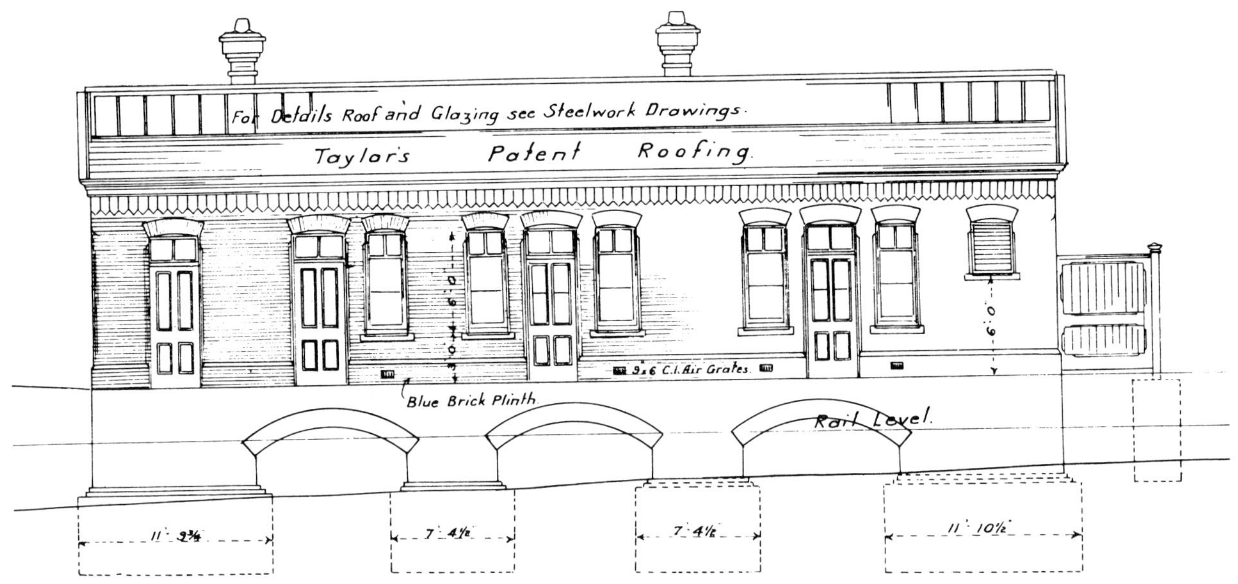

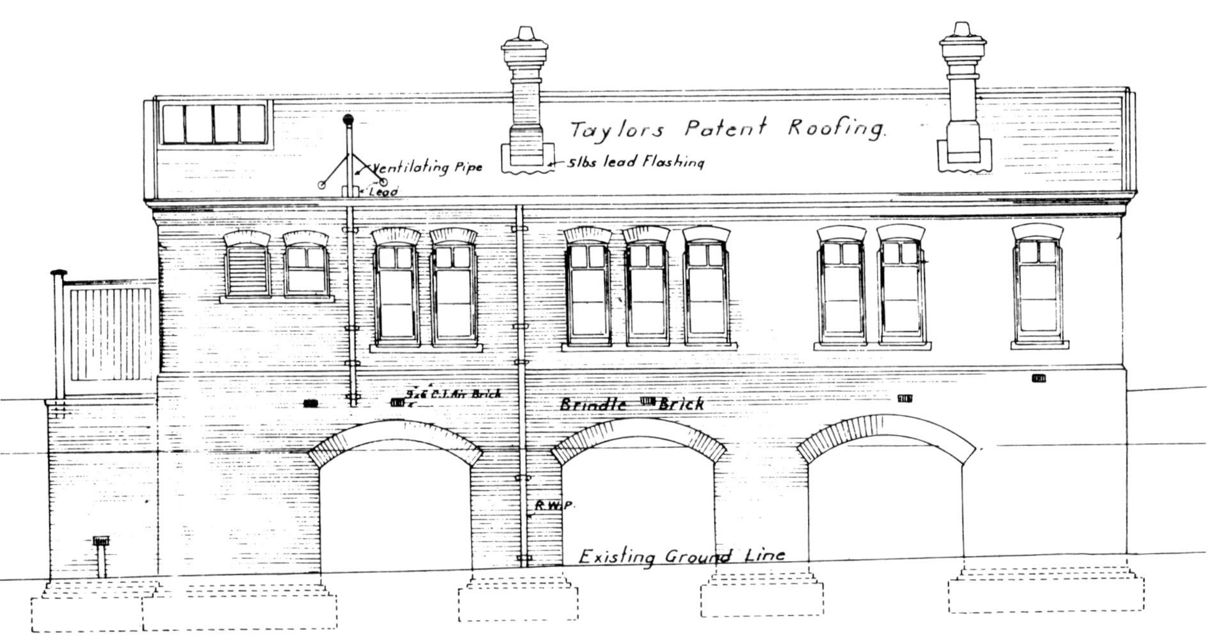

Plate 233
Official drawings of Lambourn station.

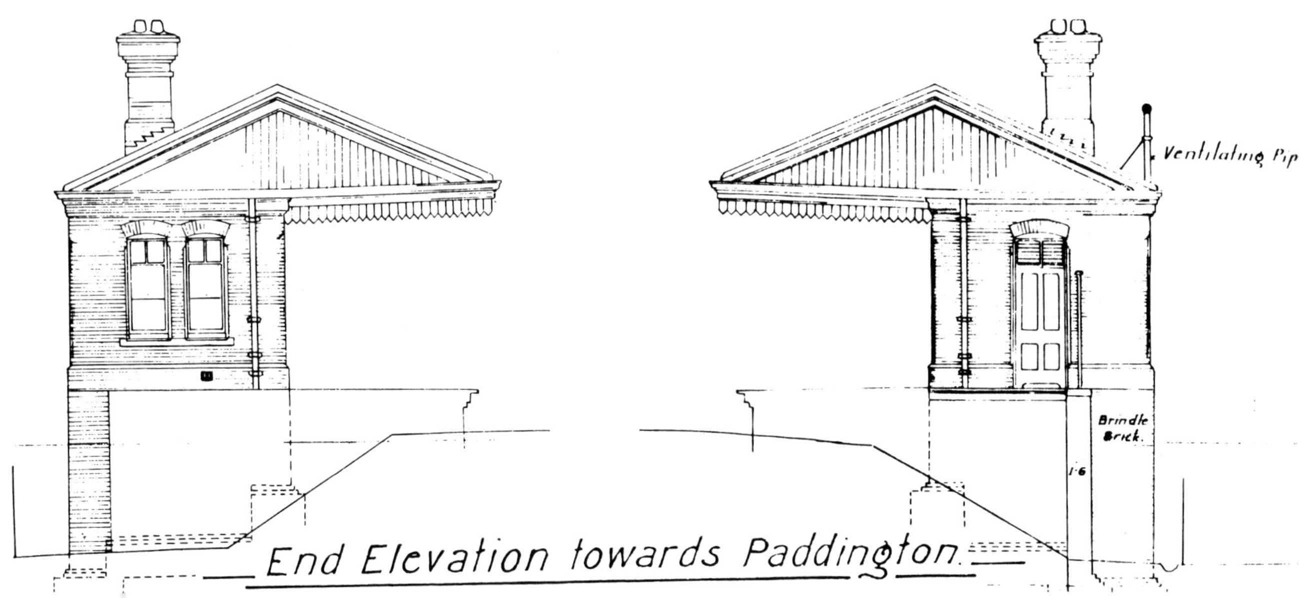

Plate 234
The first station on the site at Abingdon was built, not by the Great Western Railway, but by the Abingdon Company. It looks a dismal place and was, over the years, subject to many letters of complaint to the Company. As if to emphasise the need for a new station, trains occasionally hurled themselves at its modest fabric. On 22.4.08 a goods train carried out an attack, assaulting the station buildings and causing them such harm as to force the Great Western Railway, owners of the station for the past four years, to build a new station. It is interesting to note that, although the Company's standard plan for small stations had been in use since 1902 this station was a unique design. The line had always been a very profitable concern and this may have had some bearing on the Company's building decision.

British Rail

Abingdon

Plate 235
The new station had brickwork in English bond for strength, and never again did a train attempt to ram it, windows dignified by good proportions, a simple cornice round three sides of the building and a round pediment enclosing the station's name. Gutterings and down pipes are in cast iron with a good shape, the guttering complementing the cornice below. The chimneys are sturdy with cornice and fillet for water run-off purposes and decoration.

British Rail

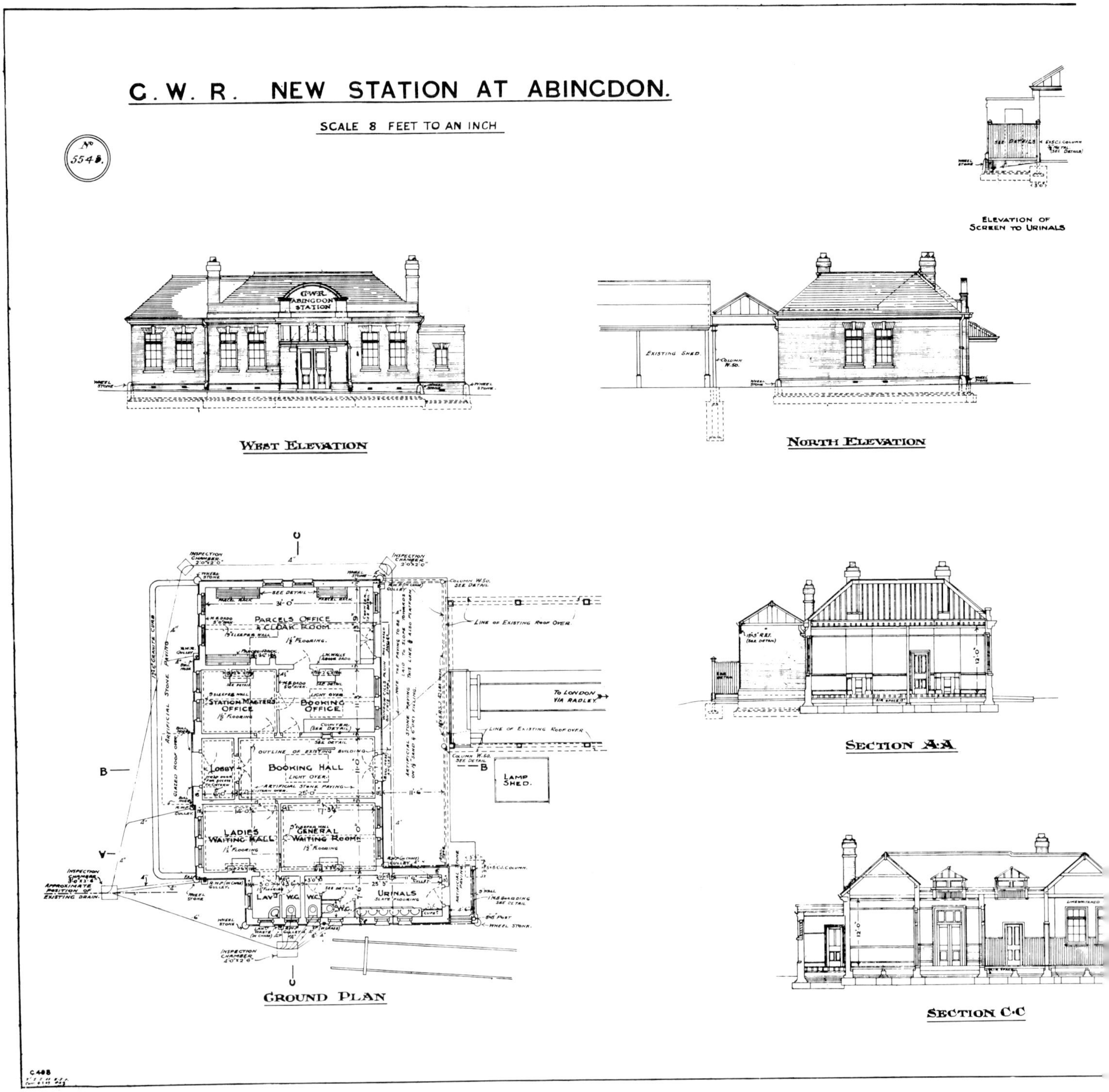

C. W. R. NEW STATION AT ABINGDON.

SCALE 8 FEET TO AN INCH

No 554B.

ELEVATION OF SCREEN TO URINALS

GWR ABINGDON STATION

WEST ELEVATION

EXISTING SHED

NORTH ELEVATION

PARCELS OFFICE & CLOAK ROOM

STATION MASTERS OFFICE

BOOKING OFFICE

LOBBY

BOOKING HALL

LADIES WAITING HALL

GENERAL WAITING ROOM

LAV. W.C. W.C.

URINALS

LAMP SHED.

To LONDON VIA RADLEY

LINE OF EXISTING ROOF OVER

ARTIFICIAL STONE PAVING

INSPECTION CHAMBER

WHEEL STONE

GROUND PLAN

SECTION A-A

SECTION C-C

C 488

Plate 236
Official drawings of Abingdon station. They were produced by W.W. Grierson.
British Rail

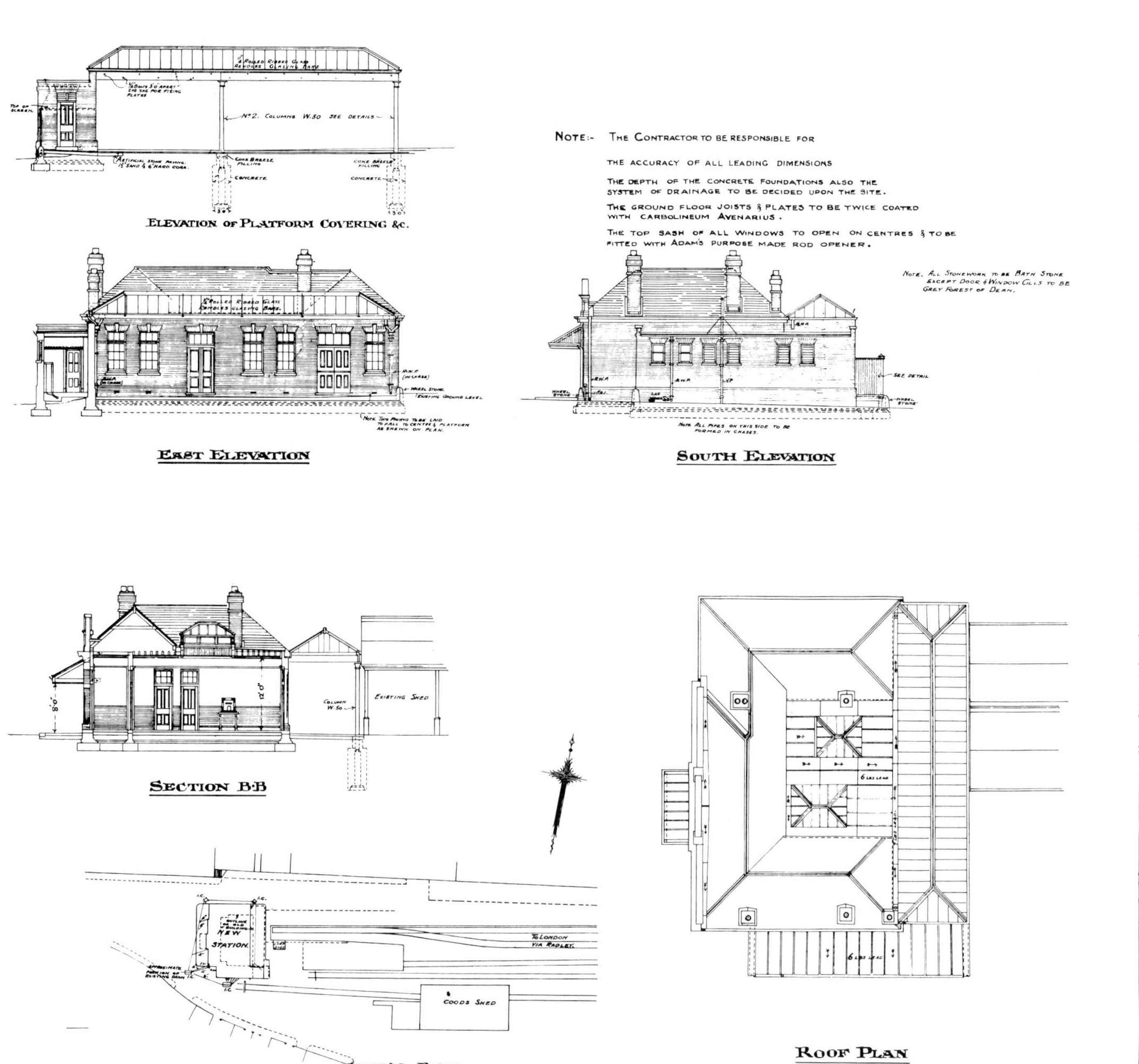

Plate 237
Continuation of *plate 236.*

Plate 238
Abingdon station quite new and ready for years of public service. Note the Goods Shed just appearing on the right.
British Rail

Plate 239
A new canopy between the station building and the old train shed was erected. In this picture the roof looks very strong and well made, the tiles evenly laid and the gutters clean and sharp looking in new cast iron.
British Rail

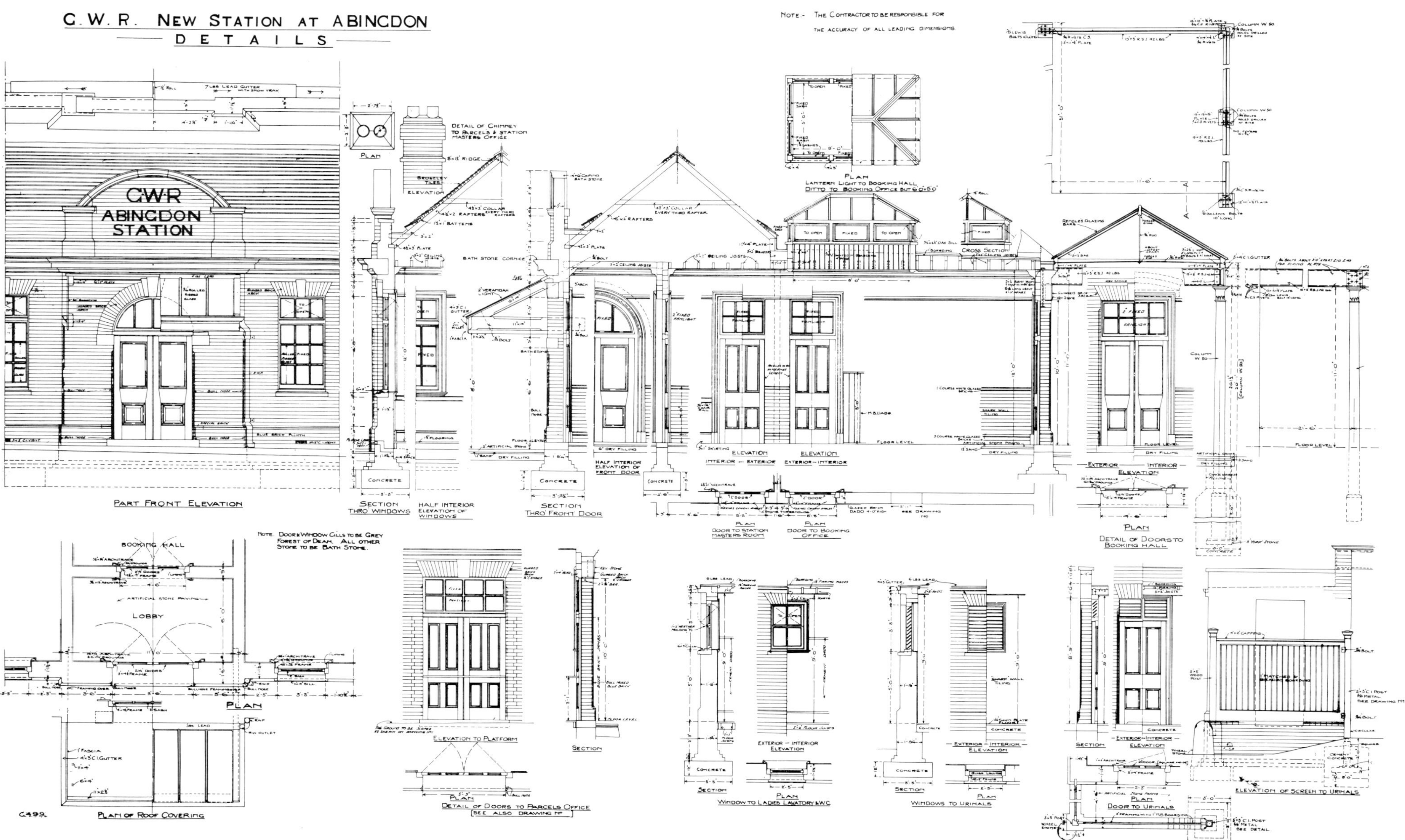

Plate 240
Official drawings of Abingdon station.

Badminton

Plate 241
The station buildings, looking west, probably before the line was open to traffic. The station master's house (see *plate 289)* has not yet been built but will soon occupy a site close to the public road to the left of the station approach. The station stood 100 miles from Paddington, high and remote amid the magnificent Cotswold farmland of the Dukes of Beaufort whose coat of arms were emblazoned on a limestone plaque set in the wall of the upside buildings—those on the right of the picture.

British Rail

Exeter St. David's

Plate 242
There have been three stations on the site of Exeter St. David's. The original (1844) was a Brunel one-sided affair. This was demolished and a new station was built by the engineer Francis Fox for the Bristol and Exeter Railway, this being replaced by the Great Western Railway between 1910 and 1912. This plate shows the Fox overall roof still in position and the new towers to carry a footbridge almost complete. The urns upon the wall in the background are part of the Fox station. In the station there is a goods van, panelled and in two colours, London and North Western colours in fact. The roof board proclaims, 'Manchester-Bristol *via* Severn Tunnel'.

British Rail 1910

Plate 243
Exeter St. David's station rebuilt into the form that is to be seen at this present time. Fox's wall has been retained complete with urns and the Great Western Railway has built a remarkable wooden building along its length above the awnings. Some of the old buildings can be seen in the right foreground and these may date from 1844. One bears an advertisement, 'Pears Soap', and another is to the rear, behind the platform wall. The illustration also shows the perfectly laid sidings and goods lines, the curves and the 'top' of the track beautifully smooth. The locomotive in the centre foreground is No. 1432 but the 'Star' in the down platform is unidentifiable. In the left foreground there is an interesting van bearing the legend 'Locomotive, Carriage and Wagon Dept. Exeter'.

British Rail 1910

Plate 244
Exeter St. David's.
British Rail

Birmingham Snow Hill

Plate 245

There were three stations on this site at Birmingham, Snow Hill. The original was a large wooden shed put up in a hurry in 1852 and removed to Didcot in 1871 for use as a carriage shed on the site of the present engine shed. The second station, 1871, survived until 1910 when the last and biggest one for the site was constructed. This plate shows the Hotel at the station, dating from 1852 after the 1910 station had been built. An archway has been cut through the building to give convenient access to the booking hall from Colmore Row. Once the facing bricks of the Hotel were white – but that was a long time ago – now the looks of the place are saved by the Italianate outline of the flanking towers and their balconies sheltered by round pediments supported by pairs of columns. The remainder of the front is equally Italian with rows of windows, some hooded with pediments and scroll work, others plain rectangles, and others again with semi-circular arches. There were once 126 rooms in the Hotel, surely one of the finest Victorian buildings in Birmingham. In June 1974 it had ceased to exist save for some rubble filling a hole in the ground at the side of Colmore Row.

British Rail

Plate 246
This is an unfortunate photograph for it shows the station resembling a hangar for a 'Zeppelin' when in fact it was once a fine roof with glazed windscreen. The view is looking north.

British Rail

Plate 247
The Booking Hall at the 'new' station at Snow Hill. A great roof of glass supported by steel ribs of lattice-work shelters a spacious passenger circulating area. Over the booking windows is an arcade faced with glazed tiles and each ticket window has a pediment which gives them the look of a classical portico.

British Rail

Plate 248
North end of Birmingham Snow Hill showing the superb roof construction.
British Rail

Plate 249
The roof of the booking hall at Snow Hill station showing the arching ribs bearing on a latticework girder which is in turn supported by the stout brick walls and at intervals by pillars which may be solid brick or brick clad steel girders.
British Rail

Plate 250
Looking north along platform 5 at Birmingham Snow Hill. This illustrates perfectly the spacious conception of the plan which must be the last truly great station built, or rebuilt, on the Great Western Railway – Paddington included. Anyone going to see the station now, having gained entry past the car park attendants, would surely be angered to see this superbly well-made station devastated by vandals and reduced to serving as a car park.
British Rail

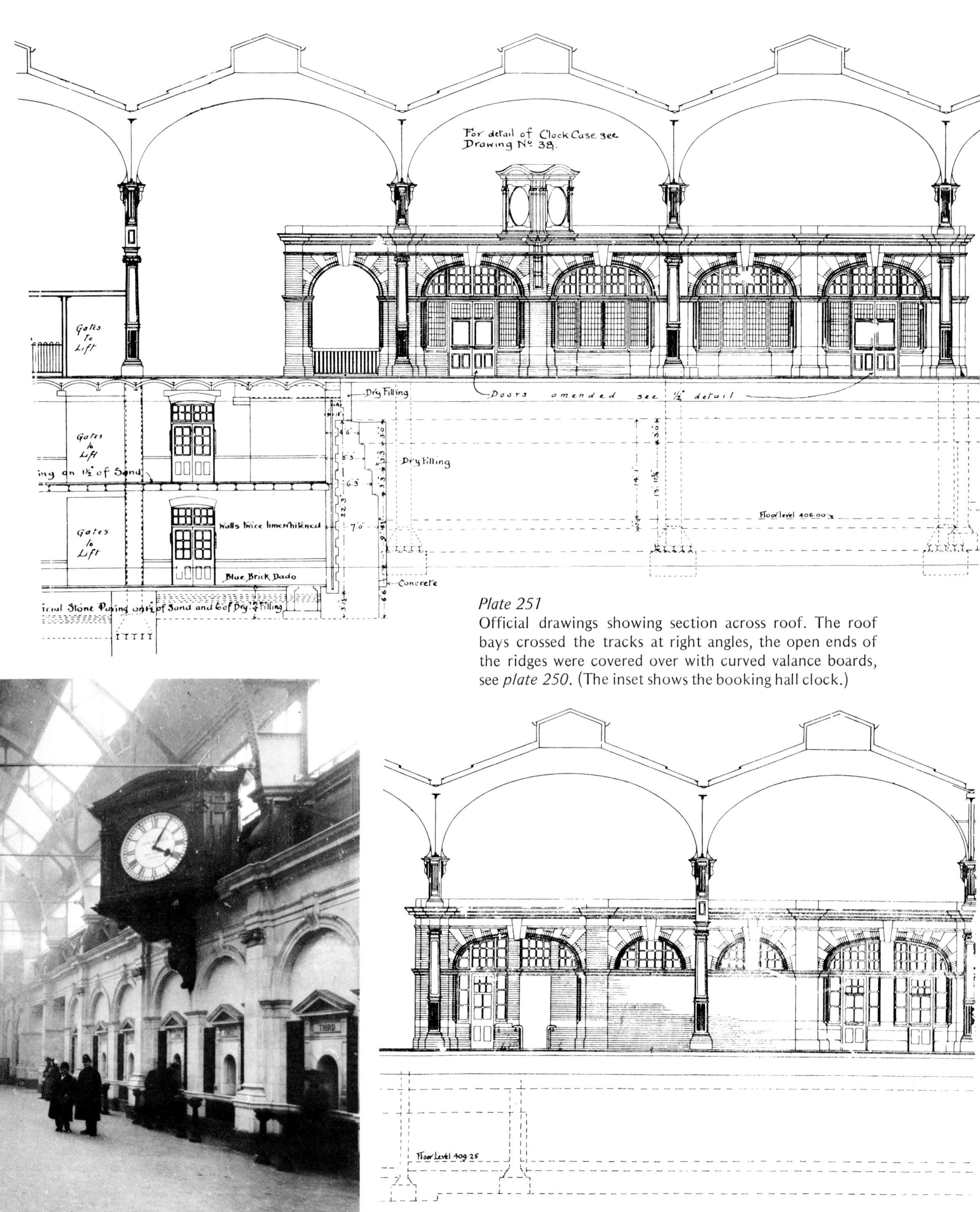

Plate 251
Official drawings showing section across roof. The roof bays crossed the tracks at right angles, the open ends of the ridges were covered over with curved valance boards, see *plate 250*. (The inset shows the booking hall clock.)

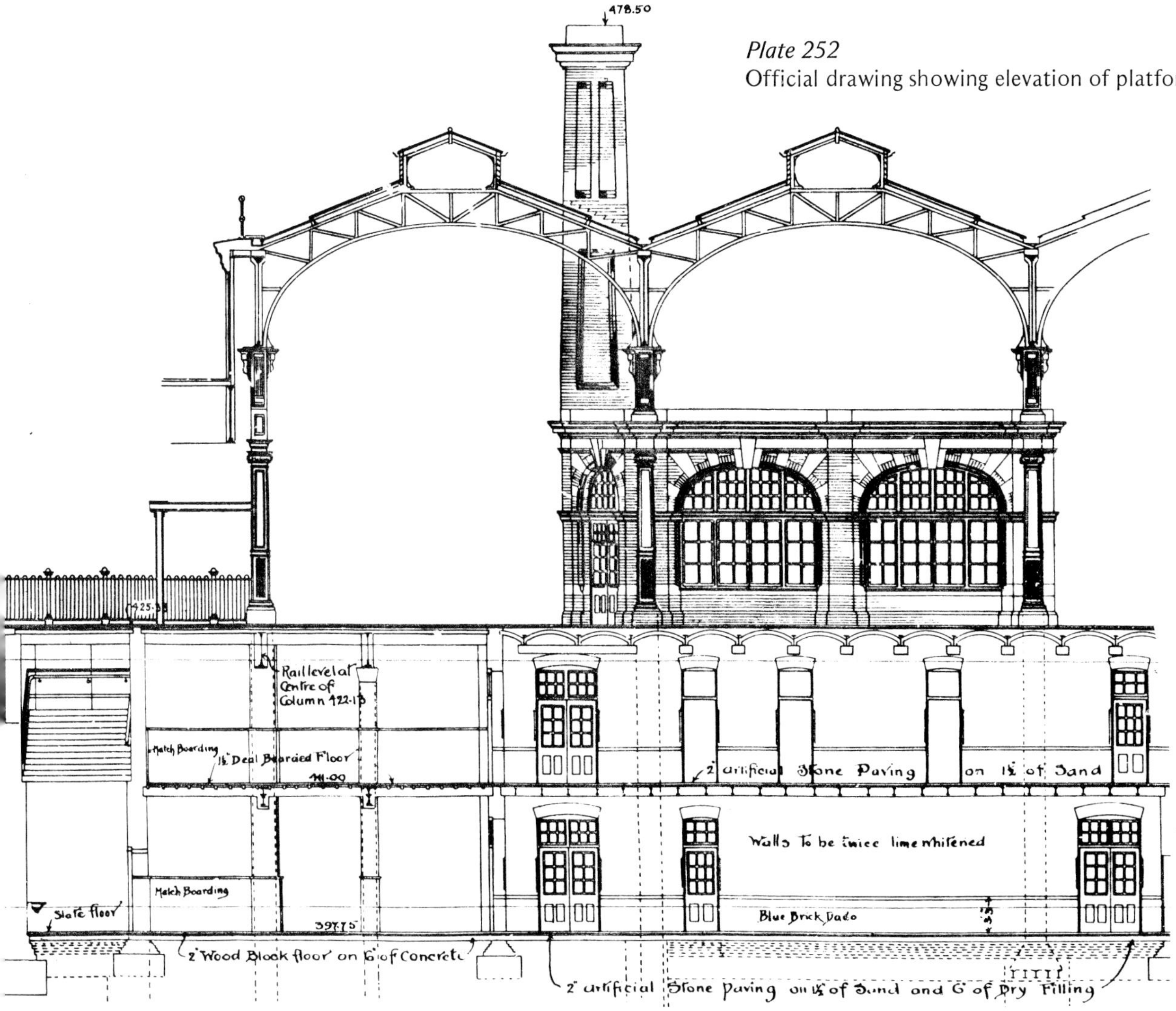

Plate 252
Official drawing showing elevation of platform buildings.

Plate 253
The station as seen from Livery Street. Looking north.

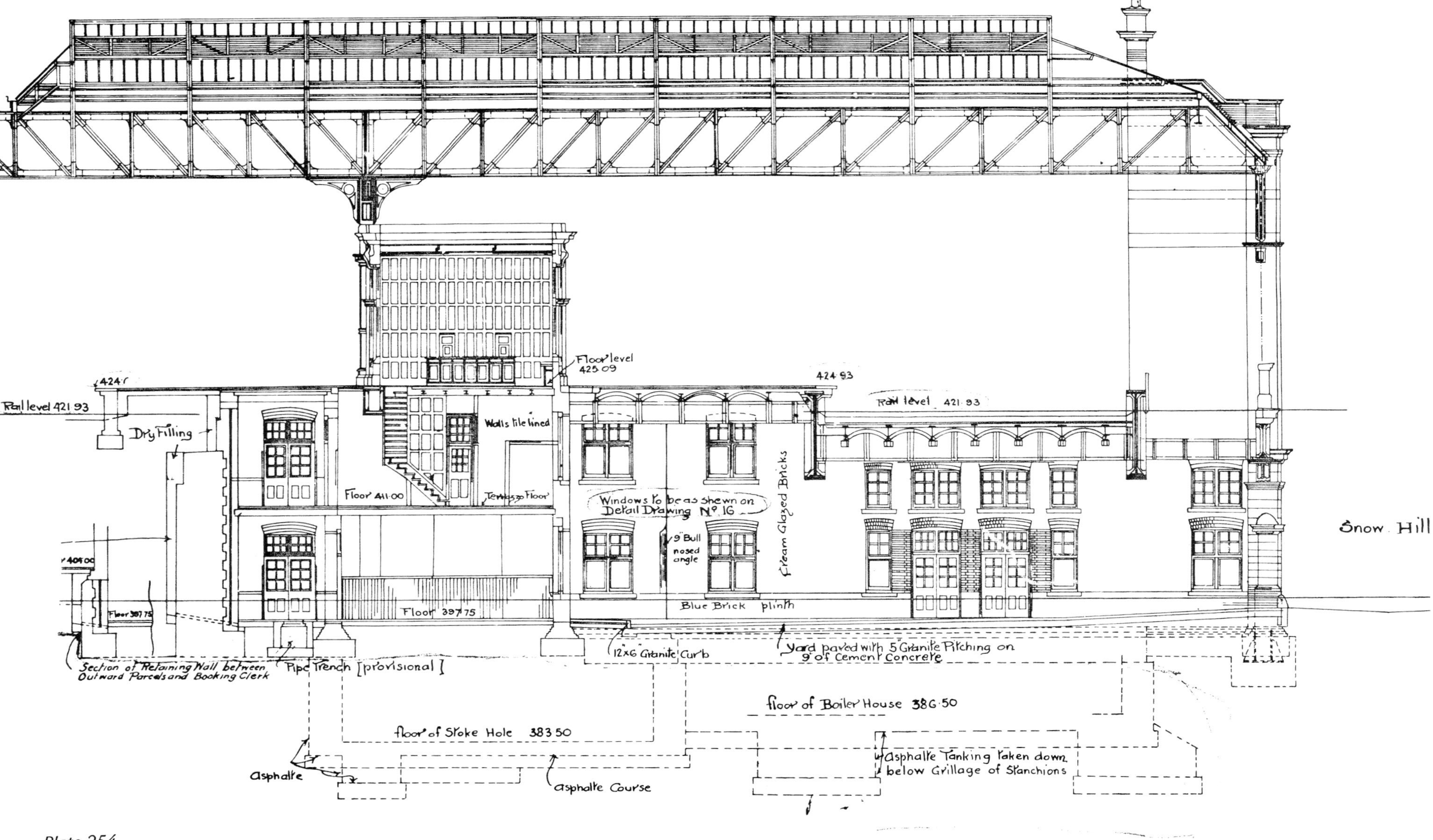

Plate 254
Elevation showing roof, platform buildings and tracks.
Snow Hill (Street) on right.

British Rail

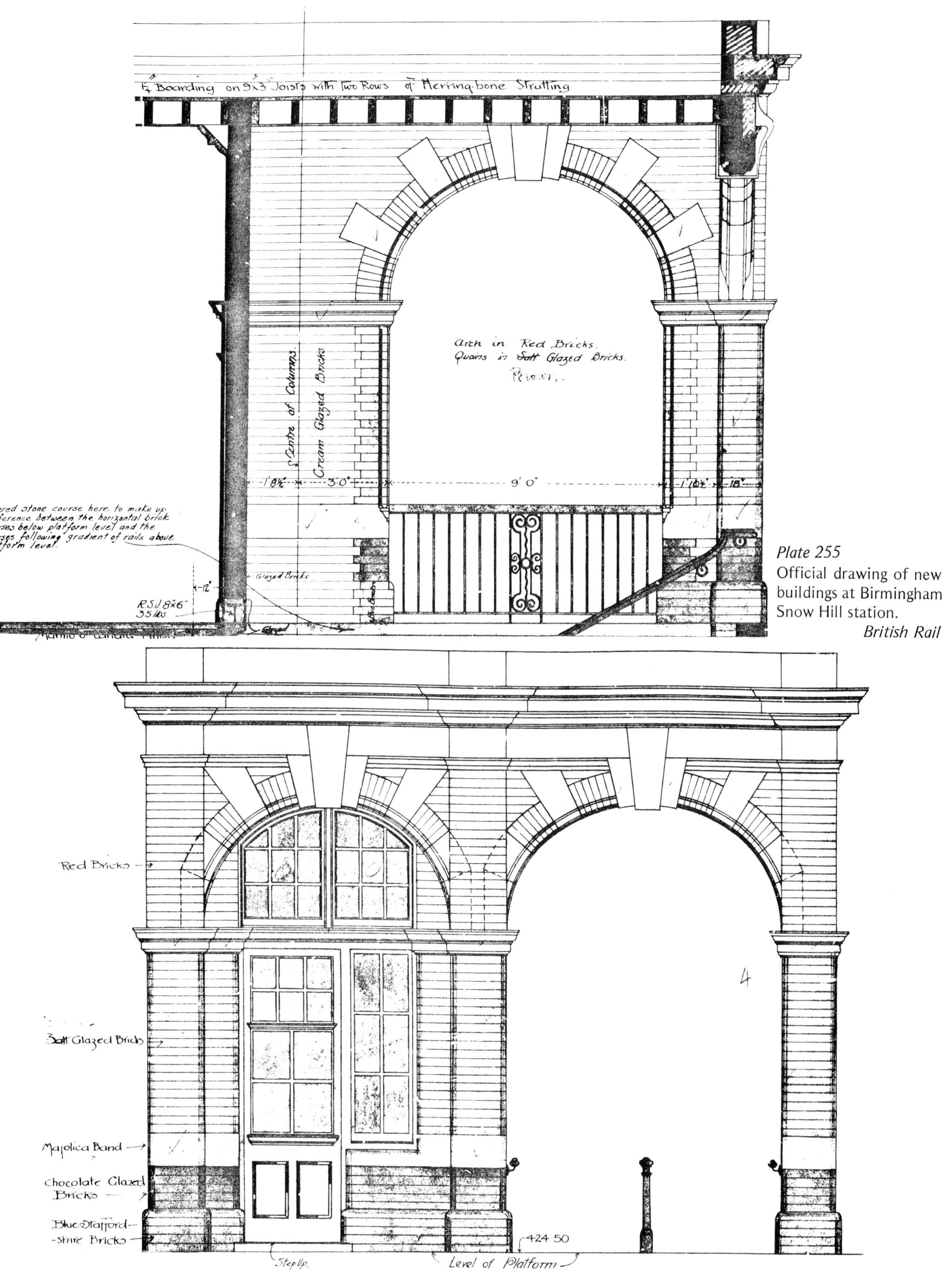

Plate 255
Official drawing of new buildings at Birmingham Snow Hill station.
British Rail

Plates 256/257
Birmingham Snow Hill station soon after it had been completed but before the electrically operated signalling system had been brought fully into use. The signal on the extreme right has an 'out of use' cross on the arm. The illustration shows the manner in which the platform buildings have been decorated with terracotta blocks and dark red brick.

British Rail

Parson Street

Plate 258
At the time that Bristol Temple Meads station was being enlarged and re-signalled, various outlying stations in the area were also rebuilt or modernised. Parson Street, shown here, was particularly important as an alternative starting point for excursion trains because they could reach any part of the country without the need to be routed through the busy station of Temple Meads. The building style used is similar to that employed in the new signal boxes at the main line station.

British Rail

Challow

Plate 259
The original station at Challow was built in 1840, a timber building, and demolished in 1932 when the tracks from here to Wantage Road were quadrupled. The new buildings were very simple, built in plain, unadorned brick. The style employed was somewhat reminiscent of that used in the much larger station at Wellington (Som.). The plate shows Challow looking east.

British Rail

Plate 260
Bourton-on-the-Water station was rebuilt in the 1930's using Cotswold stone in a remarkably solid looking style. The fashion for plain lines in building suits this area very well and I think this is a remarkably successfully designed station.

British Rail

Bourton-on-the-Water

Plate 261
Bourton-on-the-Water with an 84XX pannier tank entering the platform from Kingham.

British Rail

Stoke Canon

Plate 262
Stoke Canon station east of Exeter, was built about 1931/32 as a replacement for a station erected there in 1893. The 1932 station is a very tidy looking building, much nicer than either Challow, Wellington (Som.) or Parson Street and it seems a pity that this design could not have been more widely used on the system.

British Rail

The first halt bearing the name 'Defiance' was built against the far side of the left hand arch in the picture, by the crew of H.M.S. Defiance, a torpedo training school ship moored in the Lynher River below the railway. The sailors used plans and materials supplied by the Great Western Railway. It was a standard platform with one 'pagoda' shelter standing beside the single line between Saltash and St. Germans and came into use early in 1905. However the Company were soon to build the St. Germans-Saltash deviation slightly to the north of the original line, the new line to be double track, avoiding the many timber viaducts and steep gradients of the old line. Within 18 months of the completion of the first halt a second had to be built. Note that the diagonal struts along the length of the platform shown in the official drawing dated 1907 are not included in Defiance Halt though the building was constructed early in 1907. The old line can be seen through the arch and may still have been in use when this picture was taken. The new Defiance Halt came into use with the opening of the deviation line in May 1908.

British Rail

Plates 264/265/266
Three more typical 'pagoda' halts on the system. *Top:* Radipole Halt. *Bottom left:* Horspath Halt. *Bottom right:* Large pagoda huts at Long Sutton & Pitney.

Plate 267

As an experiment the Great Western Railway built this 'pagoda' shelter with Messrs. Taylor's of Birmingham patent 'Universal Roof Covering and Building Material'. The shelter was in use early in 1907.

British Rail

Plate 268

End view of the 'pagoda' at Appleford. View looking north.

Author 1973

Plate 269
Combe Halt, north west of Oxford on the route to Worcester, probably dates from the early 1930's or was rebuilt at that time. The platform, shelter support piers and fence posts are made from old sleepers which present a very rough appearance. Various halts were built in this fashion including some on the Hereford-Shrewsbury section. A concrete post bears the winding gear for a 'Tilley' lamp. In the left hand distance the Combe Siding, a trailing connection in the down main worked from a one lever ground frame, runs back into a saw mill. *British Rail*

Plate 270
Abingdon Road Halt seen here in 1914. Passenger trains ceased to call here after 1925. The platforms were situated against the south side of the bridge two miles south of Oxford station. Note the interesting station lamp.
W.L. Kenning 1914

Plate 271
Not a halt, but built in pre-cast concrete to a similar design to the traditional timber platform. In fact this was the 'staggered' down platform at Silverton.

British Rail

Plate 272
Clyne Halt, just north of Neath on the route to Aberdare and Merthyr. This is heavily constructed with sleepers but carries standard fencing, lighting and shelters.

British Rail

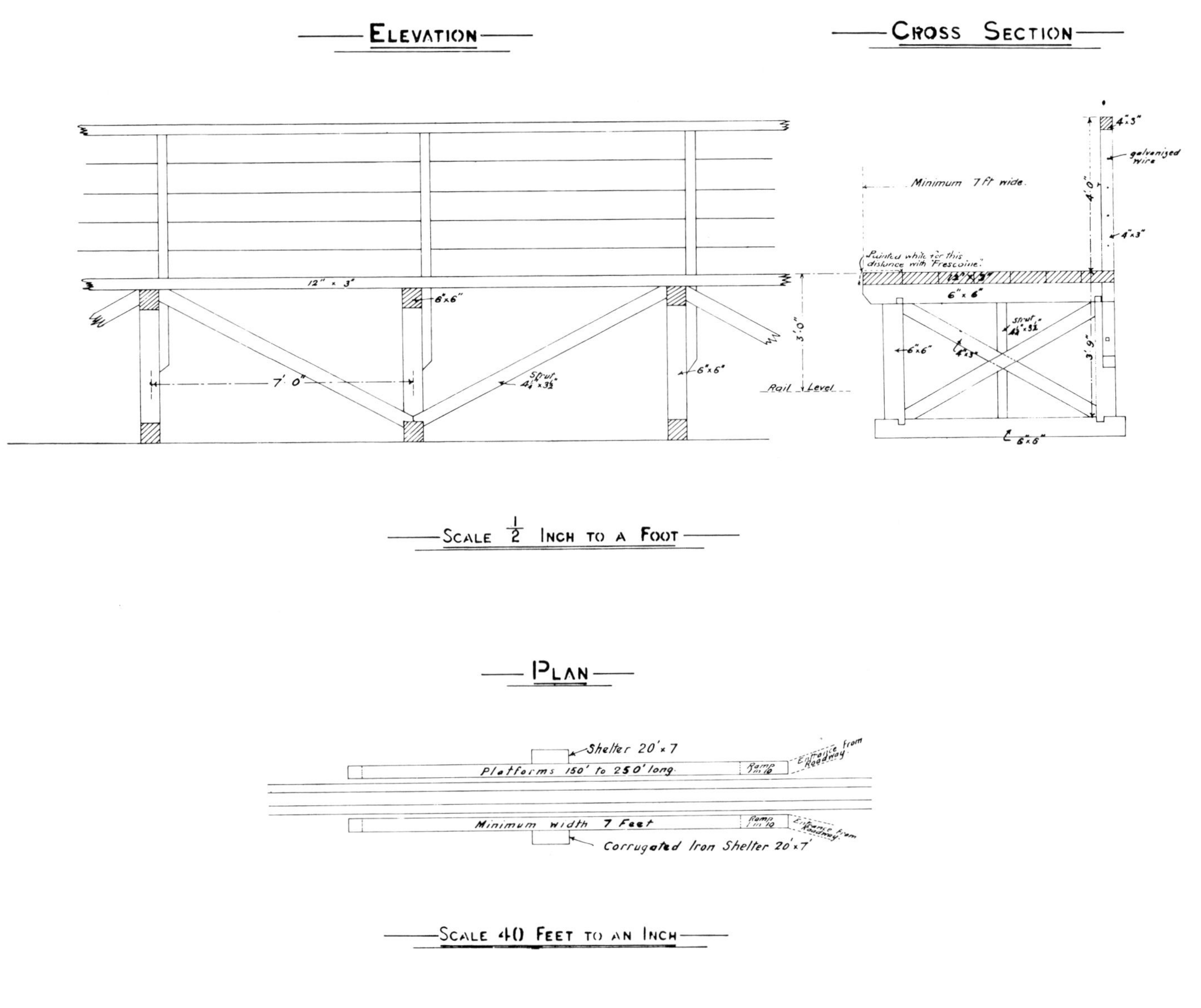

Plate 273

The Great Western Railway decided in 1903 to inaugurate a system of rail cars and halts to serve remote country areas. The first such service was operated between Gloucester and Chalford. Lineside platforms were designed to be constructed cheaply and the rail motors were single carriages powered by a vertical boiler supplying steam to two 9" x 12" cylinders. The halts were placed where a lane ran alongside, or over, or under the railway, so that people could just 'hop on a train' at a point specially chosen to be as close as possible to the village or group of houses in which they lived. The plan was very successful. Being cheap to install and operate, many halts were built and the scheme became widely known and used by the public. In 1905 there were 43 halts, in 1908 there were 80. This plate shows an official drawing of the standard halt. The platform was not less than 7' wide made up of 12" wide planks, 3" thick. A rectangular timber frame stood beneath the platform, one such frame every 7'. This was constructed of 6" x 6" timber braced diagonally with struts 4" x 3". The posts at the back of the platform which carried the fence wires were also 4" x 3". Longitudinally there were diagonal bracings 3½" x 3½" though as has been seen these were not always included.

British Rail

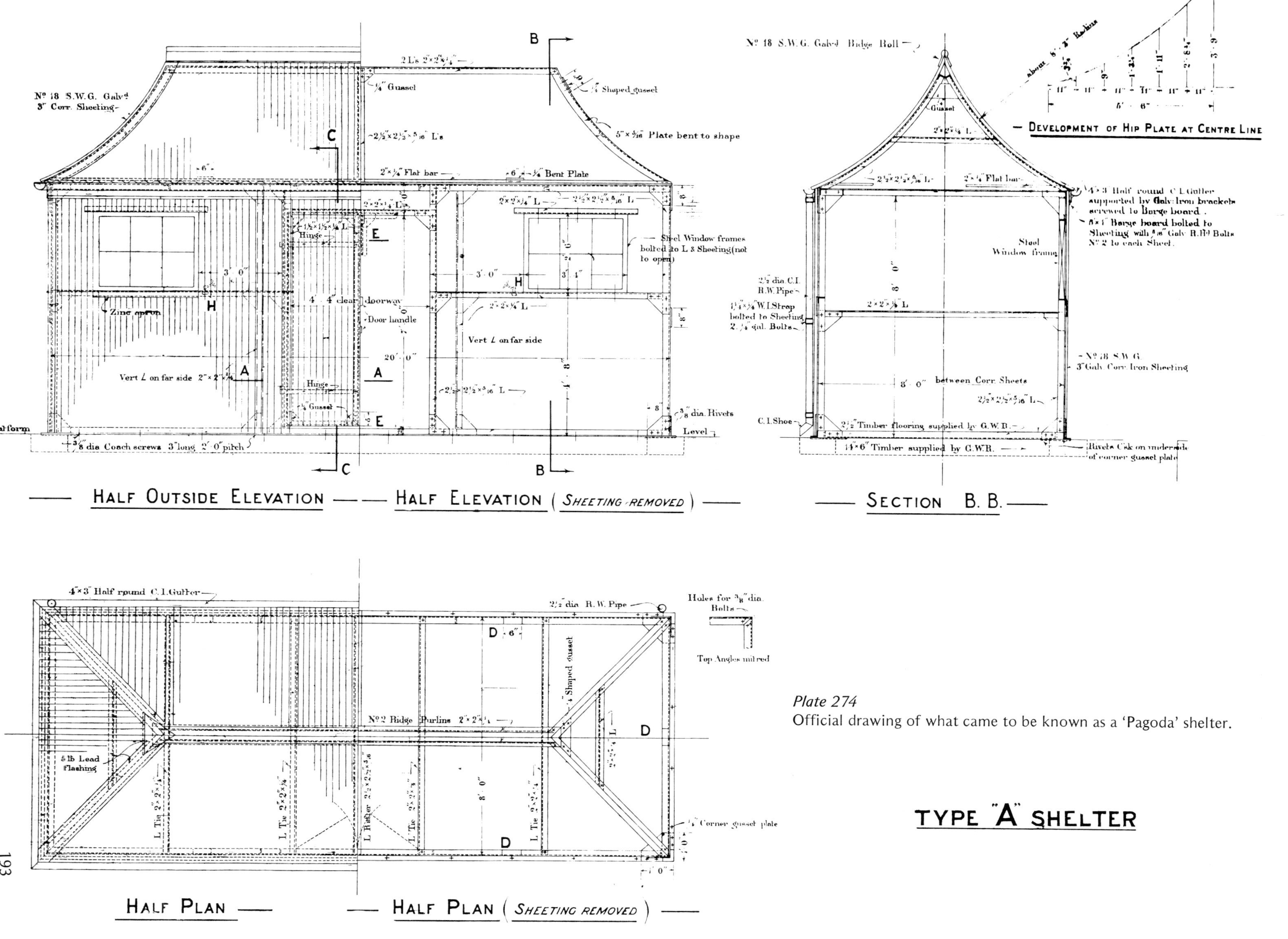

Plate 274
Official drawing of what came to be known as a 'Pagoda' shelter.

G. W. R. MOTOR CAR SHED.

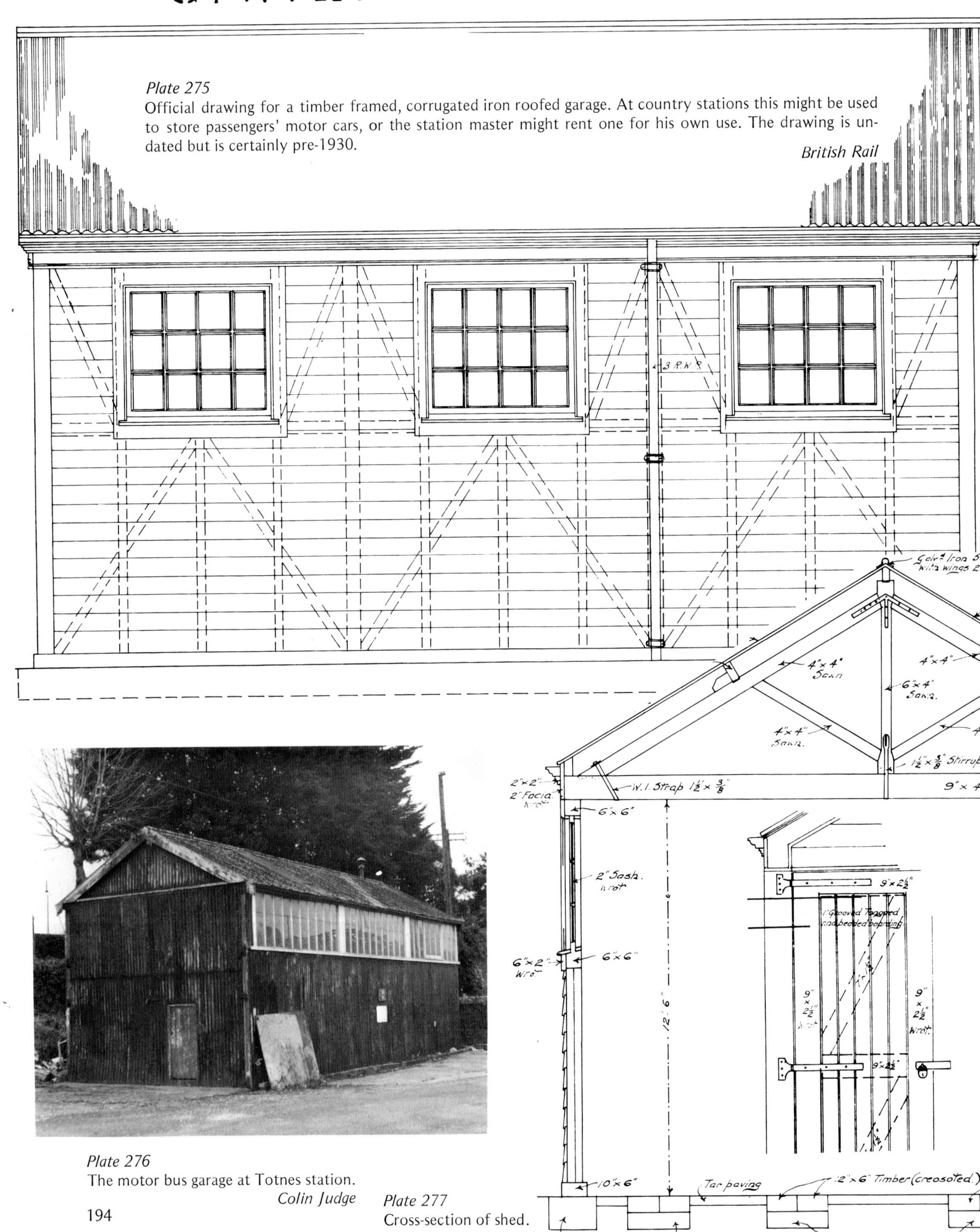

Plate 275
Official drawing for a timber framed, corrugated iron roofed garage. At country stations this might be used to store passengers' motor cars, or the station master might rent one for his own use. The drawing is undated but is certainly pre-1930.
British Rail

Plate 276
The motor bus garage at Totnes station.
Colin Judge

Plate 277
Cross-section of shed.
British Rail

Chapter Two

Company Residences

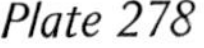

Plate 278

These flint fronted cottages were built about 1839 to house (perhaps) the stableman and porter at the Moulsford, or Wallingford Road, station. This is now disused and stands at the side of the A329 as a transport cafe. The cottages are a plain version of Brunel's 'Tudor' style and include the characteristic features of a steep, sharp gable with slit window centrally placed therein, and mullioned windows.

Author 1974

Plates 279/280

This house was built to Brunel's designs for the Superintendent of the Line and subsequently altered inside to accommodate the offices and Board of Directors. Dating from 1837/39 it had all the characteristic marks referred to in the last plate but these are expanded and added to in order to produce a very much more dignified building. The steep gable here is complicated by a square and stepped shape, the slit window is retained. Over the tall bay window is a tiny gable, a device that was to have been used at Temple Meads (see *plate 3*). The bay windows are similar to those used at several stations including Bath and Cirencester, though in the latter case they were more ornate. Brunel used chimney stacks in both diamond and hexagonal shapes, following his Tudor prototype, and here at Steventon he has used both kinds simultaneously. The only jarring feature is the mid-Victorian red brick carbuncle at the side of the limestone house. (*See plate 280.*) The last Board meeting was held in the house in January 1843 but the station retained its status 'first class' until the opening of the Oxford branch in 1844. Since then, and until 1964, the house was occupied by the station master but was sold out of service around 1970.

Author 1974

Plate 280

Plate 281
Stables at the disused Moulsford station. In the background is the old station hotel building. Note that the gable over the hay loft door is built faithfully to the 'Tudor' motif.
Author 1974

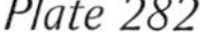

Plate 282
Brunel's hotel for Wallingford Road station. While he followed his principle of hotel accommodation for passengers, he does seem to have watered down his 'Tudor' style here and has produced a building which is in the early Victorian mould. There are steep gables with the ubiquitous slit window, but the obvious 'Gothic-ness' is lacking. There is an entrance porch facing the railway which has slightly pointed arches and a curious, indescribable shape, but in fact, the building has little of the usual character of Brunelian buildings. It is built in brick and has been white painted overall so it may have looked more characteristically 'Brunel' in its original state. The station platforms were below, at the end of a sloping drive, and had no offices but a simple shelter. Obviously passengers waited at the hotel, bought their tickets, rugs, food and hired horses all within the hotel building.
Author 1974

Plate 283
House built about 1850 for the keeper at the Causeway level crossing, Steventon. Mean looking, with tiny rooms, one 'large' downstairs room and a kitchen and two small bedrooms upstairs and also an outhouse, it was as good as any other house built at that time for the working people of the railway. The house was demolished in 1975 and a modern timber and glass shelter for the level crossing keeper was erected on the site. At the same time the old gates seen here – and those at Stocks Lane a quarter of a mile away – were replaced by lifting barriers, the man at the Causeway shelter operating both sets of booms.

Author 1974

Plate 284
A similar house at Upton Lovell near Codford on the Westbury to Salisbury route. This seems to be slightly taller allowing higher ceilings and looks more attractive for not having been faced with cement.

Author 1974

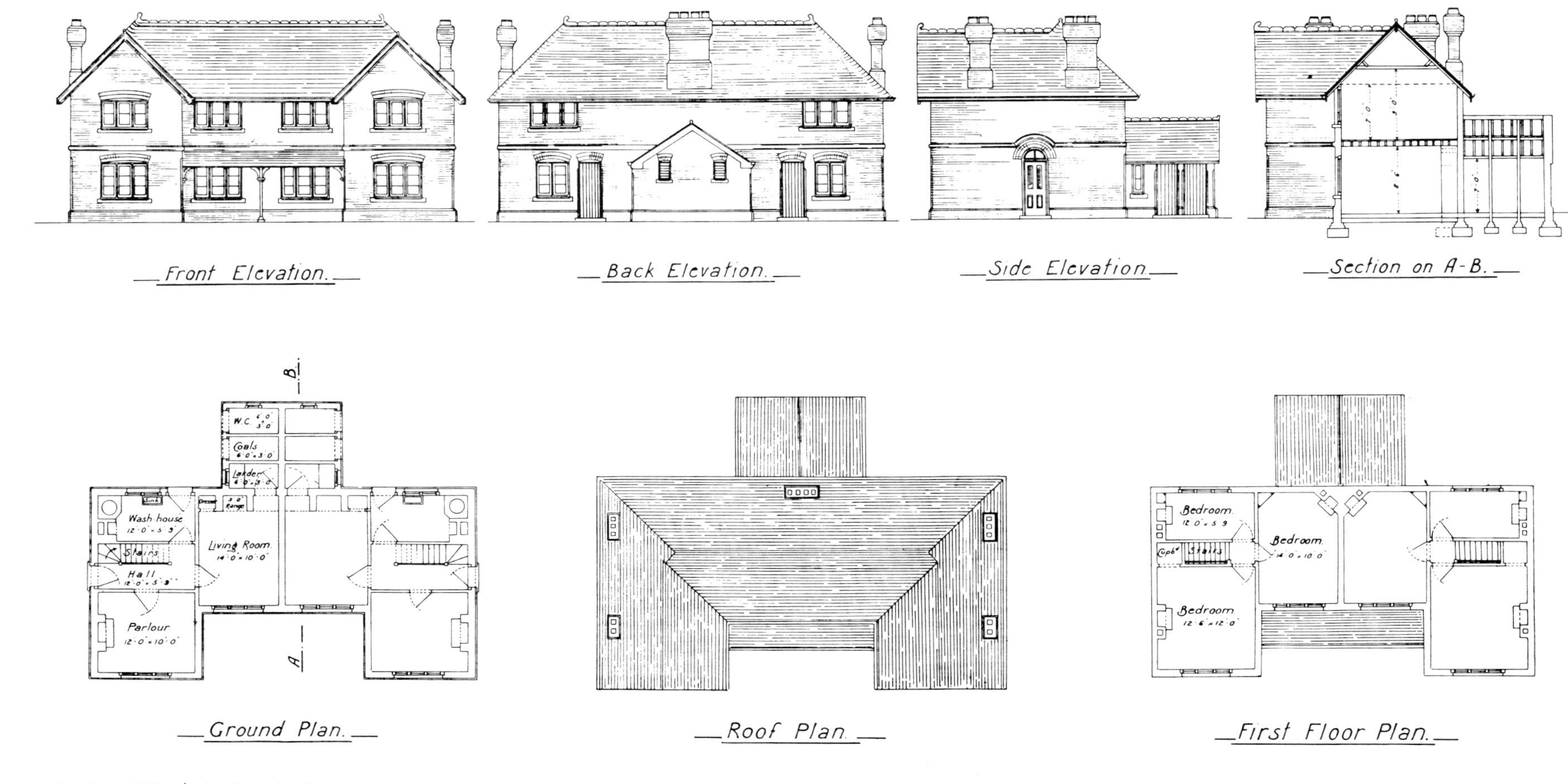

Plate 285
Official drawing of the Badminton staff cottages built between 1900/02. They are still in use but modern additions now fill the recess shown at the front of the house.

British Rail

Plate 286
Side view of the Badminton cottages. The houses are very well constructed and have, by modern standards, large rooms. Downstairs they are 12′ x 10′ and 14′ x 10′ for parlour and living room respectively, while the three bedrooms are 12′ 6″ square, 14′ x 10′, and 12′ x 5′ 9″. Outside they had brick wash-houses, essential in those pre-electricity days, a W.C. and a coal-house. The Company did not skimp their early 20th century houses but built heavily and strongly right up to the well proportioned chimney stacks and cock's-comb ridge tiles. It was Great Western Railway policy to build some staff housing in areas where there was likely to be a shortage of accommodation but there were never enough for everyone and those lucky enough to be allocated a house prized it and kept a good garden.

Author 1974

Plate 287
Official drawing of a station master's house similar to that illustrated in *plate 291.*

British Rail

Plate 288
Rectangular section downpipe with ornate fastenings at the station master's house, Badminton.

Author 1974

Plate 289
The front of the station master's house at Badminton built 1901/02. It seems so well made that it would not be out of place in some 'stock broker belt' at Amersham or Maidenhead, especially when glimpsed from the road through its screen of flowering shrubs and chestnut trees. The house is well cared for by Mr. and Mrs. Saunders with whose permission I took these photographs.

Author 1974

Plate 290

G.W.R. houses on the north, or upside, of the line at Taplow built to a similar design to those at Badminton.

Author 1974

Plate 291

At Wantage Road station, the station master had lived in a house at the side of the Wantage-Oxford Road on the bridge, from 1840 till about 1907 when a new house was built (illustrated here). The house is of a standard design which was varied slightly from place to place as regards details such as the porch or verandah, sometimes the latter were omitted altogether. There are two large living rooms and a fair sized kitchen, downstairs W.C. and a scullery. Upstairs the house is equally roomy with a bathroom/W.C., and three bedrooms leading off a long landing. In the kitchen of this particular house there are 5 bells in decreasing order of size hanging over the door with wires from each to a certain part of the house — obviously the station master at one time employed a servant or two.

Author 1974
Courtesy of Mr. Ken Fuller

Plate 292/293

This house was built for the Booking Clerk at Uffington station in the latter half of 1888 for £450 and the bay windows were added during November 1900 for £30. It had a compact, well-made look, with its sturdy hip roof and ornamental use of yellow bricks to relieve the main bulk of red brick.

Author 1973

With the kind permission of Mrs Stella Tanner.

Plate 294
Savernake station master's house. The building date I do not know but the style appears to date from 1912. These houses are smaller than those of 1896/1907 and one wonders if rising costs were beginning to be felt or if they were ordered for the less important stations and were therefore smaller.
Author 1974

Plate 295
A rear view of the station master's house at Challow, built to the identical design of that at Savernake.
Author 1974

Plate 297

Station master's house at Hullavington, a design I have not encountered elsewhere on the railway. Built in 1901/02 with the rest of the 'Badminton and South Wales Direct Railway'.

Author 1973

Plate 296

Porters' and signalmen's cottages at Challow, building date unknown, but certainly pre-1914. They are built in brick with slate hung fronts and are curious in that, rather than building the front and back walls wide enough apart to allow decent sized rooms, the designer relied upon the gabled projections at the front and a brick 'lean-to' arrangement running the length of the back wall to provide the necessary room space. They are not, in my opinion, good houses, though many good railwaymen have lived in them. The houses are now sold out of service.

Author 1973

Plate 298

Staff cottages at Hullavington built 1901/02. They have features in common with the Badminton cottages — all the buildings on this line have their 'family likeness', the dark, purple/red bricks, bull nosed string course and heavy looking roof. The upper parts of the walls seem to be of a harder brick than that employed in the lower parts.

Author 1973

Plate 299

Plate 300

Plate 301

Plates 299/300/301

Standard 'C' house for the station master of Culham built in 1898. Another of this type was built at Henley and one wonders if this most handsome of the Great Western Railway houses was designed specially for aristocratic areas. It has the looks of an early 19th century vicarage or farm house with its beautifully proportioned 'squareness' and cap-like roof, but it must be said that it is disappointingly small inside. The bricks used in its construction are very good, well coloured and smooth, the area around the back door is laid with these bricks which have taken on a time worn appearance from scores of years scrubbing which looks very attractive.

Author 1973

Plate 302

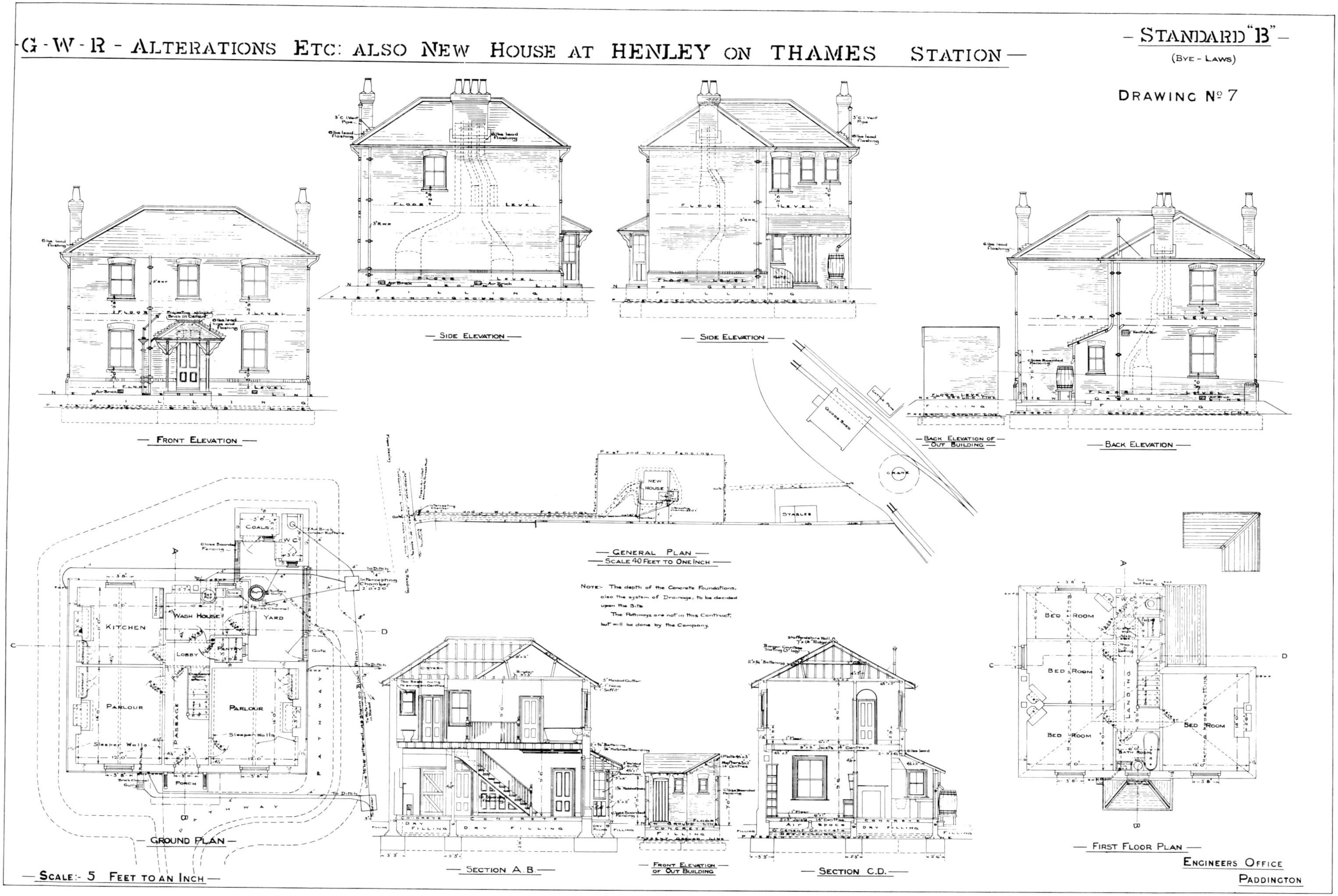
G-W-R - ALTERATIONS ETC: ALSO NEW HOUSE AT HENLEY ON THAMES STATION
STANDARD "B"
(BYE-LAWS)
DRAWING Nº 7
FRONT ELEVATION
SIDE ELEVATION
SIDE ELEVATION
BACK ELEVATION OF OUT BUILDING
BACK ELEVATION
GENERAL PLAN
SCALE 40 FEET TO ONE INCH
NOTE:- The depth of the Concrete Foundations, also the system of Drainage, to be decided upon the Site.
The Pathways are not in this Contract, but will be done by the Company.
NEW HOUSE
STABLES
GOODS SHED
CRANE
KITCHEN
WASH HOUSE
YARD
LOBBY
PANTRY
PARLOUR
PASSAGE
PARLOUR
PORCH
COALS
W.C.
PATHWAY
Interceptiing Chamber 2'0"x2'0"
GROUND PLAN
SCALE:- 5 FEET TO AN INCH
SECTION A.B.
FRONT ELEVATION OF OUT BUILDING
SECTION C.D.
BED ROOM
BED ROOM
BED ROOM
BED ROOM
LANDING
BATH ROOM
FIRST FLOOR PLAN
ENGINEERS OFFICE
PADDINGTON

COTTAGE FOR SIGNALMEN OR PLATELAYERS. STANDARD "D"

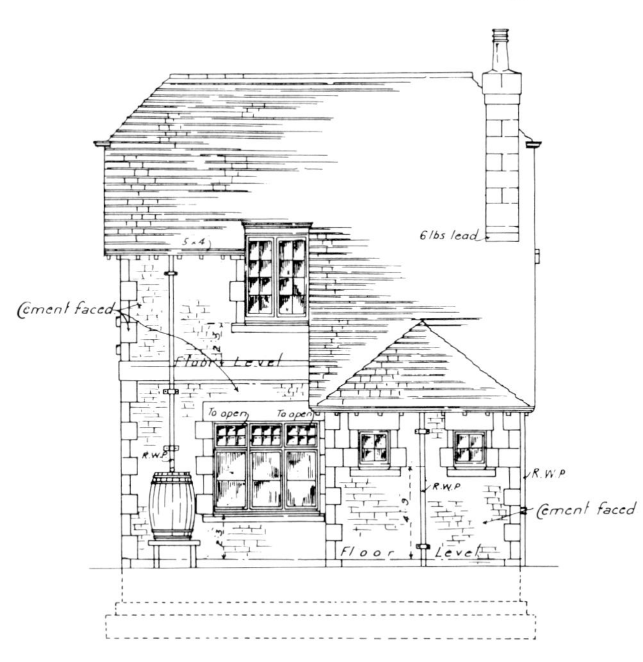

Back Elevation.

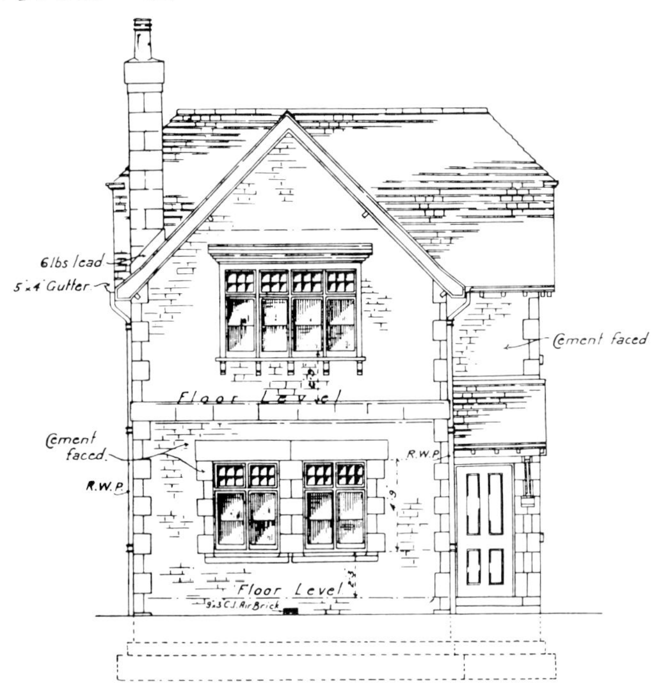

Front Elevation.

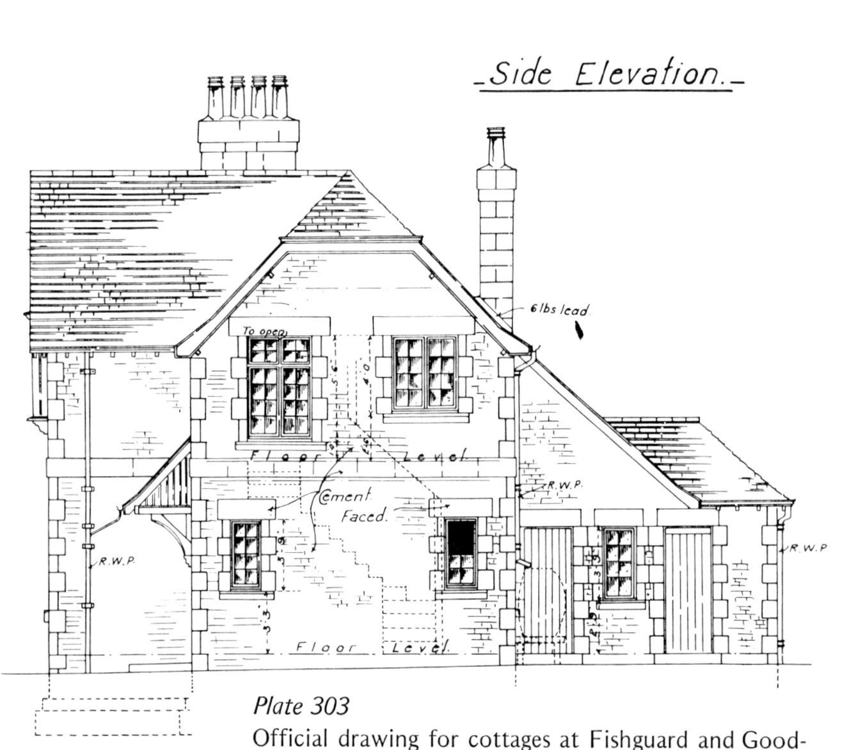

FRONT ELEVATION

Plate 303

Official drawing for cottages at Fishguard and Goodwick station. It appears that they were intended to be built in local stone with dressed stone quoins. I feel they would look well in Cotswold stone.

British Rail

C. W. R. CLYDACH PONTARDAWE & CWMCORSE RLY.

LABOURING CLASS DWELLINGS AT TREBANOS.

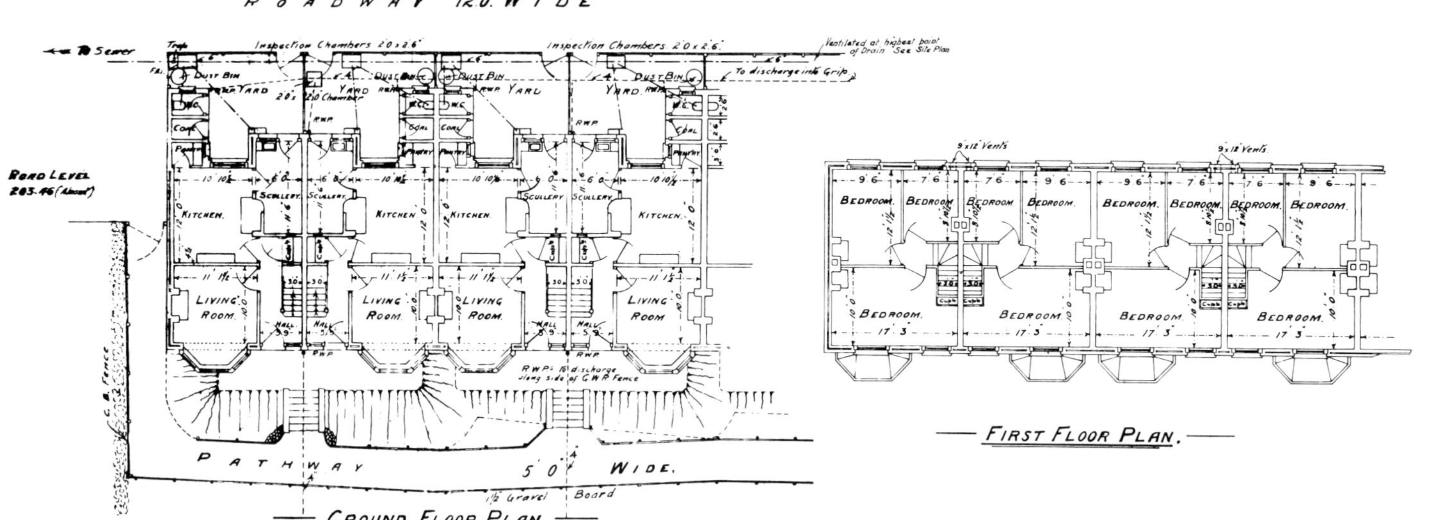

SCALE 8 FEET TO AN INCH.

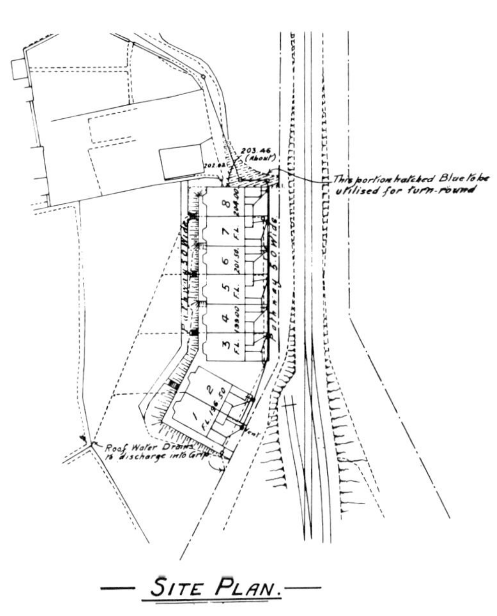

Plate 304

Official drawing for small terrace of 'Labouring class dwellings'. The rooms provided were: Kitchen 10′ x 12′, Living room 10′ x 11′. The three bedrooms measured: 9′ 6″ x 12′ 1½″. 7′ 6″ x 12′ 1½″, 17′ 3″ x 10′ which seems a careless way to space out rooms. They were planned in brick with a small bay window. Date unknown.

British Rail

Plate 305
On Pen Cw, Fishguard, the Great Western Railway built a 'garden village' overlooking the bay. There were 112 houses on 13 separate sites because, as the site of the village was so conspicuous, the Company did not want to show lines of 'barrack' like houses. The Company also provided a reading room which could be used for plays, and a library which accommodated the debating society and the amateur dramatic society. Bazaars and concerts were also encouraged.

British Rail

Plate 306
Staff housing at Penzance, probably built in the early 1930's. Note the bay windows with sash type openings.
British Rail

Plate 307
(*a*) Official drawing of chimney stack 1902.
British Rail
(*b*) Chimney on parcels office, Goring 1892.
Author 1973
(*c*) Chimney on weighbridge house, Badminton 1902.
Author 1974

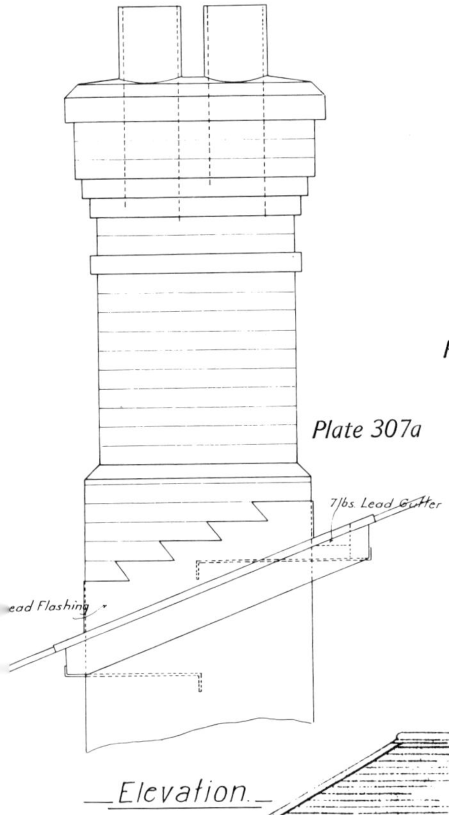

Plate 307a

Plate 307b

Plate 307c

Plate 308
Official drawing of a terrace house.
British Rail

Plate 309a

Further pictures of company houses just after construction.

Plate 309b

Chapter Three

Selection of Footbridges

It seems unlikely that footbridges were generally provided before 1880 and that after that date they were provided in the various "standard" forms illustrated on the next few pages. This is not to say that there were no footbridges before 1880 or that there were no non-standard designs after that date, but 1880 seems to be the date that a standard footbridge became part of the equipment of practically every station on the line. There appear to have been two types—as far as the layman can discern: the plate sided kind and the more ornate latticework-sided bridge. Stairs were built with timber treads and risers, the tread sometimes having a non-slip portion made of small cubes of very hard wood. The stairs rested on steel "stringers", though on very early bridges these were in timber and the rising passage-way was then fenced in with cast iron balusters, lattices or plate steel. Roofs on footbridges varied, but, plain or decorative, they were always distinctively Great Western. A standard footbridge was designed owing to the multiplicity of "one-off" jobs often made of timber or in cast iron to a very unsuitable design. In the former case the timber at ground level would inevitably rot and new wood would periodically have to be spliced in to replace the unserviceable part. If they were lucky the Company carried out this operation before someone was hurt and demanded compensation. In the latter case, cast iron was liable to failure without warning and it was very heavy so that superstructures were kept light. Such a bridge was at Uffington for 101 years. It was a cast iron arch with the lightest footpath and handrail possible; the walls were only a foot high with a handrail above. To be caught on that bridge when a steam hauled express passed beneath, engulfing one in thick fog, was to feel very precarious. The advent of cheap steel enabled the Company to produce a design for a really first class footbridge which did not require any degree of intrepidness on the part of the passenger using it and sheltered him from smoke and the inclement weather.

Plate 310
Detail of iron work in the footbridge at Taplow.
British Rail

Plate 311
The footbridge at Taplow framed in the curve of the station's canopy.
British Rail

Plate 312
Taplow station footbridge from the north, up relief line, side.
British Rail

Plate 313
From the south, down main line side.
British Rail

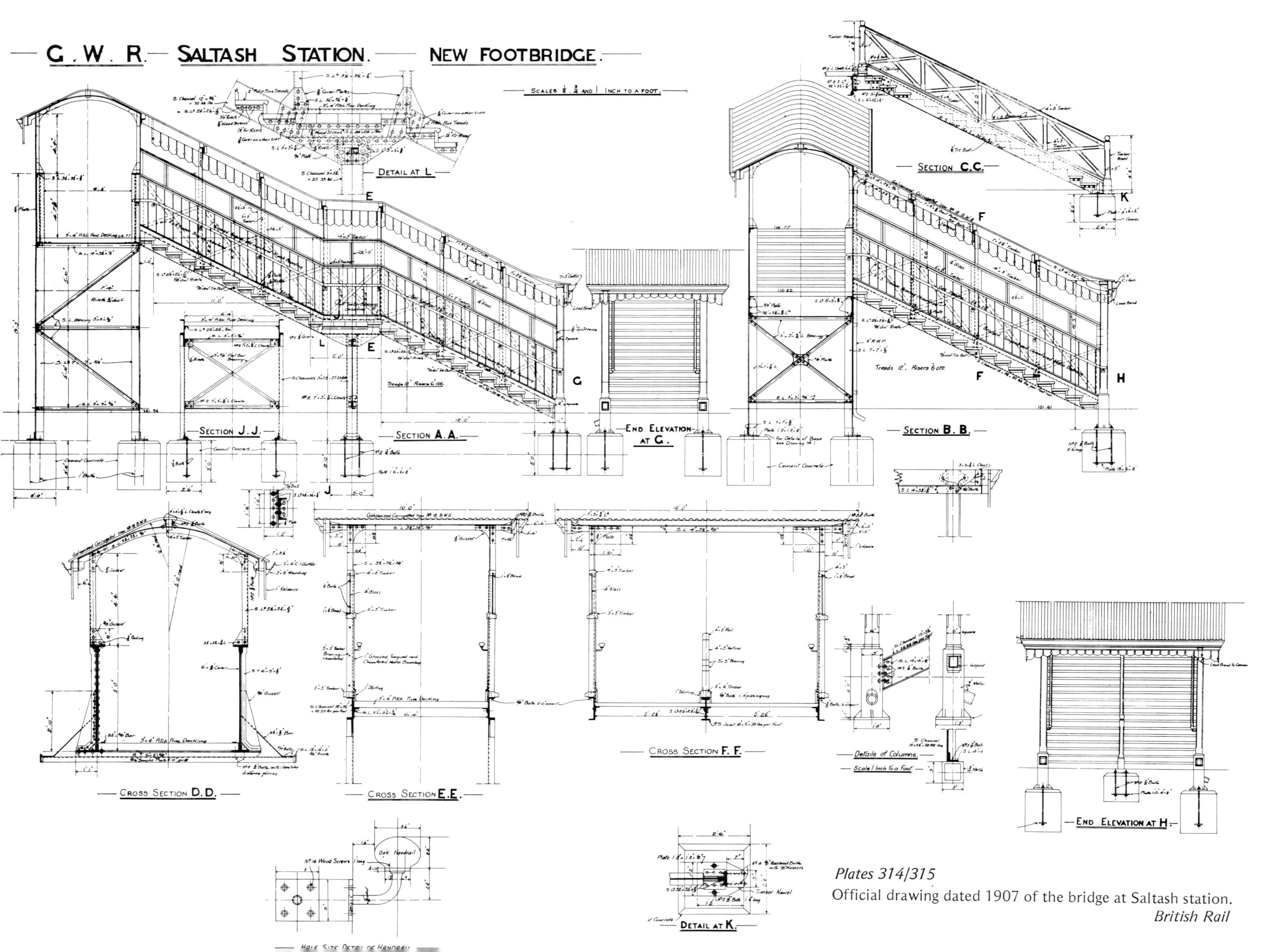

Plates 314/315
Official drawing dated 1907 of the bridge at Saltash station.
British Rail

G.W.R. — SALTASH STATION — NEW FOOTBRIDGE
ELEVATION
Staircase to Down Platform
Treads 12" Risers 6 1/2"
SECTION e e
SECTIONAL PLAN at f
SECTIONAL PLAN d d
Note 5/8" Rivets 4" Pitch
Section thro Glazing
Note Smoke Plates to be fixed over Centre of Rails
SECTIONAL PLAN at g
SECTIONAL PLAN
Scales 1/2 and 1 1/2 to One Foot
Public Road
Up Platform
Down Platform
Way Out Path
Plan of Site
Scale 40 Feet to an Inch
DETAIL AT C
END ELEVATION AT B
Cement Concrete

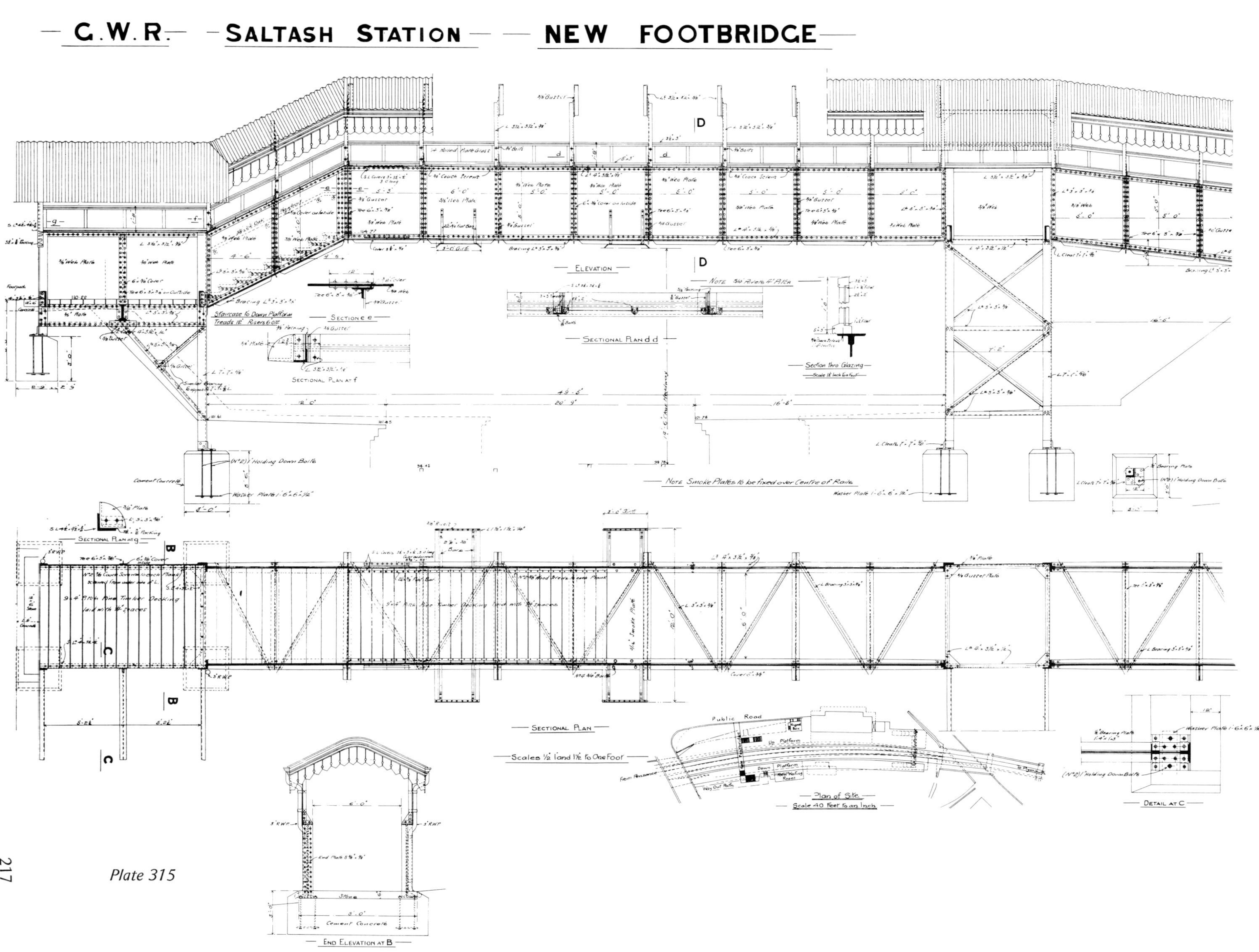

Plate 315

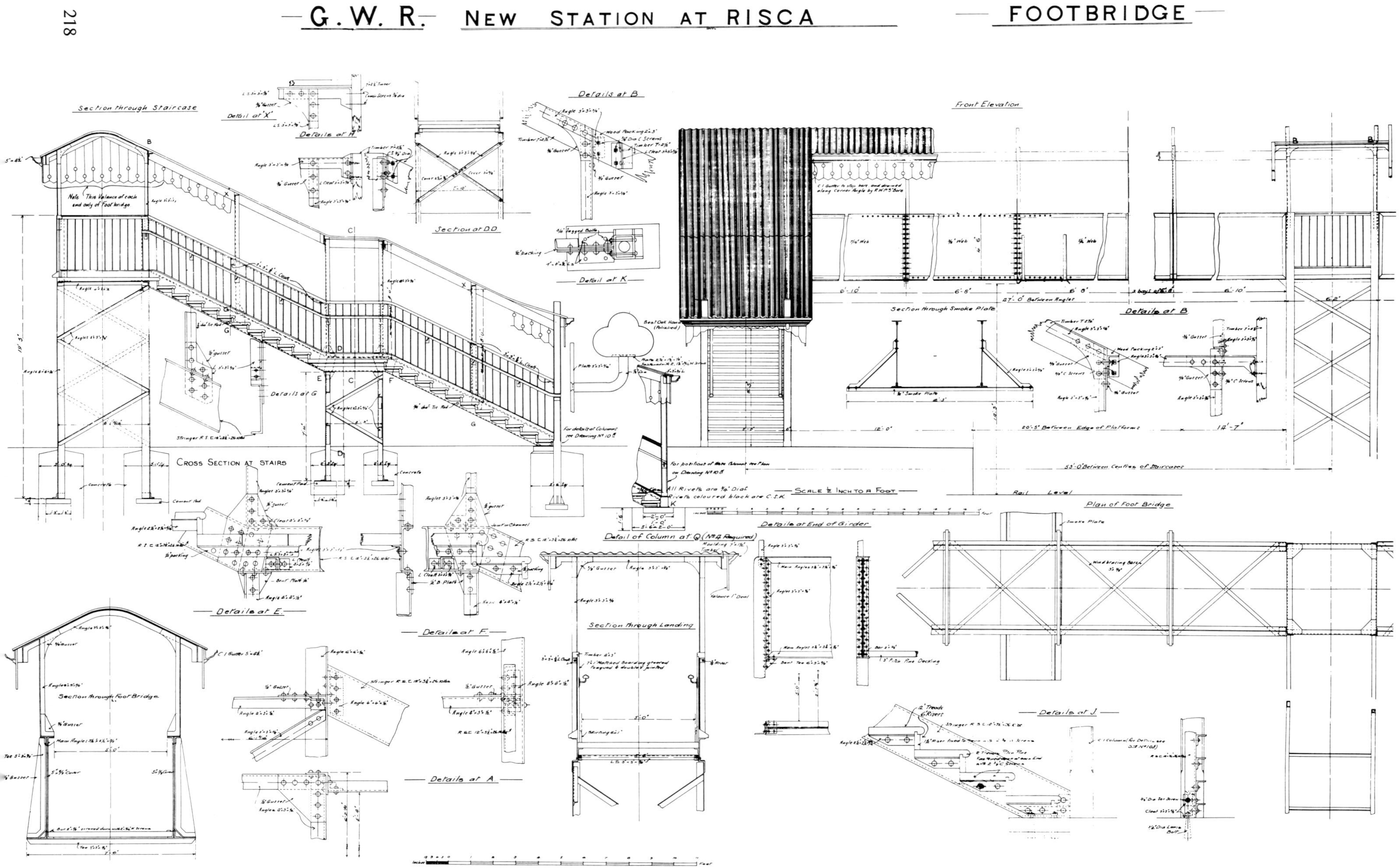

G.W.R. New Station at Risca — Footbridge

Section through Staircase

Note This Valance at each end only of Foot bridge

Detail at 'X'

Details at H

Section at DD

Details at B

Detail at K

Front Elevation

Section through Smoke Plate

27'-0" Between Angles

20'-5" Between Edge of Platforms

55'-0" Between Centres of Staircases

Rail Level

Plan of Foot Bridge

Details at G

Cross Section at Stairs

All Rivets are ⅝" Dia. Rivets coloured black are C.S.K.

Scale ½ Inch to a Foot

Details at End of Girder

Detail of Column at Q (No. 4 Required)

Details at E

Details at F

Section through Landing

Section through Foot Bridge

Details at A

Details at J

Plate 316

Official drawing of the footbridge erected at Risca about 1907. Minor differences in detail can be noted between this drawing and those at Saltash, for instance the width of staircase – 5′ at Risca as against 9′ 4″ at Saltash, the cross section of the handrail. Under the landings the Saltash bridge has a diagonal bracing where Risca has cross-bracing.

Plate 317
Plate sided footbridge at Tilehurst apparently dating from 1892 with the rebuilding of the station. The station master's house can be seen beneath the soffit of the bridge.
Author 1973

Plate 318
Stairway at Newbury. A special 'one-off' footbridge for the new 1910 station.
Author 1973

Plate 319
The stations between Reading and Didcot had special care devoted to the detail of their footbridges. Maybe the Great Western Railway had plans to develop the Thames Valley as a high class dormitory area for London? Whatever the reason the balusters on the staircases were very well executed. This plate shows the staircase at Goring & Streatley station.

Author 1973

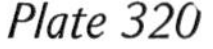

Plate 320
Elegant as a tightly rolled parasol, this beautiful cast iron pillar supports the handrail at Tilehurst station.

Author 1973

Plate 321
The footbridge at Wootton Bassett station. The bridge, dated 1880, is constructed in plate steel with a corrugated iron roof. The landings are supported by cast iron columns while beneath the stairs are timber supports. The stringers are in steel-girder form. Ornate cast iron balusters support the handrail. The station buildings are quite new, ready for the opening of the 'South Wales Direct' line. Beyond the left hand platform one can see the new signal box, the old one is on the platform, and the bracket signal for the diverging line still has the 'Not in Use' crosses on the arms. The photograph must have been taken soon after rebuilding. The repainting was just completed because there is no trace of locomotive smoke on the bridge or station buildings.

Plate 322
A plate sided bridge at Hungerford which is rather different from the one shown above. The landings are supported with angle steel and the stringers may well be timber beams. Up to the landings most of the construction is wooden until the bridge itself springs upwards and outwards. This part is in steel plate for the sides, with timber decking resting diagonally on the steel walls and angle steel beneath. An odd little bridge, probably erected when the new waiting rooms on the far platform were built in the early 1900's. The station building on the left is interesting in that it dates from 1847, designed as the terminus of the 'Berks and Hants' line (a position it held for 15 years). The building is in red brick with an arcade of segmental arches in yellow brick over doors and windows, a feature of several stations on the 'B. & H.' line. These were usually under a roof which also served as a platform canopy. As this is not the case at Hungerford it is conceivable that Hungerford had an overall roof originally. The small canopy shown on the station has cast iron brackets steadying the support beams, these brackets having a delightful 'ear of wheat' motif and may well have been put up when the overall roof had to be removed in consequence of a re-alignment of the rails. Note that the near platform has been widened to meet a less severely curved track, an adjustment which may have become necessary when the terminal became a through station in 1862.

Truro

Plate 323a

Flax Bourton

Plate 323b

Plate 323c

Wilmcote

Plate 323d

Plate 323

(a) Truro looking west, about 1952.

(b) Flax Bourton with an early 20th century footbridge.

(c) Flax Bourton. Unorthodox footbridge in timber on brick piers. Timber struts added later.

(d) Wilmcote circa 1952 with a very fine footbridge dating from the 1880's.

(e) Thame about 1952 looking towards Princes Risborough under a steel footbridge built to replace the original timber one, sited beneath the station's roof.

(f) Patney & Chirton about 1952. Looking east with a very plain footbridge probably dating from the early 1930's.

(g) Witham circa 1952. Looking east with East Somerset branch bay on left and Wilts & Somerset Railway buildings behind an ancient footbridge which has been partly modernised.

(h) Devizes looking towards Holt Junction about 1952.

Plate 323 continued

Thame

Plate 323e

Patney & Chirton

Plate 323f

Witham

Plate 323g

Devizes

Plate 323h

Plate 324
Lattice work and monogram at Taplow.
Author 1973

Plate 325
A wealth of lattice work at Newbury Race Course station, a cheaper form of footbridge, as official records state!
Author 1973

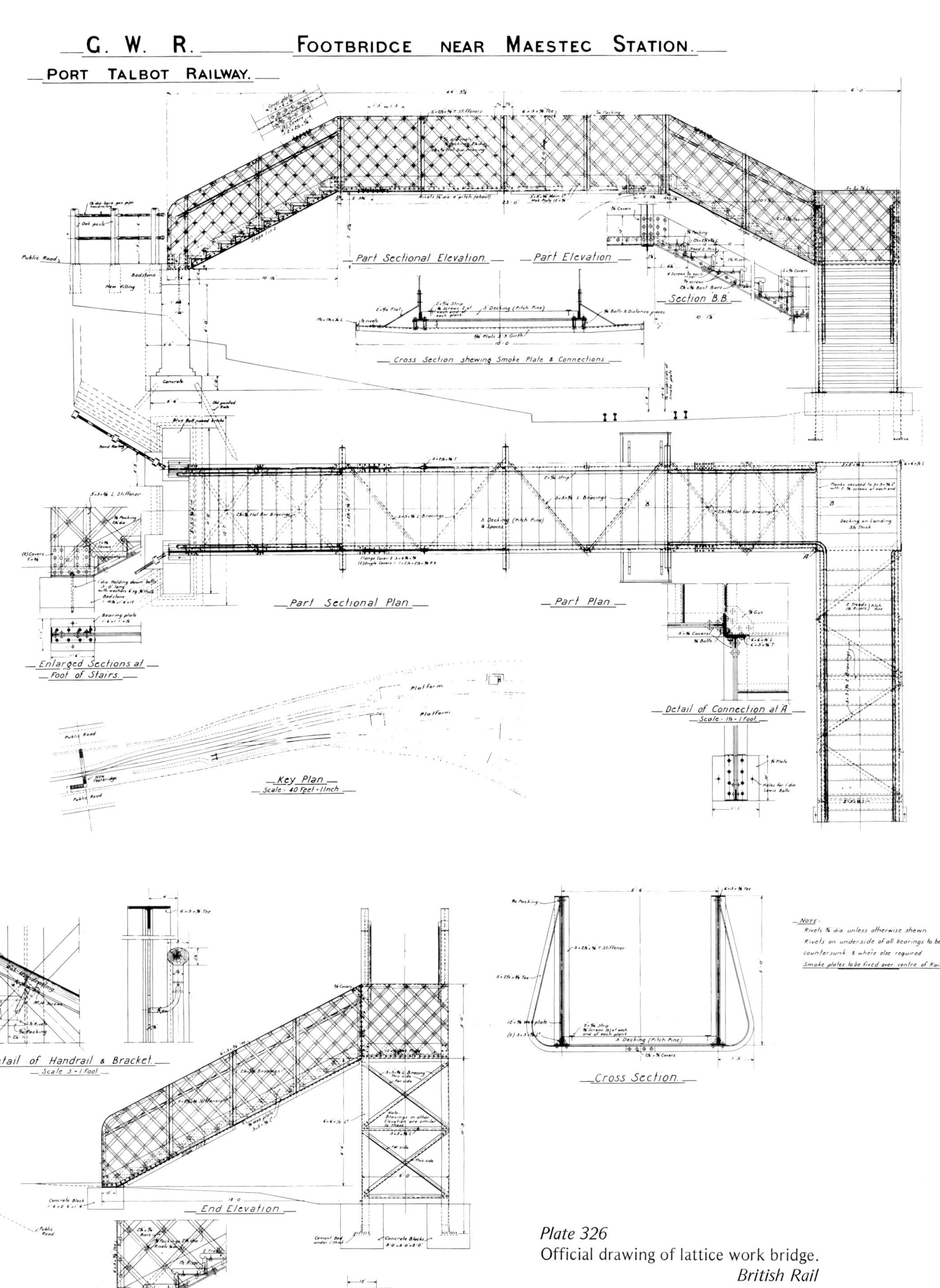

Plate 326
Official drawing of lattice work bridge.
British Rail

Plate 327
The splendid footbridge spanning four tracks and two platforms at Newbury. Steel girders rest on the brick and carry a timber superstructure which shelters the passageway. The stairs are illuminated from the glazed portions, the latter giving the whole bridge a special appearance.
Author 1973

Plate 328
A dainty footbridge at Cwmgarw, supporting wonderful gas lamps.
British Rail

Plate 329
Sturdy timber steps from the platform at Appleford Halt to the road bridge over the line, thus converting the road motor bridge into a footbridge for the Halt.
Author 1974

Plate 330
The stringers and landing supports of this bridge seem to be made of old rails. The walk way over the rails is supported by a deep lattice work girder of angle steel. To prevent passengers falling through the wide lattices timber planking has been provided. The station is that at Halesowen.

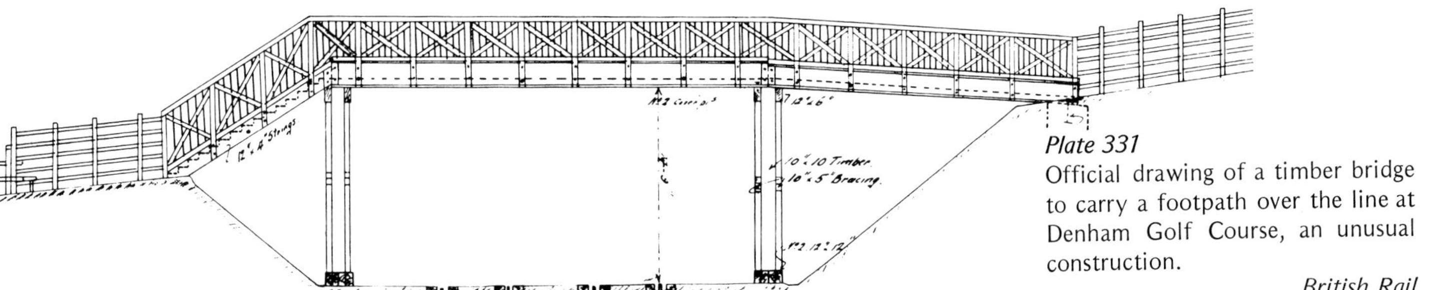

Plate 331
Official drawing of a timber bridge to carry a footpath over the line at Denham Golf Course, an unusual construction.

British Rail

Plate 332
An interesting timber construction at Dinas Powis. Heavy beams form towers which support the landings of the staircase and the cross beams of the arch. Equally heavy beams form bracket-like supports between the towers and the bed of the bridge.

British Rail

Plate 333
Heavy girders in open box form resting on steel piers and brick abutments carry the footpath over the goods lines at Adamstown, Cardiff. Built 1903.
British Rail

Plate 334
This footbridge stands at the south end of Oxford station and was probably built in the 1850's. Cast iron columns support stringers, probably of the same material, rising to brick piers upon which rests the channel carrying the footpath. It seems likely that the bridge once had a roof.
Author 1973

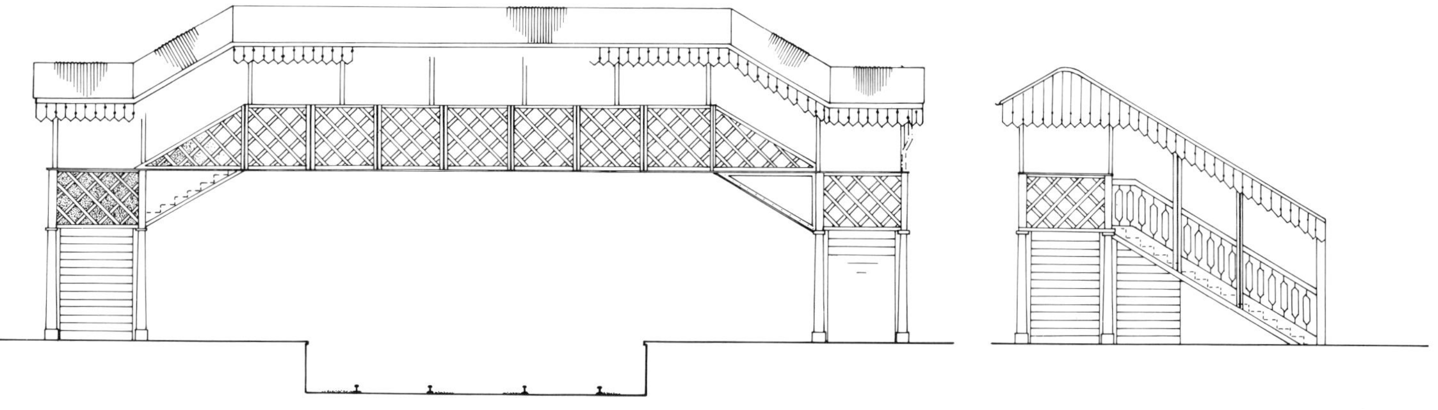

Plate 335
Lattice type footbridge at Radley. The stairs were not boxed in with timber or plate steel as was usual but provided instead with cast iron balusters. These are similar to those at Wootton Bassett.

Colin Judge 1973

Plate 336
At Wood End, on the Birmingham to Stratford on Avon route, this fine timber footbridge was probably built with the new line in 1907. The only steel used was the two girders to span the tracks.

British Rail

Plate 337
A gloomy, corrugated iron tunnel carrying the footpath over the 'New Line' near North Acton.
British Rail

Plate 338
Concrete beams and pillars, fenced with wood make up this bridge on the Kerry branch.
British Rail

Plate 339
Ferro-concrete at Highbridge. This pre-dates the Southern Railway's concrete economies by many years, as the photograph is dated with certainty 1.7.15. Note the wedge shaped end of the Highbridge West Box built thus to accommodate the track of the Somerset and Dorset Joint Railway. Hanging on the wall of the brick building at the left of the picture are some fire buckets bearing the letters S & D J R. Note the different styles of railway fencing.
British Rail

Plates 340/341
South Liberty footbridge a short distance west of Bristol was made from a footbridge lying redundant at Neath and has the appearance, in its cast iron cross beams and columns of dating from the 1850's. The staircase and its components date from the time of erection at this site, about 1932. A 'make-do' bridge.

Author 1974

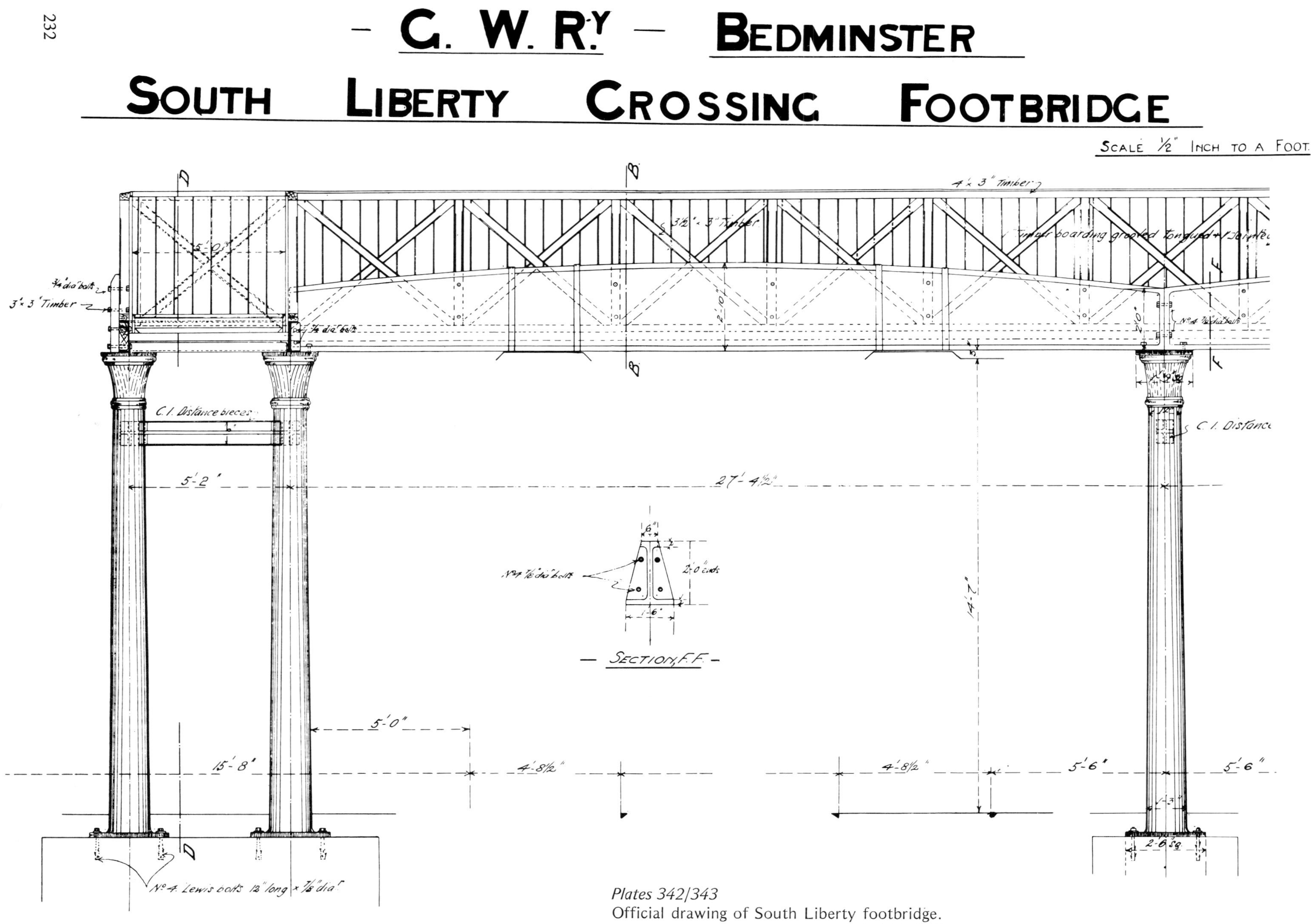

– G. W. R.Y – Bedminster
South Liberty Crossing Footbridge

Scale ½" Inch to a Foot.

4" × 3" Timber
3½" × 3" Timber
Timber boarding grooved tongued + jointed
¾" dia. bolts
3" × 3" Timber
⅞" dia. bolts
No. 4 ⅞" dia. bolts
5'-0"
2'-10"
C.I. Distance pieces
C.I. Distance
5'-2"
27'-4½"
6"
No. 4 ⅞" dia. bolts
2'-0" ctrs
1'-6"
– Section F.F. –
14'-2"
5'-0"
15'-8"
4'-8½"
4'-8½"
5'-6"
5'-6"
2'-6" sq.
No. 4 Lewis bolts 12" long × ⅞" dia.

Plates 342/343
Official drawing of South Liberty footbridge.
British Rail

No 10 C.I. COLUMNS 15'-6½" LONG. MARKED T.7 LYING AT SWINDON.
No 4. C.I. GIRDERS 28'-1" LONG MARKED N.J.2.1 LYING AT NEATH,
these to be cut to 27'-4½" long.
SECTION THRO D.D.
ELEVATION, C.C.
C.I. Distance piece
Oak Handrail
SOUTH LIBERTY COLLIERY
UP GOODS LOOP
DOWN GOODS LOOP
UP MAIN LINE
DOWN MAIN LINE
FROM EXETER
TO BRISTOL
SITE PLAN.
ENGINEERS OFFICE
PADDINGTON.

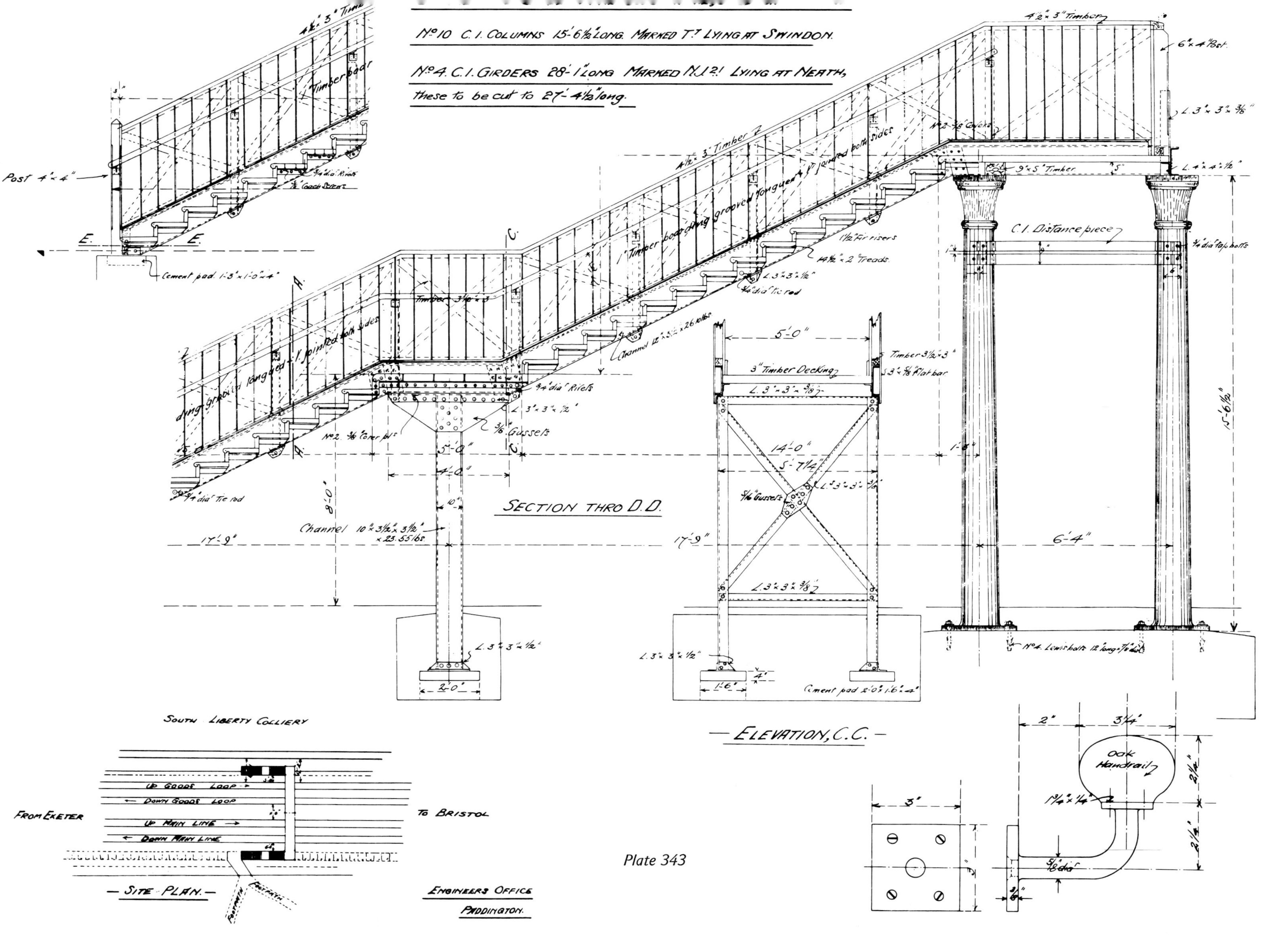

Plate 343

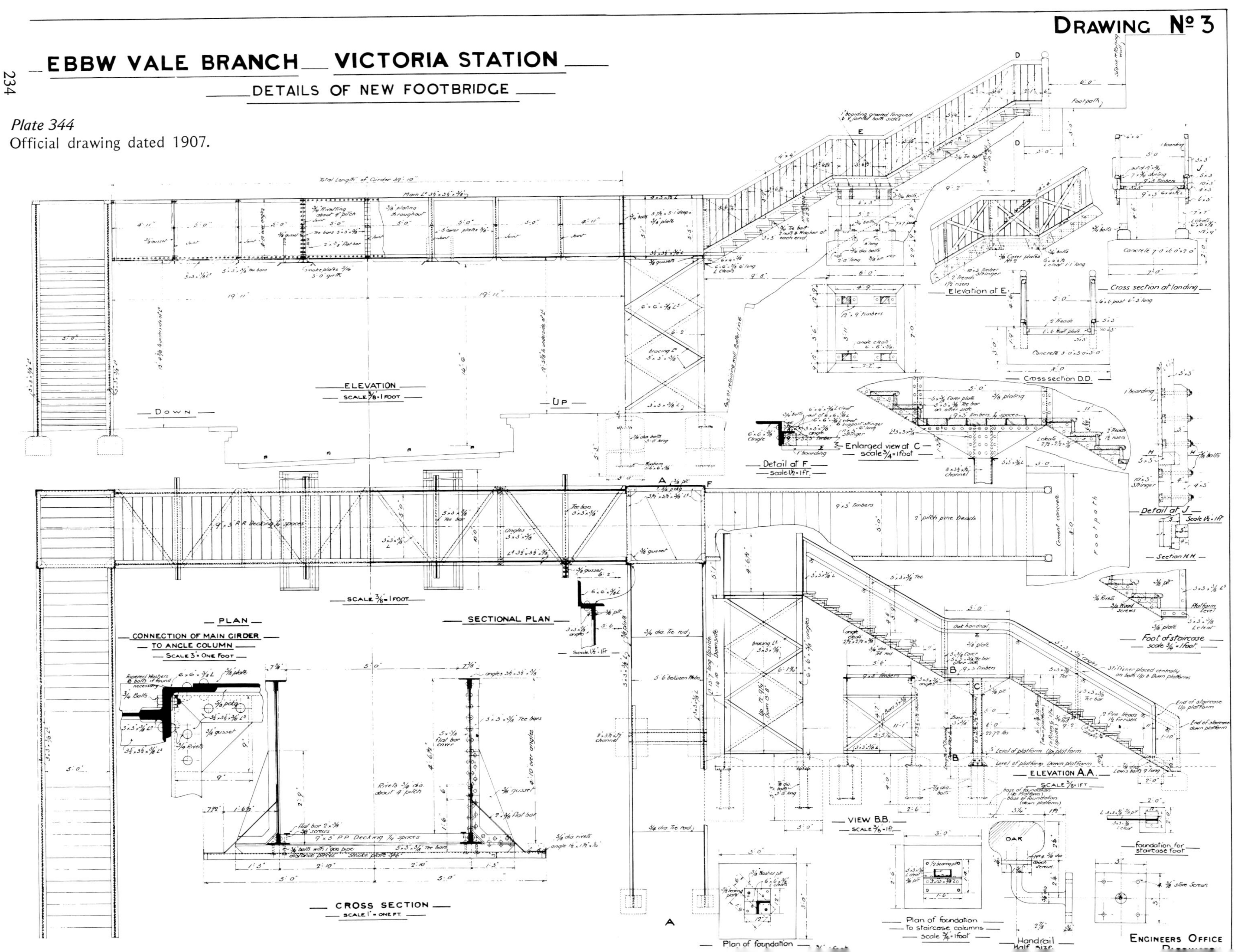

Plate 344
Official drawing dated 1907.

Plate 345

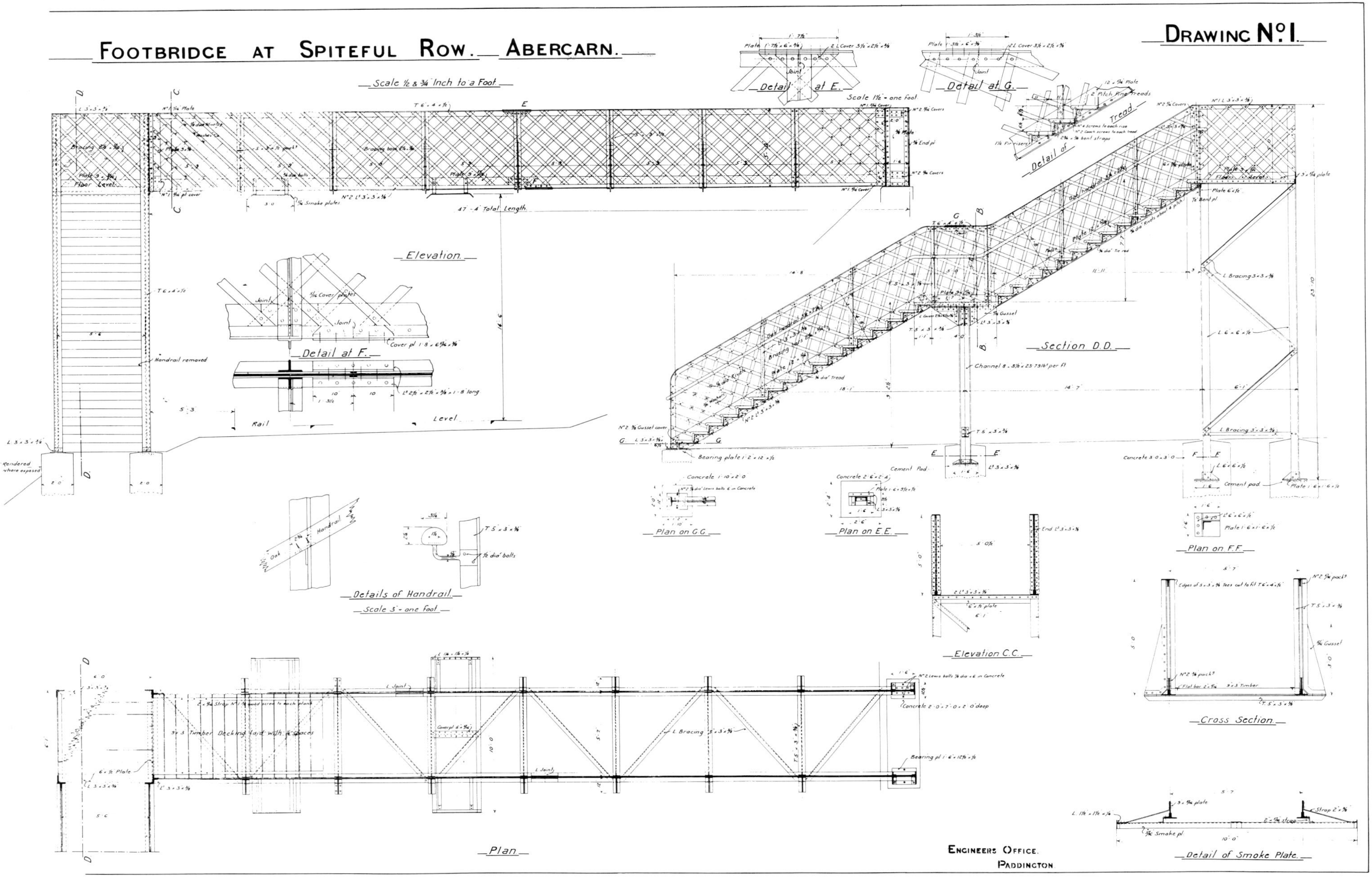
FOOTBRIDGE AT SPITEFUL ROW. ABERCARN.
DRAWING No. I.
Scale ½ & ¾ Inch to a Foot
Elevation.
Detail at E.
Detail at G.
Scale 1½ = one foot
Detail of Tread
Detail at F.
Section D.D.
Details of Handrail.
Scale 3" = one foot
Plan on G.G.
Plan on E.E.
Plan on F.F.
Elevation C.C.
Cross Section.
Plan
Detail of Smoke Plate.
47 - 4 Total Length.
Handrail removed
Rail
Level
Floor Level
Rendered where exposed
ENGINEERS OFFICE.
PADDINGTON

Plate 346
But the most beautiful of all the footbridge designs is to be found at Taplow, the picture showing the elegance of the Great Western engineer's design.

British Rail

Chapter Four

Bridges and Viaducts

Plate 347
The Wharncliffe or Hanwell Viaduct was the first great work to be completed on the Great Western Railway. This was in 1837, after fourteen months hard work. It is 300 yards long, crossing the valley of the river Brent on eight arches each of 70′ span. Brunel designed the piers in what might be called an 'Egyptian' style, a massive looking pillar, slightly tapered and stone capped at the spring. The cornice like projection of the cap once made a footing for the timber centring which had to support the brick arches till the mortar had set. 65′ above the fields can be seen the arms of Lord Wharncliffe emblazoned on the bricks. He was Chairman of the House of Lords committee on the Act of Incorporation of the Great Western Railway, and in recognition of his 'zealous and indefatigable' attention to the business thereof, the Bill authorising the construction of the Railway became law. The Company named their first great work after his Lordship in spite of his vigorous protests.

British Rail

Plate 348
Sixty five feet above the Brent valley a 'Castle' draws her train across the superb Wharncliffe viaduct.
British Rail

Plate 349
Originally the viaduct was built for double track of broad gauge, 7′ railway. The line was quadrupled during the 1870's with two additional 4′ 8½″ tracks on the north of the original tracks. The new work can be distinguished from the old by a lime mark on the underside of the arch. This plate shows the dramatic 'pylon' shape of the piers, which, with their great mass earns for them the description 'Egyptian'.
British Rail

Plate 350

Maidenhead Bridge was an early example of the designs of Brunel which were so far ahead of their time as to nearly cost him his employment, so fiercely did his critics press their charges. The river Thames is one hundred yards wide at this bridging point. He intended to span the river with two arches, their common pier resting on an island conveniently placed in the middle of the river. On a piece of cartridge paper, about 12″ x 10″, he sketched out the profile of the span, all around on the sheet he scattered a mass of arithmetic. The result was the construction of the 'flattest' brick arch in the world, the greatest brick bridge ever built. Compared with the thick wad of paper needed to hold modern bridge calculations, it could be said that Brunel designed this amazing bridge on the back of a cigarette packet. By modern standards it was worked out 'by rule of thumb' but Brunel was as accurate as the scientific development of the period would allow, he was constantly working beyond the bounds of contemporary knowledge and practice. Each span was 128′ with a rise from the springing to the crown of only 24′ 6″. Many engineers criticised the flat arches. 'The arches are supported by their centreings', they said, 'take away those and the bridge will fall down'. Brunel's Directors forbade him to remove them. Brunel readily agreed. Very few knew that the centreings had settled and were not in fact supporting the bridge at all. Trains ran over and everyone was happy because the timber framing was supporting the bridge. Brunel kept his secret and enjoyed the joke. In the autumn of 1839 a storm blew the centreings down leaving the bridge silently and gracefully confirming the genius of her designer.

British Rail

Plate 351
The bridge was widened on the south side when the tracks were quadrupled in 1890-1893. It took twelve months longer to build a slightly smaller bridge in 1890 than in 1839. The plate shows the centreing in place ready for the bricks to be laid. The tricycle in the foreground probably belongs to the photographer.
British Rail

Plate 352
Though only a small part of the bridge this tow path arch is worthy of separate study.
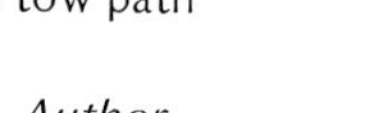
Author

Plate 353
On both banks Brunel provided flood arches at 28′ span. These are the eastern arches.
Author

Plate 354

Immediately west of Chippenham the line is carried over the main road by this massive bridge. Brunel built it in Bath stone but with the passage of time engineers brick has replaced the crumbling limestone, leaving the bridge a heavy ugly looking lump. It has a main arch of 26′ span and side arches over the footpaths of 10′. The main arch springs from piers, three abreast, which are not of uniform size, varying from 9′ to 12′ square and the whole thing is 8° skew to the road. Butting against the bridge is the six arch viaduct with spans of 26′ and one of 10′. The piers for these arches are three abreast and vary in size. The centre pier against the bridge is 8′ square and all the others on this centre line are 6′ square. The north and south outer rows of piers are all 7′ square. In 1857 an additional 10′ was added to one face of the bridge on the north side.

Author 1973

Plate 355

The viaduct arches at Chippenham.

Author 1973

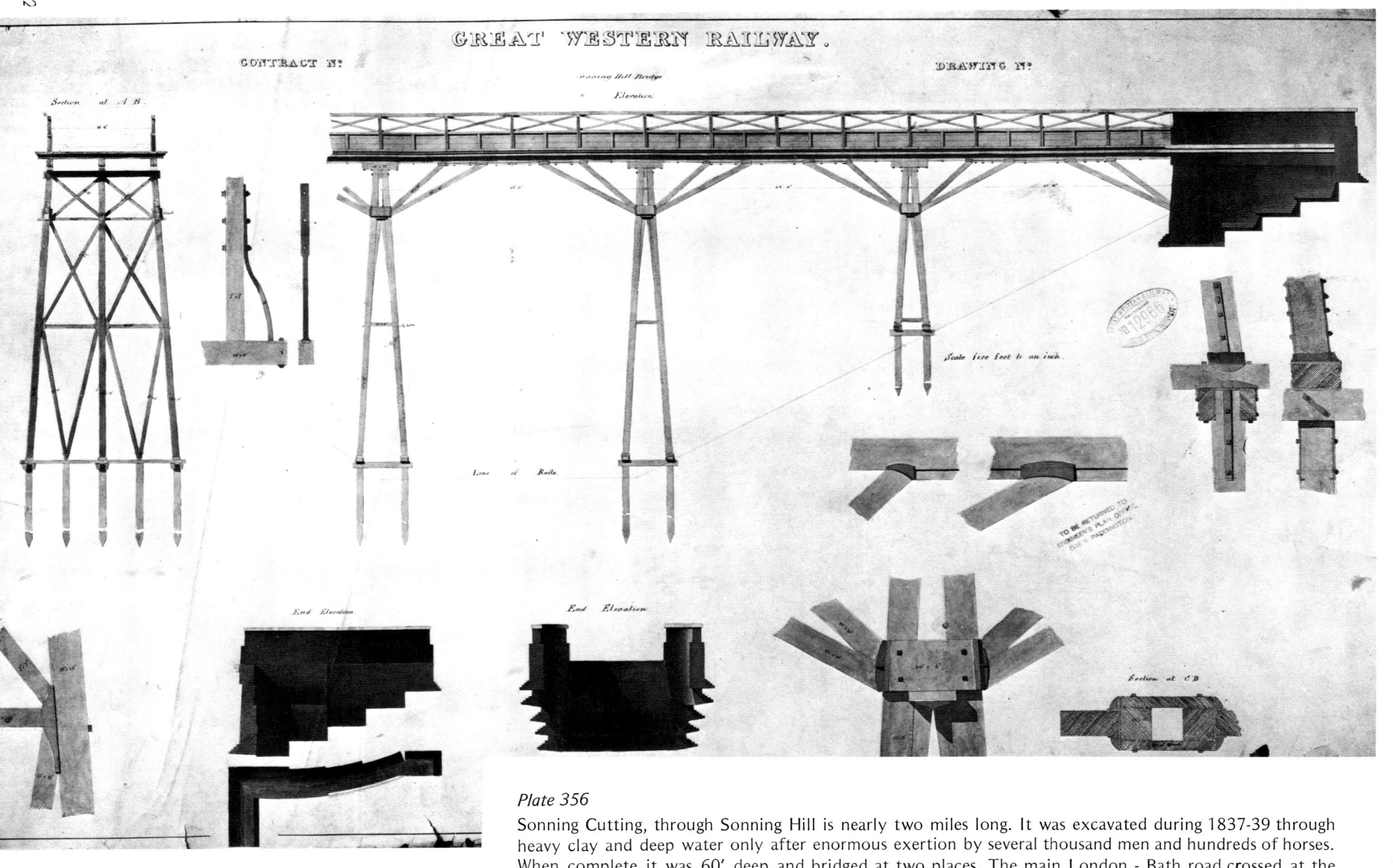

Plate 356

Sonning Cutting, through Sonning Hill is nearly two miles long. It was excavated during 1837-39 through heavy clay and deep water only after enormous exertion by several thousand men and hundreds of horses. When complete it was 60′ deep and bridged at two places. The main London - Bath road crossed at the eastern end and a by-road was carried over about half a mile from that point by the bridge shown here. One could say that this was the prototype of the beautiful timber bridges that Brunel was to use in the far West Country later. In this design he has economised in timber, as only the lightest loads would be using the bridge, by having the shortest possible struts, thus giving the bridge a very uncomfortable appearance. Notice also the lack of tie rods. The plate is a photograph of Brunel's drawing for the bridge.

British Rail

Plate 357

Plate 358

Captions overleaf

Plate 359

Plate 357

◀ The Gover Viaduct was built for the Cornwall Railway, between St. Austell and Burngullow, to the standard design of I.K. Brunel. The piers on this and all the Cornwall Railway viaducts, also the viaducts on the Tavistock branch of the South Devon Railway, were built at 66′ centres. On the West Cornwall Railway he put the piers at 50′ centres. By adhering to these dimensions it was possible to have all struts and beams a standard length according to their position in the bridge which meant that stocks of spares were easy to maintain. Brunel designed the viaducts so that any spar could be replaced without disturbing any other spar and went so far as to claim that one spar could be replaced in an hour. The Gover was a large viaduct, 230 yards long, with a maximum height of 95′. Tie rods have been fitted between the trestles so that during the passage of a train, deflections in any one trestle will be resisted by the combined strength of all the trestles. The viaduct was replaced with stone arches in 1898.

British Rail

Plate 358

◀ The course of the line between Newton Abbot and Plymouth took it over the southern slopes of Dartmoor, forcing Brunel to bridge several relatively narrow but very deep valleys which cut down off the moor to the sea at right angles to his railway. The illustration is of Ivybridge Viaduct carrying the line 108′ 6″ above the little River Erme. The viaduct is 252 yards long and in the photograph had timbers resting on piers of Dartmoor granite (from the Western Beacon) to support the track. Struts fan out to support these timbers in a manner reminiscent of the bridge in *plate 356*. Built about 1847 it represents a stage between the bridge in *plate 356* and that in *plate 357*.

British Rail

Plate 359

◀ Walkham Viaduct, on the Tavistock branch, built during 1856-58 was considered to be the most mature of all Brunel's timber trestle viaducts. It appears to have a greater number of spars and bracings than the slightly earlier versions on the Cornwall Railway and looks less spindly in consequence. It was 367 yards long and 132 feet above the ground at the highest point. It was replaced in 1910 with a steel-web girder bridge resting on the old piers.

British Rail

Plate 360

Combe Lake Viaduct.

British Rail

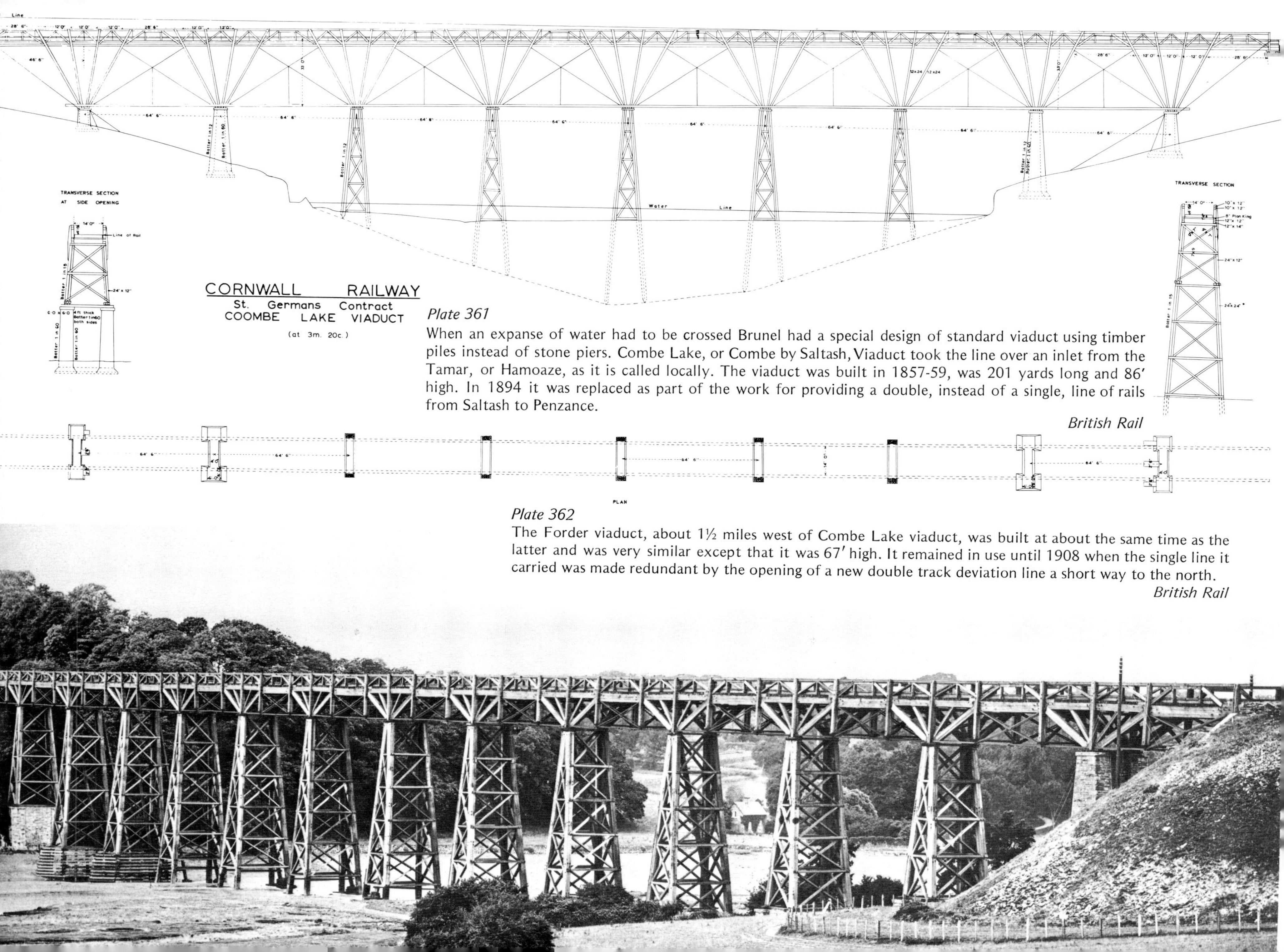

Plate 361

When an expanse of water had to be crossed Brunel had a special design of standard viaduct using timber piles instead of stone piers. Combe Lake, or Combe by Saltash, Viaduct took the line over an inlet from the Tamar, or Hamoaze, as it is called locally. The viaduct was built in 1857-59, was 201 yards long and 86′ high. In 1894 it was replaced as part of the work for providing a double, instead of a single, line of rails from Saltash to Penzance.

British Rail

Plate 362

The Forder viaduct, about 1½ miles west of Combe Lake viaduct, was built at about the same time as the latter and was very similar except that it was 67′ high. It remained in use until 1908 when the single line it carried was made redundant by the opening of a new double track deviation line a short way to the north.

British Rail

Plate 363

These marvellous viaducts were demolished for a variety of reasons. For instance they needed a very special, high quality timber which became unobtainable, thus as the old timber wore out no new parts were forthcoming. Sometimes the viaduct carried only a single track and the Company needed to double the line, so a new viaduct was built alongside. In this illustration the old double track Liskeard viaduct is being strengthened. The timber trestles still support the bridging but brick piers are rising to support the track bed. In the far left temporary lattice work is supporting the track and progressively across the viaduct one can see the various stages that the rebuilding has reached. Heavy, fish-bellied girders will be installed later. The locomotive on the bridge, spotless No. 1755, has a crew leaning nonchalantly over the 140′ parapet. They must feel fairly secure, but what about the men who have to stand on half finished brickwork laying consecutive courses, or the men walloping in rivets as a fierce Cornish wind tugs and tears at them, high above the valley floor?

British Rail

Plate 364
New stone piers rise from the ground alongside the redundant Ponsanooth viaduct on the Falmouth branch. Built in 1860-63 it was 139′ high and 215 yards long. The Great Western Railway replaced it in 1930 (see *plate 368*).

British Rail

Plate 365
Liskeard viaduct after rebuilding about 1894. It is said that the iron used in the deep fish-bellied girders was very bad for rust, and would blister and fall away no matter how much careful painting was done.

British Rail

Plate 366

Trenance viaduct, on the outskirts of Newquay, was built in 1848/49 by Thomas Treffry to carry his Mineral Railway over the Trenance valley. It was 98′ high and 210 yards long with a timber superstructure on stone piers. It carried a single line of rails. In 1874 a wrought iron superstructure replaced the timber but the viaduct was not widened. The plates illustrate the work done during 1938/39 when the wrought iron was replaced with masonry arches to carry a double line of track. In this plate you can see the additional width given to the original piers to accommodate a double line and you can also see the 1874 superstructure.

British Rail

Plate 367

Trenance viaduct rebuilt and wanting only the handrails to be finished. The old piers can be seen walled up inside the new stone work.

British Rail

Plate 368
Ponsanooth viaduct, six miles from Truro on the Falmouth branch, was originally a Brunel, timber trestle viaduct, 215 yards long and 139′ high. It was replaced by a new stone arched viaduct alongside during 1930. The plate shows that the arches on the left are completed but that the ones on the right are in various stages of development. It is interesting to see how the bricks lie in 'rings' on their wooden platforms or centring.

British Rail

Plate 369
Moorswater viaduct, between Liskeard and Doublebois stations, is about 318 yards long and 147′ high. The plate shows the masonry arches and the old Brunel piers alongside. The new viaduct was built in 1881.

British Rail

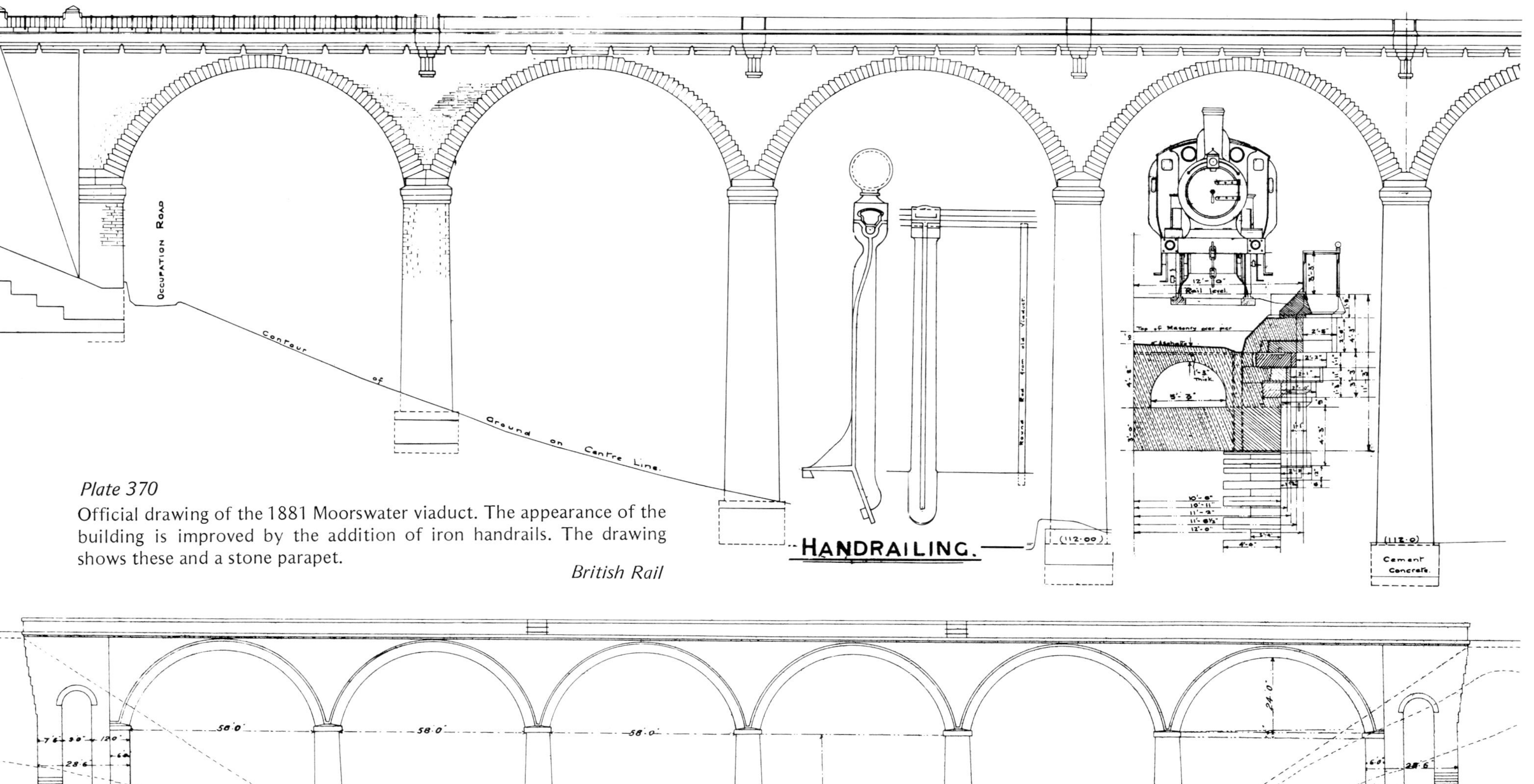

Plate 370

Official drawing of the 1881 Moorswater viaduct. The appearance of the building is improved by the addition of iron handrails. The drawing shows these and a stone parapet.

British Rail

Plate 371
College Wood viaduct on the Falmouth branch was the last of the timber viaducts to be built in the West of England. It was 318 yards long and 100' high and was 73 years old when replaced in 1934. The last surviving timber trestle viaducts were demolished in 1947, the year of Nationalisation for the Railways. These were the Dare and the Gamlyn viaducts on the one time Vale of Neath Railway.

British Rail

Plate 372
Forlorn stumps, the tops unweathered and raw, testify to their recent execution. College Wood viaduct, near Falmouth.

British Rail

Plate 373
A dramatic view of the Coldrennick viaduct which gives a good idea of what 138′ of rugged stone pillar looks like relative to tall trees. The trestles have been replaced with a system similar to that at Liskeard.

British Rail

Plate 374
This is the famous 'Cocked Hat' bridge at Wrangaton which was replaced about 1894. It has a 'frontiersman' look but was perfectly practical until engine loads increased or the timbers rotted, or both.

British Rail

Plate 375

This bridge over the River Thames at Windsor is the oldest surviving iron bridge built by Brunel. He designed it during 1847/48 and it was opened in 1849. It stands among a series of brick arches (originally timber) which carry the Slough to Windsor branch over the flat meadows of the Thames-side. It is a 'bow and string' type bridge, the three main girders being 213′ long, built up of riveted, wrought iron plates. The 'bow' girders have a 'kite' shaped section. The bridge crosses the river on the skew with a span of 202′, so the depth of the 'bow' girder from crown to decking is suitably deep at 25′. Originally the bridge rested on 12 cast iron cylinders. Each 'bow' girder rested on two of these cylinders which were placed one behind the other. Brunel provided the bridge with his own style of timber decking to carry the permanent way. Four inch thick planks rested on the flanges of the 'string' girders at right angles to the track and on top of these another layer was placed about 45° to the track. In 1908 the cast iron piers were replaced with brick abutments and Brunel's decking gave way to steel.

Author 1973

Plate 376

After 125 years Brunel's rivets are as tight as the day they were closed up. The original double track has now been singled and Royal Trains over the bridge, once common, (if that is the right word) are now rare, but Brunel's bridge continues to give good service.

Author 1973

Brunel's Wye Bridge

The first bridge over the Wye at Chepstow was designed by I.K. Brunel and erected under his supervision for the South Wales Railway during 1851/52. The overall length of the bridge was 600 ft., 300 ft. over the mudflats on the Monmouthshire side, and 300 ft. over the deep water to the cliff bank on the Gloucestershire side of the river. When completed it carried a double track 7 ft. gauge railway.

There were several difficult problems to be overcome before the bridge was completed. Approaching from Gloucester, the line passed through a deep cutting which terminated in a sheer drop to the river. The bank here was 120 ft. high. Opposite, the land is a muddy flood plain. Therefore in neither case could an orthodox or simple approach be made to the bridge. In 1850 coastal shipping passed upstream to Monmouth, and the Customs House too was upstream of the proposed bridge so a mast room of 50 ft. at high water was necessary below the bridge. The Wye has the second highest tidal rise in the world with a difference of 40 ft. between low and high water. This was a problem when the piers upon which the bridging was to rest were being sunk. Foundations for these piers were reached only after passing through a 40 ft. layer of slimy mud, the bedrock was 84 ft. below high water. Thus, while sinking piers, Brunel had the constant worry of a fierce rapidly rising tide inundating the works. The piers closest to the deep water were sunk first using Brunel's usual technique. A cast iron tube with a cutting edge was weighted as it stood on the mud so that it sank slowly, more tubes were added as the preceding one disappeared until bedrock was reached. The interior was then cleared of mud down to the rock which was then excavated till the tubes rested in a rocky socket. They were filled with concrete to form a massively strong pillar. By this means nine cast iron tubes were placed, three abreast, in three rows with 100 ft. between the rows.

Brunel intended to suspend his 300 ft. river span from chains which were to be attached to tubes, one over each track, the tubes to lie on towers built at each side of the deep water channel. The tube is ideal as a shape for withstanding the forces of compression. Robert Stephenson had used a box form tube to bridge the Conway estuary in North Wales. Here the span was 400 ft. and the line had only to be 12 ft. above the water. Each tube was a rectangular box 18 ft. x 14 ft. with an inner and outer shell at the top and undersides. The distance between these was 21 ins. This cavity, 21 ins. high by 14 ft. wide was divided into narrow tunnels by plates, so as to give a cellular construction and therefore rigidity to the otherwise unsupported 400 ft. span. It was the duty of an examiner to crawl through these cells to inspect them for rust and other damage. There were two such tubes, one for each line and they weighed over a thousand tons each. At the Menai Straits Stephenson had to bridge a wider gap. The same construction was used as at Conway but the largest spans were 460 ft. long and 100 ft. above high water. The total length of the bridge was 1511 ft., all of which had to be crawled by a bridge examiner in those ghastly 21 ins. tunnels. These spans weighed over 1500 tons each.

Brunel, who had been present at the raising of these bridges, had rather more finesse. He did not want to raise vast weights over 120 ft. nor did he want to waste his Company's money, and last but not least, he did not want his passengers trundling through abominably noisy iron tubes when they could be admiring the beauty of the Wye gorge. So he used circular tubes. These were very strong in compression so that they could be made lightly and therefore cheaply and the bridge would be suspended from them. Their disadvantage was that they could not support themselves and the bridge, so Brunel designed struts from the tubes to the bridge plate girders to give the necessary support. Also, the tubes were not as wide as the track beneath, so that the chains hung downwards and outwards to the track. Thus there arose friction where the chains passed through the downstruts and against the side of the plate girders. This was overcome by placing rubbing strips of gunmetal at the friction points. When completed each tube was 312 ft. long and weighed 138 tons constructed of riveted wrought iron plates.

The chains were lengths of wrought iron 20 ft. long and 10 ins. deep. These links came in two thicknesses, ¾ inch and $\frac{11}{16}$ inch, and they were assembled into suspension chains 14 links across. The work of forging these links, which was done in one piece with no welded additions, a very unusual feature for that time, was carried out in Dublin at the Seville Iron Works (see *plate 381*). Brunel had had to go over to show the foundrymen how to carry out his novel idea.

The tubes were fabricated parallel to the river on the Monmouthshire bank and manhandled into a position at right angles to the river, lying on a temporary staging between the riverward piers. On this staging was a railway track and a rail mounted trolley while on the river were six iron barges in position under the nose of the tube. On the morning of April 8th 1852, at about 9 a.m., the tide was rising and soon brought the barges into contact with the tube. Now was the time to give the signal "heave away" and with one end of the tube floating and the other on the rail trolley it was a fairly simple matter to draw the great tube across to the foot of the cliff. Once arrived, with the tide rising all the time to bring the tube nearer the cliff top, lifting tackle was attached and the tube lifted up to the level of the railway. By the following day it was in position on top of its towers (see *plate 377*).

There were two towers, the one on the cliff was built of stone and on the riverward pier it was of iron. The latter had roller bearings to allow the tube some movement under the forces set up by braking and acceleration of trains beneath. One would have thought that the masonry pier was the stronger and therefore should have had these bearings, but Brunel did not trust the strata in the cliff to remain stable under load. When the bridge was rebuilt in 1962 the bearings were again put on the riverward pier.

With the tubes in position over the tracks, the wrought iron plates were riveted together to form the trough or bridging through which the trains would run. As I said earlier, the tubes were ideally suited to resist the compression forces set up by the inward drag of the chains but they could not support themselves over the long span. Without vertical struts for support they would have bent about their centres. The suspension chains passed through these verticals via square apertures and at these points Brunel had large wedges hammered in to bear down on the chains. This had the effect of tensioning, or bowing, the tube which was then even better suited to withstand compression and resist buckling. The rise from tip to centre of the tube was 30 ins.

The bridge lasted for 90 years before the first plates buckled. In 1944 part of the Monmouthshire span bent slightly under the stress of heavy wartime traffic, weights undreamed of in Brunel's day. The fundamental problem is that being a suspension bridge it moves under the unequal loading of a heavy train moving across. The loading of one section unloads another in a wave pattern which causes severe strains in the structure. For many years a 25 m.p.h., and later a 15 m.p.h. restriction was imposed and the bridge survived. In 1948 the Monmouthshire spans were re-girdered but the main bridge remained intact. In 1962, exactly one hundred years to the day since the first tube was launched, the Chief Civil Engineer began a 14 week operation, without interfering with the train service, during which time the old trusses were dismantled and the present construction erected. The new bridge was tested by two King class engines, No. 6011 *King James I* and No. 6018 *King Henry VI*. Within a year they too had been sent for scrap.

CHEPSTOW BRIDGE
FLOATING AND LIFTING TUBES

1ST POSITION
2 ND POSITION
FINAL POSITION
3 RD POSITION
SECTION A.A
A
A

Plate 377
Sequence of events in raising the tubes at the Wye bridge, Chepstow.

British Rail

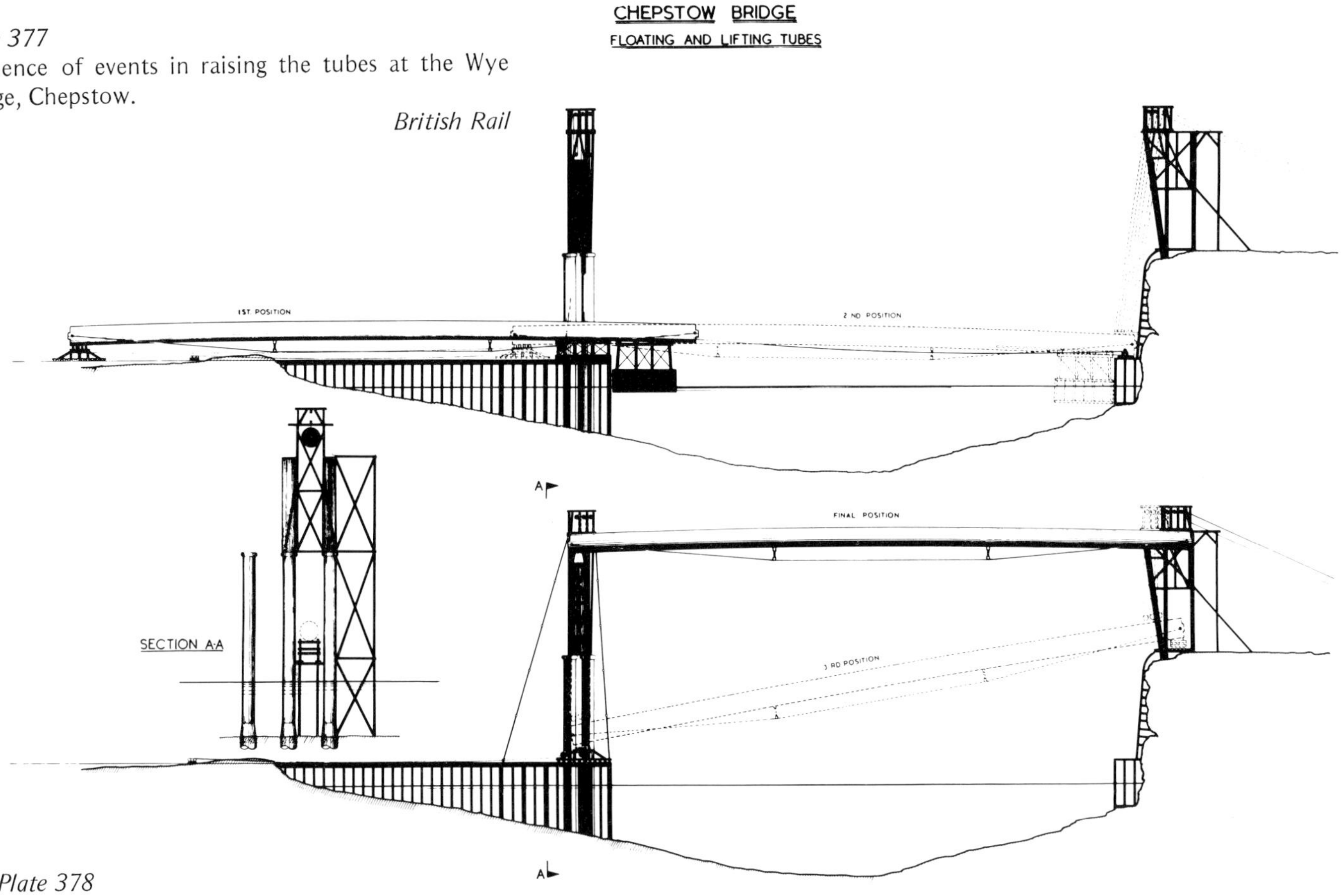

Plate 378
The Wye bridge from down stream. The suspension chains pass through the struts and are fixed to the base of the bridge at two points, these being marked by a red navigation lamp over each bolt.

British Rail

Plate 379
A view towards Gloucester from the centre of the bridge showing how the suspension chains hung in festoons and crossed each other to effect diagonal bracing.
British Rail

Plate 380
Looking through the Wye bridge with the camera standing in the down main.
British Rail

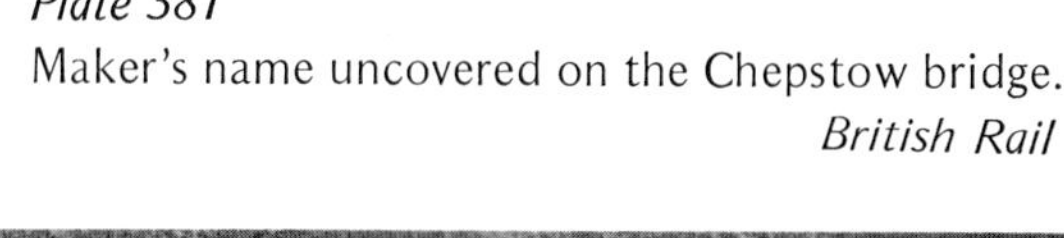

Plate 381
Maker's name uncovered on the Chepstow bridge.
British Rail

Plates 382/383

Tube's end. Brunel's wrought iron tubes were lowered to the rails in May 1962. This plate shows the pin joint for the suspension chains and part of the chains falling to the left. The tube rested, at the river-pier end, on roller bearings. An illustration of these is in *plate 383.* *British Rail*

Plate 384

Brunel's Saltash Bridge

Saltash bridge has a total length of 2,200 ft. formed by the two main spans of 455 ft. each, and 17 approach spans ranging between 69 ft. 6 ins. and 93 ft. At the period of its construction, warships under sail still used the Tamar, or Hamoaze, as it is called in that locality, and the Admiralty specified that there should be 100 ft. of mast room below the soffit of the bridge at high water. The distance to the top of the tubes from high water is 168 ft. Work commenced on the bridge in 1848 when a small coffer dam was sunk down to bedrock to excavate foundations for the central pier. A small piece of masonry was constructed but money to prosecute the work further was lacking and the project lapsed. In 1854 a new coffer dam, 35 ft. in diameter was sunk over the rock that was to make the foundation for the central pier. The dam was in the form of an inner and outer iron tube, sealed at the top and open at the base, which, when bedded into mud, was sealed against further ingress of water. The contents of the tube could then be pumped out and dug out until bed-rock was reached and the work of excavating the foundations could begin. Compressed air was pumped into the tube to keep out any trace of water once the dam was occupied by workmen. They had to shovel through mud and sand and hack through dense beds of oyster shells till eventually bedrock was reached. They were nearly drowned when excavating the bedrock when they breached a fresh water spring which overcame the air pressure in the dam and nearly overcame the pumps too. Before the picks and shovels won the day, the men had got the better of such obstacles as the compressed air atmosphere in which they worked, under 70 ft. of water, the icy cold, the gloom, tides, mud, sea shells, primitive tools and lighting, until at last a solid tower of stone reared its head above water. At this stage the iron tube of the coffer dam simply unbolted and was towed away in two halves, another clever idea by I.K. Brunel.

While all this was going on the great truss for the Cornish span was being constructed on the river bank. Its tube was elliptical in section, 12 ft. 3 ins. high and 16 ft. 9 ins. broad so that the chains to the bridging could hang vertically—a lesson learned from Chepstow. Eleven pairs of vertical struts connected the bridging and the tube, passing through the suspension chains and riveted solid at each end.

Ten pairs of intermediate hangers were attached to the chains and the bridging, making the bridge truly a suspension bridge—the only one of its kind in the world surviving to carry a railway. Where the hanger plates of the main struts passed through the chains at the centre of the bridge, they were quite inaccessible to paint, with the inevitable result that they rusted and broke. The failures occurred during the 1939-45 War as at Chepstow and were patched up. In 1960 an entirely new design of hanger was fitted to the verticals whereby the plate passing through the chains was dispensed with and a pair of straps, like a bridle iron, passed outside the chains and were fixed to the bridging and verticals by pin joints. Brunel tended to overlook the necessity of paint and hid many important areas behind iron cladding or simply made them inaccessible to anything but the rain. After the 1960 operation, the bridge is stronger than when it was built. To restrain the tendency to longitudinal movement inherent in suspension bridges when a moving load passes over, Brunel introduced diagonal bracing between the main verticals. They were wrought iron rods fixed by pin joints at the tubes. Curious to relate, these pins were made $\frac{1}{8}$th inch smaller in diameter than the holes they were to fit resulting in a very slack joint. This has been a source of trouble ever since. Whether Brunel was ill, or away supervising his S.S. Great Eastern is not known but the blunder was made and is with us still. In the tubes, about quarter the way up their sides are a series of ventilation holes 2 ins.—3 ins. across. If one is inside the tube one will see the camera obscura effect of these as they focus a view of the Tamar on the opposite side of the tube.

Some of the chains for the bridge came from the Clifton suspension bridge, the company attempting to build this having got into financial difficulties, and sold them to the Cornwall Railway for the Royal Albert Bridge. The rest were constructed by Ravenhill, Howard and Co. of Rotherhithe at the "King and Queen" iron foundry. They were 1 inch thick and 7 ins. deep and hung in two tiers, each being 15 links wide, from the towers at each end (see *plate 385*).

The main spans, or trusses, constructed at the water's edge had a dock cut round them into which were floated pontoons of iron pressurised with air. These were attached to the underside of the trusses at each end, and to facilitate this a section of the bridging was lifted up above the level of the rest. Having got the truss afloat in the dock it was possible to tow it out onto the river using ships and land based winches. Conducting this operation (for which special printed instructions had been issued) was Brunel, standing on the side of the truss with two signallers above him. On the 1st September 1857 the strange vessel set out on its short voyage, watched by a crowd of thousands who kept perfect silence in accordance with Brunel's wish. The great truss was manoeuvred into position between its land and river pier without any untoward incident but with perfect accuracy as if those involved carried out such performances every Thursday afternoon. From now on hydraulic jacks would raise the truss as course after course of stone was laid beneath it until its soffit was 100 ft. above high water mark. The truss weighed 1060 tons. The Devon span was floated in July 1858 and took eight months to reach its final position, the Cornish span having taken five months. Brunel had been too ill to supervise the second launching which was controlled by the second in command, Brereton. When the bridge was complete, and the crowds with their flags and their cheering had gone, Brunel rode across his bridge, lying on a special flat trolley drawn by a Gooch 'Single', for the great engineer was dying. In September 1859, five months after the bridge was completed Brunel was dead. He had planned his work so well that from the digging of the first sea sand to the driving of the last rivet in the Devon span the cost to the Cornwall Railway company had not exceeded £225,000. By comparison, Robert Stephenson's "Britannia" bridge over the Menai Straits, built for double track 4 ft. 8½ ins. gauge with a span 600 ft.

shorter than that of the Royal Albert, had cost its owners £601,865. Brunel had built the bridge at the cost estimated at the start, in spite of extraordinary difficulties and the general novelty of the various operations.

Today the bridge is recognisably the one which Brunel erected but it has had a great deal of bracing added in an attempt to restrict the movement to which suspension bridges are subject. The timber decking was strengthened in 1892, the approach spans were renewed in 1928/29 and in 1960 the centre hangers had to be renewed owing to rust. In 1968 further bracing was added but the great tubes and basic struts and bracing remain after 115 years, the only rail link into Cornwall. It is carrying axle loads in excess of 22 tons so it was not the Royal Albert that kept the "Kings" out of Cornwall. The following is an extract from the half yearly report of the Cornwall Railway and will do splendidly to sum up Brunel's achievement in building this bridge.

"Since the last half year meeting you have lost the services of your celebrated engineer Mr. Isambard Kingdom Brunel, whose works of extraordinary genius had earned for him a European reputation, and whose death will be a loss, not only to the Company, but to the general interests of science throughout the world. It is an act of justice to the memory of Mr. Brunel, to place on record that the whole cost of the erection of that stupendous and beautiful structure, the Royal Albert Bridge, which has elicited the admiration of the whole scientific world, has not exceeded £225,000.

Considering the extraordinary difficulties which were overcome and the magnitude of the operation, it is believed that there is no engineering work in existence which has been more economically completed."

Plate 385

There was a problem concerning the suspension chains of which Brunel was aware. How did one pull the two parts of the chain together at the centre in order that the eyes in all the links would be in line and thus receive the locking pin? The weight of iron in the chains from the top of the tube to the centre of the bridge would be measured in tons. The answer was to forge in one end of each link the shape as seen in this plate. The lug would give a place for a rope to grip and pull. All the links had one end fashioned in this manner so that there would be no complications with having special links for certain parts of the chain. This system is believed to have first been used by Tierney Clark in his pretty suspension bridge over the Thames at Marlow.

British Rail

Plate 386

Compare the bracing in these two photographs. The upper picture shows the original construction of eleven vertical struts per truss and ten pairs of intermediate hangers from the suspension chains to the bridging. Light horizontal and diagonal bracing between the verticals is the only other bracing.

British Rail

Plate 387

In 1968 additional bracing was introduced to try and restrict the movement of the bridge under 22½ tons axle loads from the new 100 ton tanker wagons. Much heavier section metal than hitherto has been used between the verticals and a long, horizontal stay has been introduced to tie the verticals and arrest longitudinal movement.

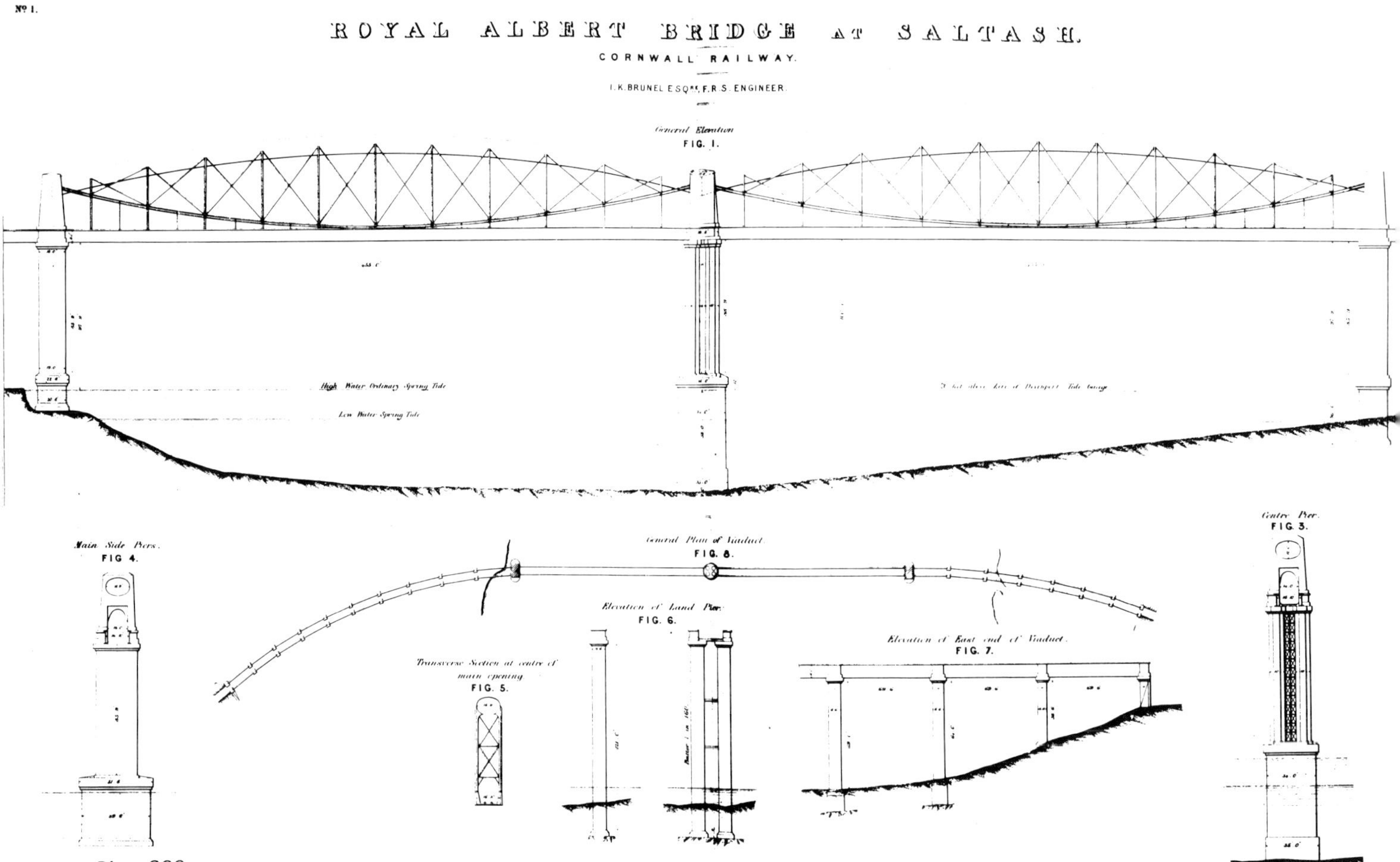

Nº 1.

ROYAL ALBERT BRIDGE AT SALTASH.

CORNWALL RAILWAY.

I. K. BRUNEL ESQRE. F.R.S. ENGINEER.

General Elevation
FIG. 1.

High Water Ordinary Spring Tide

Low Water Spring Tide

Main Side Piers.
FIG. 4.

General Plan of Viaduct.
FIG. 8.

Elevation of Land Pier.
FIG. 6.

Transverse Section at centre of main opening
FIG. 5.

Elevation of East end of Viaduct.
FIG. 7.

Centre Pier.
FIG. 3.

Plate 388

Photographs of Brunel's drawings for the Royal Albert Bridge show the original construction much clearer than my attempts at explanation. The bottom left hand diagram shows how the central hanger was made totally inaccessible to paint (see *plate 391*).

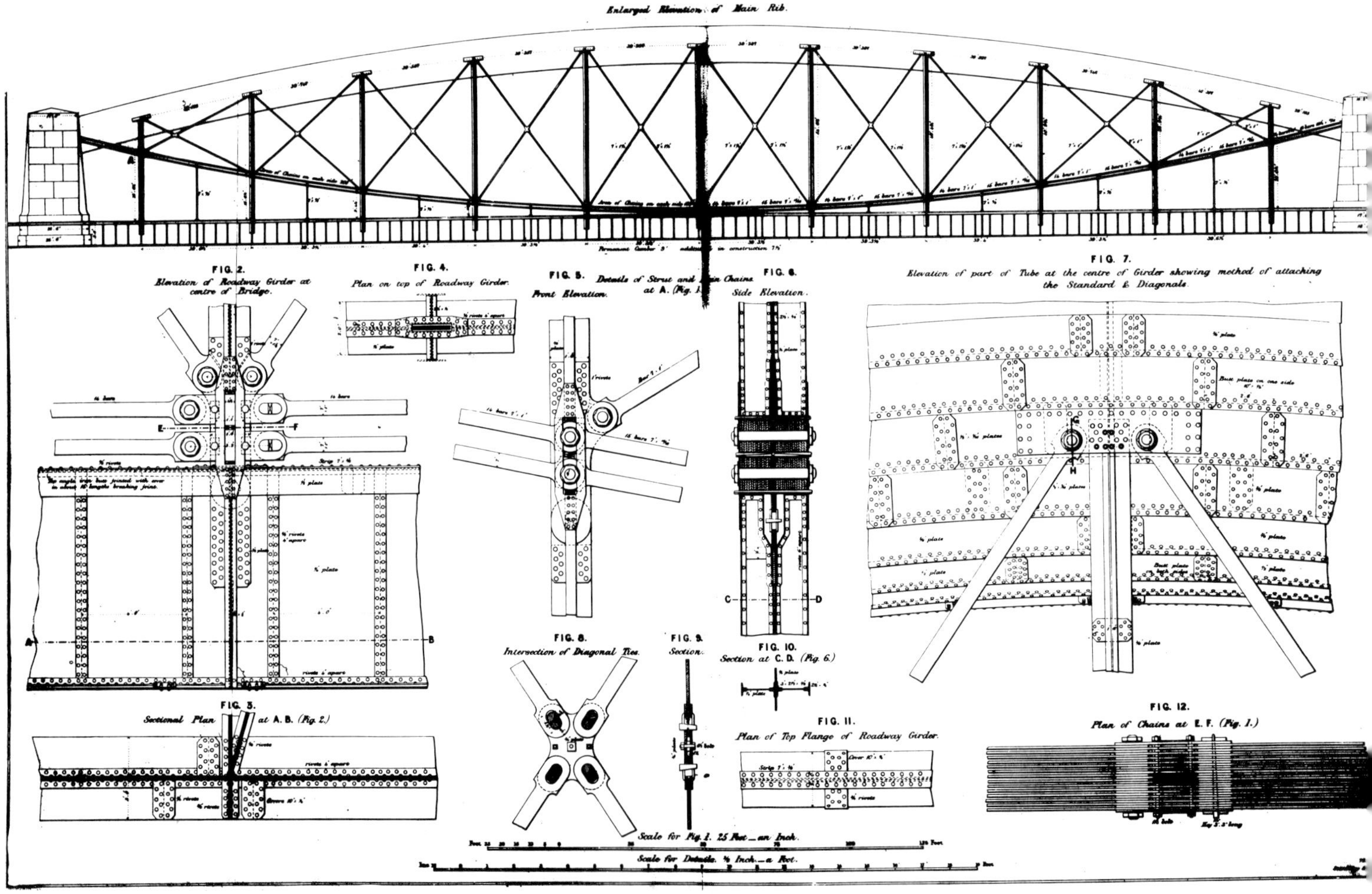

Enlarged Elevation of Main Rib.

FIG. 2.
Elevation of Roadway Girder at centre of Bridge.

FIG. 4.
Plan on top of Roadway Girder.

FIG. 5.
Details of Strut and Main Chains at A. (Fig. 1.)
Front Elevation.

FIG. 6.
Side Elevation.

FIG. 7.
Elevation of part of Tube at the centre of Girder showing method of attaching the Standard & Diagonals

FIG. 8.
Intersection of Diagonal Ties.

FIG. 9.
Section.

FIG. 10.
Section at C. D. (Fig. 6.)

FIG. 3.
Sectional Plan at A. B. (Fig. 2.)

FIG. 11.
Plan of Top Flange of Roadway Girder.

FIG. 12.
Plan of Chains at E. F. (Fig. 1.)

Scale for Fig. 1. 25 Feet ... an Inch.

Scale for Details ¾ Inch ... a Foot.

Plate 389
One part of the bridge just prior to being lifted into place.

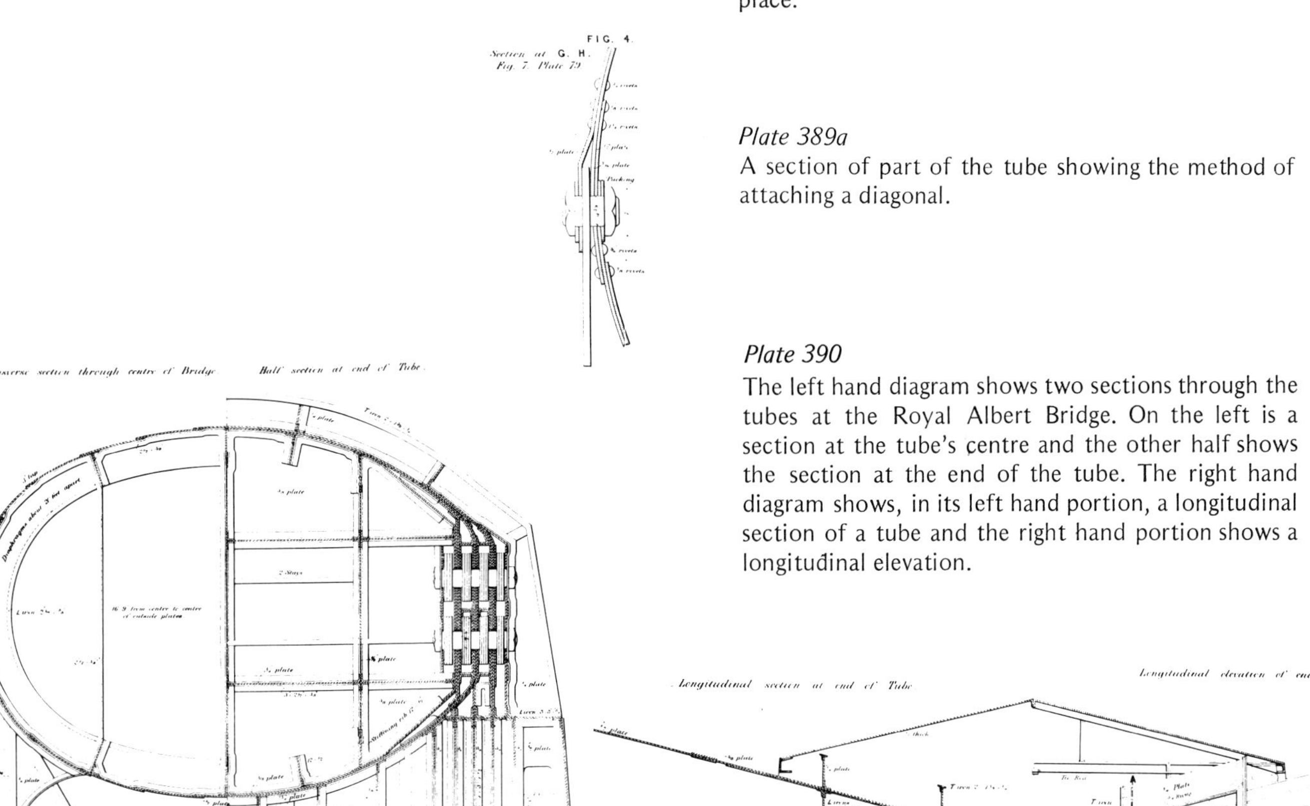

Plate 389a
A section of part of the tube showing the method of attaching a diagonal.

Plate 390
The left hand diagram shows two sections through the tubes at the Royal Albert Bridge. On the left is a section at the tube's centre and the other half shows the section at the end of the tube. The right hand diagram shows, in its left hand portion, a longitudinal section of a tube and the right hand portion shows a longitudinal elevation.

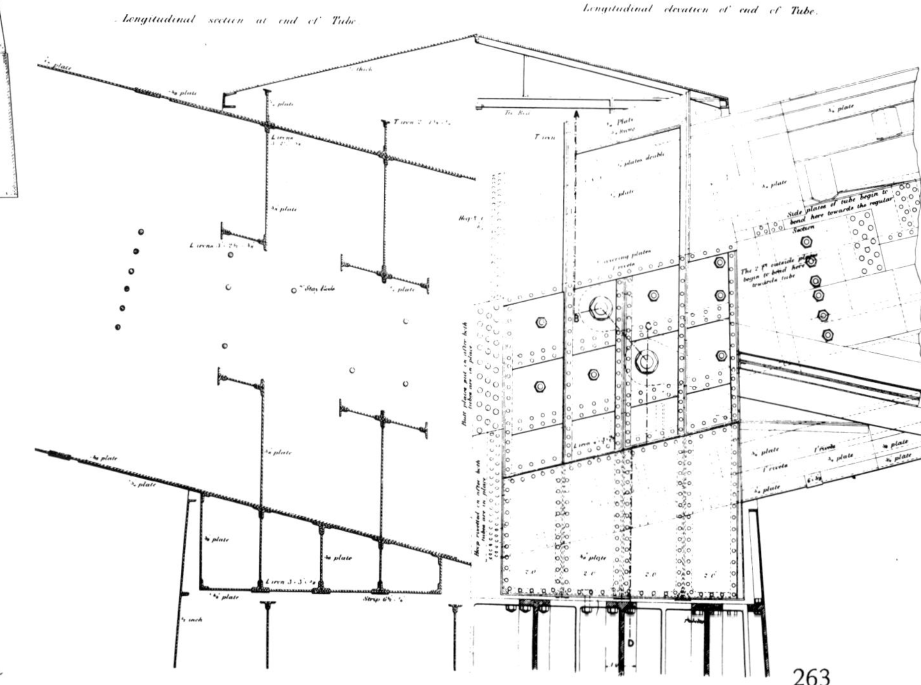

Plate 391
Brunel's original design of hanger connection to bridging. Where the hanger passed through the chains it was out of reach of paint and rusted away in consequence.

British Rail

Plate 392
A new joint was designed and installed whereby nothing passed through the chains but a bridle iron connected the hanger with the bridging. Here Fred and George are tightening up the nut with a mammoth spanner.

British Rail

Plate 393

The photographer took this picture with his heels on the rungs of a tiny iron ladder, his back to the bridge. Both his hands were occupied in holding a half plate (6½" x 4¾") camera which required a relatively large amount of movement to operate, plate holders to be changed and stowed in pockets, racking in and out of the focusing and adjustment of the shutter and aperture. The former probably meant tilting the heavy camera over on its side to see the readings and the latter meant reaching forward to the lens. Whilst thus employed, craning his head and balancing on the narrow ladder 140' above the Tamar, a man standing on top of the tube had a rope under the intrepid cameraman's armpits. There is nothing upon the tube for the ropeman to hold onto except an iron bar 4" above the tube under which he could thrust his toe. Men walking across the bridge via the upper side of the tubes had no handrail, only this low bar which, I should have thought, was more likely to trip them up than provide security. An interesting point is that the tubes are straight between each vertical strut as can be seen from this photograph.

P.S.A. Berridge

Plate 394

One of the massive portals of the Royal Albert Bridge, Saltash. The 'Egyptian' style pylon and its archway has some slight echo of Chepstow and foreshadows the chain towers at Clifton, yet to be built.

British Rail

Plate 395
Brunel's timber built skew bridge over the Avon immediately west of Bath station. The roof of the station goods shed can be seen above the parapet of the bridge. The work commenced on the bridge in the spring of 1840. Brunel's method was, as usual, unusual. Here is J.C. Bourne's description taken from his 'History of the Great Western Railway' 1846. He says, 'The angle at which the bridge crosses the river is so considerable that, although the space from quay to quay is only 80 ft, the space traversed by the railway is 664 feet. The bridge is two arches, each of 80 feet span. Each arch is composed of six ribs placed about five feet apart and springing from the abutment and a central pier of masonry. Each rib is constructed of five horizontal layers of Memel timber held together by bolts and iron straps. The end or butt of each rib is enclosed in a shoe or socket of cast iron, resting with the intervention of a plate upon the springing stones, the shoes on the middle pier are common to the two ribs. The spandrils of the four external ribs are filled up with an ornamental framework of cast iron supporting the parapets. The interior ribs are connected by cross struts and ties. The cornice and parapet are both of timber; the latter is framed in open work of a lozenge pattern. The abutments are flanked by plain turreted piers, and the tow path is carried on an iron gallery beneath the western arch.' This bridge was replaced in 1878 which, in its turn, has been superseded by the present construction. Brunel had to build the bridge in double quick time because the line was ready for opening except that there was no bridge to carry the line over the Avon. No contractor would take the job on and so Brunel, at the last minute, had to 'run one up' for the Company. It is strange that he should have been able to do so quickly when everyone else seemed to be afraid of the job.

British Rail 1878

Plate 396
The eastern approaches to Bath were beautifully thought out by Brunel who designed the various arches and walls with a quiet grandeur. The bridge is immediately east of the station and spans the Avon with an 88′ arch. To the east of this is a long viaduct of 37 arches to the handsome London Road bridge.

British Rail

Plate 397
London Road bridge.

Plate 398
Beyond the London Road Bridge the line runs on an embankment, through two short tunnels of 99 and 77 yards respectively, under Bathwick Hill, until the line comes out into Sydney Gardens. This area, at the time of the railway's construction, was very close to the houses owned by members of the Royal Family and aristocracy which accounts for the elegance with which the railway was endowed. There are three bridges over the tracks in the Gardens. The one illustrated here is, in my opinion, the best. It carries a footpath, 10′ wide over a span of 30′ on the three arches of cast iron of ¾″ thick cross section. The arches support a bed of cast iron plates laid in two rows, each row being made of 5′ square plates. Each has stiffening webs and at the outer edge has a channel shape. Upon the top flange of the channel stands the cast iron stanchions which support the handrails. These stanchions are hollow, and a bolt 3′ 8″ long passes through the space to be bolted to the cast iron channel already mentioned. The bridge rests on a massive abutment and on the cutting retaining wall (see *plate 399*). The latter is an interesting feature of this section of line. It supports the Kennet and Avon Canal which runs on the bank above the railway. This is not the canal's original line but was diverted to its present course so as to clear the way for the Great Western Railway which then ran in the Canal's old bed for a short way. The thickness of the masonry of the wall varies with the height of the cutting and therefore the weight of earth to be held back. At its greatest the wall is 27′ above rail level and is 5′ thick.

Author 1973

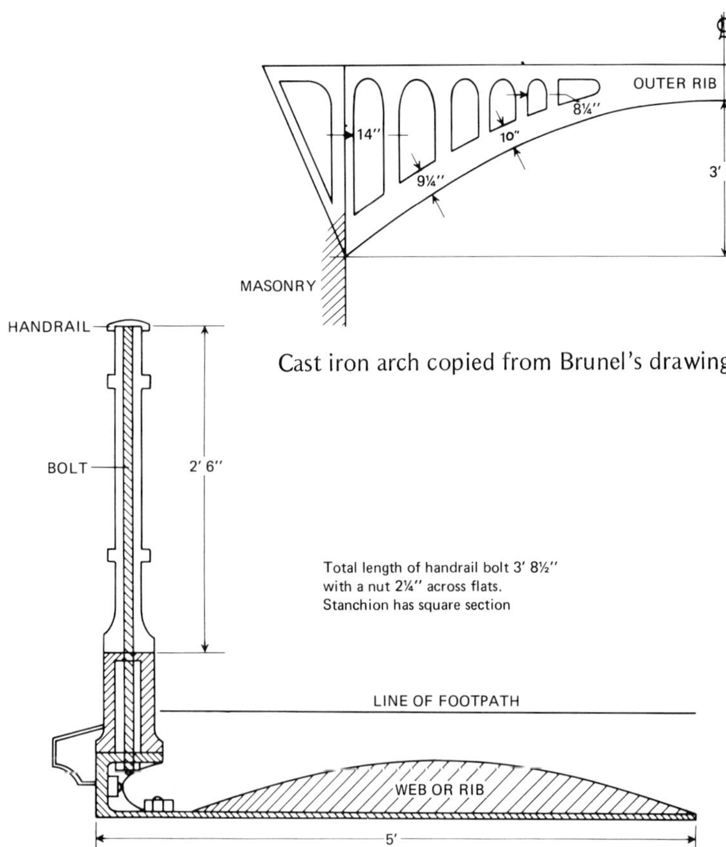

Cast iron arch copied from Brunel's drawing.

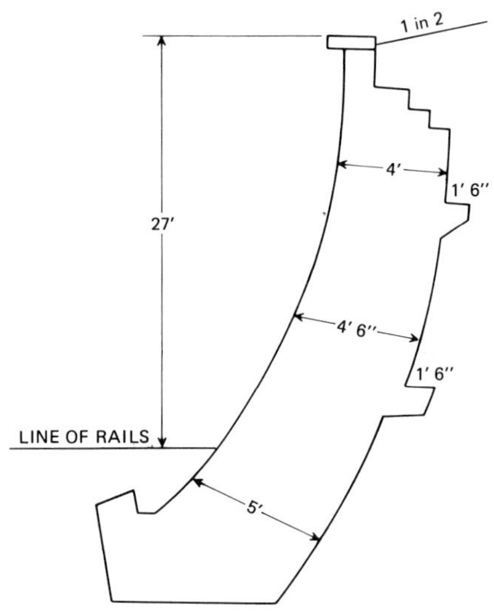

Sydney Gardens. Canal/cutting retaining wall. Weight of masonry varies with height. Its maximum height is 27′ with a thickness of 5′ 0″. Copied from Brunel's drawing.

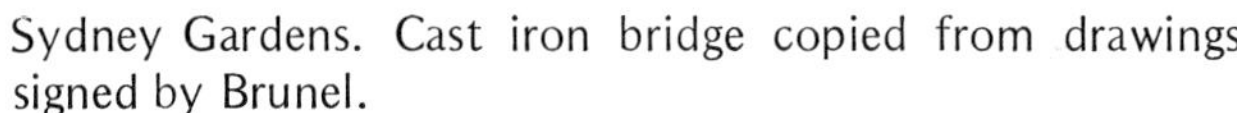

Sydney Gardens. Cast iron bridge copied from drawings signed by Brunel.

The Great Western Railway had to divert the course of the Kennet & Avon Canal and apparently sold a piece of land to be the site of that course to the Canal company. This diagram is copied from the Deed of Conveyance dated 25th June 1839.

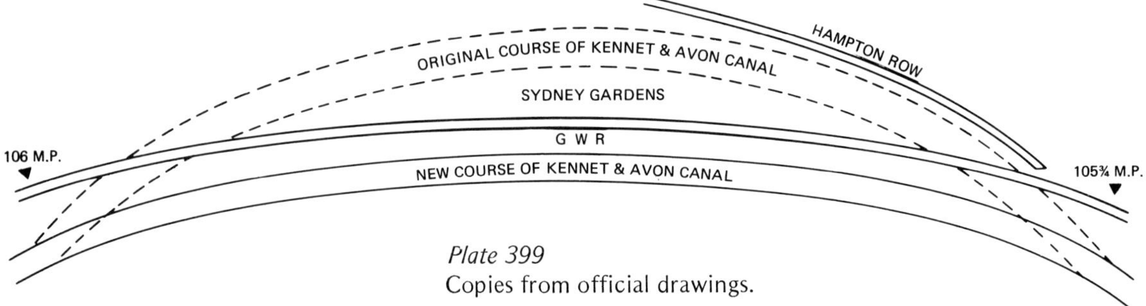

Plate 399
Copies from official drawings.

Plate 400
Stone arch in Sydney Gardens, Bath. This one i immediately east of the cast iron arch. The heigh from rail to spring is 14′ and 8′ 6″ from thence to th crown. The span is 30′. These measurements are th standard for the broad gauge though Brunel did no always follow them. The bridge seen through thi arch is a 29′ 6″ span.

Author 197

Plate 401
Gothic passage under the railway.

Plate 402
Part of South face of viaduct.

Plates 401/402/403
Westwards from Bath station the line passes over a fine viaduct, details of which are illustrated here. Though now largely faced with brick, it was originally stone covered and features Brunel's 'Gothic' style. There are fine arches, heavy buttresses with plate like water tables, crenellated towers and 'arrow slit' windows. Various road improvement schemes have affected parts of it; as far back as 1901, alterations were made, but the viaduct is strong enough and large enough to endure these changes without losing its personality.

Author 1973

Plate 403

Plate 404
Detail of cap. North face of viaduct adjacent to station platform.
Author 1973

Plate 405
Crenellated turrets in north face of viaduct.
Author 1973

Plate 406
General view of south face looking towards the station.
Author 1973

Plate 407
A footpath in Sydney Gardens.
Author 1973

Plate 408
Detail in the south face.
Author 1973

Plate 409
The stone bridge and cutting retaining walls at Parson Street, Bristol, looking east before the 1934 widenings.

British Rail

Plate 410
In 1893 the Great Western Railway widened the lines through Sonning Cutting from two to four tracks. In consequence the timber bridge shown in *plate 356* was demolished and replaced by this graceful cast iron arch which rests on tall, brick abutments. In the distance is the arch carrying the London-Bath road. A 'Star' class engine is approaching on an up express.

British Rail

Plate 411

At Knowle and Dorridge, this handsome, typical brick arch stood until the widenings of 1930. It would appear that the central arch has become very slightly crippled over the years due to movement of the abutments or of foundations.

British Rail

Plate 412

Just after leaving Southall station on the Brentford Branch the line passes under the road and the Grand Junction Canal at Windmill bridge. This branch, having been planned by Brunel, was authorised by Parliament in 1855 and opened to goods traffic on 18th July 1859. The scene is made to look additionally complicated by the arches supporting the cutting walls. The brick wall in the background with its curved steps like the running plate of a Great Western Railway locomotive seems to be a fine piece of work, though not necessarily built by the Company.

British Rail

Plate 413

'lates 413/414/415
ections of the old main line from Padding-
)n to Bristol are distinguished by their
articular type of over-bridge. Plate 413
iows a Bath stone faced bridge with simple
ornice and brick patching on the arch, just
ist of Corsham. Plate 414 is of the bridge at
ie site of Bathampton station, the original
one partly replaced with brick though the
ath stone parapet and curved wing walls are
tact. In plate 415 a bridge just west of
hingley Junction, brick work has almost
ntirely replaced the stone and a Second
'orld War period steel girder bridge has
een added to span the once extensive
dmiralty sidings here.

Author 1973

Plate 414

Plate 415

Plate 416

On the 'Wilts Somerset & Weymouth' railway there was a standard type of bridge built in hard limestone with a soffit profile very similar, if not the same, as those on the Great Western Railway main line. The building material gives these bridges a distinctive character so that they could not be mistaken for a bridge from any part of the early Great Western system. This one is in perfect order, quite unpatched by brick after 120 years and stands at Hawkeridge Junction, Westbury.

Author 1973

Plate 417

A Cornish stone arch over the main lines and goods loop at Tremabe, between Liskeard and Doublebois.

British Rail

Plate 418

Whether this bridge carrying the Corsham-Lacock road was built in Bath stone would be difficult to say, the parapet is, but the remainder is in brick with a pattern of triangular dentils at the parapet base. Judging from the type of brick used, one could say that the bridge was refaced at the turn of the century.

Author 1973

Plate 419

This style of arch was used by Brunel for all the bridges between Bath and Bristol. The masonry side walls are 5′ 6″ thick. The span varied between 29′ and 31′ 6″. From rail level to the spring was 8′ 6″ and from the spring to the crown was 10′ 5″. It is not a good shape as stress forces usually follow the parabolic curve. There is also no room for track slewing owing to the sloping shoulder. Apparently aesthetics had priority.

Author 1974

Plate 420

'West of Bath Gothic.' A culvert under the line which can be reached easily from the A4 at Newton St. Loe traffic lights. Through the arch one can just make out the bridge carrying the Midland Railway line over the Avon into Bath.

Author 1974

Plate 421

Harbury Cutting, south of Leamington, was commenced in 1847. When completed in 1852 it was half a mile long, and no less than 110′ deep, terminating at the south end in a 73 yard tunnel. On the left hand side, as the camera is looking, is Bull Ring Farm, cut off from Harbury village by the railway. This fine, brick bridge was built purely to give the occupants of the farm access to the village. The inset shows a detail of the right hand pier of the main arch with the chamfered corner bricks and blocked apertures.

Author 1974

Plate 421 (inset)

Plates 422/423

Immediately west of Box station the London-Bath road crosses the line on this excellent bridge to plans of Brunel. It has a wide cornice, bead moulded soffit and a keystone decorated with an acanthus leaf pattern, the whole faced in Bath stone.

Author 1974

Plate 422

Plate 423

Plate 424
Bridging the Avon just east of Bradford is this plate steel, riveted girder with what appears to be a modern concrete parapet and railings. The embankment is encased in stone retaining walls to protect the otherwise soft earth from the under-cutting action of the river. Note that these walls are simply but effectively ornamented with pilasters and smooth stone courses in low relief.
Author 1974

Plate 425
A footpath from the village of Box passes through fields to cottages in woodland a mile or so away. Brunel designed this culvert to pass the path under the tracks. Monotony is kept at bay with a segmented arch and bold keystone all in Bath stone.
Author 1974

Plate 426
At Stratton station on the Highworth branch is a rebuilt bridge using concrete with an artificial stone parapet. Only one line of blocks is used which gives a 'shoddy' look. Do take a good look at the station buildings through the arch!
British Rail

Plate 427
Dropping down from the ironstone ridge and Ardley tunnel (1,150 yards), the Great Western Railway's 'New Line' from Princes Risborough to Aynho Junction passed over two viaducts. One was 400 yards long with twenty-four arches spanning 40′ each, the other was 300 yards long with eighteen 40′ spans. The latter is illustrated here. It was built between 1809/10 as part of a new route from Paddington to Birmingham taking eighteen miles off the distance by rail between those two places. It is thought that the main building material used was common brick which has been faced with weatherproof engineer's brick. This type of brick was introduced around 1890 and is made from a special clay fired at a higher than usual temperature which produces a hard, almost glassy finish. The disadvantage of the bricks lies in this, that they require specially skilful laying as they do not absorb any water from the mortar, which remains soft for much longer than normal, thus giving the bricks a chance to slide along the courses and produce bulges. There are no bulges in this structure due, no doubt, to the plentiful supply of craftsmen at the time it was built.

Plate 428
Looking through the central arches of the viaduct one can perceive the slight curve on which the viaduct is built. It seems a wonderful thing to me that such a massive construction should be able to follow such subtle delineations!

Author 1974

Plate 429
One arch of the viaduct. The road to a peaceful farm house passes under here. Looking through the arch one can see the farm and the quiet buildings grouped around, looking the other way you can see the road turn, rise, and fall behind the low hills. It was a wonderfully silent, sunny day when I took these photographs, walking through the fields to this magnificent viaduct.

Author 1974

Plate 430
Transformation at Parson Street. This bridge replaced that shown in *plate 409* around 1933 as the tracks were quadrupled. The arch is probably concrete faced with brick. Beyond the arch is West Depot yard and the junctions to the Portishead line.

British Rail

Girder Bridges

Some of the plates that follow illustrate steel girder bridges built by riveting steel plates together. The riveting was not new, it had been in use in the 18th century, but for many years rivets were thought of as a pin through a hole rather than as a clamp. Brunel was far ahead of his time when he deliberated before a Royal Commission on bridges, saying, "I believe that in riveting plates together where they (the plates) will be exposed to tension, the rivets should not be considered as pins or bolts to be exposed to a cross strain, and holding the plate through which they pass merely as a bolt through the eye of a link, but they should be treated, and disposed accordingly as clamps which compress the plates powerfully together, and produce an adhesion laying hold of the surface of the enclosed plate as if in a vice; to produce this effect the rivets must be of large diameter, which is well known to make the strongest work, and the workmanship generally must be good; but with proper precautions and the rivets judiciously disposed, and by crossing the joints of the different plates I believe there is hardly any limit to the approach which may be made to obtaining the entire strength of the plates, and such riveting, I believe, will be entirely unaffected by ordinary vibration or by oxidation." Brunel here was foreshadowing the modern friction-grip bolted joint. In this speech, and the very fact that a Royal Commission was investigating bridges, one gets the distinct impression that railway construction in the first half of the 19th century was operating at the extreme edge of scientific knowledge, and that it advanced knowledge as rapidly as in later years war has done. In the case of Brunel and this particular speech, he was beyond accepted science, operating in a sphere of his own. By the late 19th century riveted plates had been used for bridges, and more important, ships' hulls. Important because they are subject to great strain and therefore the technology to build such hulls needed to be more advanced than to build a bridge by riveting. Brunel, of course, built the first iron, riveted hull. The rivets were driven in red hot and hammered up tight against the metal plates. Thus when they cooled and therefore contracted they clamped the plates tightly together. A hot riveted bridge was robust, had some degree of flex to act as a "safety valve" if bad strains were imposed but was very heavy and required a great deal of equipment to build. Many different types of steel sections were needed to build such a bridge; equal angle, unequal angles, tees, channels and other rolled sections. Thousands of holes had to be centre-popped, drilled and reamered. The drawings for the bridge were even expensive to produce. Templates were necessary to site the holes accurately and the template loft required a large area of floor space with many men employed. The riveting gangs had their boys, who carried and threw the red hot rivets from the heating furnace to the riveters. This was a fine art, throwing and catching a single rivet with speed and dexterity so that it would not have cooled before it was driven in and closed up. There were pom-pom gun riveters, rivet squeezers, stitching bolts, crows foot chisels and all manner of ancillary equipment. The riveter man needed a solid footing and something to brace his back against as he walloped rivets or held a pom-pom gun tool. This required strong scaffolding to every part of the bridge, which could be a terrific additional expense in the construction costs. After the Second World War it was very difficult to get riveters and this accelerated the adoption of the welded, prefabricated steel bridge. Though never actually used by the Great Western Railway, bridges using this technique were designed at Paddington by men who had previously worked for that Company; indeed for years after nationalisation, Western Region of British Railways was the Great Western in disguise. Welding was cheaper and lighter than riveting. It dispensed with a host of ancillary equipment and used less steel. In the early days of the technique there had been fears for safety. A weld cannot be checked for flaws, just like cast iron a century earlier. But the development of radiography and ultra-sonic testing removed this objection. Welds are quite rigid, have no "give" and therefore the designer must be very careful and take all stresses and strains into account in his calculations, which was not the practice in earlier riveting. Given this care a welded bridge is just as reliable as the riveted kind, costs less at first and requires less maintenance. The first welded bridge on the Western Region was over the Holy Brook, a few miles west of Reading on the "Berks and Hants" line. This was erected in 1952. In 1960 the decision was taken to rebuild the Wye bridge at Chepstow and it was decided that this too should be a welded, prefabricated structure. The various parts were welded at Fairfield's yard, Chepstow, the descendants of the firm that built much of the ironwork for Brunel's bridge in 1852. On site the members were bolted together using the "Torshear" bolt. This was the invention of a small engineering firm at Banbury who had been producing precision machine tools for high class firms like Rolls Royce. The bolt has a groove cut in it so that at a certain tension, as the nut is being tightened, the bolt breaks leaving the assembly tightened to exact requirements. These are more expensive than ordinary bolts but far fewer are needed and no skilled labour is required, or even physical strength in tightening them, a wrench driven by compressed air is used to turn the nut. These bolts, used in some of the greatest bridges in the world, were first used by the Western Region of British Railways in a bridge at Wheatley in 1960. Western Region was not the "Great Western" in disguise for nothing—they really did pioneer engineering techniques in the tradition of Brunel. The Wheatley bridge was a second span to an existing bridge as the County Council were going to build the A40, at that point, into a dual carriage way. The existing span was a riveted bridge built in 1927. The comparative figures of these spans are interesting.

	Wheatley 1927	Wheatley 1960
Floor	Plate deck with asphalt	Plate deck with waterproofing
Design	Riveted	Welded
Basic tensile stress	8.00 tons/in^2	9.00 tons/in^2
Live load inc. impact	340 tons	454 tons
Weight of one steel truss	33.43 tons	21.96 tons
Complete span exc. bearings	107.29 tons	85.80 tons

In the case of the Chepstow bridge, the Brunel structure had weighed 558 tons without track and ballast, the 1962 bridge weighs 292 tons.

Plate 431
This bridge, at Shifnal, was built for the Shrewsbury and Birmingham Railway between 1846-49, by William Baker, a pupil of Robert Stephenson. Stephenson was once in trouble for using cast iron composite beams in a bridge over the river Dee. The bridge collapsed. He had bolted three, straight, cast iron beams together to span a 60 ft. gap. In this straight form the iron was subject to tension when loaded and, being unable to flex, snapped. Shortly after the Dee bridge disaster, Baker erected these composite, cast iron arches. They are built up in three pieces, the junctions being covered by rectangular caps. Cast iron in arch form is perfectly safe as it is subject only to compression, and provided it is kept painted and free from rust it will last indefinitely. The openwork filling the spandrels is made in sections of cast iron bolted together, each rib through the bridge having one of these sections resting upon it and rising to track bed level. In 1948 or 1949 this fine bridge was replaced with a mundane plate steel girder type span.

British Rail

Plate 432

About a mile to the west of Dolgellau the Great Western renewed an old Cambrian Railway bridge with this standardised steel plate girder bridge. It is spanning Afon Wnion.

British Rail

Plate 434
Plate girders on cast iron cylinder type piers over the estuary of the river Gwendraeth near Kidwelly. The piers look as if they might have been designed by Brunel or one of his assistants.

British Rail

Plate 433
◀ Between Devizes station and Bromham and Rowde Halt the line crossed the Kennet and Avon Canal (which had just come down its marvellous 'staircase locks' on Dunkirk Hill) on the bridge, known enigmatically as 'Foxhanger'. This bridge was built in 1894 to replace one with a lifting span.

British Rail

Plate 435
A standard plate steel riveted girder bridge near Chipping Campden. The outer plate girder is deep, and has stiffening webs. Under the bridge are two rail bearer girders spanning the road and transverse to these are many cross girders. Both types of girder are of 'I' section.

British Rail

Plate 436
The Bourne End viaduct, built by the Great Marlow Railway, officially, but doubtless designed at Paddington. It was opened on the 28th June 1873. The manner of its construction follows closely that of the earlier timber viaduct on the Oxford Railway of 1843 at Nuneham Reach. See *plate 437.*

British Rail

Plate 437
This was the bridge built to replace that shown above, the timbers of which can be seen in the background.

British Rail 29.10.95

Plate 438
Cast or wrought iron valances on the bridge over Foregate Street, Worcester, give the impression that an arch is carrying the rails across the street, but they are in fact carried on a bed of girders. The bridge was reconstructed thus in 1908. Four girders span the 50′ 6″ gap with no support apart from their deep channel shape. Transversely, there are channel girders closely spaced. If this is the case, as it appears to be, then this is a remarkable bridge. The photograph shows the bridge before the tops of the pilasters were rebuilt in cast iron.

British Rail

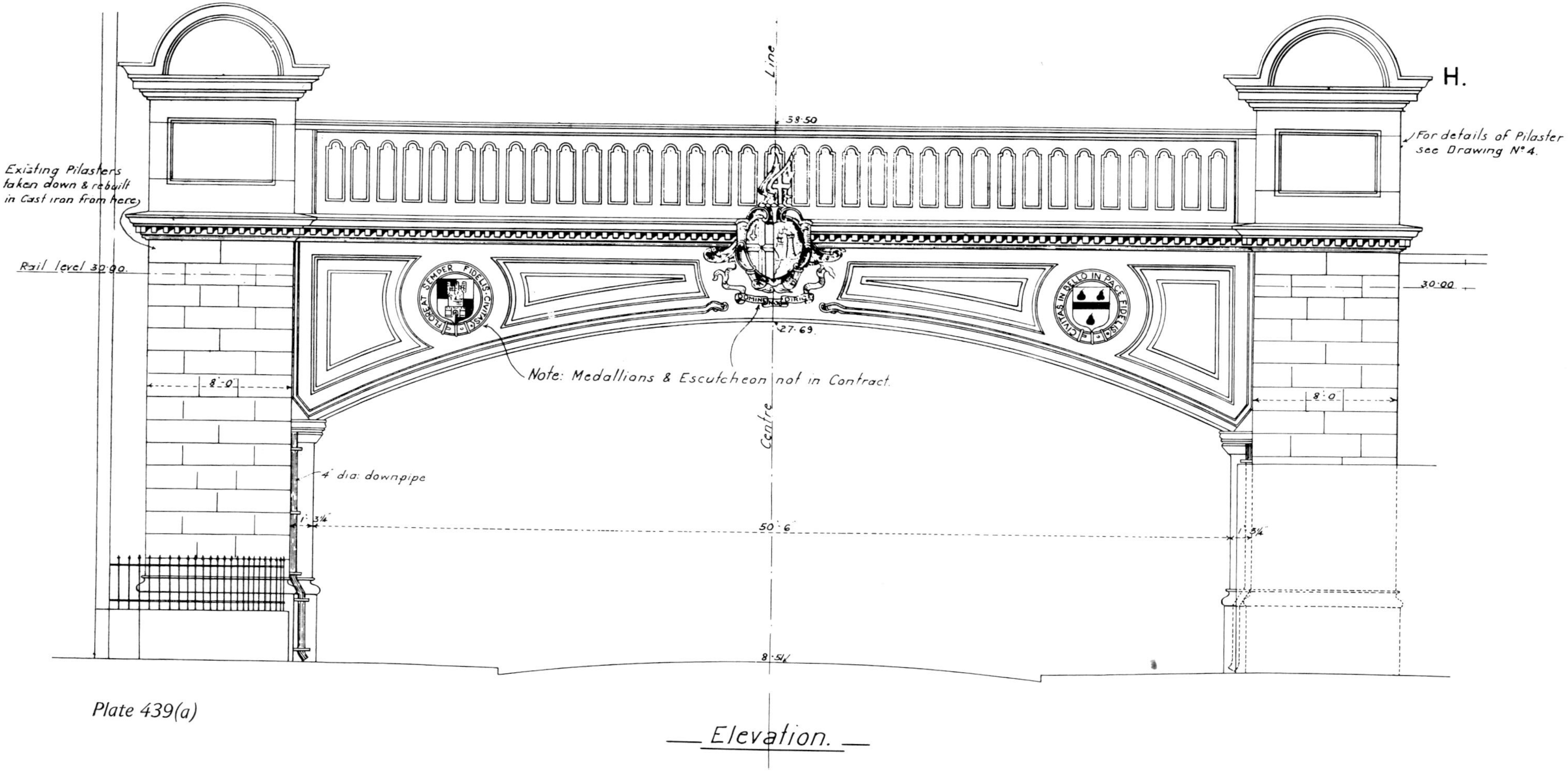

H.

Existing Pilasters taken down & rebuilt in Cast iron from here

For details of Pilaster see Drawing N° 4.

Rail level 30·90.

30·00

38·50

27·69

Centre Line

Note: Medallions & Escutcheon not in Contract.

8′·0″

8′·0″

4″ dia: downpipe

1′·3¼″

50′·6″

1′·3¼″

8′·5¼″

Plate 439(a)

Elevation.

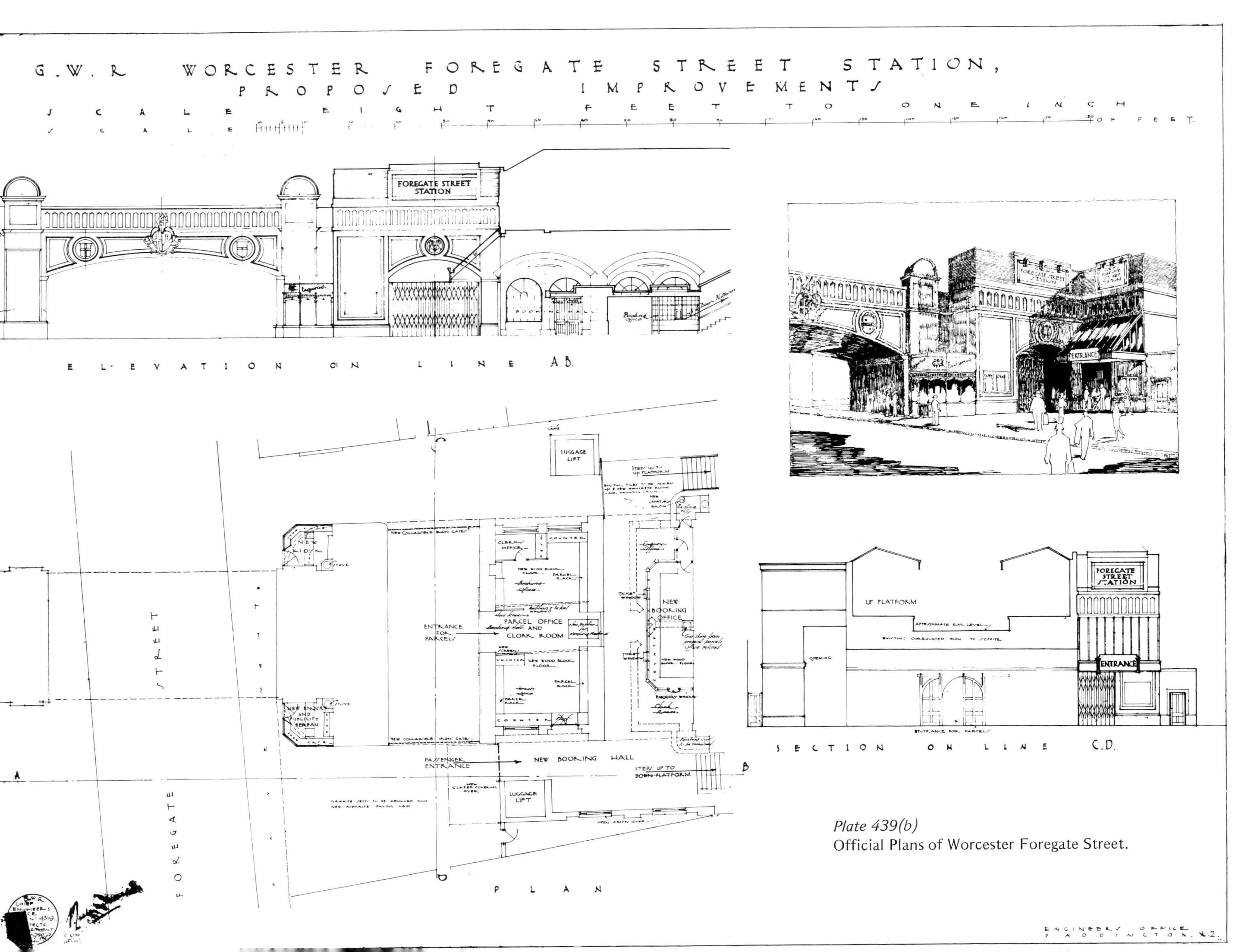

Plate 439(b)
Official Plans of Worcester Foregate Street.

Plates 440/441

The girders employed in the 'bow' of Westbourne bridge were the longest to have been used on the Great Western Railway since the erection of the Royal Albert Bridge at Saltash. The steel, 'N' girder bridge has two spans sharing a common central pier. The southern girders are about 230' long and the northern, furthest from the camera, is about 240' long. The roadway across the bridge is 50' wide. Cast iron ornaments adorn each end of the bridge and the central columns, but though these are handsome, engineers frown on them as they prevent the painters from getting at the girder ends. The present bridge replaced an eleven arch brick construction which was seriously hampering track improvements in the vicinity of Paddington station. The total weight of the two spans is no less than 2,150 tons.

British Rail

Plates 442/443
Fine riveting on the river Thames bridge near Appleford Halt.
Author 1973

Plate 444
Originally the river was bridged at this point by a timber viaduct similar to that shown in *plate 436.* About 1860 this was replaced with a wrought iron plate girder construction on screw girders. In fact there were two such bridges, built side by side, for the up and the down line respectively. In 1929 the decision was taken to replace this ancient bridge as it was slowly sinking into the river and the ballast piled on the bridge to keep the track level with that on the 'land' at each side was getting ridiculously high. A similar bridge a few miles to the north at Nuneham (Radley) had been replaced in 1907. Coming from the south, the line passes over four brick arches with spans of 18′, then the 'bow string' bridge spanning 168′ and finally, on the Oxfordshire side one brick arch of 14′ span. The steel bridge rests on roller bearings. It was erected by Messrs. Jackman of Slough.
British Rail

Plate 445
'Bow and string' bridge over the tracks at Taunton West Junction.

British Rail

Plate 446

Brunel designed in 1852 the first lifting bridge over the Teify at Carmarthen for the South Wales Railway. The single lifting span was approached by a timber viaduct on both sides totalling thirteen spans covering 385′. The present bridge, illustrated here, was built during 1909/11 and is a steel bascule bridge. In the action of rising the span it also rolls back from the waters edge to give 50′ of clear waterway. The fixed spans of the bridge have a headroom of 9′. They are constructed of steel plate girders, cross girders, rail bearers and steel trough decking resting on cast iron cylindrical piers at 60′ centres. There is a lattice work parapet. The end of the spans furthest from the lifting section widens to accommodate the diverging tracks of the rail junction into or avoiding Carmarthen Town, the points being situated on the bridge. Concerning the bascule portion one can describe the main girders as steel lattice work tapering eastwards to meet the fixed span. The superstructure is steel plate cross girders and rail bearers with intermediate 'T' bearers. The decking is of timber and the space between those large rectangular boxes is braced to give lateral stiffness against the wind. Alternate cross girders project from beneath the bridge to give support to diagonal outriggers to the main girders. The rectangular boxes referred to are known as 'Kentledge' or balance boxes. These are filled with cast iron blocks run in with asphalt. During construction additional iron blocks were attached to the boxes to achieve an exact balance. The advantage of this type of bridge is that the means of raising the span are situated at its rolling centre and therefore a comparatively small amount of energy is required for its operation. A cast steel rack on the curved end of the bridge, (see *plate 447*) is engaged by a pinion driven through differential gearing by an electric motor. The apparatus is very low geared so that a small power plant is capable of performing the task. Current for the motor is, or was, supplied by a battery of accumulators charged by a paraffin engine driving a dynamo. In case of failures a handwinch was also provided; and thereby, doubtless, hangs a tale. I think the simplicity of operation and independence from a central supply of power are two very important factors in this bridge and points well worth consideration today in our highly technical, specialised world. The bridge was opened for traffic on 11th July 1911 having been tested by four, six coupled tank engines when the structure was measured to have deflected $\frac{3}{8}$ th inch. The first train over the new bridge was a Fishguard Ocean Liner special carrying passengers from a Booth Line trans-Atlantic liner.

Plate 447

G.W.R. GLOUCESTER DOCKS BRANCH.
LLANTHONY SWING BRIDGE AT 0M 74CHS
Level of High Water at Ordinary Spring Tides
Low Water at Bridge

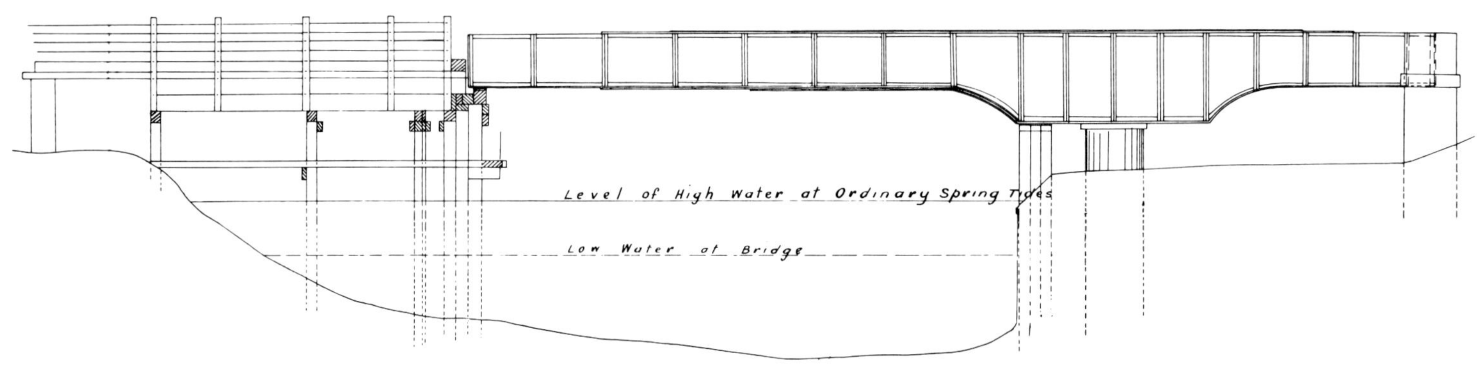

Plate 448
Official drawing of a swing bridge.
British Rail

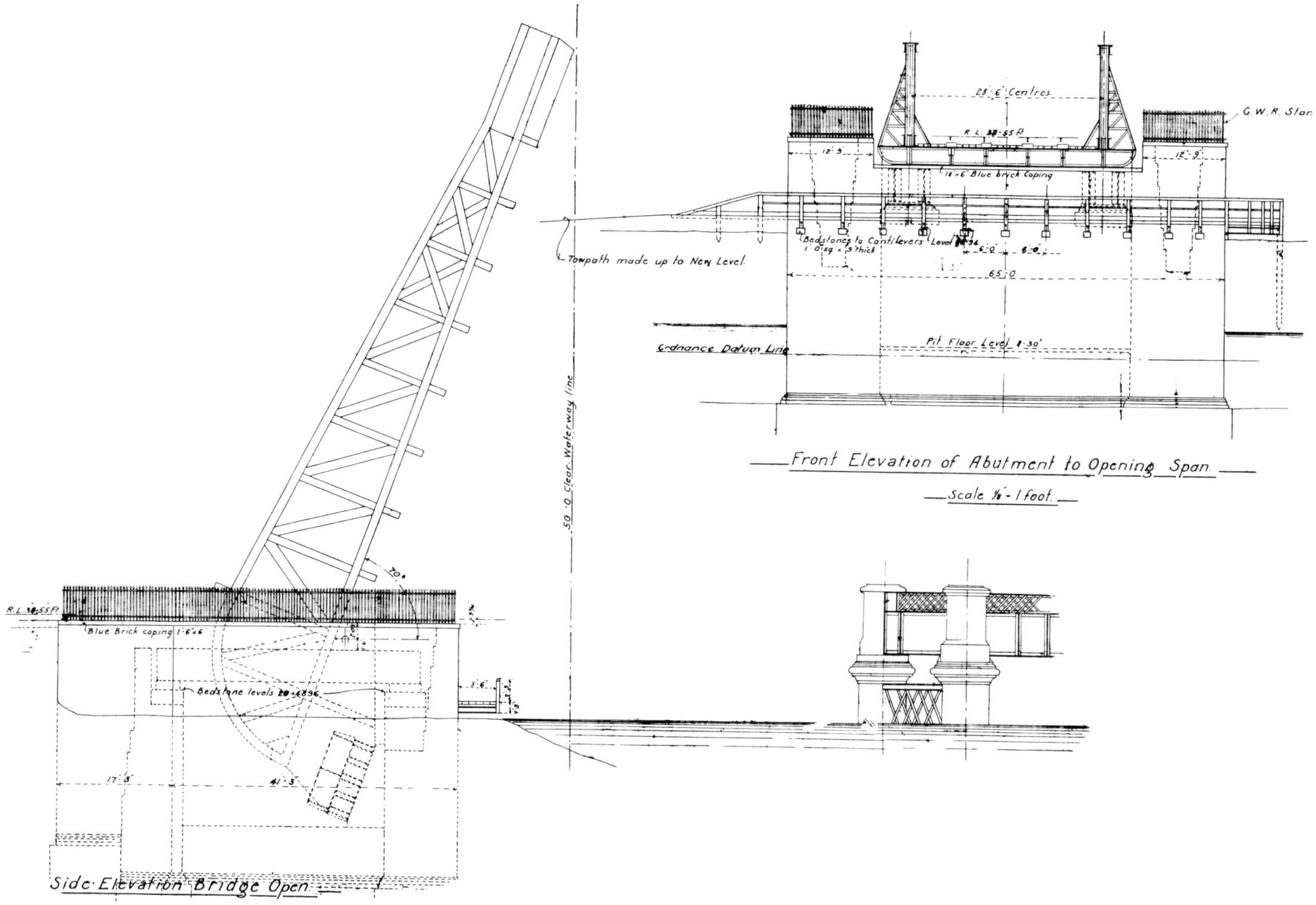

28' 6" Centres
12' 9"
12' 9"
Towpath made up to New Level.
65' 0
Pit Floor Level
Ordnance Datum Line
Front Elevation of Abutment to Opening Span
Scale 1/8" - 1 foot
50' 0" Clear Waterway line
Blue Brick coping 1'6"x6"
Side Elevation Bridge Open

C.W.R. Bridge over River Avon at 106M 12C Nearest Station Evesham.

Scales 1/8" & 1/4" to 1 Foot

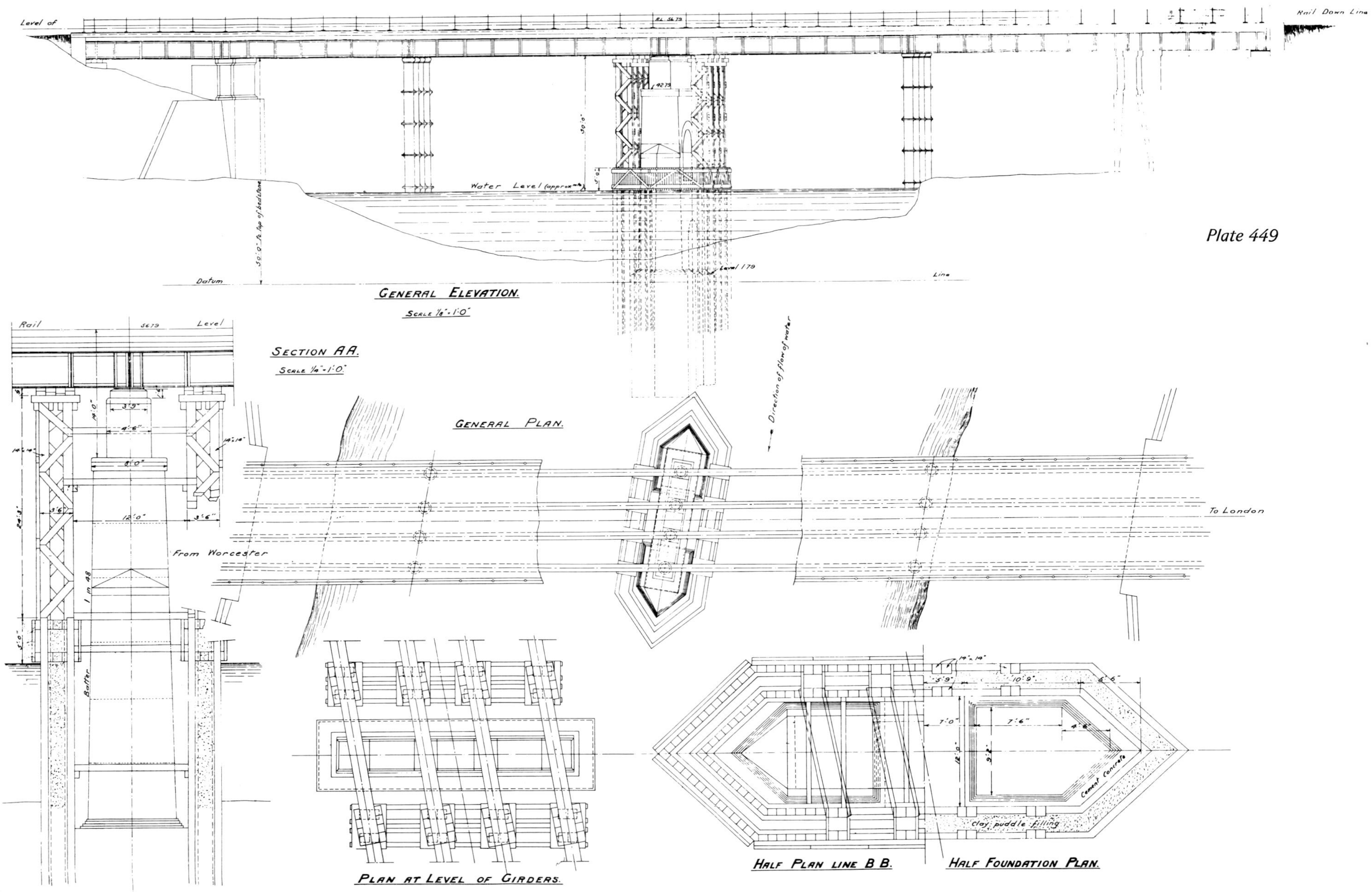

Plate 449

Level of Rail Down Line

R.L. 56.73

42.73

30'.0"

5'.0"

Water Level (approx.)

30'.0" to top of bedstone

Level 17.9

Datum Line

General Elevation.

Scale 1/8" - 1'.0"

Rail 56.79 Level

Section AA.

Scale 1/4" - 1'.0"

3'.9"

4'.6"

8'.0"

14'.0"

14" x 14"

24'.3"

3'.6"

12'.0"

1 in 48

Batter

5'.0"

From Worcester

General Plan.

Direction of flow of water

To London

Plan at Level of Girders.

5'.9"

10'.9"

7'.0"

7'.6"

4'.6"

12'.0"

9'.2"

Cement Concrete

Clay puddle filling

Half Plan line B B.

Half Foundation Plan.

Chapter Five

Engine Sheds and Water Towers

THE FIRST ENGINE SHED AT PADDINGTON.

Plate 450
Basingstoke shed, a view taken from the Great Western Railway signal box at that station. The building is constructed in timber and brick and was open for traffic about 1850. Mixed gauge tracks were laid in the shed. Facing the camera, the wall is of timber but the rear wall is built in brick, all under a slated, hip gabled, roof. The shape of the water tower and its plinth have something in common with that at Neyland (*plate 453*). Against the plinth is the timber coaling stage, open to the weather, and upon this one can see three iron tubs for coal and the little crane for lifting and swinging them onto the low tenders of early locomotives. Though they would reach over a little 2,500 gallon tender, I should think that coaling a 3,500 gallon tender would have been difficult and almost impossible where a 4,500 gallon tender was concerned.
British Rail

Plate 451
A timber framed and weatherboarded shed similar to that at Oxford and probably built around the same time (circa 1850). The location is unknown but I believe it is in the Newport area.
British Rail

Plate 452
Chippenham shed was opened in 1858, and while the roof was almost certainly renewed during its 106 year existence it seems equally certain that the walls were never altered.

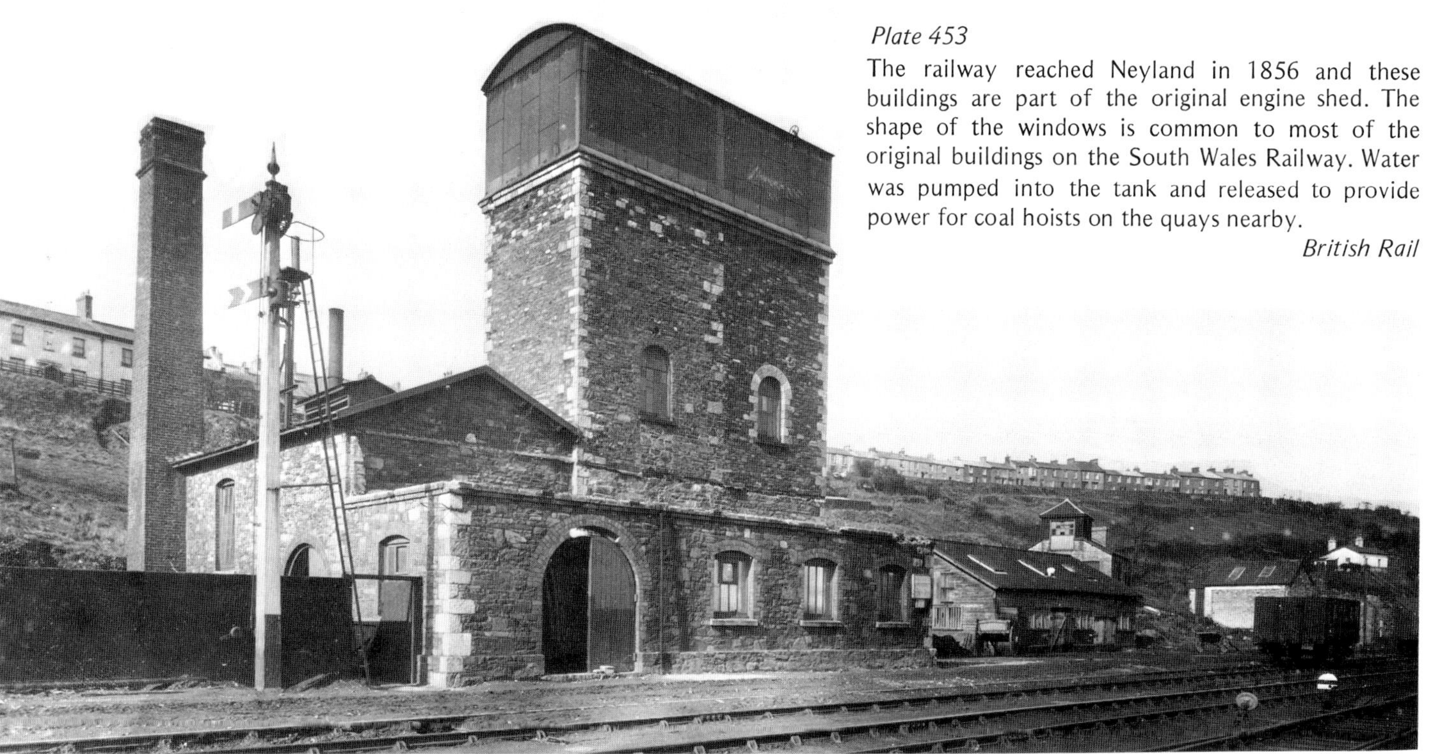

Plate 453
The railway reached Neyland in 1856 and these buildings are part of the original engine shed. The shape of the windows is common to most of the original buildings on the South Wales Railway. Water was pumped into the tank and released to provide power for coal hoists on the quays nearby.

British Rail

Plate 454

One of the four turntables inside the round house at Old Oak Common shed. 'Old Oak' was the largest locomotive shed on the Great Western Railway and was built in the standard pattern. This was a cunning device to be put together in a single unit or grouped, as shown here, into four, without altering the basic design. The four turntables were interconnected by a line of rails so that an engine could move from one to the other and gain access to any corner of the building. A 'road' also came in through the door in the left and right hand wall to a turntable, one such 'road' leading directly to the repair shops. Thus there was an 'escape road' if the main entrance to the shed was blocked. At a busy shed such as this with a constant turnover of important locomotives for the express train working out of Paddington, it was essential that an engine should never be blocked in. The shed was opened to traffic in March 1906, after four years building work, and judging by the smoke free appearance of the ventilators this photograph was taken before the opening.

British Rail

Plate 455

A panoramic view of the running and maintenance depot at Old Oak Common. The coal stage and water tower were the largest on the Great Western Railway and double track coaling roads, for standing the coal wagons, passed beneath the tank, allowing two ranks of engines to be coaled at once. At the buffer end of the coal ramp is the shed master's office and stores; to the left is another detached building, the general office where a platoon of clerks were kept busy with time sheets, duty logs and maintenance records of the engines, to name but a few of their duties. The engine shed is seen behind the general office and behind the arches of the coal ramp is the repair shop.

British Rail

Plate 456

A standard coal stage at Oxley. This seems to me to be a triumph of draughtsmanship. Bear in mind that, although it is a 'Churchward' standard, some unknown designer prepared the plans and submitted them to 'the Chief', who passed them, thus initiating the 'Churchward' standard water tower. He has relieved the monotony of the massive brick bulk supporting the terrific weight of tank and water, by introducing sunken panels with corresponding pillars, yellow brick arches over windows, and a strong, bull nosed brick, string course. The three courses of brick immediately beneath the tank, while utterly functional, do lend a decorative effect as do the round tops of the tanks, which are probably there to run off rain water and prevent puddles forming which would rust the metal. The snap headed rivets make a pattern which is both functional and decorative, their duty being to clamp the steel plates tightly together and to rigidly hold the wall support brackets on the inside of the tank.

British Rail

END ELEVATION A
FRONT ELEVATION
END ELEVATION B
PLAN AT COALING LEVEL
REAR ELEVATION
CROSS SECTION
74250 Gallon
Water Tank
Coaling
Level
Store
steel floor
Tips
Overflow
Outlet
Elec. Box
Inlet
Messrooms &
Stores under
paved
slope
Notes
1. Colour Scheme
Cream – Tank, Coaling Canopy.
Brown – Doors, Tank Lining
2 Dimensions taken
from Didcot M.P.D.
G.W.R. COALING STAGE
Scale
Drawn
Date
Surveyed
DRG. NO.
DID/70/2

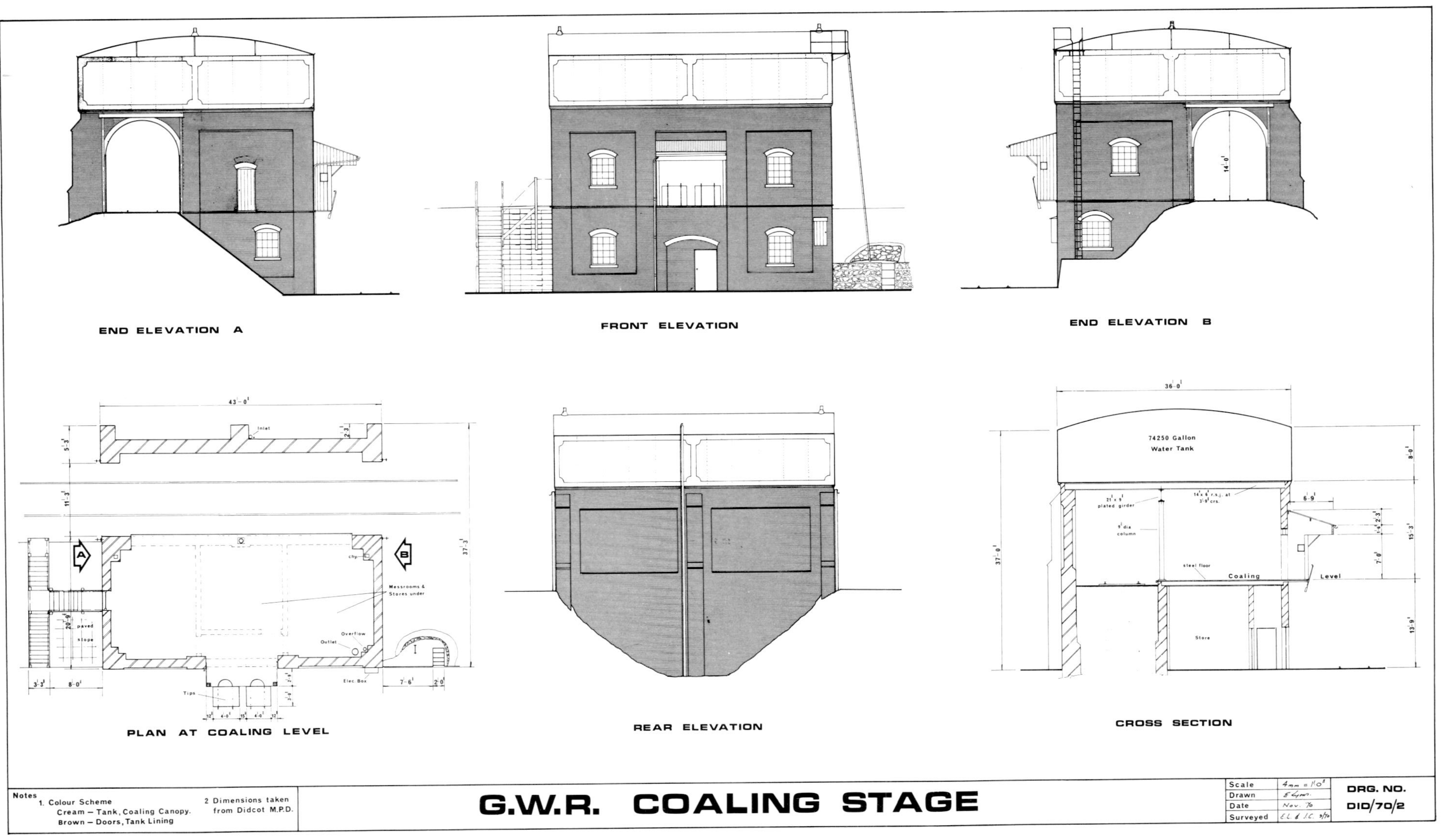

Plate 457

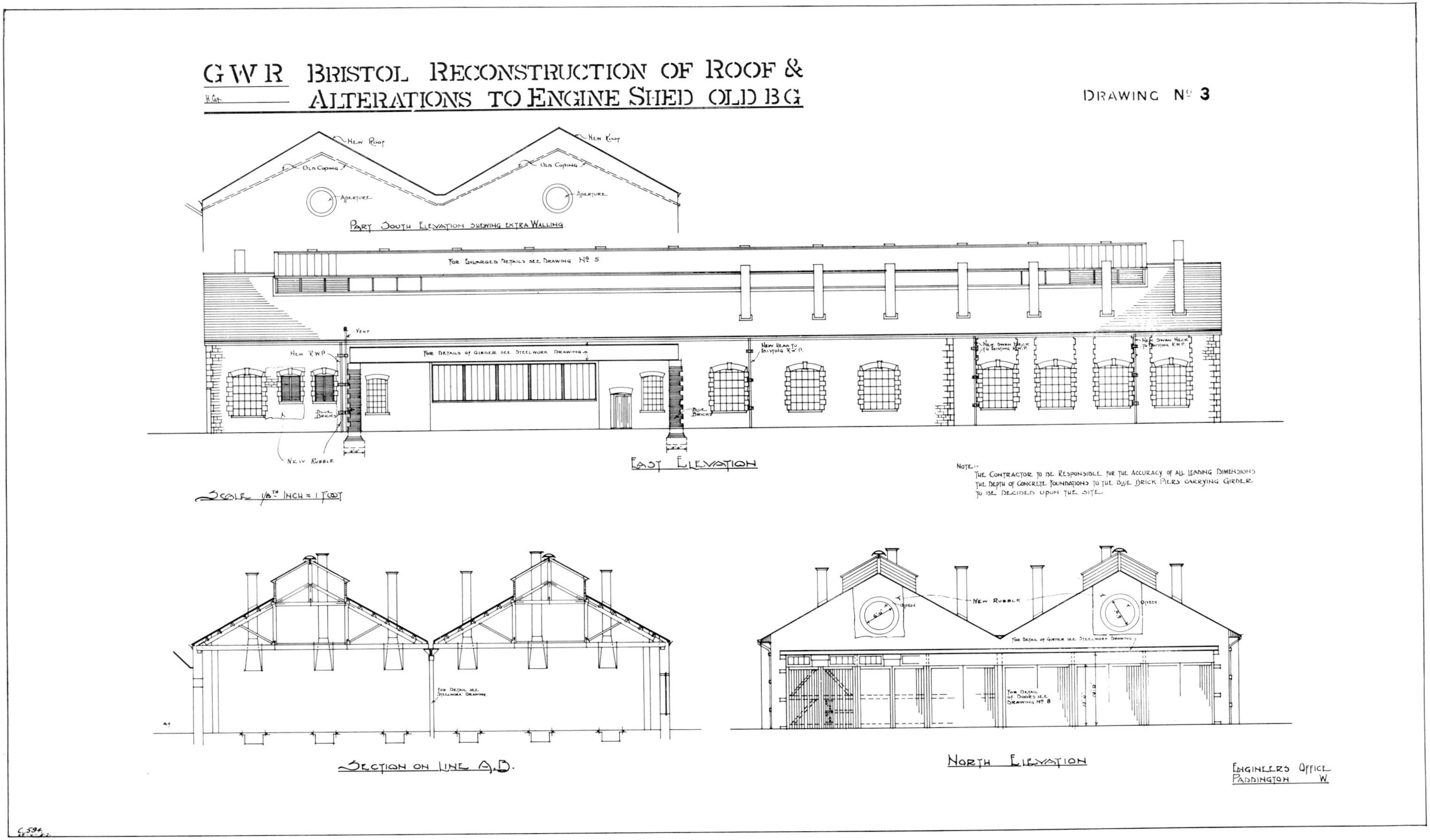

GWR BRISTOL RECONSTRUCTION OF ROOF & ALTERATIONS TO ENGINE SHED OLD BG

DRAWING No 3

New Roof
Old Coping
Aperture

PART SOUTH ELEVATION SHEWING EXTRA WALLING

For enlarged details see Drawing No 5

Vent
New R.W.P.
For details of girder see Steelwork Drawing
New head to existing R.W.P.
New swan neck to existing R.W.P.
Blue bricks
New Rubble

EAST ELEVATION

SCALE 1/8TH INCH = 1 FOOT

NOTE:- The Contractor to be responsible for the accuracy of all leading dimensions. The depth of concrete foundations to the blue brick piers carrying girder to be decided upon the site.

For detail see Steelwork Drawing

SECTION ON LINE A.B.

New Rubble
Open
For detail of girder see Steelwork Drawing
For detail of doors see Drawing No 8

NORTH ELEVATION

Engineers Office
Paddington W.

Plate 458
Official drawing.

Plate 459

Severn Tunnel Junction shed as new in 1908. The building is to Churchward's standard pattern and consisted of two bays covering four tracks which terminate within the building. There is no repair shop that one can see and no water softening plant. The shed, with the coaling plant and water tank form only the very basic facilities for locomotives. Those who knew the place during the 1930's and after may be surprised to see (a) how clean the shed looked, and (b) how small it was. In 1931 an additional bay covering two more tracks was built and perhaps at that time all the shed lines were taken through the building instead of terminating inside. In later years a water softening plant and repair shop was added and a great many sidings filled the empty space shown in the foreground of this picture.

British Rail

Plate 460
Reading shed.
British Rail

Plate 461
Swindon stock shed.
British Rail

Plate 462
Marlborough High Level station engine shed and water tower.
Author 1962

Plate 463
Wallingford engine shed.
Colin Judge

Plate 464

Oswestry shed was originally built by the Cambrian Railway and was modernised and extended over the years after 1929 by the Great Western Railway. This coal stage was built by the latter, in 1928. It seems likely that the water tank was sent second-hand to Oswestry from another shed. In the background can be seen the old Cambrian shed and two ex-Cambrian locomotives. One of these, a 4-4-0, is standing by the sand drying furnace.

British Rail

Plate 465

Cardiff, Cathays shed has a steel framed, brick filled coal stage dating from the 1929 period of Government loans for railway improvements. Looking at this makes one realise that the Churchward stages were very handsome!

British Rail

Plate 466

Kidderminster coal stage was another installation built during the Loans and Guarantee Act period of the 1930's. The method of construction is unusual though there were similar designs, at Cheltenham for instance. On the roof, right of the handrail is a pulley from which is suspended a ball and chain. The chain goes inside the tank terminating in a float so that the rise and fall of the internal water level is imitated by the position of the ball outside. This tank appears to be full.

British Rail

SECTIONAL ELEVATION A·A
END ELEVATION C
SIDE ELEVATION B
END ELEVATION D
doors open
Shed Master
Foremen
Lobby
Stores
Enginemen
Boilersmith & Fitters
Mechanics
Chargeman Cleaner
Shedmen
Washroom
Toilet
sliding door
ARRANGEMENT OF ACCOMMODATION
Timber Rafters
EAVES BEAM
TRUSSES
purlin runs & smoke troughs omitted
VALLEY BEAM
ROOF
temporary
side
21 Bays at 10·0' – 210·0'
PLAN
glazing
smoke vents
walkway
corrugated metal sheeting on boards
valley gutter
asbestos slates on boards
smoke troughs
corrugated asbestos sheeting
beam
post
CROSS SECTION
scale 4mm – 1·0'
Notes
1. Colour Scheme
Grey – Slates, Sheeting & Smoke Vents
Brown – Doors
2. Dimensions taken from Didcot M.P.D.
G.W.R. STANDARD RUNNING SHED (1932)
Scale 2mm = 1·0'
Drawn
Date
Surveyed
DRG. NO.
DID/70/1

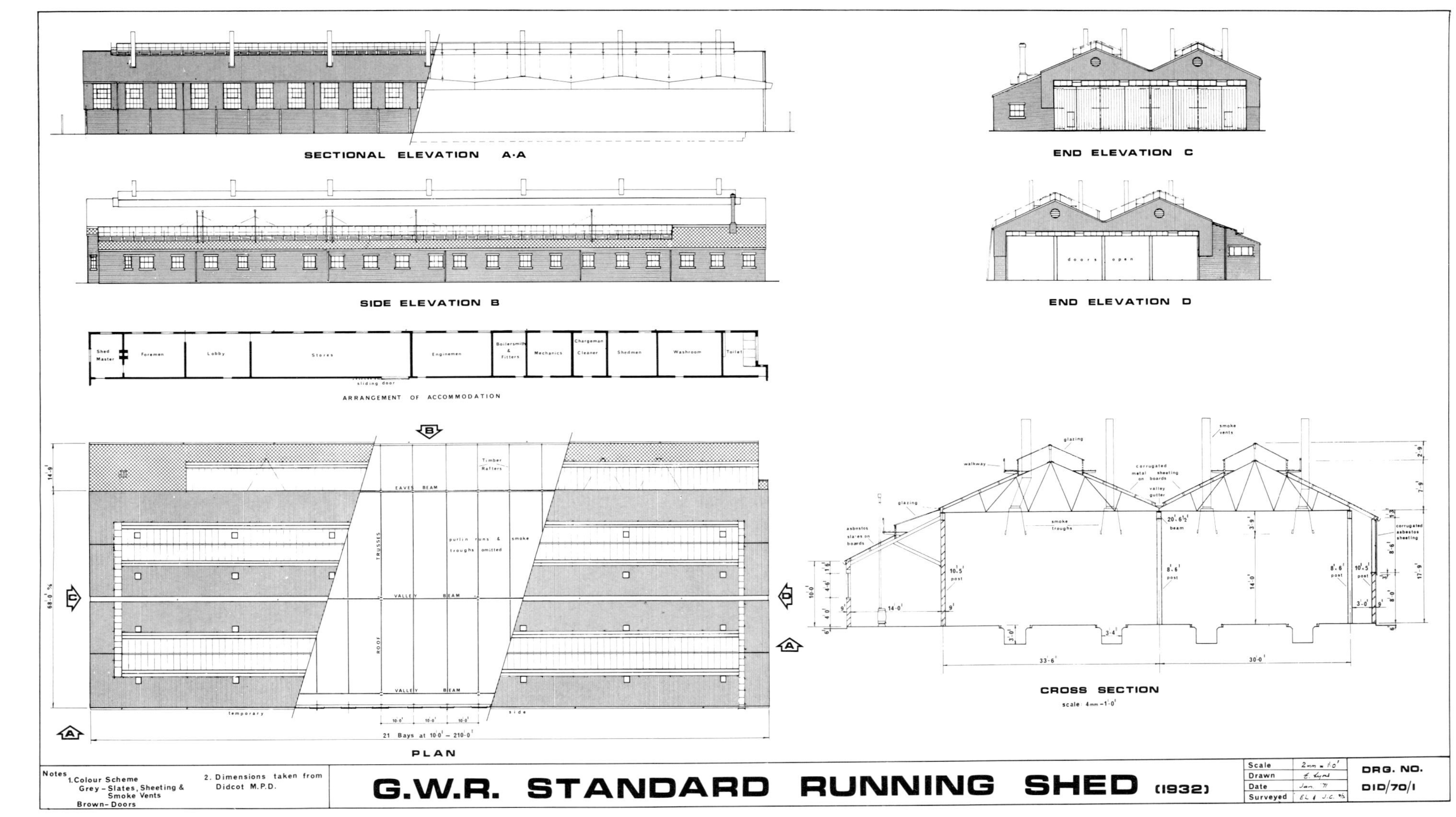

Plate 467

SIDE ELEVATION A
SIDE ELEVATION B
7 Bays at 12'0" = 84'0"
stores
stove
Gable format as other end
pit
coal
Corrugated Metal Sheeting
SECTIONAL PLAN
Corrugated Asbestos Sheeting
GABLE ELEVATION
Glazing
Asbestos Slates
10 x 6 posts
9' walls
50ton Hoist
Boiler House
SECTION C-C
Notes.
1. Colour Scheme
Grey - Slates & Sheeting
Brown - Doors
Black - Boiler House
2. Dimensions taken from Didcot M.P.D.
G.W.R. STANDARD REPAIR SHOP (1932)
Scale
Drawn
Date
Surveyed
DRG. NO.
DID/70/3
Plate 468

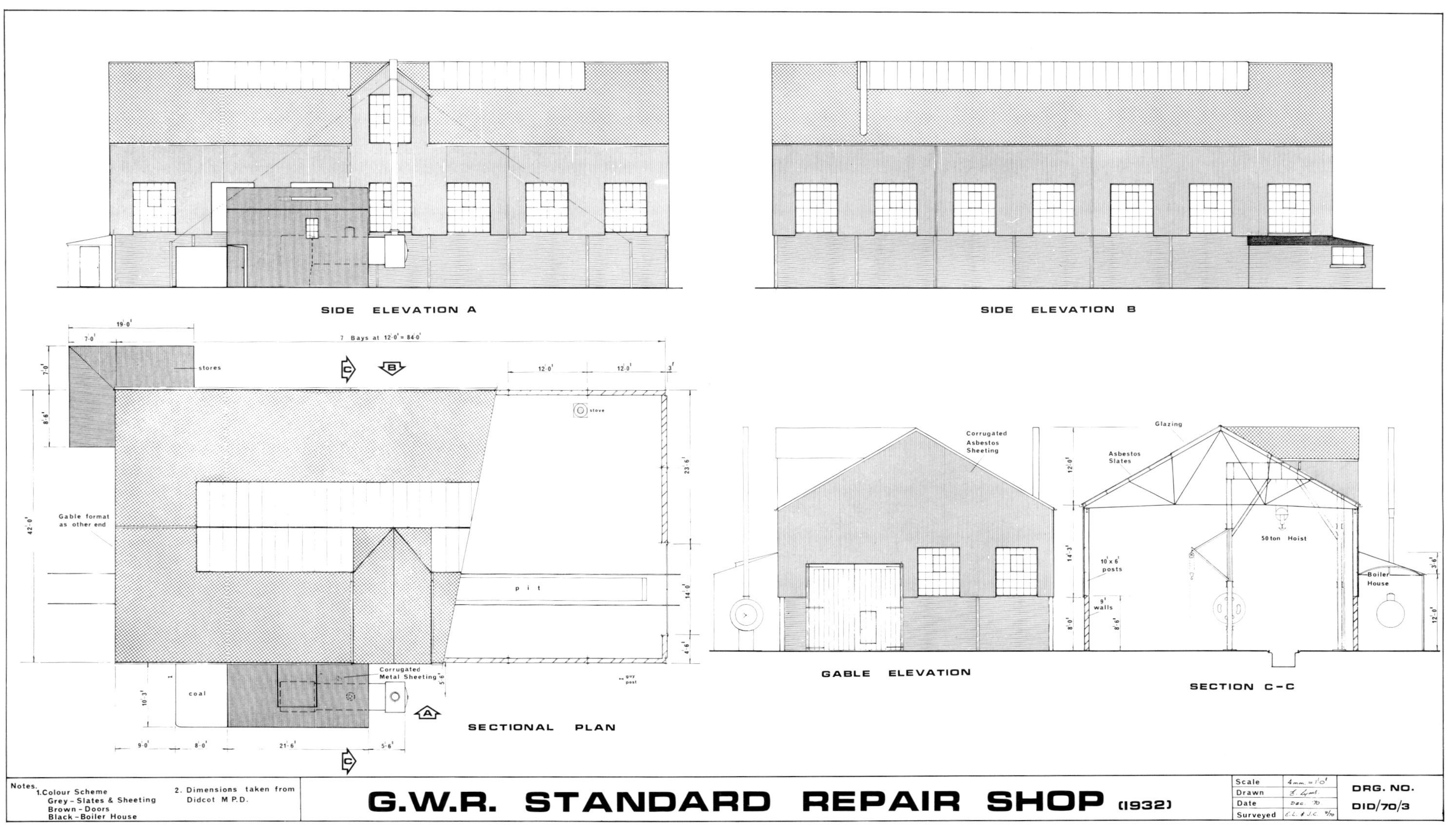

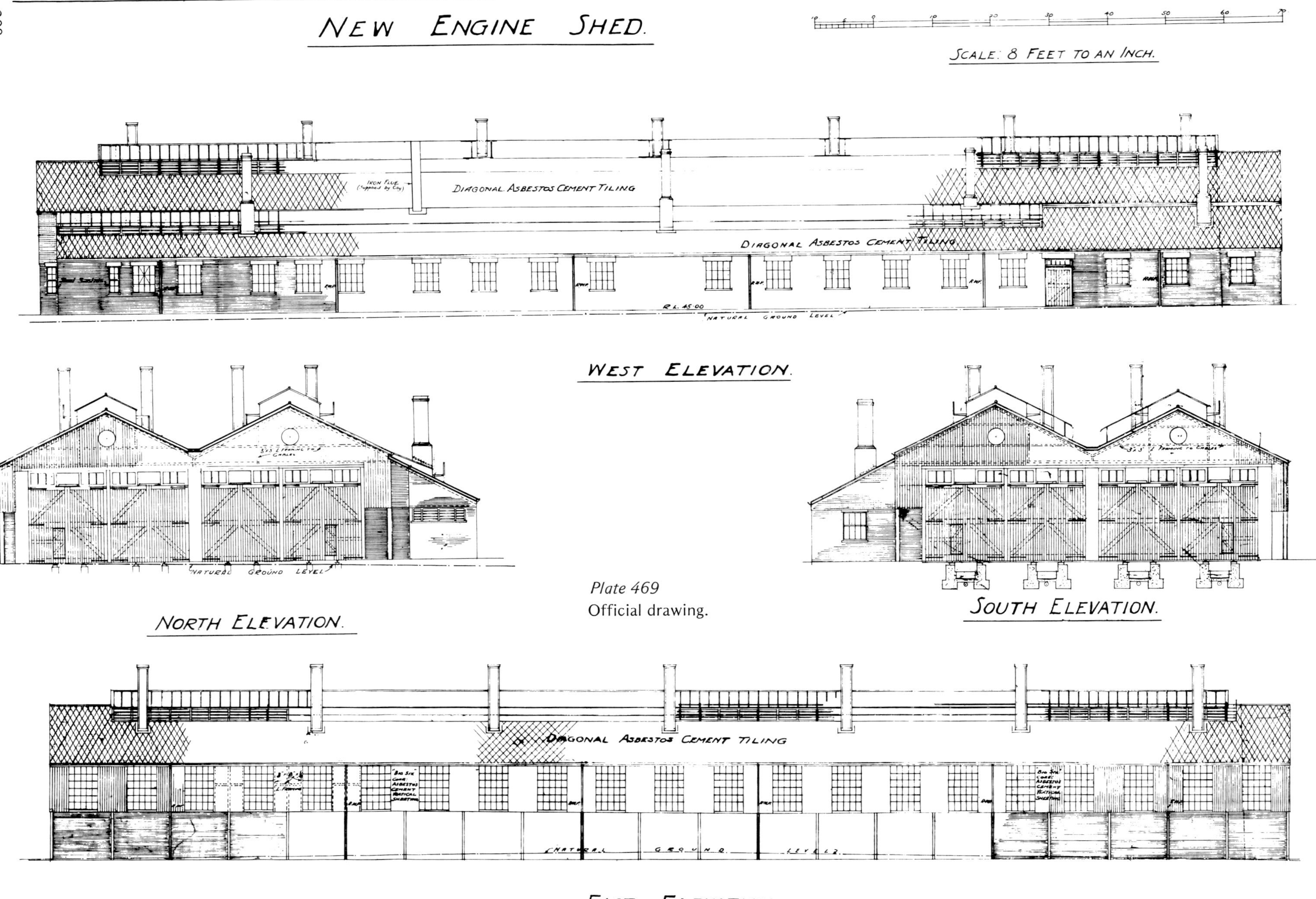

Plate 469
Official drawing.

Plate 470
Stratford-upon-Avon engine shed in the early 1900's.
British Rail

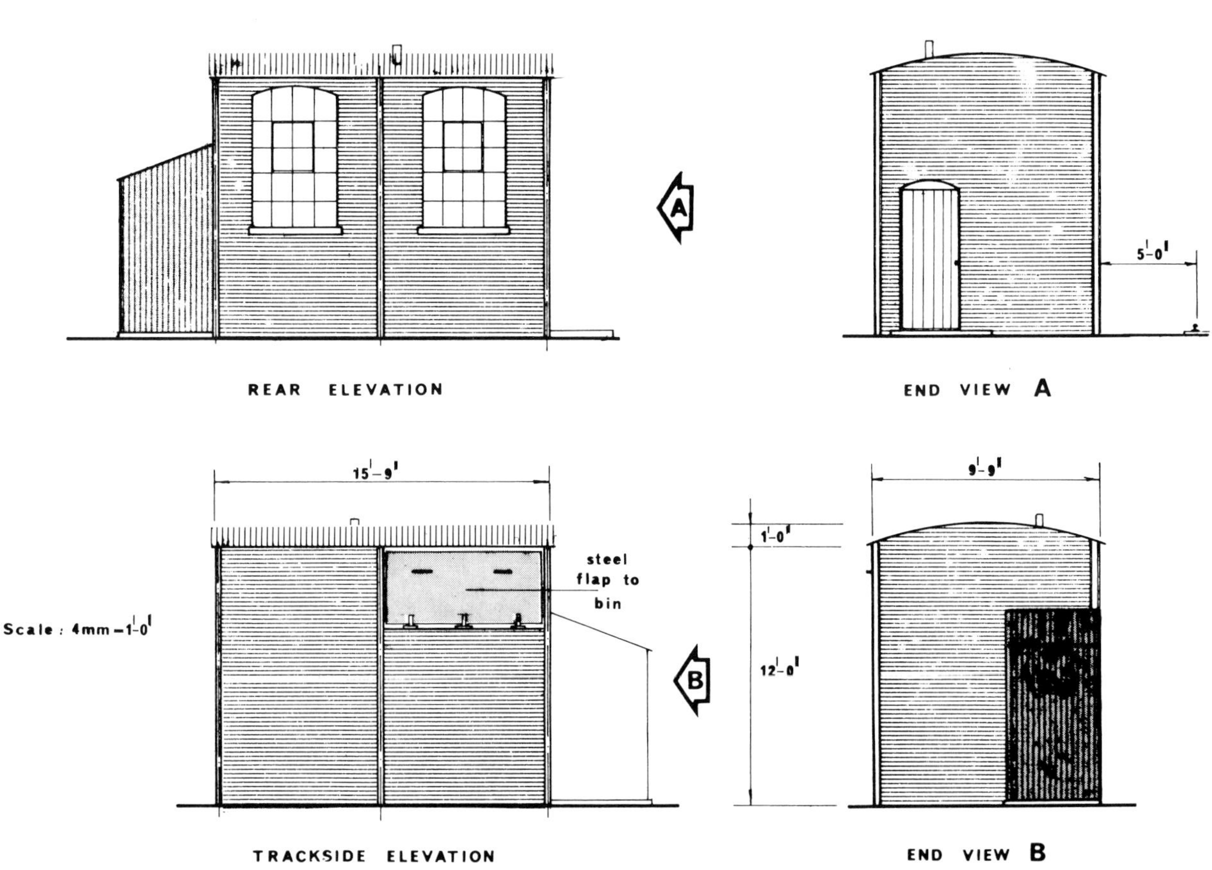

Plate 471 **SAND BIN & FURNACE (1930 Pattern)**

SIDE ELEVATION
END ELEVATION
10 Bays at 12'6" = 125'0"
12" step in pit
pit
TWO LEVEL PLAN
Corrugated Metal Sheeting
Corrugated Asbestos Sheeting
9" x 4" posts
4½" wall
31'-3" between walls
CROSS SECTION
Notes.
1. Colour Scheme :-
Black – Roof Sheets
Grey – Side Sheets
2. Dimensions taken from Didcot M.P.D.
ASH SHELTER
Scale 4mm = 1'0"
Drawn
Date Nov. 70
Surveyed
DRG. NO.
DID/70/4

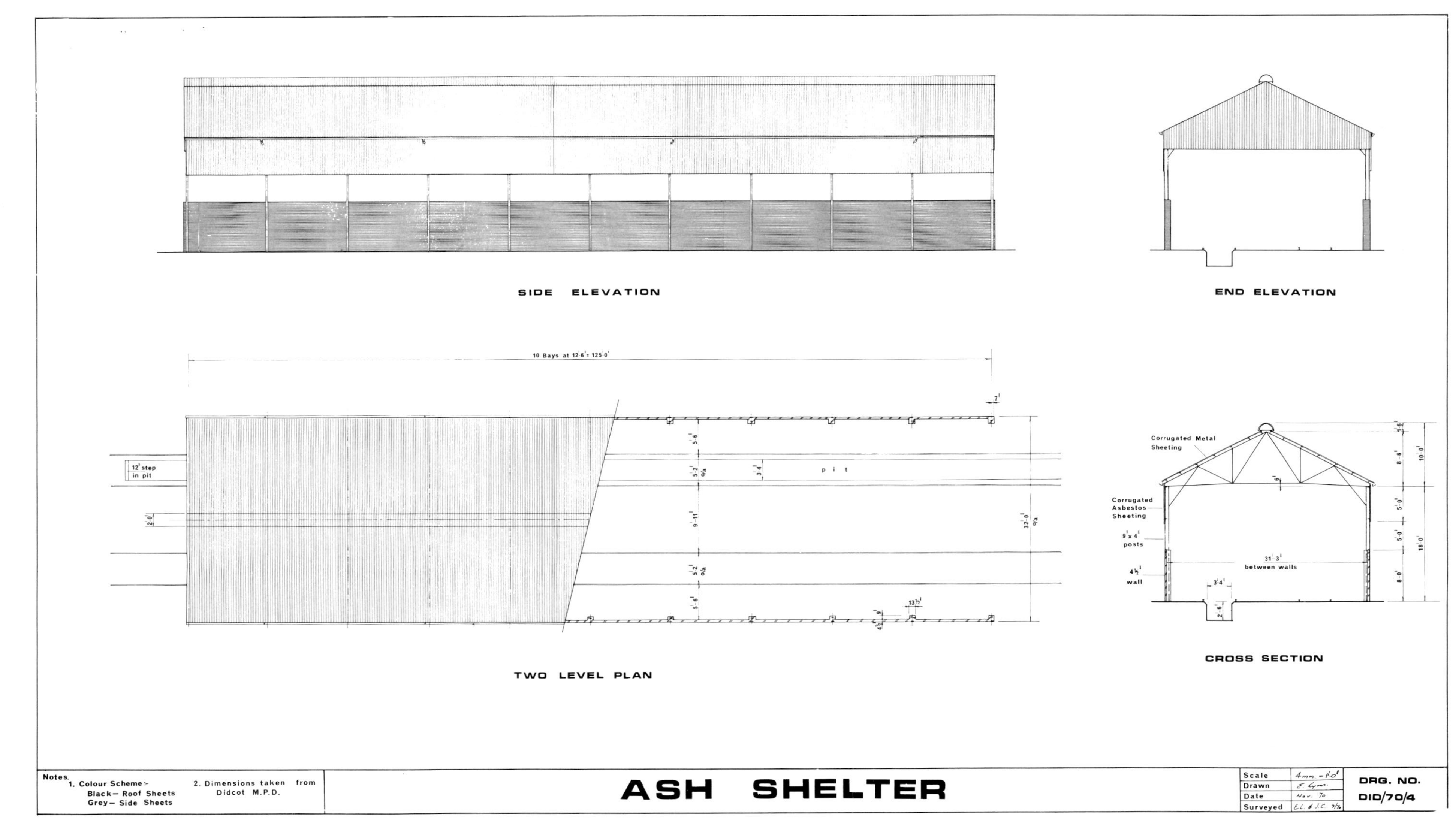

Plate 472

Plate 473
Swindon 'Water sidings', on the up side, at the east end of the station had this water tower and crane.

British Rail

Plate 474
Water tower on the upside of the line at the eastern end of Reading station.

British Rail

Plate 475
Drawings of typical water towers and columns.

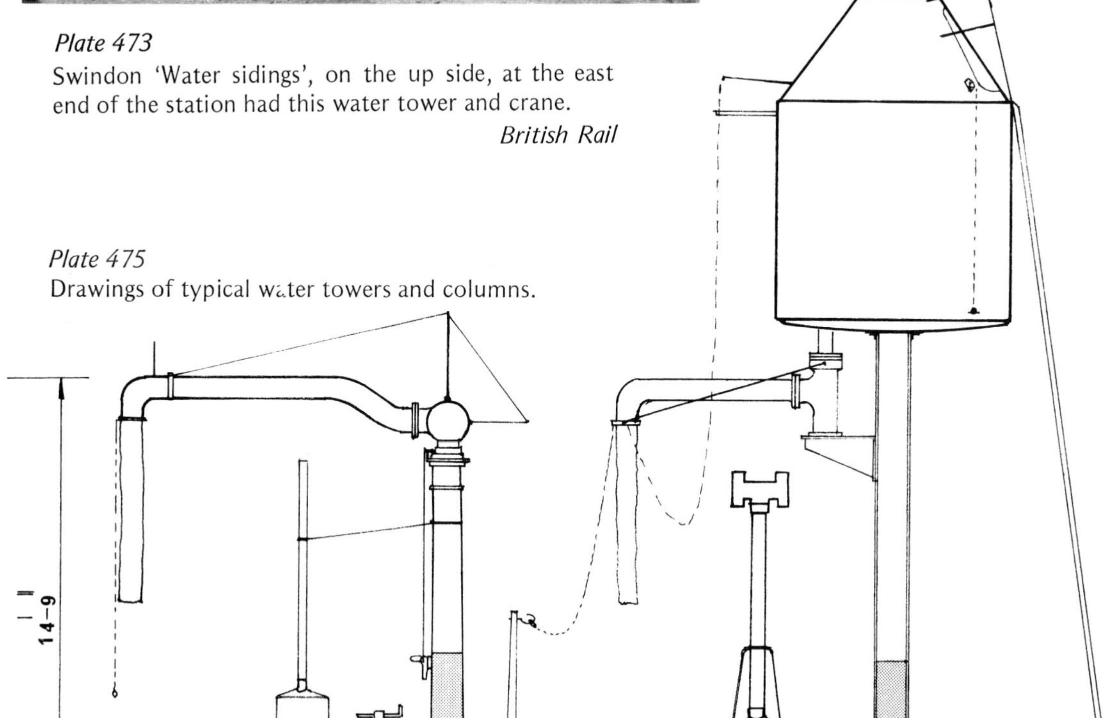

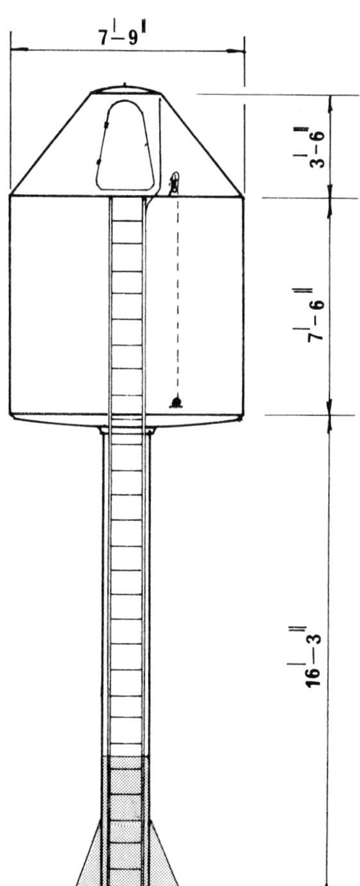

Plate 476a
Broad gauge period water tank at Clevedon.
Colin Judge

Plate 476b
Water column at Wells Tucker Street.
Colin Judge

Chapter Six

Tunnels

This is only a selection of the more interesting facades or portals erected at the mouths of tunnels. It is only a small selection because most tunnel portals tend to look alike—plain but decent. However in the early days of the Great Western Railway Brunel was able to design many beautiful facades for his tunnels, probably the finest being those at Box and Middle Hill Tunnels. During their excavation large quantities of fine building stone were removed which went to build bridges, stations, embankments and the decorative portals of the tunnel/quarries themselves. West of Box the land required tunnels and in the 18 miles from there to Bristol no less than eleven tunnels were bored, though some of these were very short. The eleven were:— Box, 3,212 yards: Middle Hill, 200 yards: two under Bathwick Hill, Bath, at 77 and 99 yards: Twerton, 264 yards: Saltford, 176 yards: two more unnamed tunnels at 37 and 53 yards long, but these were opened into cuttings by 1894: Fox's Wood No. 3, 1017 yards: No. 2, 154 yards: and No. 1, 326 yards long. For the tunnels between Box and Bath, Brunel used a kind of "Classical" architecture, except that the east portal of Box was quite plain, even ugly. From Bath to Bristol he used either a Romanesque arch as at Saltford or the "Castle Keep" style as at Twerton. An example of the former can be seen in MacDermot's *History of the Great Western Railway* Vol. 2, facing page 203. The west end of No. 2 Tunnel was never completed by Brunel. Bad weather had forced the work to be abandoned for the winter and by next spring a landslide had demolished part of the intended medieval gateway. Brunel was taken by the impromptu "ruin" and had ivy planted on it in the best traditions of the Victorian folly. This human gesture was taken away in 1900 when a business-like engineer decided to have a "proper" portal built instead.

These business-like engineers were the death of fantastic tunnel mouths. Even the mouth of the greatest underwater tunnel in the world, the Severn, has no more than the vestige of decoration, and that is at the English end, the Welsh having nothing to look at at all. A great deal has been written about the Severn Tunnel, usually by engineers who know what they are about, so I have included a rare picture of a tunnel *beneath* the Severn Tunnel and one of the English portal.

Tunnels are exciting. The west end of Box, seen from the A4 road outside the village is a majestic sight, at close quarters it is awe-inspiring. Ardley Tunnel, which pierces the ridge of ironstone hills of Oxfordshire, can be seen distantly from the canal side fields at Aynho, high up there on the horizon, a deep cavern, silent in the hills. The tunnel is as dramatic as a springing viaduct, it is a token of human determination and courage; to sit high on the cutting side above the tunnel entrance, whether in rural stillness or as a train rushes screaming into the black throat—a tunnel remains powerfully attractive.

Plate 477

Western portal of Box tunnel. From a lithograph by *J.C. Bourne 1842*

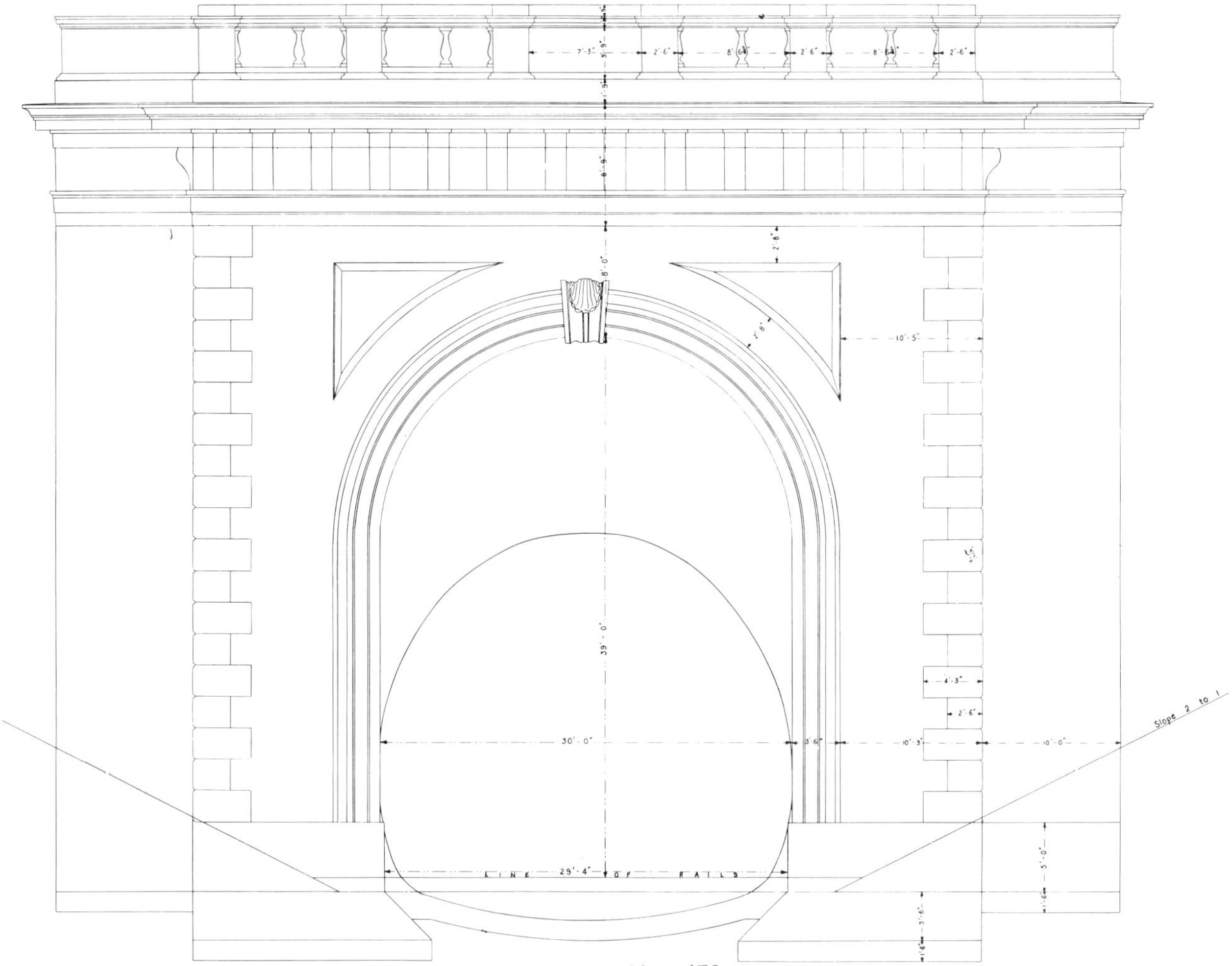

Plate 478
Official drawing of the western portal of Box tunnel.

Plate 479
The western portal of Box tunnel in 1948.
British Rail

Plate 480
This plate is made from the original, water colour tinted drawings produced by Brunel as his original plan for the western portal of Box tunnel. He has shown, from the left, section through entablature. Elevation of a truss. Elevation of a baluster. Front elevation of the keystone. Side elevation of the keystone. Below the last two items are, on the right, a section of the spandrel moulding and a section of the rustication.

British Rail

Plate 481

Western portal of Box tunnel showing the rusticated quoins, sunken panels at spandrel, the acanthus leaf carved keystone (a feature of the bridge west of Box station), trusses beneath the cornice and ornamental balustrading for a parapet.

British Rail

Plate 482

The western portal of Middle Hill tunnel. The proportions of the facade are similar to that at Box, but Brunel has varied the detail to produce a unique design. The arch is divided into segments with a scroll pattern keystone. Pilasters rise to the parapet which is very simple, unlike that at Box, but Middle Hill has these fasces like mouldings on the face of the pilasters.

Author 1973

Plate 485 (overleaf)

A view eastwards from above the eastern portal of Box tunnel.

British Rail

Plate 483

Side view of Box tunnel, western portal showing wide cornice and trusses beneath.

Author 1973

Plate 484

Middle Hill tunnel, west front.

Author 1973

Plate 485

Plate 486

Front and side elevation of Twerton tunnel, east end. The plate is made from the water colour tinted working drawings which, in this case, were made from pencil and ink sketches drawn by Brunel. The right hand drawing is a longitudinal section of the tunnel portal. According to the drawing the dimensions of this facade are as follows. From rail to crown of arch 30′. Span of arch 30′. The towers are set at 50′ centre, the tallest being 65′ from rail level to top of crenellations. Both towers are octagonal tubes of stone, 10′ 6″ across the 'flats' with a brick dome, hidden behind the battlements, sealing the top of each tube.

Plate 487

No. 1 tunnel, Bristol, western portal, from a sketch by Brunel. The tunnel was 326 yards long and was opened into a cutting in March 1889 as a result of track widenings due to the opening of the Severn Tunnel in September 1886. Traffic for London from South Wales now came via Bristol over the old Bristol and South Wales Union Railway which had been doubled as a consequence. Additional tracks had been laid from the branch to the Bristol-London main line, creating the famous Dr. Day's Bridge Junction, to Feeder Bridge Junction which became known as North Somerset Junction. A new marshalling yard was built on the up side of the line between the latter and the wall of red sandstone which was pierced by the No. 1 tunnel. To provide additional siding accommodation this cliff was excavated and the tunnel, as a result, opened into a wide cutting. During the demolition of the tunnel, trains were not prevented from using the line.

Plate 488
Eastern portal of Twerton tunnel.
British Rail

Plate 489
Twerton tunnel, west end provided an excellent example of Brunel varying a design to achieve individuality while retaining the 'family likeness'. A comparison of the two portals shows that the west end has a taller, more pointed arch and that its flanking towers are also taller and thinner. The brick hut on the left is very probably the base of the old Twerton tunnel signal box.
British Rail

Plate 490
The line in South Devon had been doubled in 1893 with the exception of the stretch along the sea wall between Dawlish and Teignmouth where it passes through five short tunnels. The tunnels were widened during 1905, the work of excavation continuing without interrupting the train service. They had been built to clear the 7′ gauge. A centring of rails, bent to shape and resting on wheels was moved gradually along inside the tunnel from which the workmen could work and cut away the roof and walls while the trains passed slowly beneath. There are no ventilation shafts in these tunnels, how those men must have choked and wheezed in fumes of hot sulphur. This plate shows the western portal of Parson and Clerk tunnel as widened with a fish bellied beam of cast iron supporting the parapet.

British Rail

Plate 491

At the east end of Parson and Clerk tunnel the original arch was retained, which dated back to 1846 and the atmospheric railway of the South Devon Company. Excavation for the double line has resulted in this curious 'half arch' if a layman may use such an expression. This delightful eccentricity from an age of business-like engineers is sadly no longer visible. In the 1920's a landslide occurred and this end of the tunnel was extended to form an avalanche shelter, a similar method of construction being used to that in 1905 which allowed the train service to continue running.

British Rail

Plate 492

A typically business-like tunnel portal of a type to be found all over the country, not only on the Great Western Railway. This shows Old Hill tunnel, Birmingham.

British Rail

Plate 493
An old print showing the western portal of Fox's Wood Long tunnel (known officially as No. 3).

British Rail

Plate 494
During the time Brunel was engaged in building this tunnel, (or is it an underbridge?) he referred to it as 'a tedious and difficult operation'. His problem was to cut through the embankment carrying the Kennet and Avon Canal at the Dundas Aqueduct in order to bring the branch from Bathampton to Bradford and Avon during the 1840's. The arches are brick faced with stone though no real attempt has been made to blend the railway bridge/tunnel portal with the magnificent arch the canal Company had built.

Author 1973

Plate 495
A short tunnel of 159 yards took the Wilts, Somerset and Weymouth line into Bradford-on-Avon beneath the streets of that town. The plate shows the western portal, an example of Brunel's work constrained to work on a 'shoe string' budget. He has made an imposing front using large blocks of rough dressed stone so that the effect is anything but constrained.

Author 1973

Plate 496
This tunnel at Harbury, on the Banbury to Leamington section, built in 1850/52, once had a moulded pattern in the Norman style on the arch. Now only the Norman or Romanesque proportions remain. The portal is also noteworthy for its unusual wing wall which is also a retaining wall owing to the 110′ depth of the cutting.

Author 1974

Plate 497
The Clifton Down branch in Bristol was a joint G.W.R./M.R. venture. This is a ventilating shaft from the Clifton Down tunnel. The tunnel was 1,738 yards long.
British Rail

Plate 498
Chipping Sodbury tunnel passed beneath the fields of the Duke of Beaufort for 4,444 yards. There are six of these crenellated vents in an impressively long line across the meadows.
Author 1973

Plate 499
The English portal of the Severn tunnel. A contractor's locomotive is emerging from the arch.
British Rail

Plate 500
The Severn Tunnel, showing one of the small water culverts.
British Rail

Plate 501
A culvert beneath the Severn tunnel, part of the system of drainage. Edgeways on to the camera is a massive watertight door. It is interesting to see that the tunnel has been constructed as an ellipse, this shape offering less resistance to flowing water than a circular shape.
British Rail

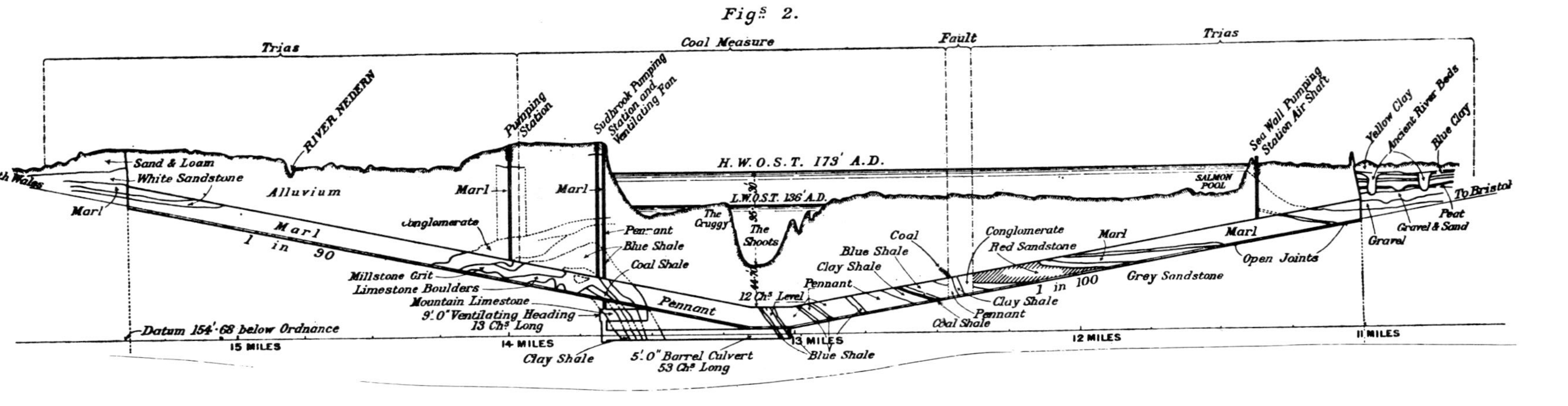

Plate 502
Longitudinal section of Severn Tunnel.
British Rail

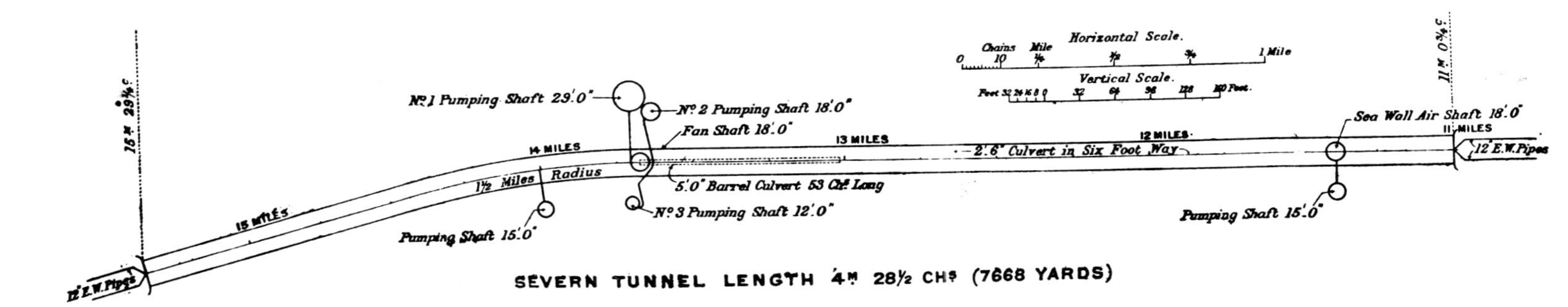

Plate 503
Plan of Severn Tunnel.

British Rail

Chapter Seven

Signal Boxes

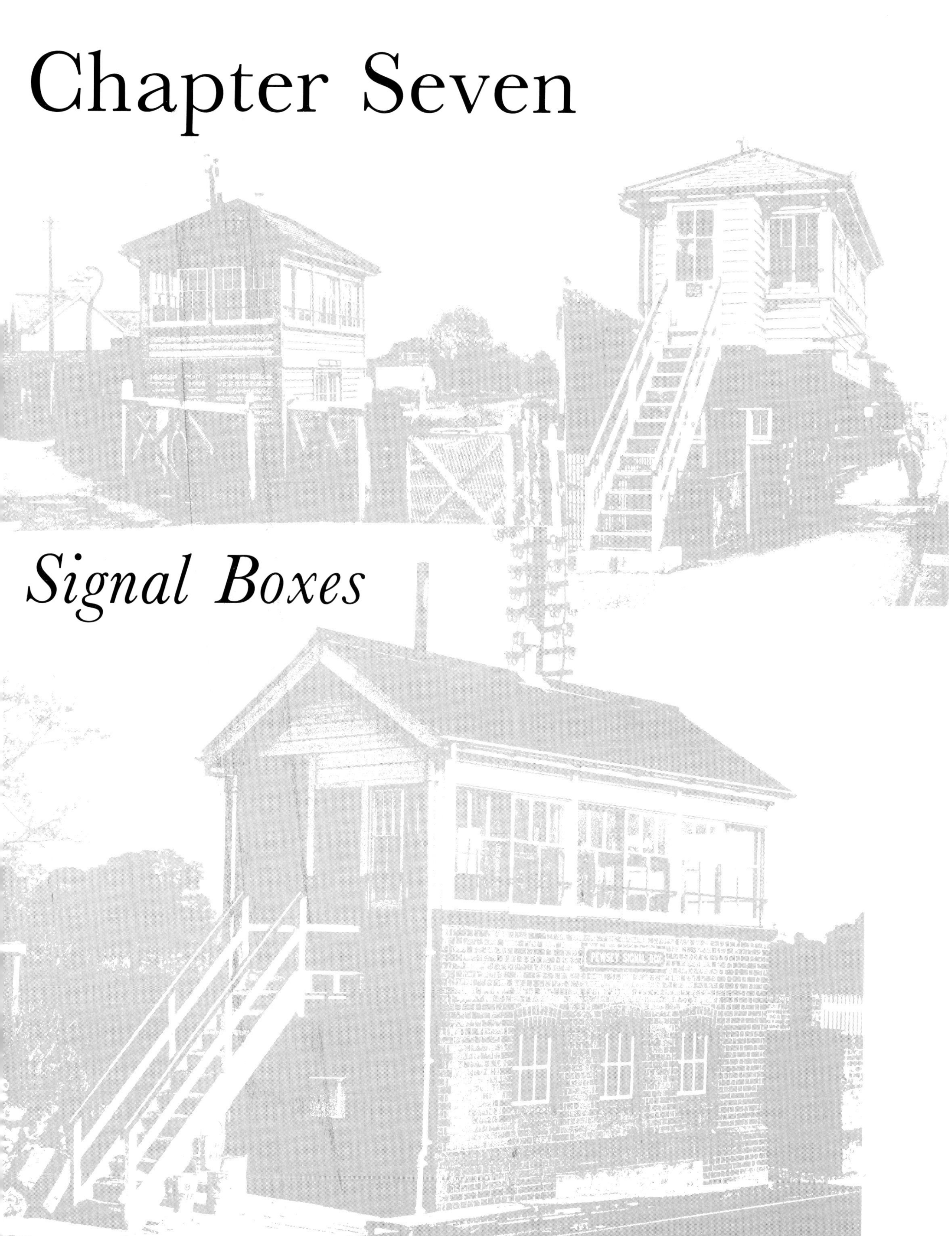

Plate 505
Frome North box was built in 1875. The plate shows an early 20th century superstructure on the old walls.

Author 1973

Plate 504
There had been a signal box at Waltham since March 1873 but it is unlikely that this structure dates from that year. I should rather say that it was erected in 1885 to accommodate, perhaps, a larger lever frame. It is entirely typical of the latter period with vertical weather boarding on a timber frame, standing on a base of rough faced red brick. It has a ventilator, adjustable from the inside, small paned windows and no porch.

British Rail

Plate 506
The signal box at Sarnau was built about 1885 and has all the marks of that period with the addition of a porch later. The ventilator, gables, windows and brickwork are all in the style of those at Waltham.

Author 1973

Plate 507

Taplow West Cabin was built with the enlarged station in 1884. The box is unusual in its siting, detail and outline resemblance to a style 20 years in the future. Steel girders support the box which appears to rest in a 'basket' of latticework attached to the footbridge. Features which are typical of the 1884 period are the vertical boarding and the small paned windows. Around the eaves is a valance to match that on the footbridge and station, this may have been a widespread practice in the London district at that time. Slough East and Paddington Arrival boxes were very similar to Taplow West and some experts believe that they were built for the Great Western Railway by Saxby & Farmer, the signalling contractors. The hip roof is lead covered. Beneath the building a timber shield has been built around the downrods, crank and pulleys to prevent passengers from becoming entangled in 'the works' and to keep the rain and dust out of the bearings of the cranks and pulleys. In front of the box there is a square section telegraph pole, painted black and white and surmounted by a finial.

British Rail

Plate 508

Bristol East Depot No. 2 signal box was probably erected in 1890/92 and is the timber version of the Great Western's new standard design of 1890. Links with earlier practice are the decorative 'cock's-comb' ridge tiles and the wooden nameplate on which metal letters are screwed. This was an intermediate stage between metal letters fastened directly to the wall of the building and the well known cast iron nameplate. Note that the form 'signal box' is used instead of the earlier style of 'cabin' or 'signal cabin'.

British Rail

Plate 509

Reading West Junction signal box photographed, when new, in 1893; a perfect example of the brick version of the 1890 standard design. It held a 100 lever frame in a floor 57ft. x 12ft. The signal spectacle has an empty frame where the green glass should be, this photograph having been taken during the changeover period from white to green to indicate "All Right".

British Rail

Plate 510

Radley signal box was built in 1896, a smaller version of Reading West Junction.

W.L. Kenning 1914
Drawings Colin Judge

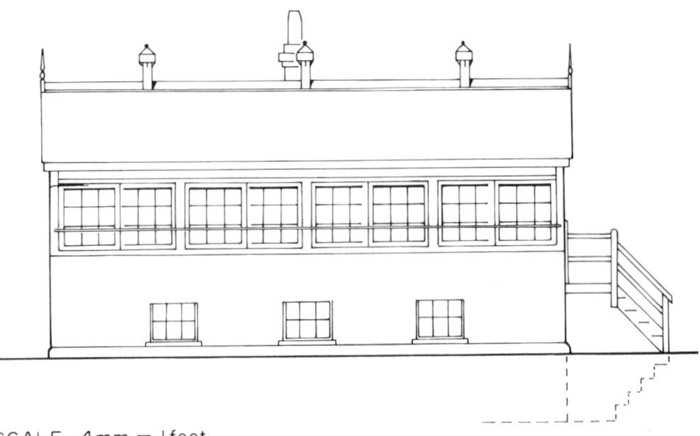

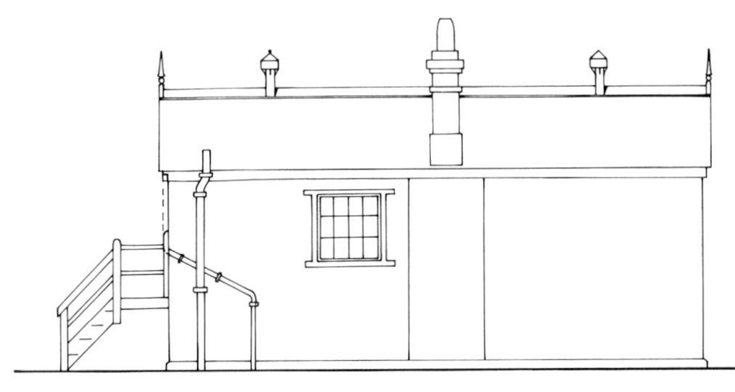

SCALE 4mm = 1foot

RADLEY STATION

(GREAT WESTERN RAILWAY)

ON THE OXFORD/DIDCOT LINE

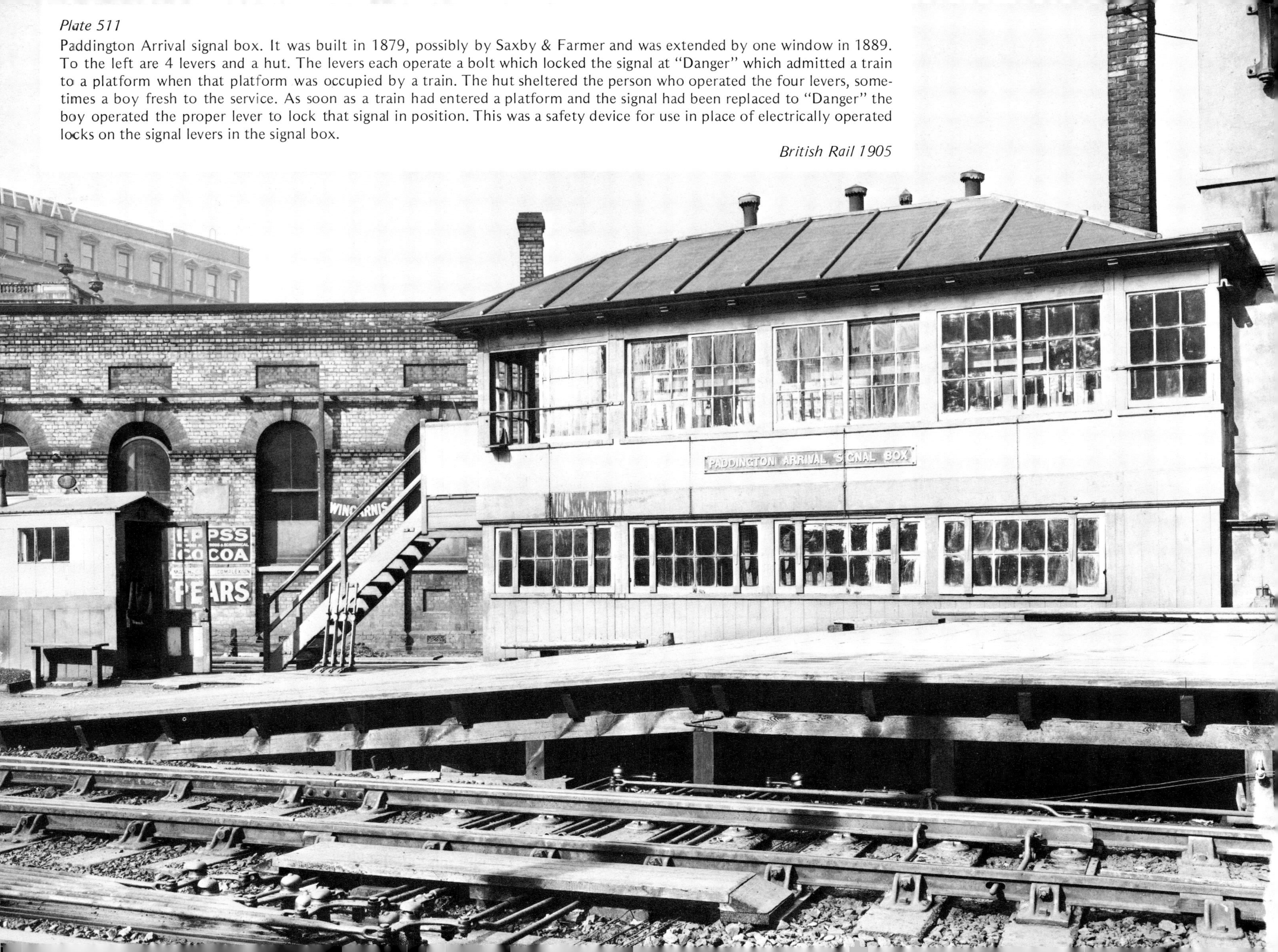

Plate 511

Paddington Arrival signal box. It was built in 1879, possibly by Saxby & Farmer and was extended by one window in 1889. To the left are 4 levers and a hut. The levers each operate a bolt which locked the signal at "Danger" which admitted a train to a platform when that platform was occupied by a train. The hut sheltered the person who operated the four levers, sometimes a boy fresh to the service. As soon as a train had entered a platform and the signal had been replaced to "Danger" the boy operated the proper lever to lock that signal in position. This was a safety device for use in place of electrically operated locks on the signal levers in the signal box.

British Rail 1905

Plate 512
The classic Great Western signal box. The second standard design, introduced in 1896. A total of 400 such boxes in brick and timber was built.

British Rail

Plate 513
The new standard box built within a platform at Shirley.

British Rail

Plate 514
Another angle on this handsome design. Midgham. Note the fine old "Berks & Hants" line station.

British Rail

– SIGNAL BOX AT CWMCORS –

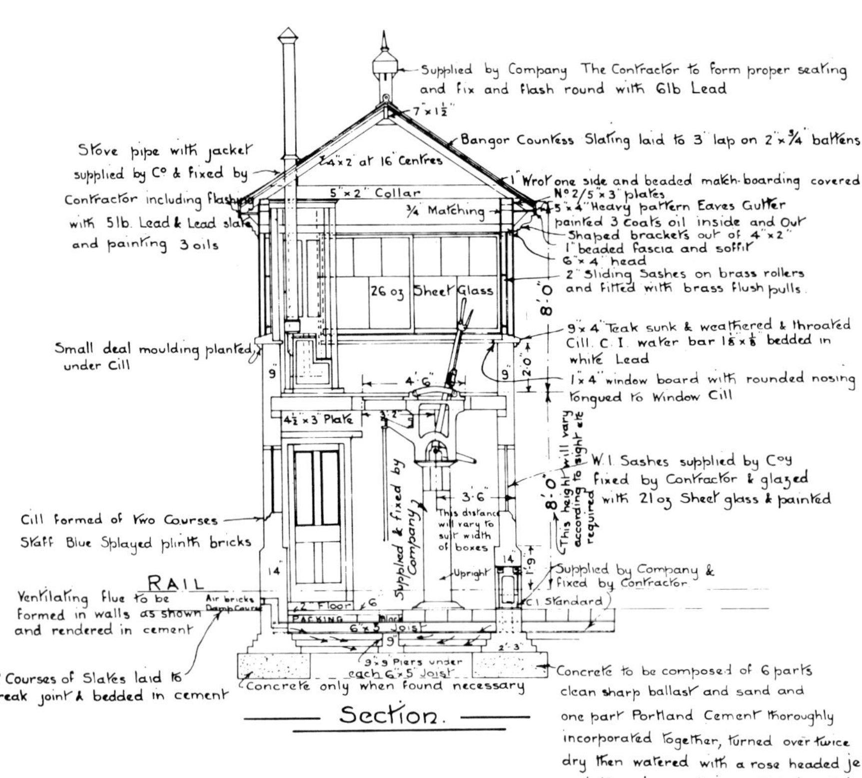

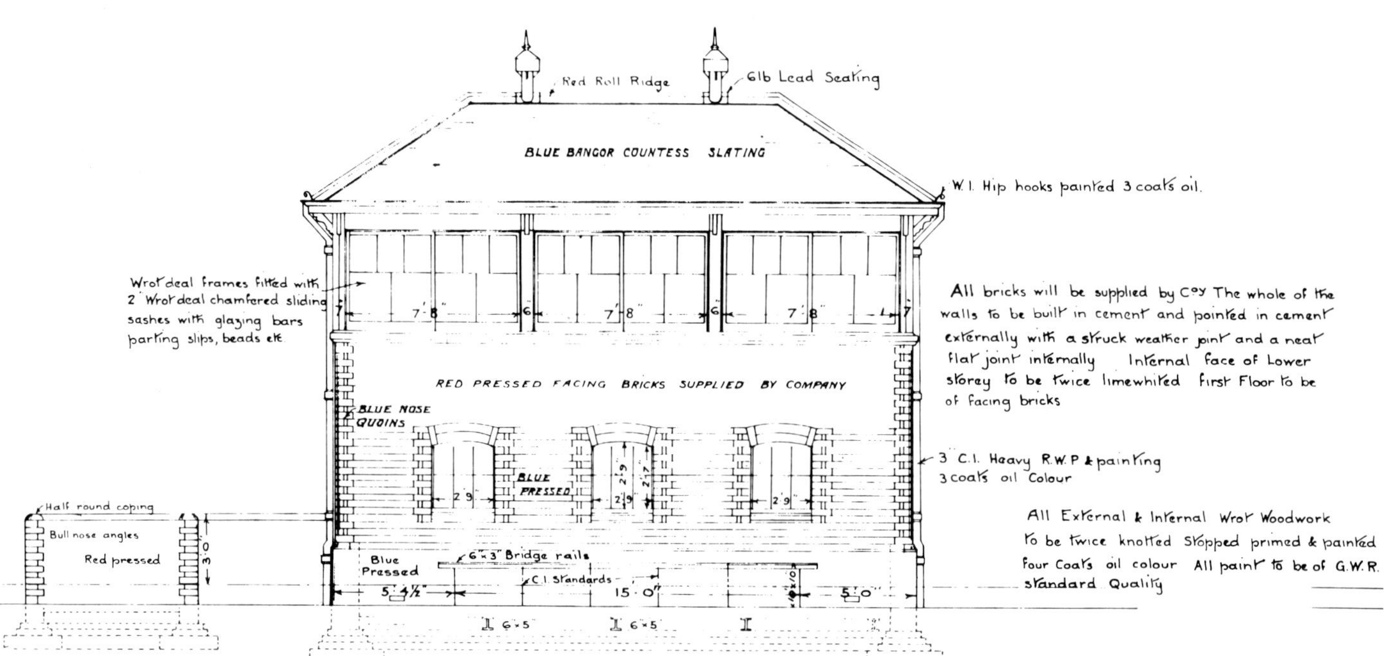

Plate 515

Official drawing of the 1896 standard design in brick. They could also be erected in timber where the site would not bear a heavy load. This box was built but never opened for use.

British Rail

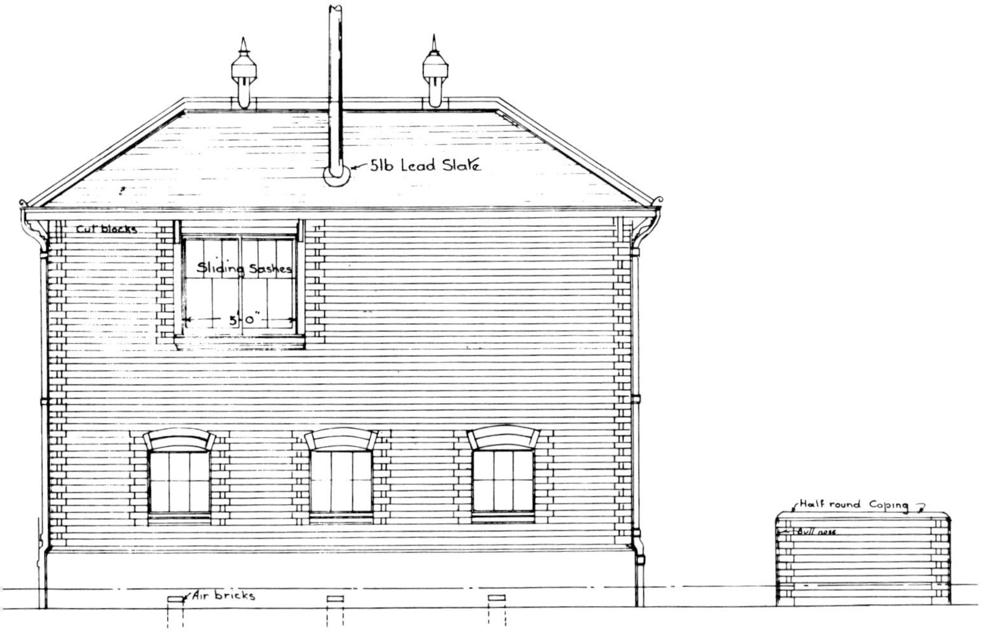

5lb Lead Slate
Cut blocks
Sliding Sashes
5'0"
Half round Coping
Bull nose
Air bricks

Back Elevation.

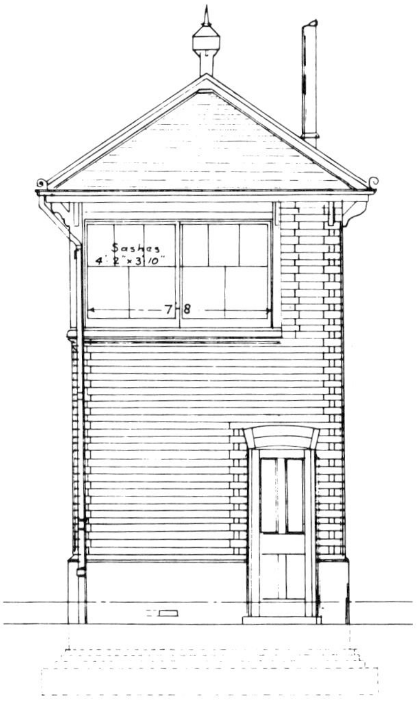

Sashes 4' 2" x 3' 10"
7' 8"

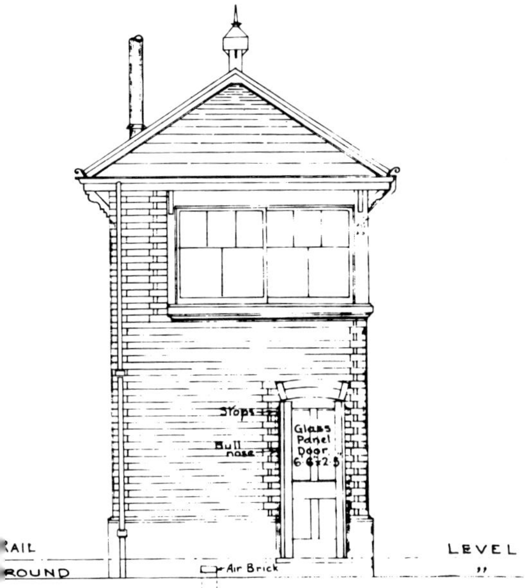

End Elevation.

Plate 515 continued
Signal box at Cwmgors.

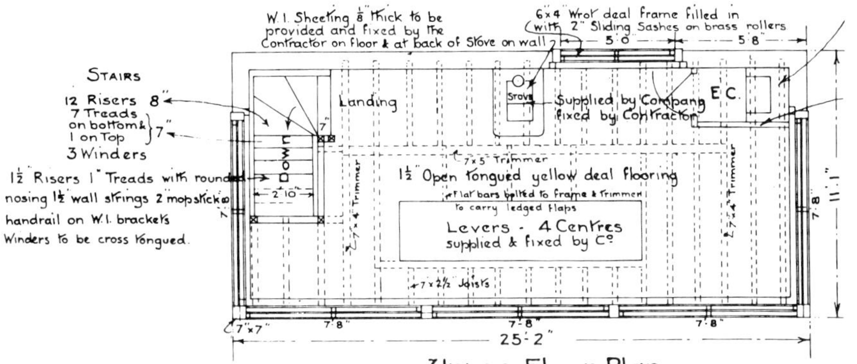

Stops
Bull nose
Glass Panel Door 6' 6" x 2' 5"
RAIL LEVEL
GROUND "
Air Brick

End Elevation

W.I. Sheeting ⅛" thick to be provided and fixed by the Contractor on floor & at back of Stove on wall
6"x4" Wrot deal frame filled in with 2" Sliding Sashes on brass rollers
5' 0"
5' 8"
STAIRS
12 Risers 8"
7 Treads on bottom & 1 on Top } 7"
3 Winders
1½" Risers 1" Treads with round nosing 1½" wall strings 2" mopstick handrail on W.I. brackets
Winders to be cross tongued.
Landing
Down
2' 10"
Stove
Supplied by Company fixed by Contractor
E.C.
7"x5" Trimmer
1½" Open tongued yellow deal flooring
Flat bars bolted to frame & trimmer to carry ledged flaps
Levers - 4 Centres supplied & fixed by Co
7"x4" Trimmer
7"x2½" Joists
7"x7"
7' 8"
7' 8"
7' 8"
25' 2"
7' 8"
11' 1"

Upper Floor Plan.

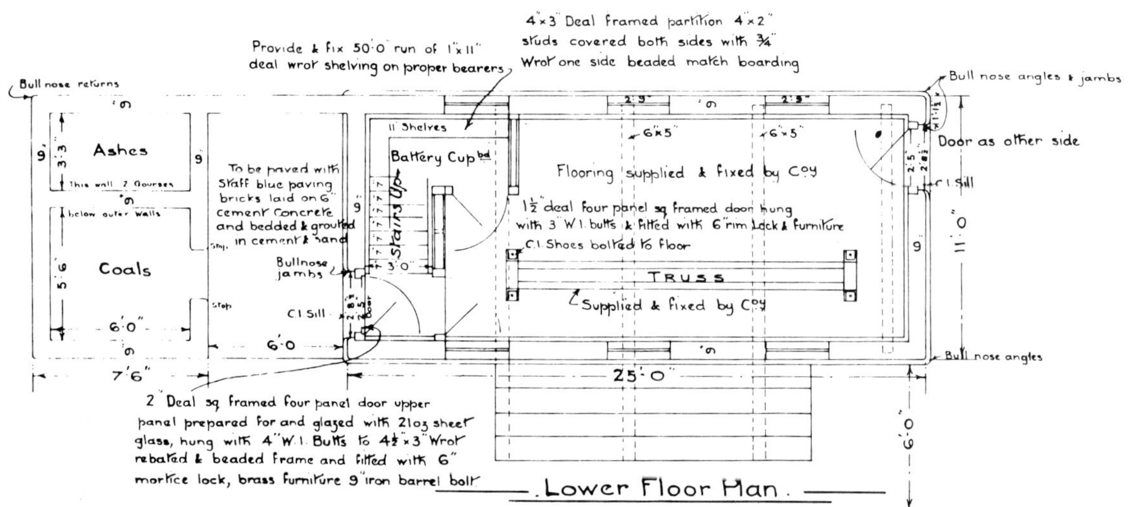

Plate 516

Highbridge signal box controlled the flat crossing of the Somerset and Dorset Railway over the Great Western line from Bristol to Taunton. The nameplate on the box is a flimsy modern replacement of the original cast iron plate. The box was ordered from the works on 18th December 1913 and is to the 'standard' design except that it has a wedge shaped western end. An 0-6-0 No. 3218 is approaching the crossing from Evercreech and is signalled to run into the Great Western Railway station at Highbridge. The latter Company's signalman operated the points in the S&DJR single line on each side of the crossing.

British Rail

Plate 517

Newport East signal box, built in 1927 to house a power operated interlocking frame. Very limited space has forced the engineer to site the box on a pedestal. The houses in the rear caused it to be placed on the pedestal in an overbalanced position hence the steel brackets under the front of the box.

British Rail

Plate 518
Wantage Road station, during the widening of the lines and the erection of a new signal box, in 1932. The old box, built to the 1896 standard design, was erected in 1916 with 35 levers. The new box, which held 52 levers, had a framework of steel, filled with concrete blocks, under a hipped roof of a patent asbestos/cement composition. These were hung diagonally to produce a pleasing pattern and, in spite of modern materials, the handsome outline of the 1896 design was cleverly preserved. The first box to be built with these materials was erected at Waltham Sidings in 1925, but it was an ugly job, having only plain gables, and was not repeated. Twenty boxes were built to the revised 1932 design, the greatest concentration of these being between Didcot and Swindon, although they were to be found as far apart as Frome and Ruabon.

British Rail

Plate 519 ▲
This view of Foxhall Junction box shows off the traditional lines of the new materials and design.

British Rail

Plate 520
Henley-on-Thames box was built to the 1890 standard design and is pictured here with later pattern windows.

M. R. Romans

Plate 521
At the same time as the steel and concrete boxes were being built at a score of different locations, the Great Western Railway was erecting these very traditional signal boxes at Taunton. This is Taunton East Junction, one of six boxes built at the station during its rebuilding about 1932. It would appear that the Company revived a 30 year old design here, perhaps because they thought it would look better at the fine new station they were building. Unless one knew that they had been put up in 1932, one would be fully justified in saying that they dated from 1912.

Author 1974

Plates 522/523

Hawkeridge Junction signal box. This was built in the early part of the 1939-45 War and is rather more substantial than similar boxes at Heywood Road, Fairwood Junction etc., built in peacetime 8 or 10 years previously. The box was built in a hurry in 1942 using a quick, cheap, asbestos roof, materials and parts originally intended for a new box at Whitland. The concrete lintels over the locking room windows are a sure sign of wartime construction. The tubular steel signals demonstrate two styles of Great Western design.

Author 1973

Plate 524

Reading Goods Lines East box was built during the 1896 improvements to Reading station. In style, it matched the huge 'East Main' and 'West Main' boxes at each end of the station, with matching red and yellow bricks, 'cock's-comb' ridge tiles and ornate finials. There is a dwelling house feeling about this box which is strengthened by the heavy, cast iron gutter pipes. The three boxes were quite unlike anything else on the Great Western, as if the Company wanted to make a special impression at Reading, and it has been suggested that the 'un-signal box-like' design is the result of the plans coming from the Chief Civil Engineer's office at Paddington, rather than from the Signal Department's drawing office at Reading.

Author 1974

Plate 525

Fifty years later on from the goods line box at Reading, the Great Western Railway had to build a new box at Oxford South. A war was in progress and a new marshalling yard had to be constructed just south of Oxford, at Hinksey. The style shown here was used in most boxes built during the 1939-45 War, from little ones like Hampstead Norris, on the Didcot-Newbury line to 72 lever boxes at Oxford. This box, officially, replaced the existing box a few yards to the north— Oxford South, and therefore took that name, but before it was operating the name had been changed to Hinksey North.

Chapter Eight

Goods Depots, Sheds and Warehouses

Plate 526
Gateway to South Lambeth goods depot. This photograph was taken during construction when twelve and a half acres of a sewage farm were cleared and laid down with miles of sidings and thousands of square yards of warehouse space. The gateposts are nicely done, even overdone to modern eyes, with limestone caps, and a central sunken panel deep enough to hold a statue. To prevent damaging honest horses as they laboured in and out of the depot, the corners of the pillars are made with bull nose bricks, and to prevent carts from damaging the plinth of the gate pillars granite fenders have been installed. The arch over the gate seems aggressively ornate, the lettering a triumph of Edwardian draughtsmanship. The gentlemen of this profession at the period in question were very fond of flowery lining and lettering but someone has excelled himself here. The outline of the letters is unusual and to make a stronger impression the face of each character has been scooped out to make, as it were, two outlines for each letter. This style of lettering was used on the Windsor station windscreen (*plate 220,* Chapter One) and over an identical entrance built for a new freight depot at Cardiff about 1908.

British Rail

Plate 527
The original goods shed at Bristol, designed by Brunel, a master in the use of timber. It is difficult not to get excited about Brunel's work and this, to me, is an exciting building. He has used timber to support the roof with brick walls on three sides. These are pierced by his famous 'Gothic' arches. A row of timber columns supports the roof at the cart entrance with timber brackets giving an appearance of a 'Gothic' arcade, similar to that at the passenger station. The rafters spring almost daintily from massively proportioned timber and form a pattern of rectangles with the purlins intersecting. In this manner, quite functionally, Brunel has brought an echo of a 16th century panelled ceiling from a great house into a goods shed of the 19th century. *British Rail*

Plate 528
The goods shed at Bristol in the steel age. Brunel would recognise only the horses, I feel. *British Rail*

Plate 527

Plate 528

Plate 529
Swindon goods shed, a steel framed corrugated iron covered building with a 'traditional' awning over the loading bays.
British Rail

Plate 530
Paddington goods shed with, in the foreground, corrugated iron roofs built within the shed of an older building. This view was taken from a window in the Goods Agents offices.

Plate 531
Reading King's Meadow goods depot.
British Rail

Plate 532
Llanelli goods shed. The building in the foreground is probably not as old as the shed in the rear which was part of the original South Wales Railway and therefore almost certainly designed by Brunel. The office block has a 'modern' treatment of stone blocks and the windows are certainly from a period later than 1850.

British Rail

Plate 533
An unidentified, early Victorian goods shed.
British Rail

Plate 534

Bath goods shed. Massive in an unrecognisable stone which one supposes to be Bath stone, the buildings stand surrounded by the organised chaos of a busy yard as virtually the entire imports/exports of the neighbourhood pass through.

British Rail

Plate 535

The goods shed at Newbury was almost certainly built to Brunelian designs for the 'Berks and Hants' line in 1845 and was demolished without a word of reproach in 1974 to provide room for the fabrication of points and track in connection with a multiple aspect signalling scheme — or maybe it was simply no longer required, owner having no further use for same. The interesting little offices in the foreground were later additions of at least two periods. The original office was the usual 'lean-to'.

British Rail

Plate 536
The marvellous timbered interior of Newbury goods shed had good beams supporting the roof in an unmistakably Brunelian manner. Chamfered corners and decorative caps are only 'finish'.
Author 1974

Plate 537
Archway to the loading bay, Newbury goods shed.
Author 1974

Plate 538 ▲
Exterior of Newbury goods shed showing the typical 'B & H' line style of brickwork, the semi-circular arches over the windows picked out in yellow brick. The 'lean-to' shed behind the engine has window openings in the same shape as in the brick walls and could be the original office for the yard.
British Rail

Plate 540
The goods shed at Challow was the largest rural goods shed between Paddington and Bristol. It was made of good brick, if rather weathered, well buttressed, the walls pierced with 'Gothic' arches and massive timbering supporting the roof. There is no doubt in my mind that this was designed by Brunel. Other features which support this view are the brick 'lean-to' office with its period windows, and the style of chimney stack high up on the point of the gable. Though made in brick, these points are very similar to the obviously Brunelian shed at Trowbridge. A double line of rails passed through the shed, there was a good deal of decking and floor space and a stable built in at the western end. It is quite likely that this shed was twice the size and height of the one provided at Wantage Road. I never measured either, but worked in both. The reason for the size of the Challow shed was that for twenty years after the station was opened it acted as the railhead for the market town of Faringdon six miles to the north. The dear old building was demolished by a colourful band of contractors about June 1965. In the right hand corner of the picture one can see part of the original, i.e. 1840, timber station. Brunel stood on this platform and saw the first fatal crash in the history of the Great Western Railway. The little dark, brick signal box (middle centre) probably dates from 1873 when the 'block telegraph' was installed here; the new box which was to last until mid1965 is on the left. The photograph was taken during work to quadruple the line between here and Wantage Road.

Plate 539
Challow goods shed with the last goods train ever to use it.
H.O. Vaughan 1964

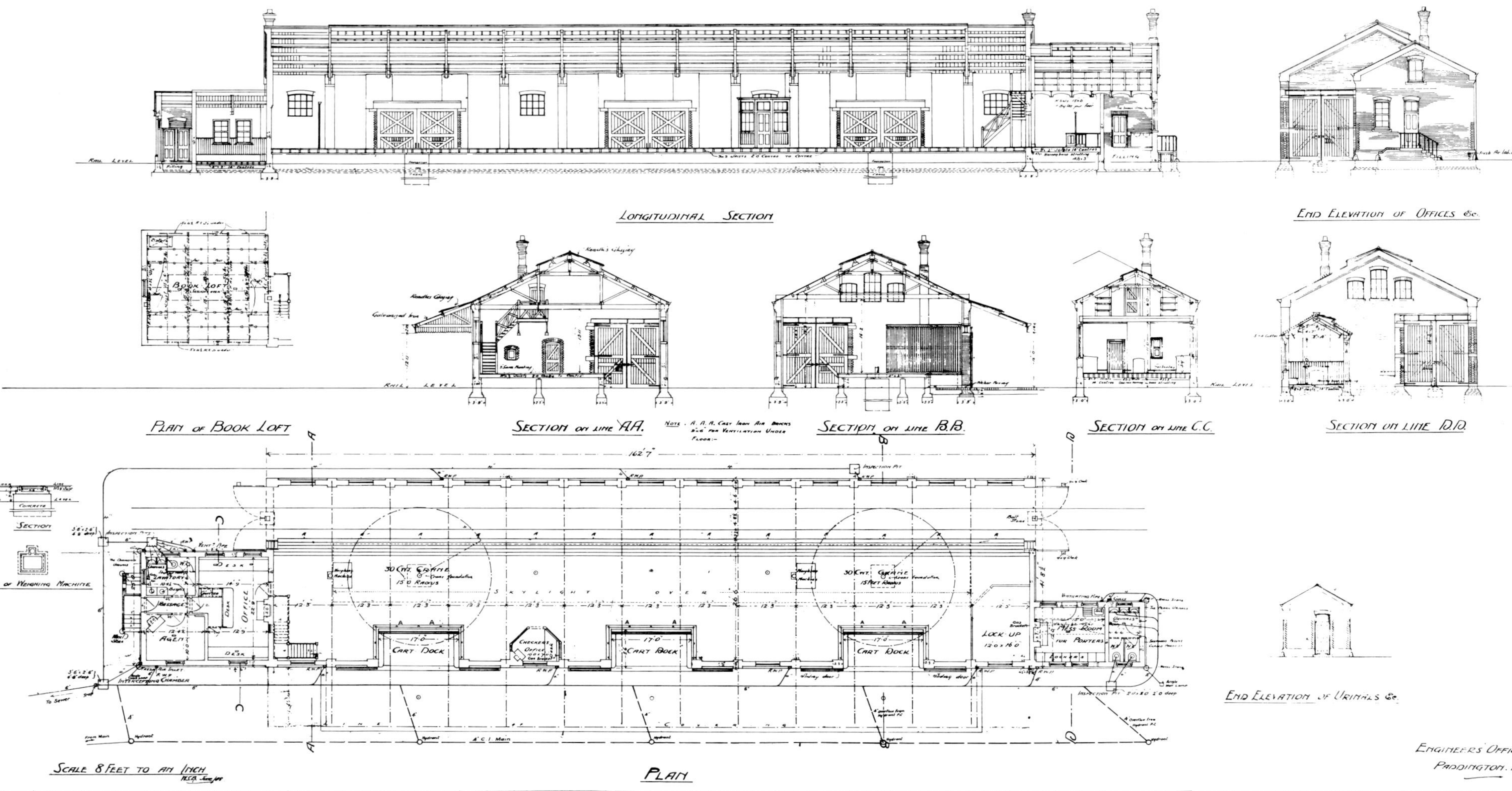

G. W. R. NEW GOODS SHED AT REDRUTH.
DRAWING Nº 1.
GAS LIGHTING
* Indicates The 20" Windsor Lamps, with Suggs Duplex Nº 4 burners and Ball trap door over each Crane :-
Ditto Suggs "Wilton" Single burner lamps with box trap door and Nº 4 burners
Ditto "Harp" Lights with single Inverted burners in Offices Mess Room and Book Loft.
NOTE.
The Contractor to be responsible for the accuracy of all leading dimensions :-
The Depth of the Concrete Foundations also the System of Drainage to be decided upon the Site :-
The Floor Joists and Plates of Offices & Mess Room to be twice coated with "Carbolineum Avenarius" and the Floor joists and Plates to Shed to be Creosoted -
The Internal Walls of Shed to be Twice Limewhited also Book Loft :-
All angles of Buildings to be Bull nosed with Blue Staffordshire Bricks :-
LONGITUDINAL SECTION
END ELEVATION OF OFFICES &c.
PLAN OF BOOK LOFT
SECTION ON LINE A.A.
NOTE. A. A. A. Cast Iron Air Bricks 9"x6" for Ventilation Under Floor :-
SECTION ON LINE B.B.
SECTION ON LINE C.C.
SECTION ON LINE D.D.
162' 7"
30 CWT. CRANE 15'0 RADIUS
SKYLIGHT OVER
CART DOCK
CHECKERS OFFICE
LOCK UP 12'0 x 16'0
MESS ROOM FOR PORTERS
OFFICE
AGENT
LAVATORY
PASSAGE
DESK
INTERCEPTING CHAMBER
SECTION
PLAN OF WEIGHING MACHINE
END ELEVATION OF URINALS &c.
SCALE 8 FEET TO AN INCH
PLAN
ENGINEERS' OFFICE PADDINGTON. W.

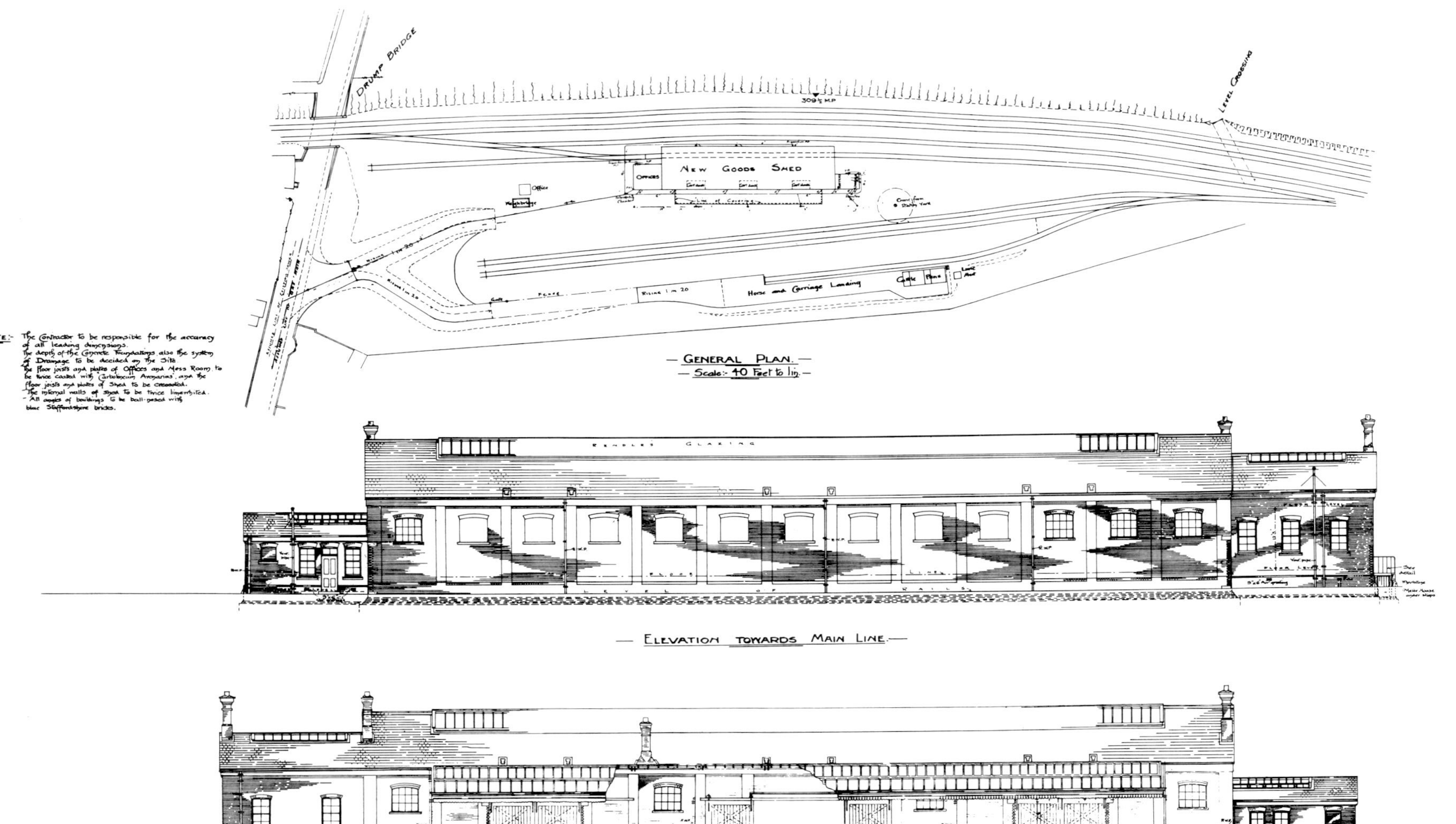
DRAWING Nº 2
G. W. R. NEW GOODS SHED AT REDRUTH.
DRUMP BRIDGE
LEVEL CROSSING
309¾ M.P.
NEW GOODS SHED
Offices
Office
Weighbridge
Horse and Carriage Landing
Rising 1 in 20
Cattle
Fence
NOTE:- The Contractor to be responsible for the accuracy of all leading dimensions.
The depth of the Concrete Foundations also the system of Drainage to be decided on the Site.
The floor joists and plates of Offices and Mess Room to be twice coated with "Carbolineum Avenarius", and the floor joists and plates of Shed to be creosoted.
The internal walls of Shed to be twice limewhited.
All angles of buildings to be bull-nosed with blue Staffordshire bricks.
GENERAL PLAN.
Scale:- 40 Feet to 1in.
RENDLES GLAZING
ELEVATION TOWARDS MAIN LINE.
ELEVATION TOWARDS CARRIAGE LANDING &c.
Scale:- 8 feet to 1 inch.
Engineers' Office.
Paddington. W.

Plate 543
Totnes station showing the goods shed.
British Rail

G.W.R. NEW GOODS SHED AT TENBY
No.
DRAWING No. 1
NOTES.
THE CONTRACTOR TO BE RESPONSIBLE FOR THE ACCURACY OF ALL LEADING DIMENSIONS.
THE DEPTH OF THE CONCRETE FOUNDATIONS, ALSO THE SYSTEM OF DRAINAGE TO BE DECIDED UPON THE SITE.
THE FLOOR JOISTS AND PLATES OF SHED TO BE CREOSOTED.
THE INTERNAL WALLS OF SHED TO BE DISTEMPERED.
APPROACH TO GOODS YARD
GOODS SHED.
WAITING SHED
UP PLATFORM
DOWN PLATFORM
STATION
REFRESHMENT ROOM
APPROACH ROAD
To Pembroke Dock
Up
Down
SECTION C C
GENERAL PLAN
SCALE 40 FT. TO ONE INCH
END ELEVATION TOWARDS PEMBROKE DK.
ELEVATION TOWARDS STATION
ELEVATION TOWARDS GOODS APPROACH ROAD
END ELEVATION TOWARDS WHITLAND
CART BAY
LOCK-UP
20 CWT CRANE
LOCK-UP
GOODS OFFICE
GOODS PLATFORM
PLAN
LONGITUDINAL SECTION
SECTION T T
SCALE 8 FEET TO ONE INCH
ENGINEER'S OFFICE

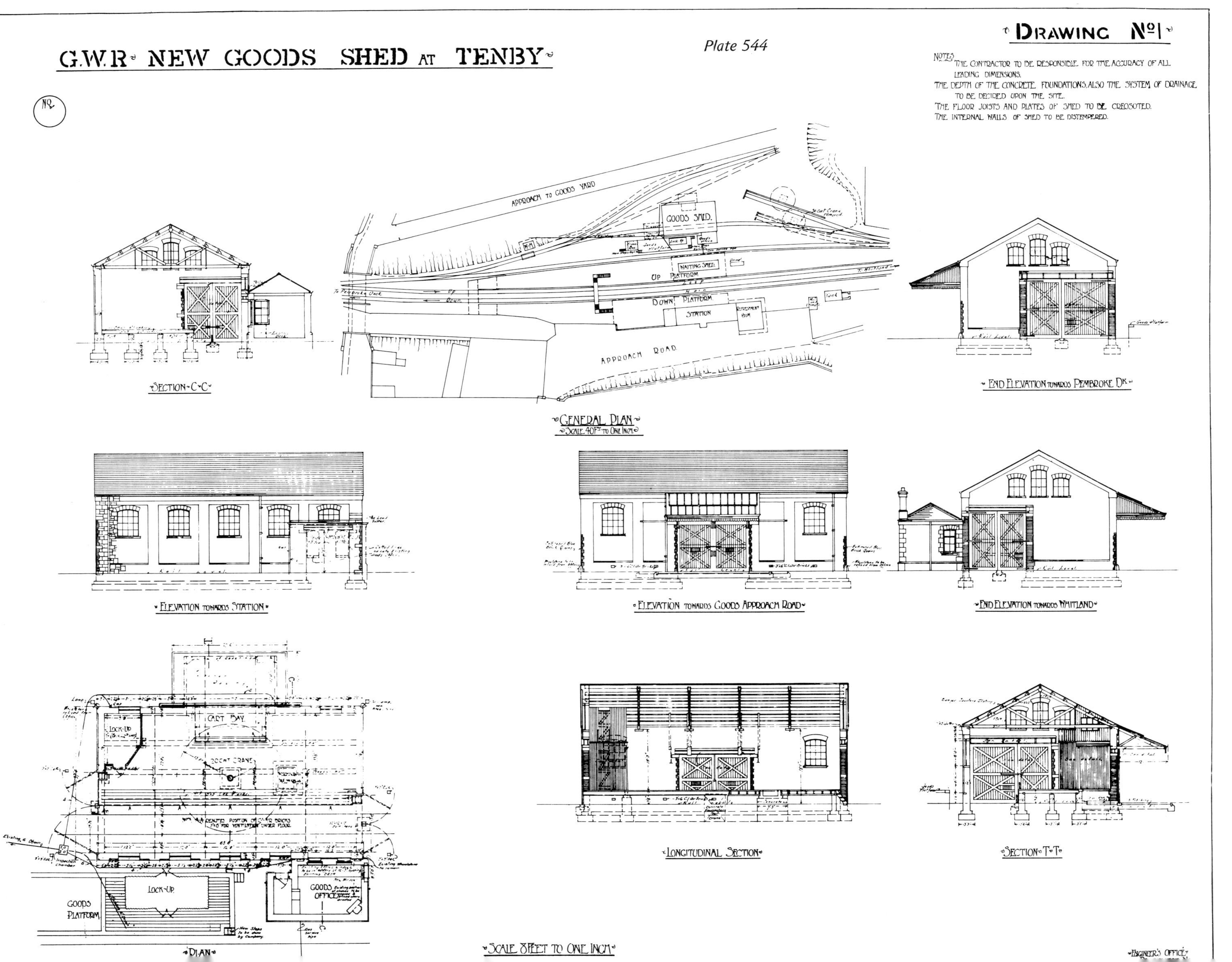

Plate 544

Plate 545
The goods shed at Trowbridge, built during 1847/48, is still standing today though not in railway use. A local firm rents it as a car park.
British Rail

Plate 546
A goods shed probably built in the early 20th century.

Plate 547
Thame goods shed. Built between 1861–64 it shows the continuing influence of Brunel's styles of architecture.
British Rail

-G.W.R.
NEW BOOKING OFFICE, GOODS SHED, AND CATTLE PEN.-
-AT GILFACH STATION.-

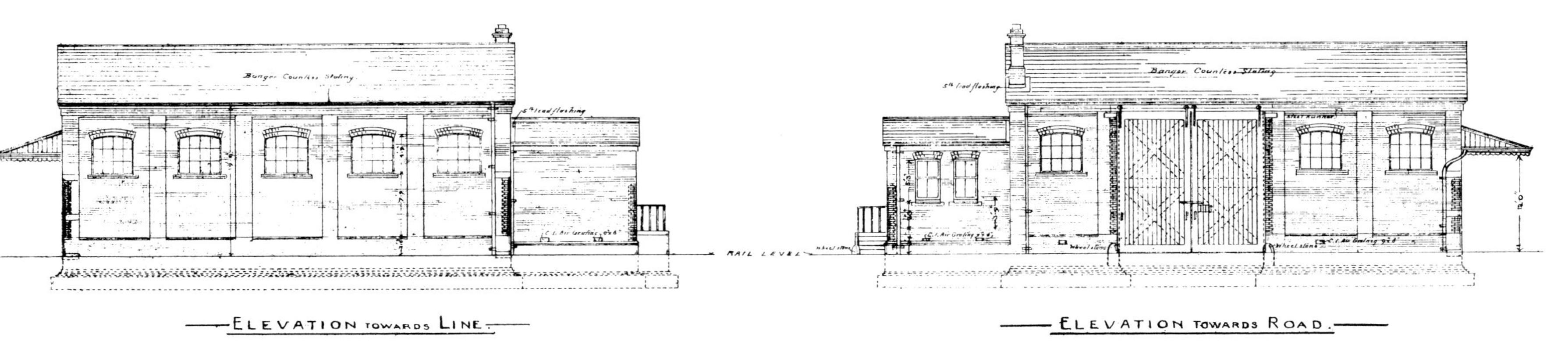

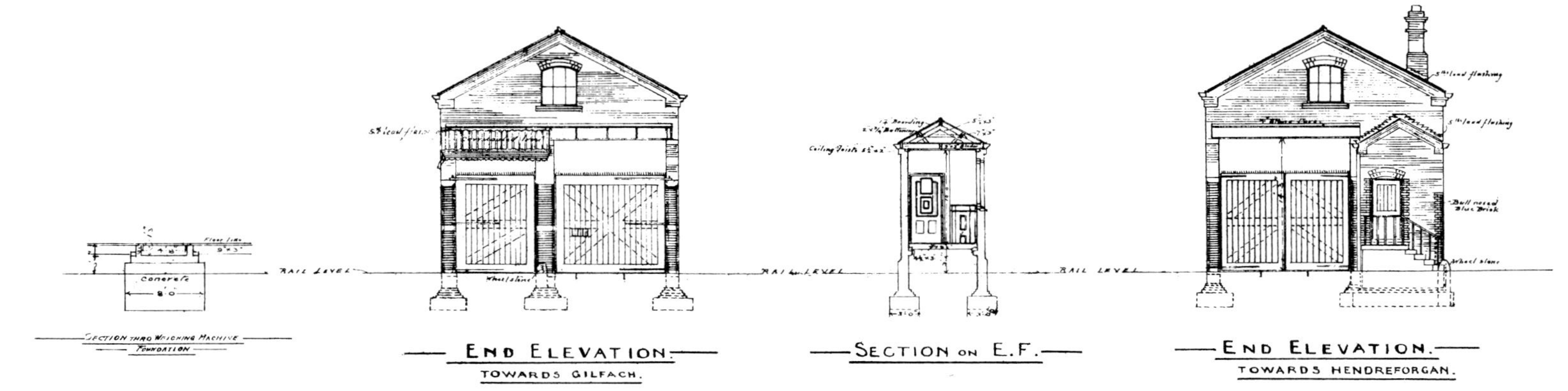

Plate 548
Official drawing. Undated.

Plate 549

The goods shed built for the new station at Birmingham, Moor Street which was opened to the public during the first decade of this century.

British Rail

Plate 550

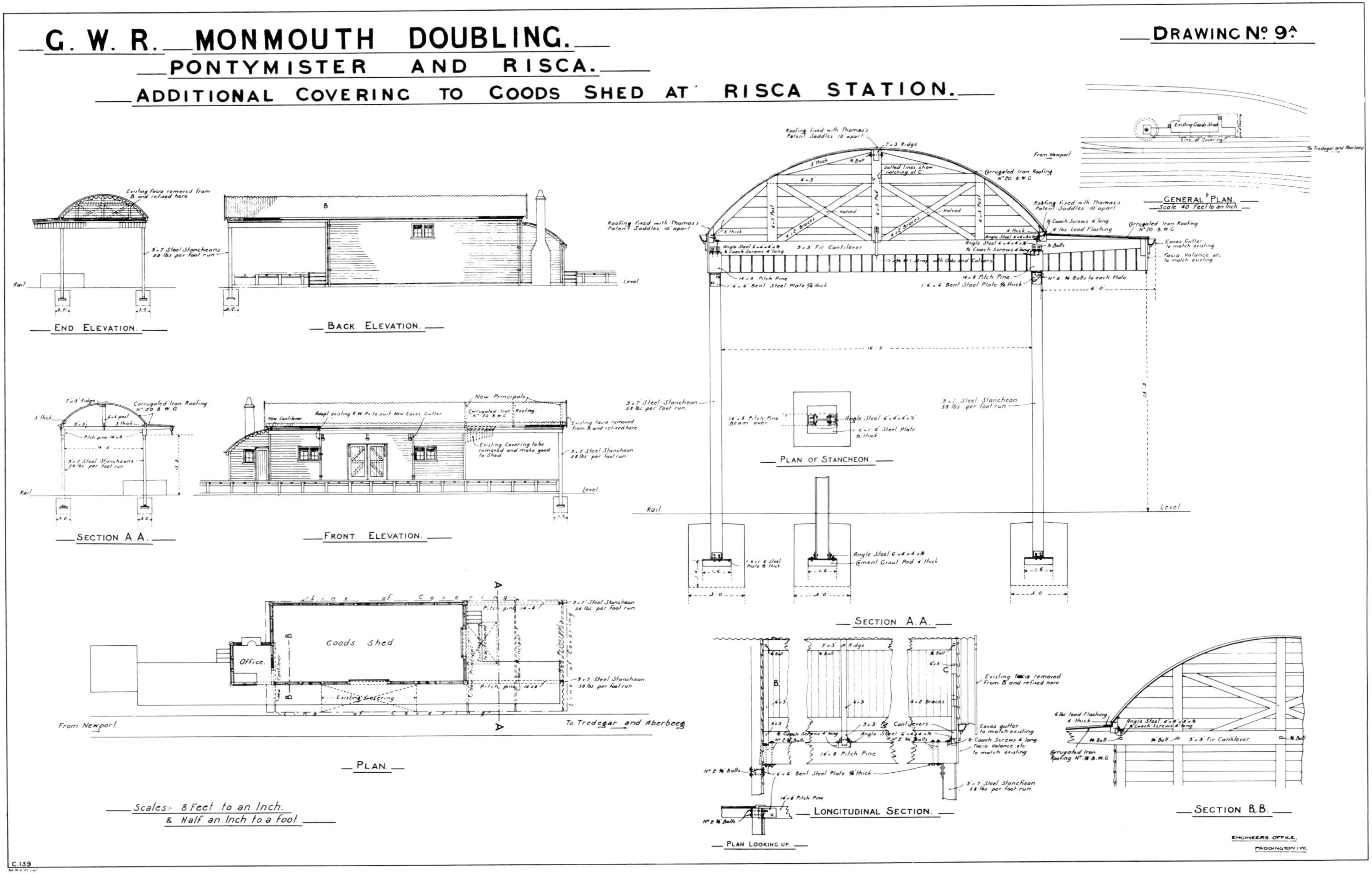

G. W. R. MONMOUTH DOUBLING.

PONTYMISTER AND RISCA.

ADDITIONAL COVERING TO GOODS SHED AT RISCA STATION.

DRAWING Nº 9ᴬ

END ELEVATION.

Existing facia removed from B and refixed here

3 × 7 Steel Stancheons 58 lbs per foot run

Rail

BACK ELEVATION.

Level

SECTION A.A.

7 × 3 Ridge

Corrugated Iron Roofing Nº 20 B.W.G

3 × 7 Steel Stancheons 58 lbs per foot run

FRONT ELEVATION.

New Principals

New Cantilever

Adapt existing R.W. Ps to suit New Eaves Gutter

Corrugated Iron Roofing Nº 20 B.W.G

Existing facia removed from B and refixed here

Existing Covering to be removed and make good to Shed

3 × 7 Steel Stancheon 58 lbs per foot run

Level

PLAN.

Line of Covering

Goods Shed

Office.

Existing Covering

Pitch pine 14 × 8

3 × 7 Steel Stancheon 58 lbs per foot run

From Newport.

To Tredegar and Aberbeeg

Scales:- 8 Feet to an Inch.
& Half an Inch to a Foot.

Roofing fixed with Thomas's Patent Saddles 10" apart

7 × 3 Ridge

Dotted lines show notching at C

Corrugated Iron Roofing Nº 20 B.W.G

3 × 3 Fir Cantilever

Angle Steel 6 × 4 × 4 × ½

⅝ Coach Screws 4" long

14 × 8 Pitch Pine

1 × 6 × 6 Bent Steel Plate ⅝ thick

Nº 4 ¾ Bolts to each Plate

Eaves Gutter to match existing

Facia Valance etc to match existing

6 lbs Lead Flashing

3 × 7 Steel Stancheon 58 lbs per foot run.

PLAN OF STANCHEON.

14 × 8 Pitch Pine Beam over

Angle Steel 6 × 4 × 4 × ½

1 × 6 × 1 6 Steel Plate ⅝ thick

Angle Steel 6 × 4 × 4 × ½

Cement Grout Pad 4" thick

Rail

Level

GENERAL PLAN.
Scale 40 Feet to an Inch

Existing Goods Shed

Line of Covering

From Newport

To Tredegar and Aberbeeg

SECTION A.A.

LONGITUDINAL SECTION.

Existing facia removed from B and refixed here

Eaves gutter to match existing

Facia Valance etc to match existing

14 × 8 Pitch Pine

1 × 6 × 6 Bent Steel Plate ⅝ thick

Nº 2 ¾ Bolts

PLAN LOOKING UP.

SECTION B.B.

6 lbs lead Flashing 4 thick

Corrugated Iron Roofing Nº 18 B.W.G

3 × 3 Fir Cantilever

ENGINEERS OFFICE.
PADDINGTON, W.

C.139

G. W. R. RISCA.

NEW GOODS SHED AND OFFICE.

Plate 551
Official drawings.

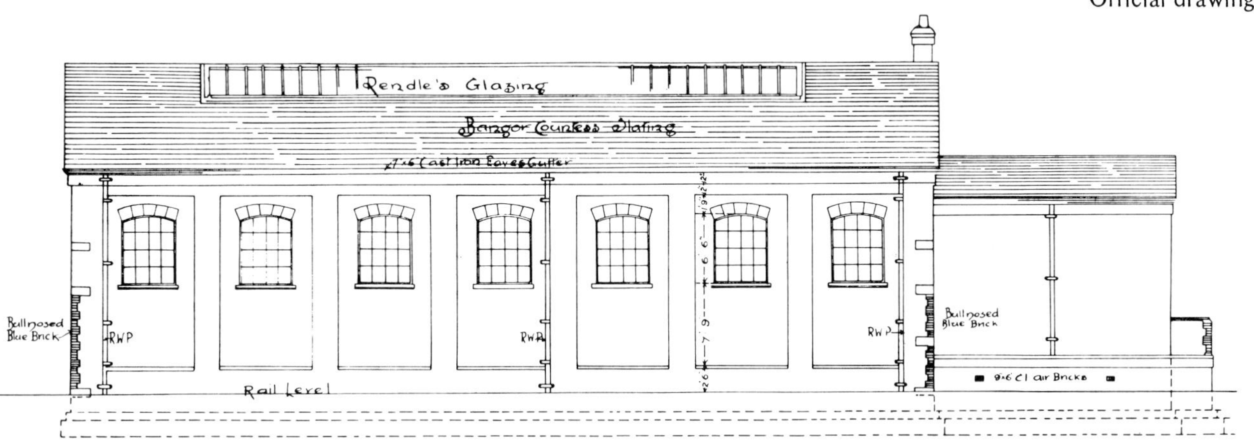

ELEVATION TOWARDS MAIN LINE

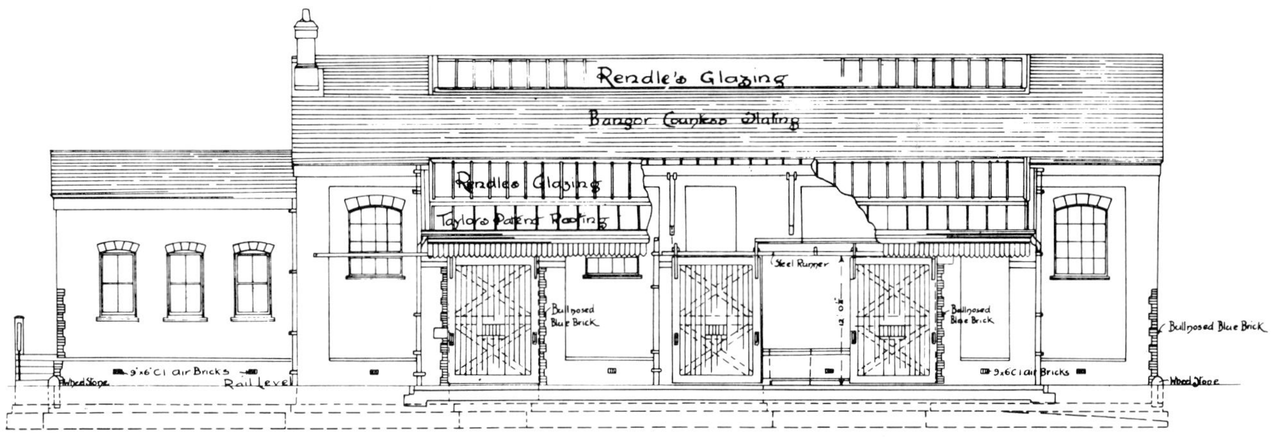

ELEVATION TOWARDS YARD

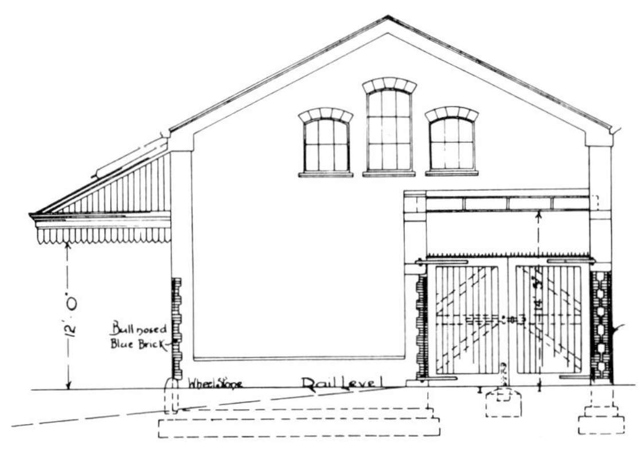

END ELEVATION OF SHED.

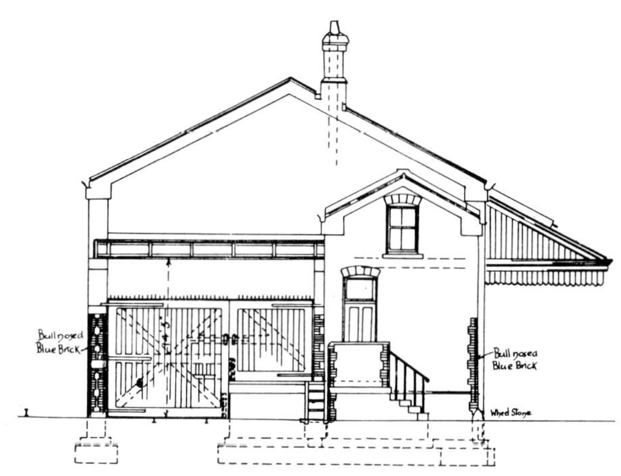

END ELEVATION OF SHED AND OFFICE

Plate 552

British Rail

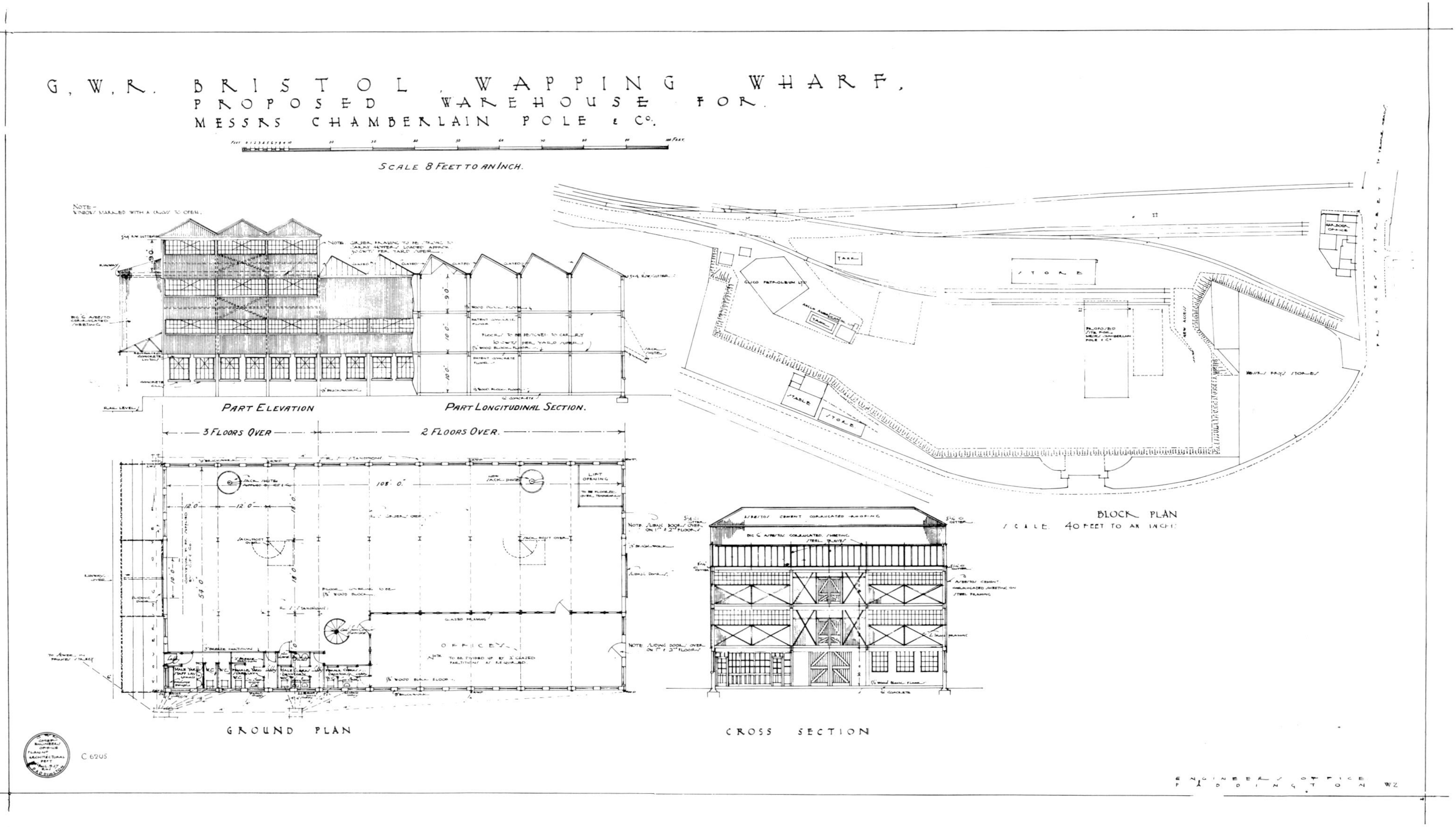
G. W. R. BRISTOL, WAPPING WHARF,
PROPOSED WAREHOUSE FOR
MESSRS CHAMBERLAIN POLE & Co.
SCALE 8 FEET TO AN INCH.
PART ELEVATION
PART LONGITUDINAL SECTION.
3 FLOORS OVER
2 FLOORS OVER.
108' 0"
54' 0"
LIFT OPENING
OFFICES
GROUND PLAN
CROSS SECTION
ASBESTOS CEMENT CORRUGATED ROOFING
BLOCK PLAN
SCALE 40 FEET TO AN INCH
STORE
TANK
STABLE
STORE
ENGINEERS OFFICE
PADDINGTON W2
C 6205

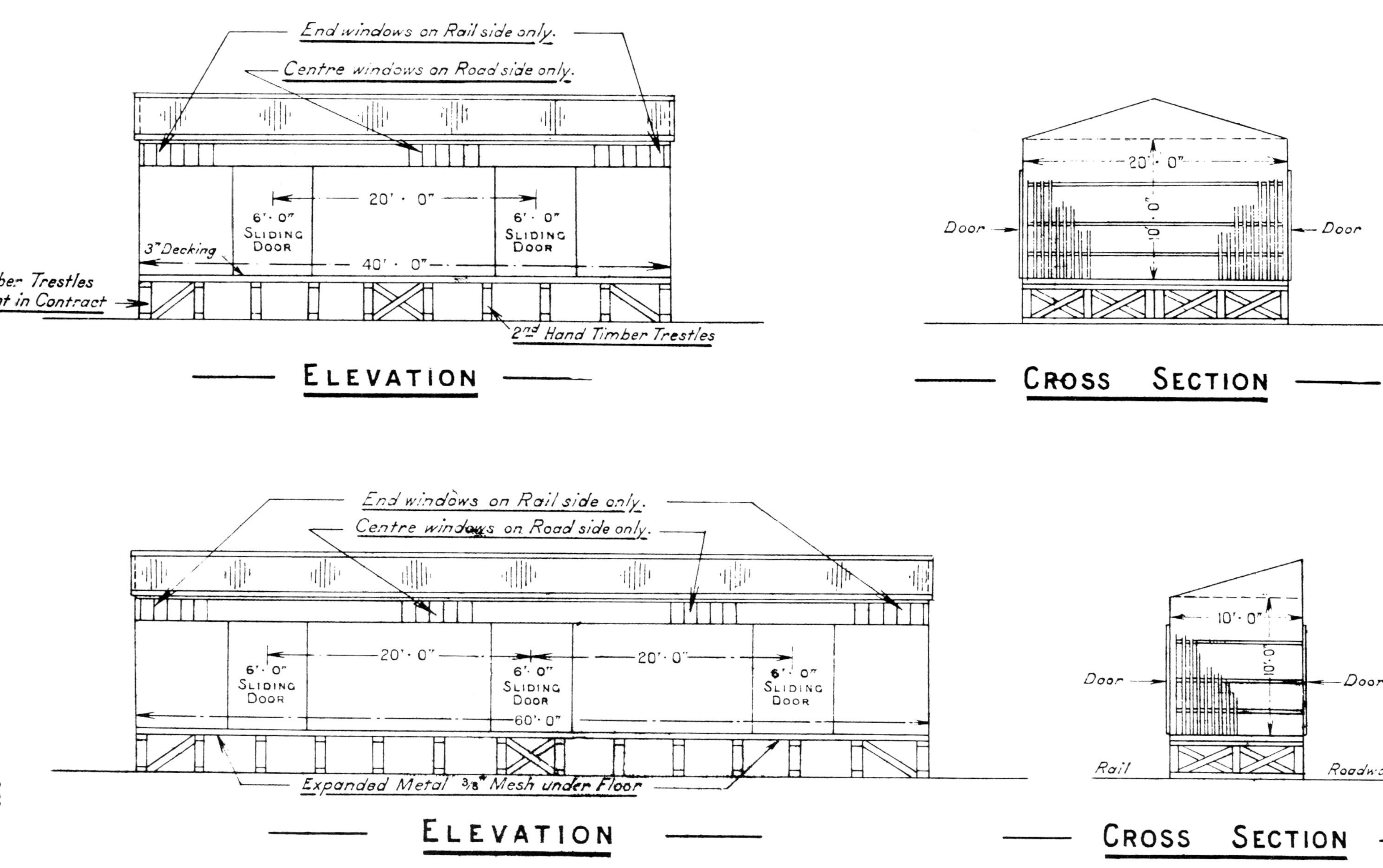

Plate 553
Official drawing dated 31.4.34.

Plate 554

Hopper mechanism shrouded in corrugated iron and mounted on a tough framework of timber to carry heavy weights of stone. This installation was at the end of an aerial ropeway in the 'Bleighert' system at a quarry, location unknown.

British Rail

Plate 555

Wagon lifts, probably operated by hydraulic pressure. Birmingham Moor Street.

British Rail

Plate 556
Another view of the wagon lift at Birmingham Moor Street.
British Rail

Plate 557
Hydraulically operated wagon lifts for transferring vehicles from the High Level to the Low Level goods yard at Paddington. The man in the foreground is standing by a wagon-hauling capstan turned by water power.
British Rail

Chapter Nine

Stables, Cattle Pens, Loading Bays, Weighbridges etc.

Plate 558
Official drawing of the stable building at Abingdon.

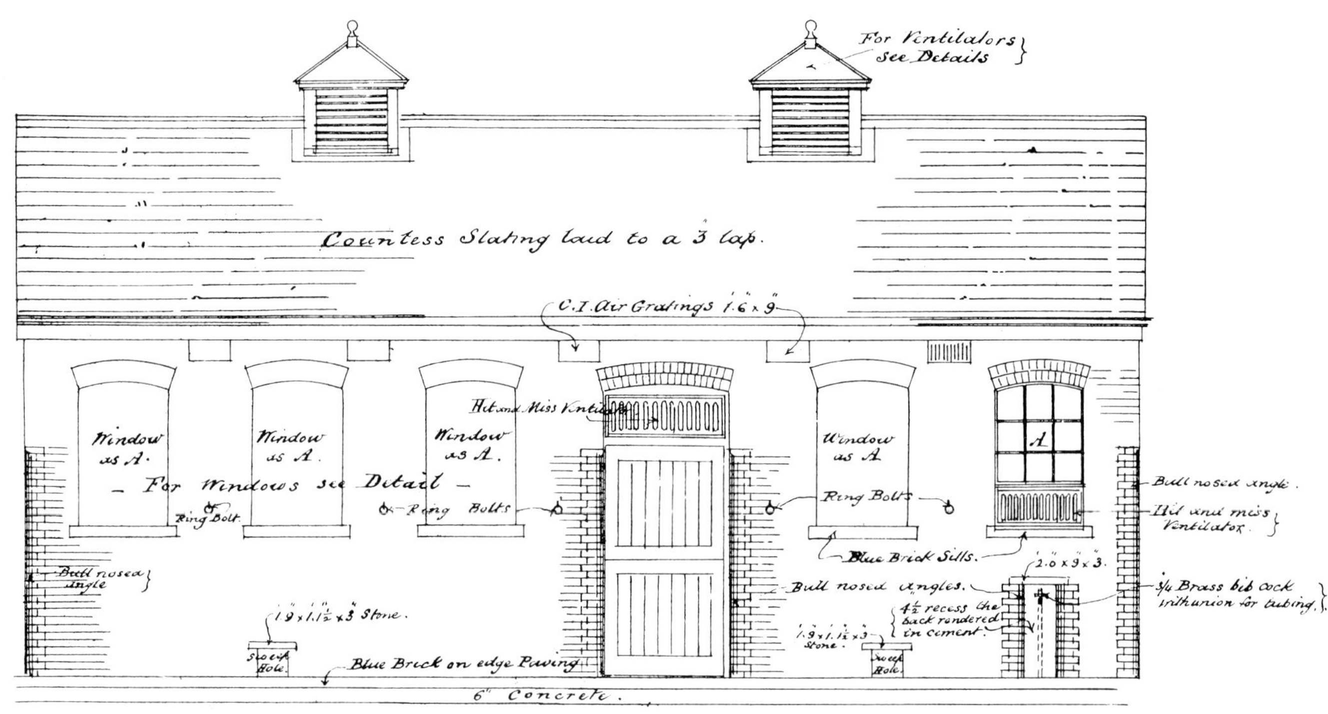

Plate 559
Abingdon stables with the horses removed and reams of printing paper substituted. The goods shed is in the background.
Author 1973

Plate 560

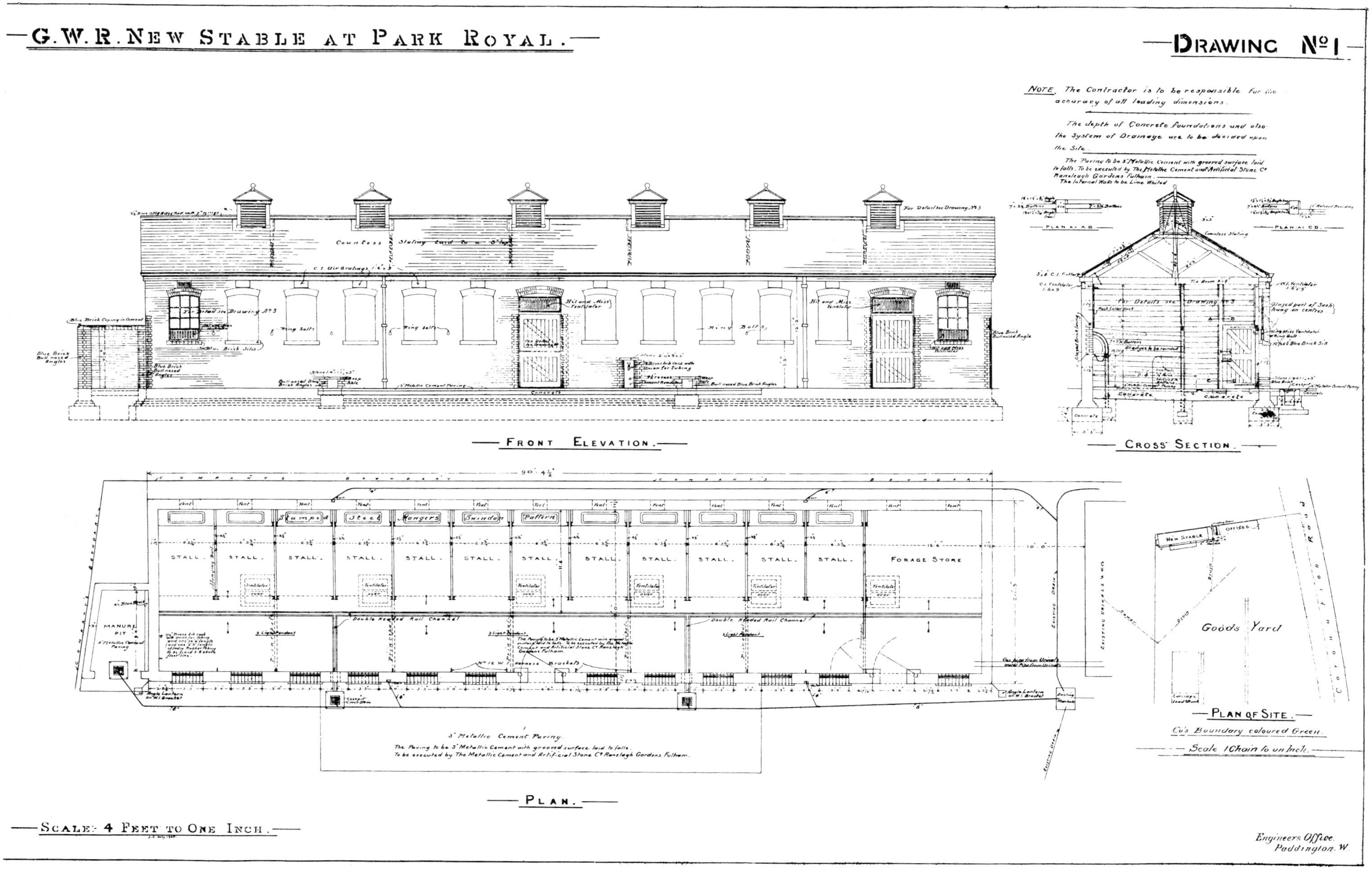

G.W.R. New Stable at Park Royal.
Drawing No 1
NOTE. The Contractor is to be responsible for the accuracy of all leading dimensions.
The depth of Concrete Foundations and also the System of Drainage are to be decided upon the Site.
The Paving to be 3" Metallic Cement with grooved surface laid to falls. To be executed by The Metallic Cement and Artificial Stone Co Ranelagh Gardens Fulham.
The Internal Walls to be Lime Whited
Front Elevation.
Cross Section.
Stall.
Forage Store
Manure Pit
Double Headed Rail Channel
3" Metallic Cement Paving.
The Paving to be 3" Metallic Cement with grooved surface laid to falls.
To be executed by The Metallic Cement and Artificial Stone Co Ranelagh Gardens Fulham.
Plan.
New Stable
Goods Yard
Plan of Site.
Co's Boundary coloured Green.
Scale 1 Chain to an Inch.
Scale: 4 Feet to One Inch.
Engineers Office. Paddington. W.

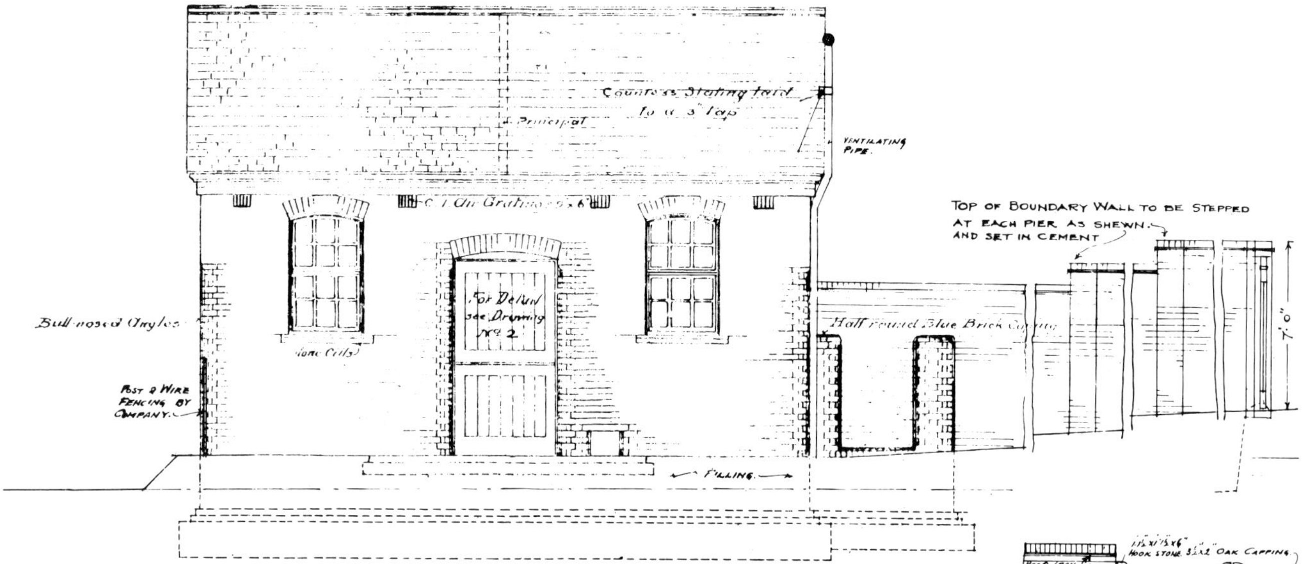

Countess Slating laid to a 3" lap

VENTILATING PIPE

TOP OF BOUNDARY WALL TO BE STEPPED AT EACH PIER AS SHEWN AND SET IN CEMENT

Bull-nosed Angles

Half Round Blue Brick Coping

POST & WIRE FENCING BY COMPANY

FILLING

FRONT ELEVATION.

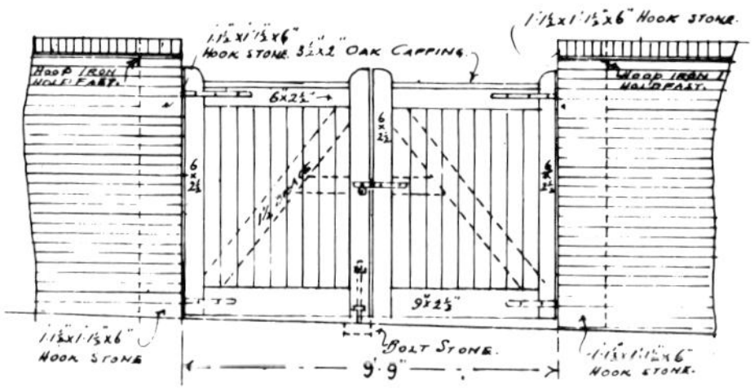

ELEVATION OF NEW GATES

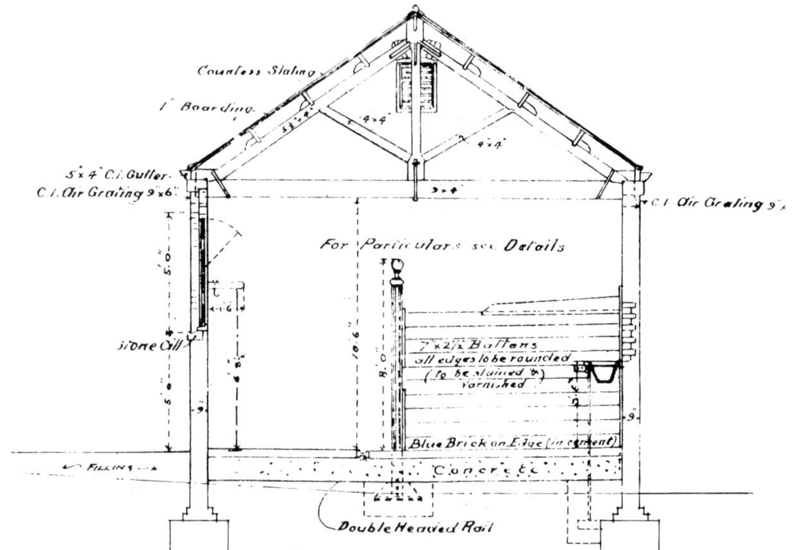

Countess Slating

1" Boarding

5"x4" C.I. Gutter

C.I. Air Grating 9"x6"

For Particulars see Details

7"x2½" Battens all edges to be rounded (to be stained & varnished)

Stone Cill

Blue Brick on Edge (in cement)

Concrete

FILLING

Double Headed Rail

CROSS SECTION.

Plate 561

Official drawings of the stable buildings at Castle Cary.

British Rail

Plate 562

The Great Western Railway had something over 20,000 horses in service before 1914 and for this vast regiment they needed tons of varied fodder. Hay, straw, oats, beans, bran, linseed, blankets, medicine, all had to pass through this central clearing house and store before being re-distributed around the system. The 'Provender Store' at Didcot had exceptionally massive walls at a time when massive walls on the railway were the norm. The place was built with the strength of a mill house because its floor had to bear the load of hundreds of tons of grain. Incidentally, the Store also made the working at Didcot West End signal box much more complicated owing to arrival and departure of provender trains and the shunting of wagons to make up the trains. The building was demolished in 1976.

British Rail

G. W. R. STANDARD CATTLE PENS.

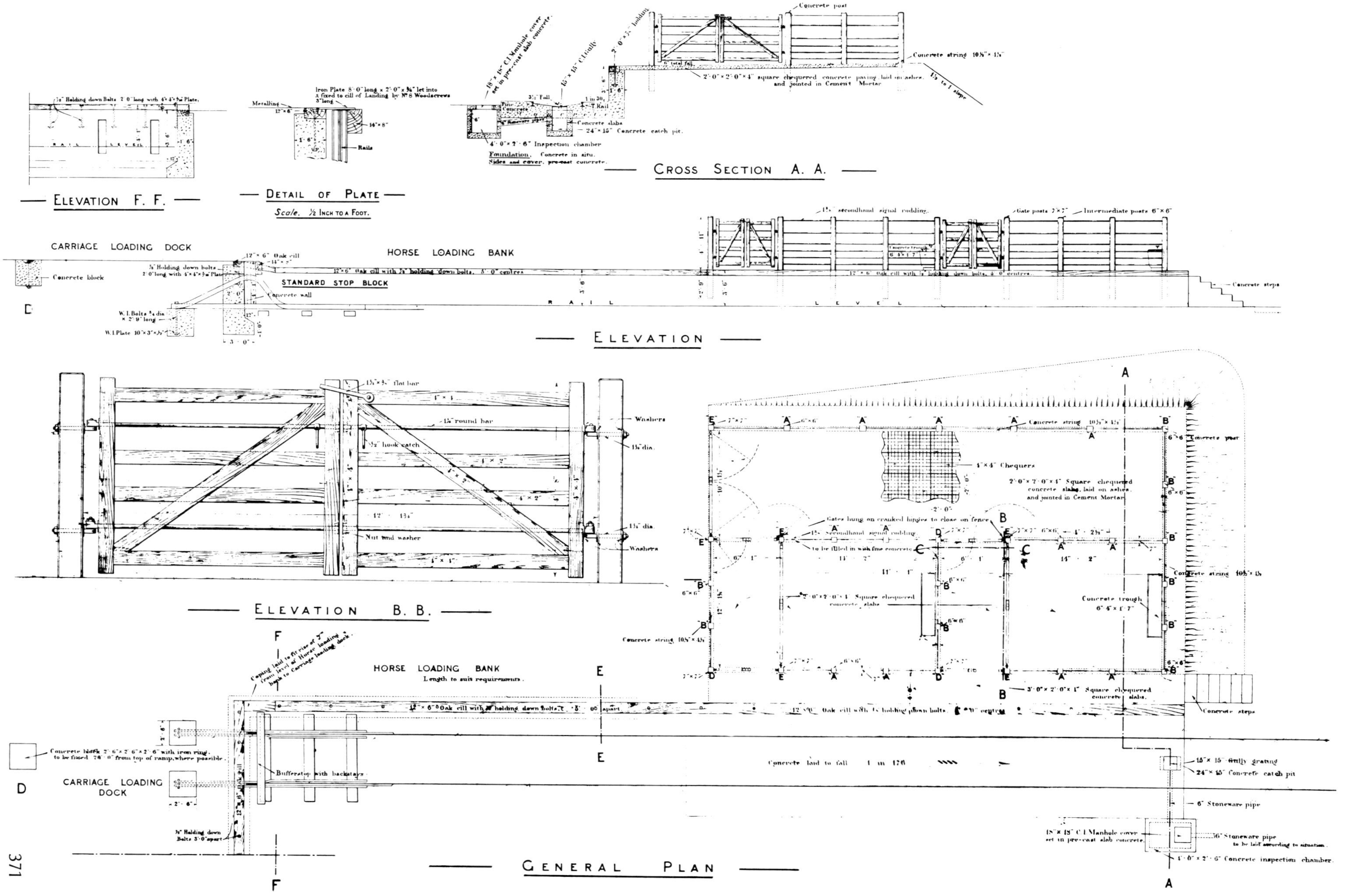

Plate 563
Official drawing of cattle pens.

CROSS SECTION A. A.

ELEVATION F. F.

DETAIL OF PLATE
Scale. ½ INCH TO A FOOT.

CARRIAGE LOADING DOCK

HORSE LOADING BANK

STANDARD STOP BLOCK

ELEVATION

ELEVATION B. B.

HORSE LOADING BANK
Length to suit requirements.

CARRIAGE LOADING DOCK

GENERAL PLAN

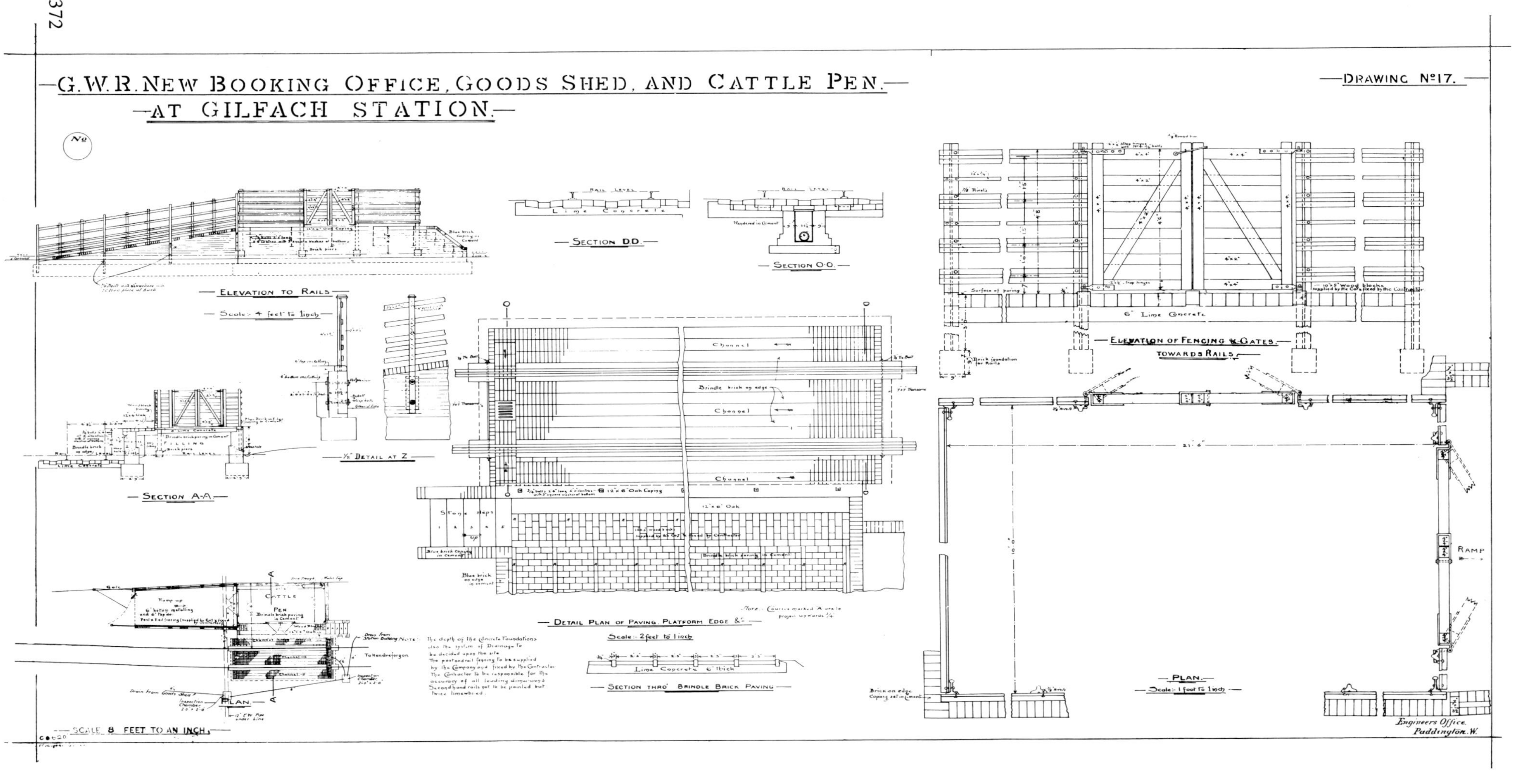

Plate 564

British Rail

Plate 565
Cattle pens, probably at Reading. A wheelbarrow by the fence is smothered in whitewash as are the pens at the end of the platform. This and the heaps of soiled straw, show that Great Western Railway policy regarding the carriage of cattle, i.e. that each wagon be thoroughly cleaned and whitewashed after every trip, is being carefully carried out.

British Rail

Plate 566
Loading gauge at Wallingford. Notice the rather ornate metal work.

Colin Judge

Plate 567
Loading gauge and weighbridge in the goods yard at South Lambeth.

British Rail

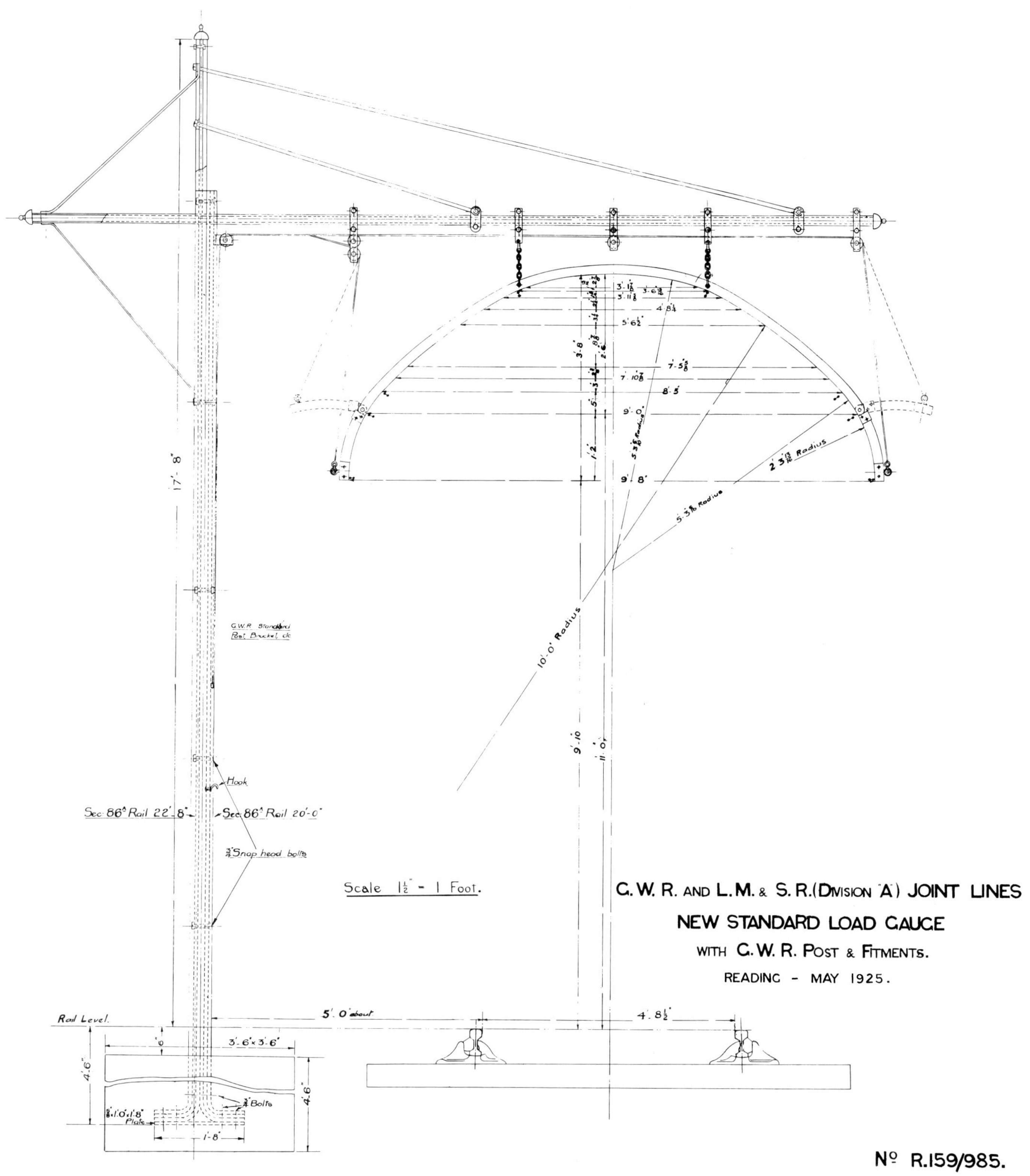

Plate 568
Official drawing.
British Rail

Plate 569

Weighbridge hut at Frome. This is well made in local stone and probably dates from 1850/60. It formed a shelter for the weighbridge man and his scales.

Author 1973

Plate 570

The Pooley scales at Badminton, with their attendant, were sheltered in this brick hut, built to the standard design of the period (1902).

Author 1973

Plate 571
Looking out through the gates of the South Lambeth depot about the time the depot opened to traffic. The small hut in the centre is the weighbridge hut.
British Rail

Plate 572
Weighbridge at Danzey in 1964.
Colin Judge

Plate 573
Weighbridge at Weston-sub-Edge (built) 1904.

Plate 574
Crane at Knightwick.
Colin Judge

Chapter Ten

Swindon– Its Works, Village and Church

"New Swindon" was built on a vacant plot of land, except for a solitary tavern, on the south side of the Great Western Railway. The Company purchased the land with the rest of the area it needed to build its locomotive works and station. By the time a contractor had been found to construct these places, the Directors had become alarmed by the high cost of building the line and so wished to economise at Swindon. J. & C. Rigby, Contractors, of London, were therefore allowed to make a strange bargain with the Great Western Railway over the work that had to be done. The contractors, the Rigby brothers, would build the factory, station and 300 cottages at their own expense on land supplied by the Great Western Railway. In return the Rigbys would receive the rents from the cottages and the receipts of the hotel and refreshment rooms to be built on Swindon station. The Company would charge the brothers one penny per annum as a lease on these rooms and in return for this agreed to stop all trains that were not travelling "express" for about ten minutes at the station so that the passengers could purchase comestibles at the refreshment rooms. The Great Western Railway further undertook not to allow any other refreshment rooms to be opened on their premises between Paddington and Bristol. One wonders if Rigbys knew of the financial straits of the Company and drove this very hard bargain as a result. The lease was signed on December 25th 1841 and within a week it had been sub-let to Mr. Griffiths of Cheltenham for a premium of £6,000 and an annual rent of £1,100. Having recouped a large part of their outlay on the station, John and Charles Rigby sat back and waited seven years to the termination of the agreement with Griffiths. Having by this time received a total of £13,700, they sold the lease outright to J.R. Phillips for £20,000. The brothers must have been formidable salesmen, and they had the Great Western Directors over the proverbial barrel in that the latter desperately needed Swindon station at a time when they were short of cash but the others didn't need Swindon. What, I wonder, did Griffiths get out of the rooms in seven years after paying John and Charles? As for Phillips handing over £20,000—no wonder the food he sold was the cheapest it was possible to buy, he had to buy very cheap and sell very dear! There were, one might say, 20,000 reasons why Swindon station got its nickname, "Swindleum."

Familiar though the outline of the buildings were on the platforms of Swindon station, the bulk of them had nothing to do with railway work but were in fact the refreshment rooms and hotel which the brothers Rigby built. The station consisted of two island platforms, four tracks separated them and the tracks of the up and down Gloucester branch passed "behind" them. On each platform was one of Rigby's blocks. These measured 170 ft. x 37 ft. and were three storeys high. The bottom floor was a basement wherein lived the refreshment room and hotel workers. The kitchens and administrative offices were also housed in the basements. The floor at platform level contained the refreshment rooms for first and second class passengers, the two grades being kept apart by elongated columns decorated with imitation wood inlay. Third class passengers did not eat. The top floor made the hotel an exceptionally inconvenient place with the sitting and coffee rooms in the block on the southern platform and the bedrooms in the northern block. Gable ends in the form of a classical pediment decorated both blocks, though the southern block had not possessed its pediments since about 1897 when a fire gutted the building and it was rebuilt with a very plain gable without so much as a line of dentils under the eaves.[1] The exterior walls of the buildings were beautifully drawn by Brunel. He used ornaments sparingly, a scroll on keystones over door and window arches, and depended on tall windows and doors, well-proportioned to produce a dignified effect. The awning over the platforms was similar to the outside canopy at Bath in that they were both in timber with very slightly tapered square section supports and a flat roof.

Passengers bought their tickets from a booking office on the south side of the line and climbed stairs to reach the down platform. To gain the up platform they had to mount further stairs to the top storey of the main building and cross the line by the covered footbridge. A new booking office and awning were provided in 1872 or 1873, the date on the drawings for this is 3-10-72, and perhaps the subway linking the booking office and the platforms was constructed at the same time. Over the years the station

[1] The Great Western Railway having just then paid £100,000 to buy the hotel company out, this parsimony is understandable.

changed little to the casual glance. Bay platforms were added at the western and eastern ends, doubtless all at different times, but all early on in the station's history. It is very likely that the east facing bay in the up platform was constructed in 1872 when the "narrow", or standard gauge rails reached Swindon from Didcot. The bay had three "roads" and these were always for the 4 ft. 8½ ins. gauge even when the rest of the tracks in the station were mixed gauge. An interesting picture of this bay appears in O.S. Nock's book "The Great Western Railway" and shows what might be a small engine shed within the bay.

Construction of the factory and working men's cottages began late in 1840 or early 1841. The original "new town" consisting of six streets between the Park and the railway station, is interesting for the following reasons. It was built early in the struggle for more healthy towns and is the practical embodiment of Brunel's conception of what such a town should be. Brunel's liberal tendencies were restrained by the Company which was already short of money and questioning the necessity of every new expense. It is to the Company's credit, therefore, that they let Brunel build as he did. Since 1838 at least, there had been a strong lobby in Parliament calling for Town Boards of Health to supervise the installation and thereafter to maintain, a piped supply of pure drinking water, proper drains and sewage disposal, and to prevent overcrowding of people and houses. "Iron man" Edwin Chadwick, who had been converted from the scourge to the defender of the poor, was vigorously pursuing these essentials in 1841 and managed, in 1848 to have a law passed setting up Public Boards of Health. Owing to Chadwick's over-zealous, overbearing manner, these boards were never popular but it was a start from which the country never looked back. Brunel's cottages pre-dated Chadwick's reforms by six years. They pre-dated the delightfully named "Metropolitan Association for Improving the Dwellings of the Labouring Classes" by several months and were 10 or 15 years ahead of the main body of early law regarding the construction and use of "labouring class dwellings". Brunel had demonstrated his fair minded and public spirited nature during the Bristol Riots of October 1831 (see L.T.C. Rolt's "Isambard Kingdom Brunel" p.59 et seq.), he showed it in his designs for Swindon "new town" and he was to show it again, in a large way, during the Crimean War (see L.T.C. Rolt's "Isambard Kingdom Brunel" p.223 et seq.).

Wide streets separated the rows of terraced cottages which Brunel had designed, so that there was not a gloomy side to any street. Each cottage had a tiny patch of ground between it and the pavement with a low wall separating the "garden" from the footpath. It is very likely that railings once lined these long walls which extended the length of the terraces. There were at least five designs of cottage, varying from the most Gothic to the square, "Lakeland" style. Those that could be described as "Gothic" had fine chimney stacks carrying batteries of diamond shaped chimneys, rather square windows, their panes recessed in a wide, exterior splay, and tall doorways, slightly narrow perhaps, with an echo of Brunel's usual Gothic hood over the lintel and around the upper part of the arch. The wall was pierced once for two front doors, these being set at about 45° to the outside walls, half facing each other. Walls of the houses were invariably constructed in stone, either "cut rubble" or "random rubble" blocks. In the case of "cut rubble" blocks the wall was built in two "skins" and the cavity between filled with stone sized ballast of quarry rubble. This appears to have been a common form of construction in the days of the Brick Tax (repealed 1850) when it was often cheaper to build in stone than brick. Looking over the length of a street of "Gothic" cottages, the ranks of sharply creased chimney stacks, "gardens" full of railwaymen's flowers, and the spaciousness of the wide street, one imagines that the new town was a new town indeed.

Whether each cottage had piped water in 1841 I do not know, it is possible, but it is fairly certain that fresh water came into every street through hydrants at intervals along the street. The Company had to bring large quantities of water for the factory and engine shed and, as the whole complex of buildings was erected at the same time, it seems certain that a water main would have been extended from the factory site to the site of the estate and then buried as building work progressed. Each cottage was built with a lavatory, or privy, as they were called then, in the back yard and it does not seem likely that Brunel would have provided a privy without some prudent procedure for procuring the rapid removal of its contents, even if it was only a bucket of water at the householder's end and a large dump at the end of a long pipe at the other. Also in the back yard was the wash-house for the weekly laundry and the coal-hole. These back yards were rather gloomy, trapped between the house and the high wall which bordered on an alley of the sort that rings to one's footsteps. The alley between the cottages facing Bath Street and Exeter Street is taken through a house at each end of its length and at its exit Brunel arranged a Gothic arch and pointed gable as a kind of gatehouse.

In the centre of the town the Company built a hospital, baths, a laundry, an adult school, a non-conformist Chapel, a market, dispensary, shops, taverns, and a coffee bar. The hospital had a resident doctor and nursing staff and a visiting surgeon. At the dispensary one could obtain medicine and bandages for a small sum or a smaller sum if you paid a weekly subscription to the Medical fund. The adult school became known as the Mechanics' Institute and taught the men the "three Rs" and more advanced technology, and there was a school for children too. The Chapel, now the Railway Museum, was out of Company ownership by 1881 having been purchased by the "New Swindon Wesleyans". I think it was remarkable that the Company allowed Brunel to build taverns for the men, when "drinking" by the lower orders was frowned upon, not without reason, by their "betters". The Directors could have saved several hundred pounds here by appealing to their consciences and forbidding all fleshpots. It is to their credit that they were democratic enough not to do this but content themselves with some counter-propaganda in the form of the "Temperance Union." The great railway companies have been criticised for "paternalism" but wherein lies the disadvantage of a kind father who builds his children "pubs" against his better judgement? The Great Western Railway seems to have been fair, very fair by the lights of their times—there are no housing estates for railwaymen being built nowadays—they gave their men a church and a chapel but did not force them to attend either, they built taverns to save their employees a long walk up the hill into "Old Town" and they gave them a health service which was to become the foundation of the present National Health Scheme.

By 1843 the new town was complete and very soon filled with families. By 1846 there were 1,800 men working in the factory. A shortage of housing existed almost from the start which was catered for by speculative builders erecting some very shoddy houses which so alarmed the Company that they began building more houses of their own. Thus the new town quickly grew in pace with the factory. In 1850 the latter extended from the junction with the main line and the Gloucester branch to a point opposite St. Mark's Church. By 1878 the buildings had reached a point now marked by the eastern edge of "A" erecting shop and soon after 1900 the latter huge building was erected. In 1850 the works extended along the main line for about a quarter of a mile and by 1910 they extended just over one mile along the Bristol main line.

As the physical size of Swindon factory grew, so did the "spiritual" life of the factory community grow. In the early times a great number of the skilled workers had come from the north of England, because there was not a sufficient supply of skilled industrial craftsmen in meadowy Wiltshire. The northerners were interlopers because they came from another part of the country, with, to the locals, a strange speech and strange customs. They were members of an industrial society, bringing a new way of life to the area and they lived in a modern "new town" with running water laid on. Quite naturally they and the town were looked upon with suspicion by the Wiltshire folk and from the earliest days in the new town a community spirit was fostered, comrades in a strange, slightly hostile country. The Company helped to create this spirit and turn it into a very useful *esprit de corps.* An annual outing to the sea by free trains was organised for members of the Mechanic's Institute, and later for labourers too. This day trip grew into an exodus of vast proportions—in 1926 25,146 men, women and children were carried to all parts of the country in 29 special trains—and tales of long ago "Trips" were retailed from year to year like the legends of Ancient Greece. The Company also gave an annual "bun fight" for anyone who wanted to attend, when swings and roundabouts were provided, tea and cakes, side shows, and races were held in a vast village fete with the Great Western Railway playing Squire. The Company used to hire the Drill Hall from the local Yeomanry regiment, nothing smaller would do to accommodate the piles of cakes that had to be cut and packed and sandwiches that had to be filled. The day before the great event, wives and sisters congregated in the big hall to prepare the food for the following day. In the 1870's it would have been normal for 20,000 people to turn up for the free food. The fair's swing boats cost a little but were largely subsidised by the Company. A tea was given in honour of Queen Victoria's Diamond Jubilee which was attended by over 20,000 people and the vital beverage was brewed in locomotive tenders specially cleaned out for the occasion. Tea leaves were poured in through the water tank filling hole and by means of specially fitted steam hose connections on the tenders' sides steam was passed into the piles of leaves. The only men who did not drink the resulting concoction were the ones who had cleaned the tanks out! Such social gatherings, attended by workmen and their families sharing a common home and a common occupation, therefore having their problems in common with their amusements, caused a terrific feeling of togetherness, a close knit family spirit within the wider affiliation of the Great Western Railway. So it was that the original settlement, built with concern for the workers, and not just the rents they could pay, in mind formed the nucleus of an army of men whose loyalty to themselves and the Company became a legend.

Swindon Tower

Plate 575

Church Place, Swindon 'New Town'. The gabled cottages on the right look out onto very typical 'Swindon Works' type walls in that familiar reddish-grey stone, rough surfaced, with smooth limestone quoins at the corners providing a contrast of colour and texture,—a dismal prospect from one's bedroom window at 5.30 a.m. on a winter's day. Yet it is strange how such apparently grim things can become friendly and familiar in time. When the factory was criticised for being no place for humans, by Alfred Williams, the famous poet and writer who worked in the foundry there, practically all the workers laughed him to scorn for his folly! Poor Alfred suggested, in his book 'Life in a Railway Factory' that it would be good for the men if they could eat their mid-day meal in a garden, away from the filth of the foundry and an angry article appeared in the Staff magazine, directed against him.

Author 1974

Plate 576

Top Bathampton Street, north side, looking east. The houses have been repaired and modernised by Swindon Corporation who now own them.

Middle I.K. Brunel's idea of chimney stacks on working men's cottages. 1840.

Bottom Backyards on the south side of Bathampton Street.

Plate 577

A cottage in Bathampton Street in what might be termed 'Lakeland' style.

Author 1974

Plate 578

The park, laid out by the Great Western Railway in 1838. In the distance, to the left, is Park House, the medical centre for the Railway, where all locomotive men, porters, signalmen and others went for their examinations prior to employment and before promotion. A famous part of the old Railway, it is now out of service.

Author 1974

Plate 579
The south front of the Mechanics' Institute rebuilt and extended in 1892. The enormous lamp and its curly bracket were standard equipment throughout the factory.
Author 1973

Plate 580
It is well known that Brunel designed ships, docks, railways and tunnels, what is probably less well known is that he also designed public houses. There were three in the original new town, the 'Cricketer's' and the 'Baker's Arms' and this, the lugubriously named 'Gluepot' once known as 'Thomas' Beer House'. These 'pubs' were interesting in the terrific community proprietorship that sprang up around them, though they were theoretically open to all and sundry, only the bravest of the 'sundry' entered them. They belonged to the factory workers who made this quite plain to any 'foreigner' that entered.
Author 1973

Plate 581

New Swindon cottages in 1881
from an official survey

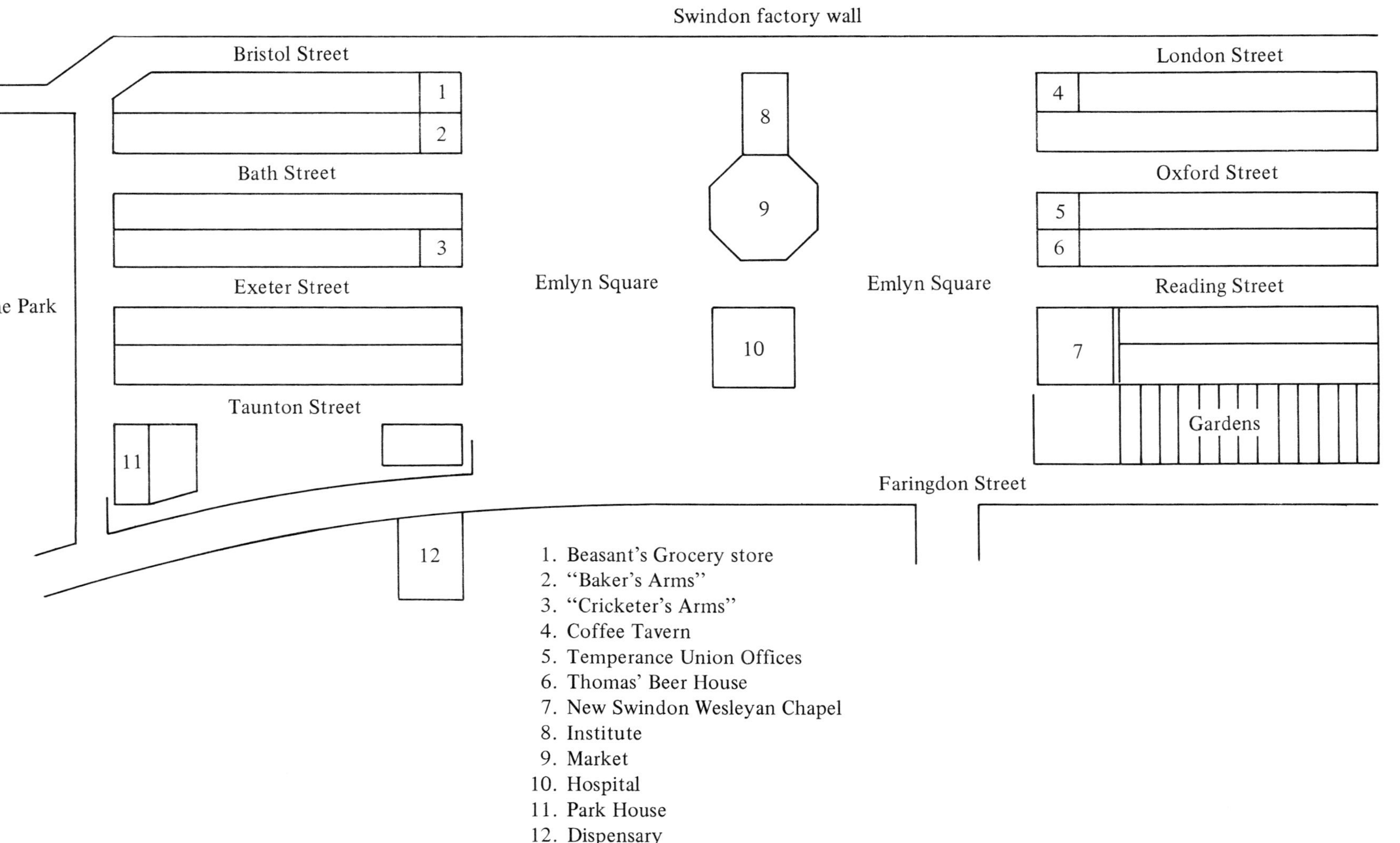

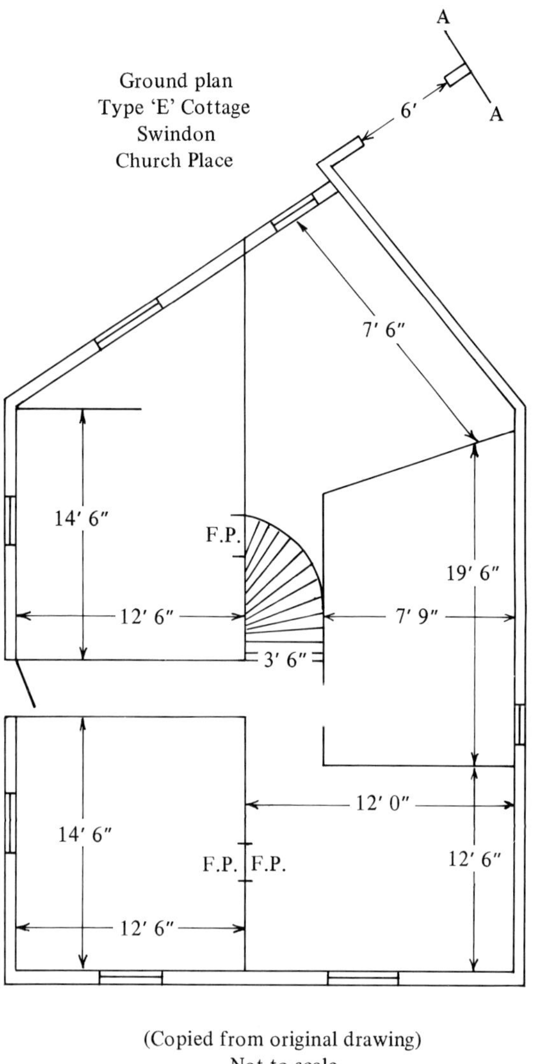

(Copied from original drawing)
Not to scale

Plate 582

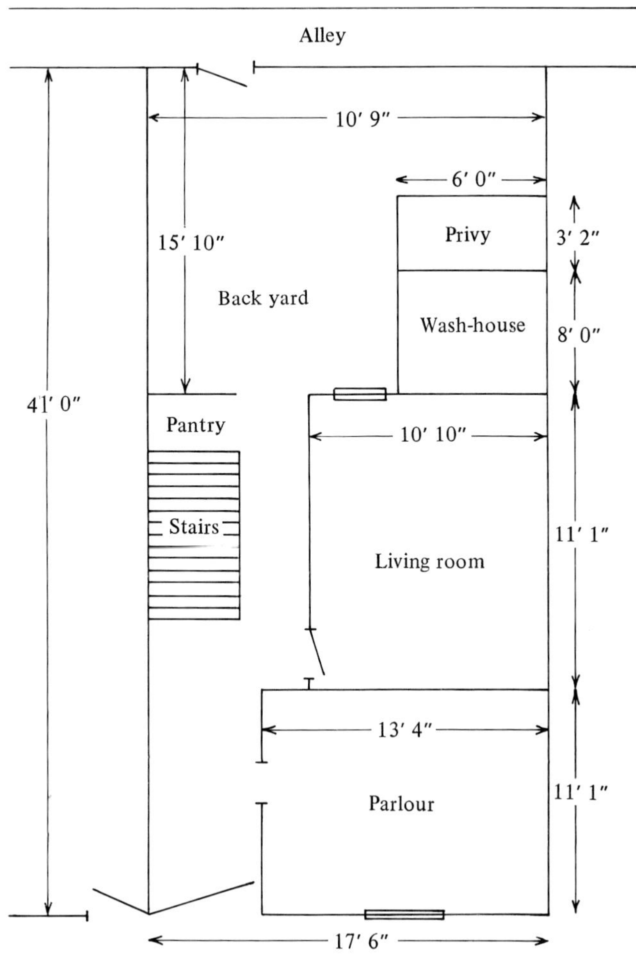

Plate 583

(Copied from original drawings)
Not to scale

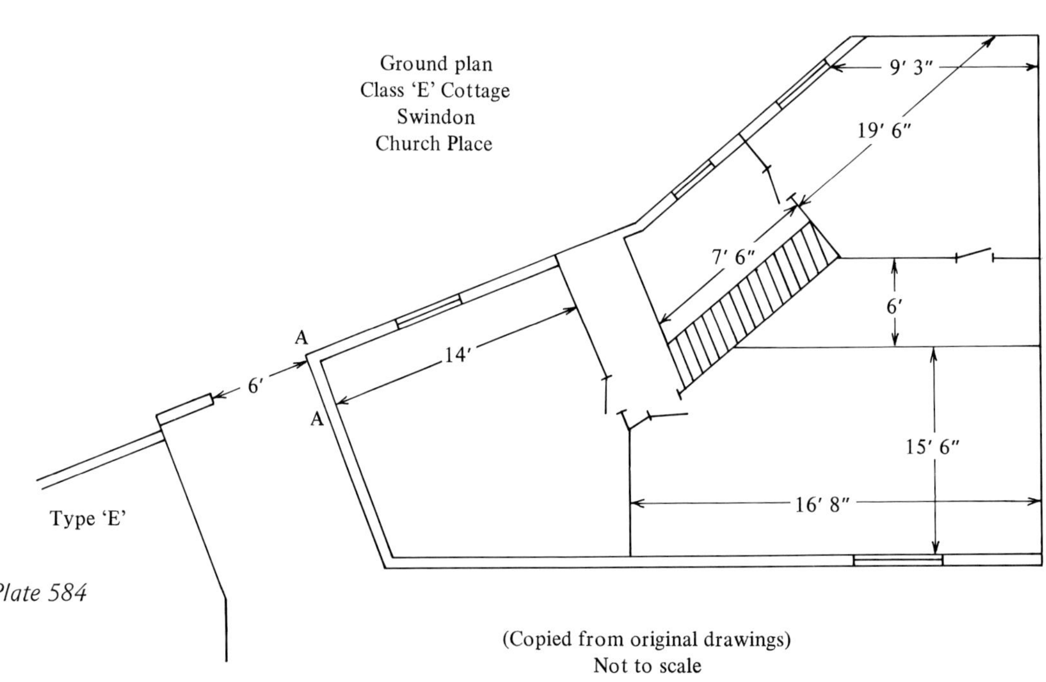

Plate 584

(Copied from original drawings)
Not to scale

St. Mark's Swindon

Plate 585

The church that the Company built for the workers was dedicated to St. Mark, a Low Church saint, while its style was after the manner of the 13th century, a High Church trait. As a sop to Low churchmen the ground plan is rectangular when, to follow the 13th century precedent, it should be cruciform. It was very well constructed, with fine, tall, nave and aisles. The latter are formed by an arcade of 'early English' arches within the church and by the 'lean-to' arrangement on the outside. The smaller rectangle at the east end of the nave houses the altar. This, the chancel, has a vaulted roof, ribbed and handsome. The designer, one Mr. Scott, (Sir Gilbert on his way up?) has not confined himself to one style but has incorporated Early English, say 1200-1250, with the later decorated style of 1250-1300, giving the impression of rebuilding and later periods that one always comes across in old churches. The work was done with restraint, the outside is plain and heavy but the interior is much more elaborate. In the belfry there is a peal of eight bells which are rung from time to time by enthusiastic campanologists from near and far. In March 1960 a new peal was composed and rung for the 2-10-0 engine *Evening Star* the last steam engine to be built at Swindon. The peal was called 'Evening Star Delight Minor'.

Author 1973

Plate 586
St. Mark's Church, Swindon. South porch.

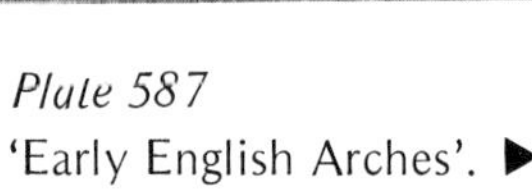

Plate 587
'Early English Arches'. ▶

Plate 588
◀ High in the west wall, a very well done window in the 'Decorated' style depicting 'Christ in Majesty' surrounded by his Saints.

Author 1973

Plate 589
The chancel arch with its fine timber vaulted roof.

Plate 590
The main administrative building of Swindon factory, now headquarters of British Rail Engineering (Swindon) Ltd. The building is 'L' shaped, the illustration showing the southern wing facing the Bristol line. At the top of the building George Jackson Churchward had his office from whence came the ideas that were to produce the finest engines of the generation and influence locomotive design for sixty years.
British Rail

Plate 591
These tablets can be seen high on the south wall of the main office block of the factory. They are very old, maybe as old as the factory itself, and have occupied a position on this building for at least 90 years. They have not always had such an elevated position and were once situated at eye level. In 1907-8 an extra storey was added to accommodate new drawing offices and the tablets were moved to their present position at that time. They each carry the representation of a Gooch 'Single' carved in limestone with considerable accuracy of detail.

British Rail

Plate 592
Entrance to the Chief Mechanical Engineer's building.

British Rail

The Drawing Office Staircase

Plate 593

The main staircase inside the main building, or 'CME's' block as it was called in G.W.R. and B.R. days. The photographs were taken on the first floor landing.

Top The stairs continue to rise to the heights of the old Great Western Railway drawing office.

Bottom Trophies on the wall. The handrail and balusters would not look out of place in a stately home. The non-slip surface on the treads is made of very hard wood cut into cubes. After 60 years they are no more worn than stone would be.

Courtesy of Mr. Roberts, Works Manager.

Author 1974

Plate 594
A view over the 'West Yard' in 1860.
British Rail

Plate 595
From the main entrance of the factory a tunnel passed beneath the tracks to come up near the main office block. This shows the tunnel exit with steps leading to the main office building.
British Rail

Plate 596

For this photograph the camera man stood on the roof of the carriage shops and faced north. It seems likely that this was a 'before' picture at the commencement of rebuilding about 1904. It shows some very old engines, having their boilers clad in asbestos lagging. Smoke box doors and front rings are leaning against the timber shed. Only one number is recognisable among the engines – saddle tank No. 2767.

British Rail

Plate 597

This was almost certainly an 'after' picture to show the CME's block with its new storey completed. It is possible to make out the contrasting colours of the old and new stone work and cement.

British Rail

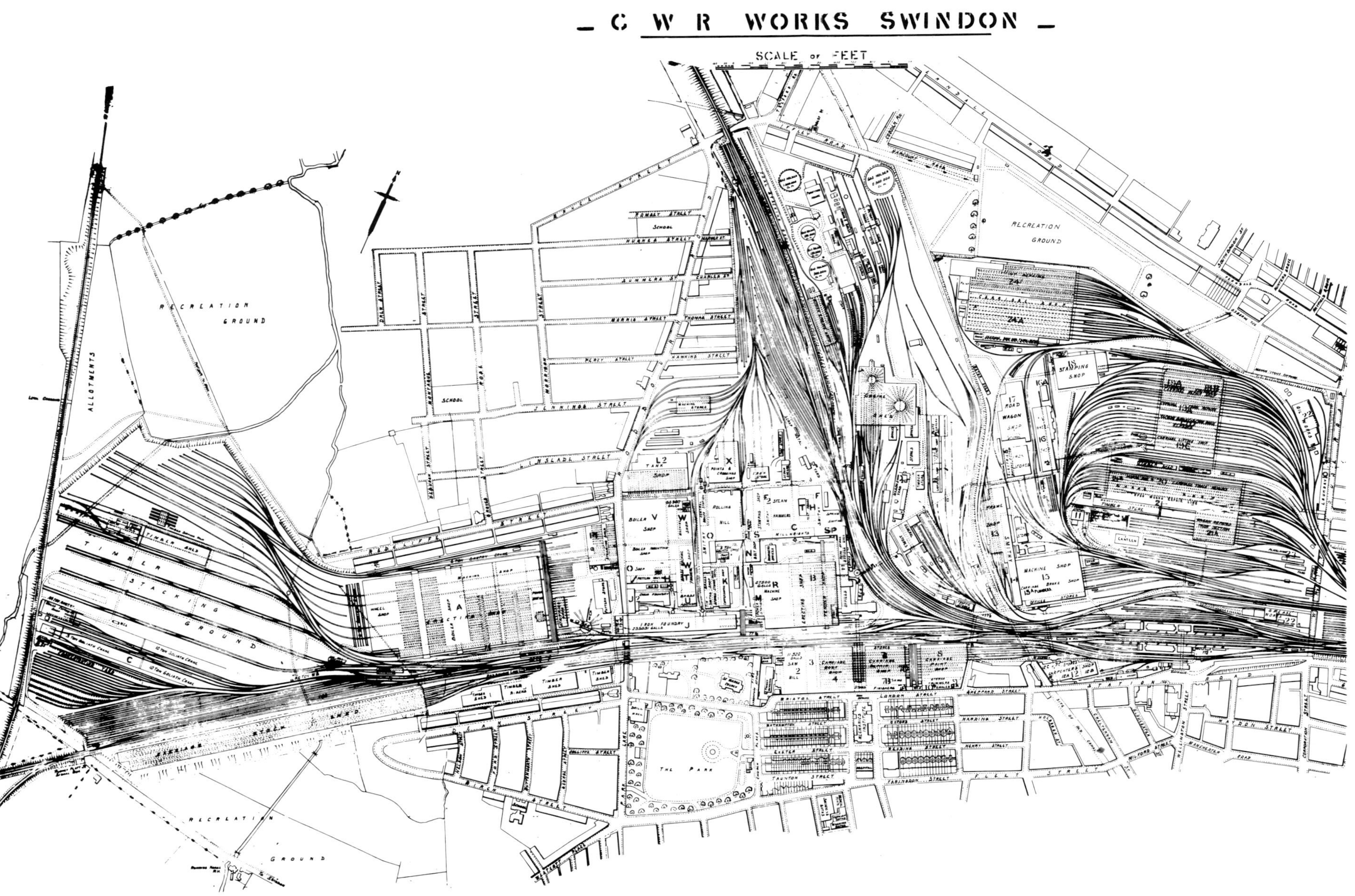

Plate 598

British Rail

Plate 599
View east from the CME's block. The carriage shops are on the right, the station with a layout differing from that of 1960 is in the centre, and the general store, containing all the necessities of daily life for the railway is on the left. The locomotive on the left is 4026 *King Richard*, her driver crouching on the running plate, tenderly pouring oil from his 'long feeder' over some part of the inside motion. Hardly anything is left of this scene today.

British Rail

Plate 600

'A' erecting shop built during the Churchward regime. Outside, shunting is in progress, No. 3855 is standing on the up goods line and No. 6008 *King James II* is about to pass on a down express. The camera man had his back to Rodbourne Lane signal box which is not a dozen yards away.

British Rail

▲ *Plate 601*

The Works Main Entrance disgorging some of the thousands of workers employed there. The view is taken from the Mechanics' Institute building.

British Rail

Plate 602

The original Mechanics' Institute seen from the wall of the Factory.

British Rail

Chapter Eleven

Pumping Stations

Pumping water was an important part of any railway's operations. Water was needed for the locomotives, of course, but in the days before a municipal supply – and indeed, long after one was available – many stations and staff houses were supplied by the Company's pumps. Swindon factory, engine shed and workers' cottages were supplied from Kemble, the pumps being housed in the "V" of the junction between the Gloucester and Tetbury lines. At Faringdon a small engine, working with steam from the branch locomotive's boiler, raised water to a tank for the benefit of the locomotive, station, cattle pens and stables. Pump houses on the Great Western Railway were not architectural gems, unless one includes – as I have done – the pumping stations of the South Devon Railway, but nevertheless they were well made and viewed today against our declining aesthetic standards in building they are admirably handsome buildings.

Plate 603
This shows a large installation for raising water, which was used in water troughs. The water in the trough will then be picked up at speed by a scoop on the locomotive's tender, or, in the case of some tank engines, on the locomotive itself. The buildings appear to be well made and indeed are quite handsome, with pear trees growing up the walls. The roof over the boiler room has a lantern light to improve the ventilation in this hot, possibly fume-laden place. A boiler from an old locomotive is jutting from the building. In the left corner of the plate is a low brick building. This houses the ball valve which is exactly at trough level and can therefore control the admission of water to the troughs.

British Rail

Plate 604

Brunel's marvellous Italianate chimney dominates all his 'atmospheric' pumping stations. Their story is too well known to require any comment from me, but please look at the water tank and the ornate trusses around the top of the tank. What might have been an ugly iron lump has been skilfully incorporated into the older stone building. The location shown here is Exeter.

British Rail

Plate 605

Totnes pump house, illustrated here, was never used as a power station. Look how Brunel used the correct tiles to be in keeping with the North Italian style of tower. Ribbed and moulded as they are they would be at home in Florence itself.

British Rail

Plate 606

This view of the Totnes pump house gives the impression of a Tuscan machicolated tower but situated in Devon. The barn like pump rooms have been arranged in a 'carefully haphazard' manner to give a series of interesting roofs and gables while all the time, in the background, the tower could be full of Lombardy bowmen.

British Rail

Plate 607
Brick built pump house built in 1909 at an unknown location, possibly part of the Severn tunnel pumping system.
British Rail

Plate 608
Garden, gardener and campanile at Totnes.
British Rail

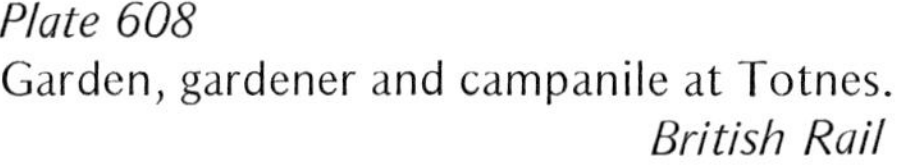

Plate 609
The No. 1 pump house at Sudbrook, Severn Tunnel.
British Rail

Plate 610
Rear view of the No. 1 pump house showing the rods and linkage to the beam of the mighty Cornish engine within.
British Rail

Plate 611

Boiler room, pump house and water reservoir of a hydraulic power plant. I believe that this nstallation provided the energy to work the 'shunting by capstan' system, the capstan and hawsers of which can be seen in the foreground. While many will find this ugly, I feel it has some dignity lent to it by the solid, well made look of the buildings, particularly the water tower, and by the clean cobbles and tidy paths.

British Rail

Plate 612
This installation stands at Reading, just beyond the east end of the platforms, on the upside of the line. Its purpose is to raise water to the large tank which is then used to operate the luggage lifts on the various platforms at the passenger station.

British Rail

Plate 613
A small water tank at St. Anne's Park, Bristol. The vantage point taken up by the photographer has given the picture the atmosphere of a perfect model railway. Every item is so well maintained as to appear unreal; observe the perfectly equal spacing of the sleepers, the rust free tank and smartly painted signal. Of particular interest to signalling enthusiasts are the outer and inner distant signals which route trains into a down goods line ahead. Owing to the curvature of the track the down signals have been placed on the "wrong" side of the line.

British Rail c1897

Plate 614
This was known officially as a wind engine, and was erected at Bicester by the makers, J.W. Titt, of Warminster in 1912. It was described as a 'Simplex' wind engine capable of lifting 10,000 gallons a day. It had fan blades 20′ diameter on a tower 60 feet tall, constructed in trellis work steel. When the wind blew it turned the fan which operated a bucket and piston type pump with a bore and stroke of 8″ x 12″. The blades had an automatic variable pitch so that, in a full gale they could be turned edgeways on to the wind thus stopping the fan, or closed fully to the wind so as to get as much 'push' as possible when the breeze was light. The Bicester engine lifted water from a depth of 120′ below the ground to the storage tank 50′ above the ground.

British Rail

Appendices

Seats

Plate 615
A platform seat at Taplow with timbers on cast iron legs in a 'tree branch' or 'rustic' pattern. The style goes back to the Victorian period when such seats were popular in gardens. It seems likely that this seat had rested passengers at Taplow platform since the station was rebuilt in 1884.

British Rail

Plate 616 (overleaf)
Beautifully made and finished seats for passengers dating from circa 1900. They were all made at Swindon, the product of the foundry and the carriage shops. The former made the iron bases, the latter the framework and upholstery.

Plate 616 (overleaf)

Top Platform seat with 'Edwardian' monogram and polished pinewood backrest. ▶

Middle Waiting room seat with hard wood frame varnished and figured to resemble oak. The upholstery is black American cloth stuffed with horse hair.

Bottom Waiting room seat *par excellence*! The upholstery may have been black or it could have been red or green. Rosette headed pins secure a binding strip in a different colour to the seat.

Plate 616

Lamps and Lamp-posts

Any improvements in lighting were always hailed as a great step forward in the Company's staff magazine. Of course, anything new that the Great Western Railway did was considered a great achievement in that publication, in the same way that "Rail News" boosts the progress of "British Rail". However, it is possible to discern special enthusiasm in connection with the installation of better lighting. At the turn of the century the Great Western Railway had four types of illumination on its premises, paraffin wick burners, gas, incandescent electric lamp and electric arc. The latter were in use at Paddington in 1900 and maybe at some other large stations. The incandescent bulb was little used, gas and the ordinary paraffin wick burner being the most common forms of lighting. The latter was very often a handsome piece of furniture but always a poor light. Many signal boxes today retain one of these for use when the mains electricity is switched off and as a signalman I can vouch for their inefficiency. Platforms were "illuminated" with a paraffin wick where gas was not available. In 1905, at a Debating Society meeting at Paddington, the general opinion was that gas was cheaper and brighter than electricity and Churchward, summing up the discussion as Chairman of the meeting, said that one day coaches might be fitted with electric light but that "at the moment the cost of conversion from gas would be too high and would result in no better a light than that already given by gas now that the new Argand burners have been installed". The opposition pointed out that gas light burned up oxygen in offices making them stuffy and that an electric lamp could be placed on each desk which could not be done with gas. Electricity was easier to install, needing simple wires rather than carefully laid and jointed piping and could be switched on at the touch of a button. The gas people replied that for desk work there was already a gas lamp without a globe (clear glass globes reduce light output by 10%) with an intensity of 50 c.p. which could be turned on by pressing a button. In the yards and on platforms a low pressure, incandescent mantle system was employed, the burner encased in glass and varying in candle power according to location, but going up to the very powerful 240 candle power.

The Company produced its own gas at some large stations and works, like Swindon, as it produced its own electricity (Park Royal), but generally it took its supplies from the "town main" in a binding agreement over a number of years. The local gas company was very often kept going only by the revenue accruing from their railway contact. At some places, signal boxes were lit by gas, the pipes of which were so old and waterlogged (a feature of gas pipes) that the supply was very erratic but the Company, and later British Railways, were unable to instal electric light because the term of the contract with the gas company had not expired.

In the early 1920's another source of lighting, as effective as gas, came into railway use—the "Tilley lamp." These were paraffin pressure lamps. The fuel in a round tank was forced by air pressure (induced in the tank by a porter or signalman with a bicycle pump) through a tube which had previously been made very hot with the result that the fine jet of paraffin vaporised and burned as gas, making a mantle at the top of the pipe incandescent. This lamp was given its proving trials at Challow station and proved so successful that they spread rapidly over the system, becoming very much part of the scene. When one was delivered new to a station it was officially described as a "Tilley (Challow) Lamp". They proved particularly useful at outlying halts where a supply of electricity was not available for they gave a light equal to that of the average street gas lamp. At Black Dog Halt, on the Calne line, one was left burning from 4 pm. till 9 am. A porter from Calne lit this lamp, filling its tank from a full one pint container which was all that was needed for the 17 hours. There were two sorts of "Tilley", all had round tanks, but some had a disc type shade and others had an inverted trough extending from each side of the burner globe. To this day these reliable lamps are in use all over the Western Region.

Plate 617

Official drawing. *Inset*. A lamp on the cattle pens at Reading.

British Rail

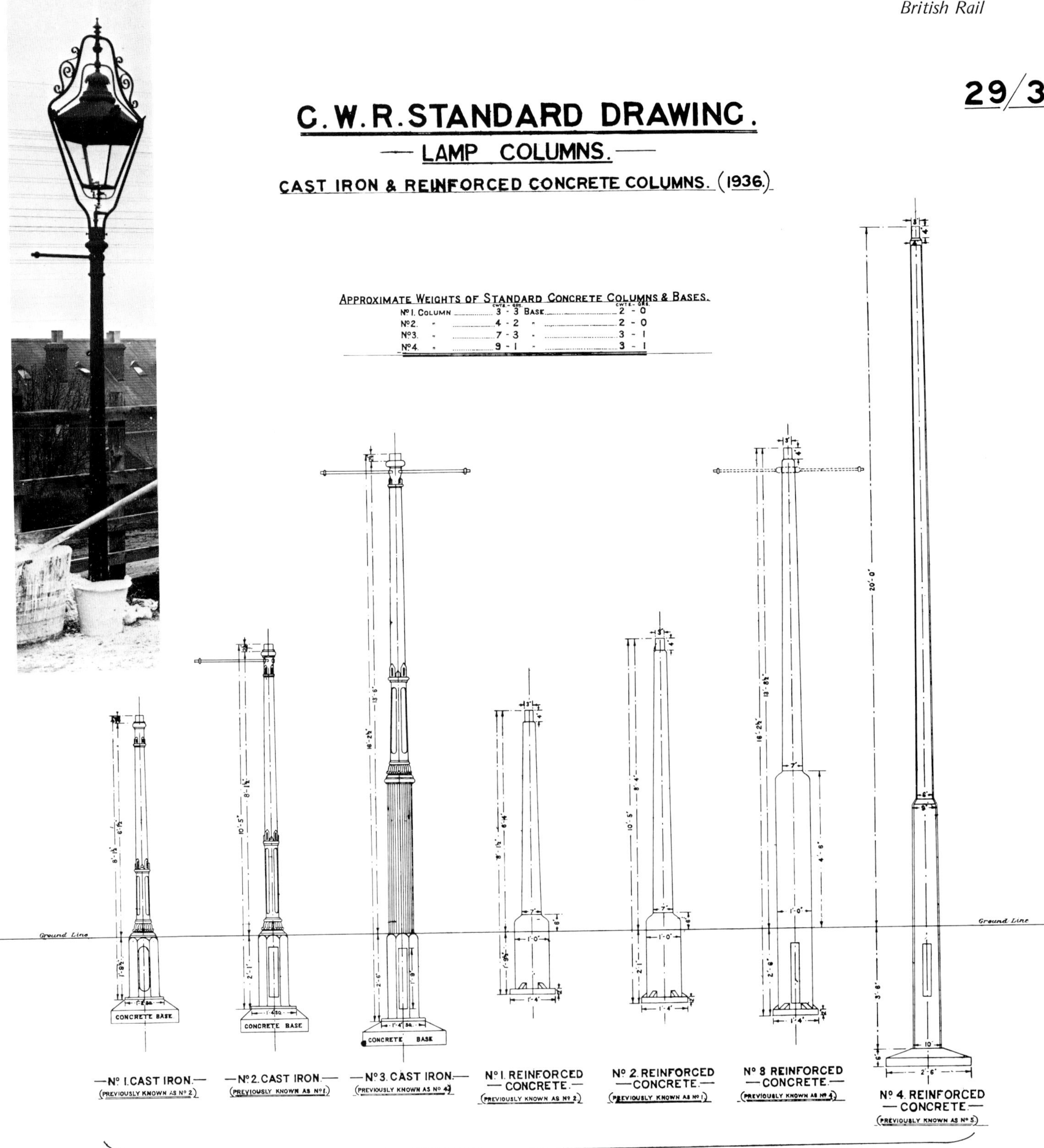

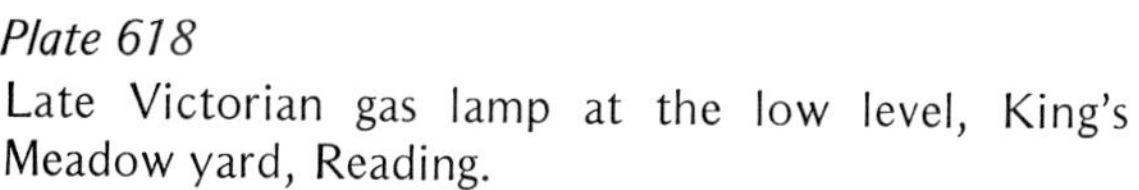

Plate 618
Late Victorian gas lamp at the low level, King's Meadow yard, Reading.

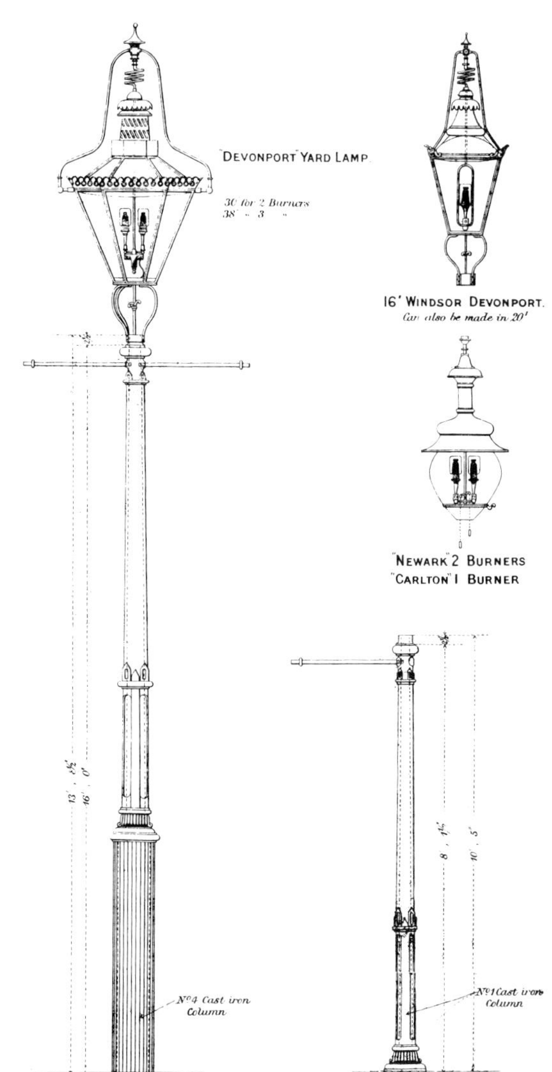

Plate 619
Official drawings.
British Rail

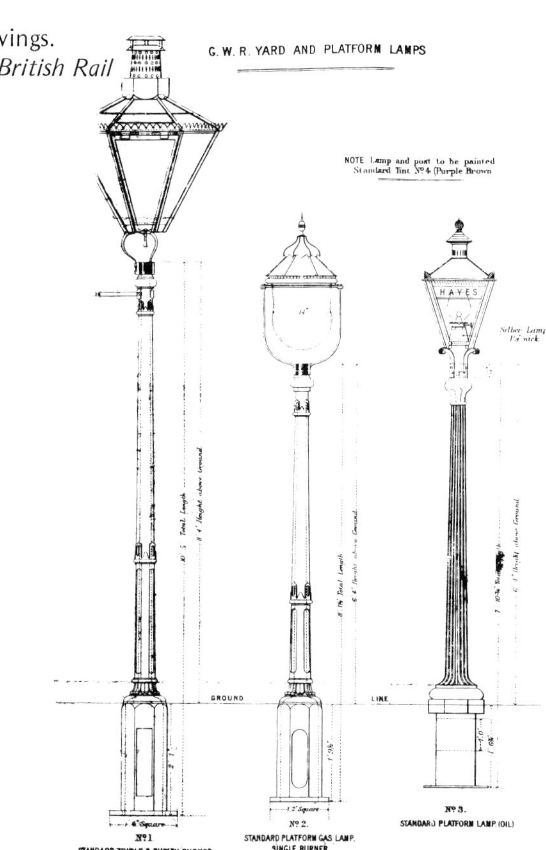

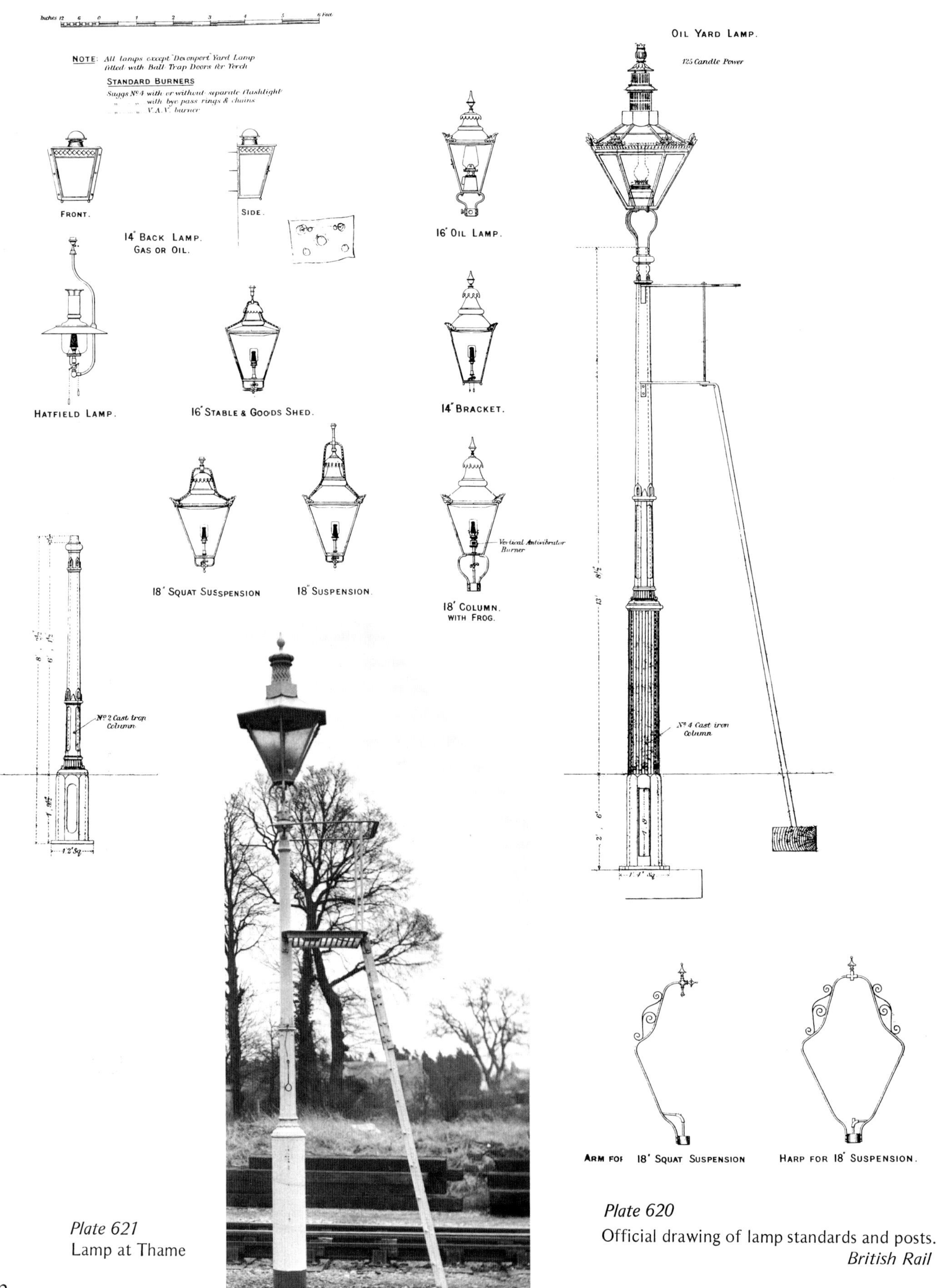

Plate 621
Lamp at Thame

Plate 620
Official drawing of lamp standards and posts.
British Rail

Plate 622
A 'full harp' at Castle Cary.
Author 1973

Plate 624
Gas lamp suspended from a 'half harp' at Castle Cary.
Author 1973

Plate 623
Details of lamp standard, Castle Cary.
Author 1973

Plate 625
At Windsor this once handsome pedestal now stands rusting and dejected on top of a grubby wall, its elegant lantern a memory and holding now only a mundane, enamelled shade for an electric lamp which has been 'vandalised'.

Notices

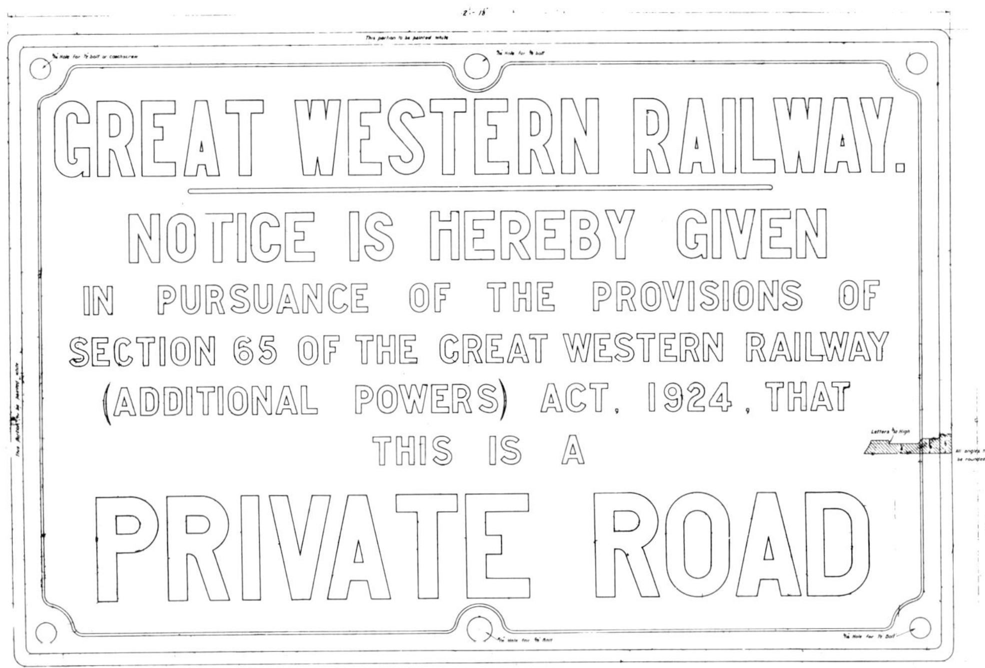

Plate 626

Until 1924, the Great Western Railway had to carry out an annual perambulation of all its roads that were non dedicated to the public in order to maintain the Company's Right of Way. Obviously this was an expensive business taking men away from their normal duties to man road blocks and inform all those passing through that this was a private road. In 1924 an Act of Parliament was passed relieving the railway companies of this obligation, it then being only necessary to exhibit the cast iron sign to preserve the Company's Right of Way over a road or lane. This is an official drawing. Note the section of the plate hatched in on the right.

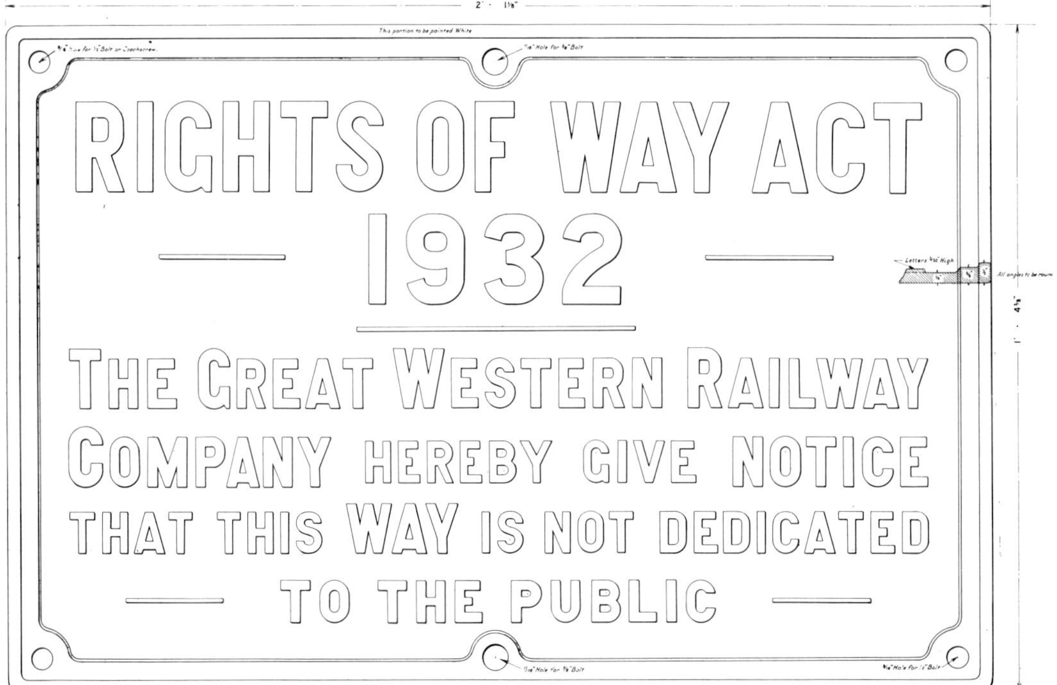

Plate 627

G. W. R. NOTICE PLATE—RIGHTS OF WAY ACT 1932.

NOTE: PLATE TO BE PAINTED BLACK WITH LETTERS AND OUTSIDE BEAD PICKED OUT IN WHITE.

Plate 628 Bi-lingual "No Trespassing" sign.
Author 1976

Plate 629
Note how the words 'Great' and 'Railway' have been painted out on this notice at Bath station.
Author 1972

Plate 630
'Sound whistle' plate for a farm crossing or footpath ahead. Hawkeridge, Westbury.

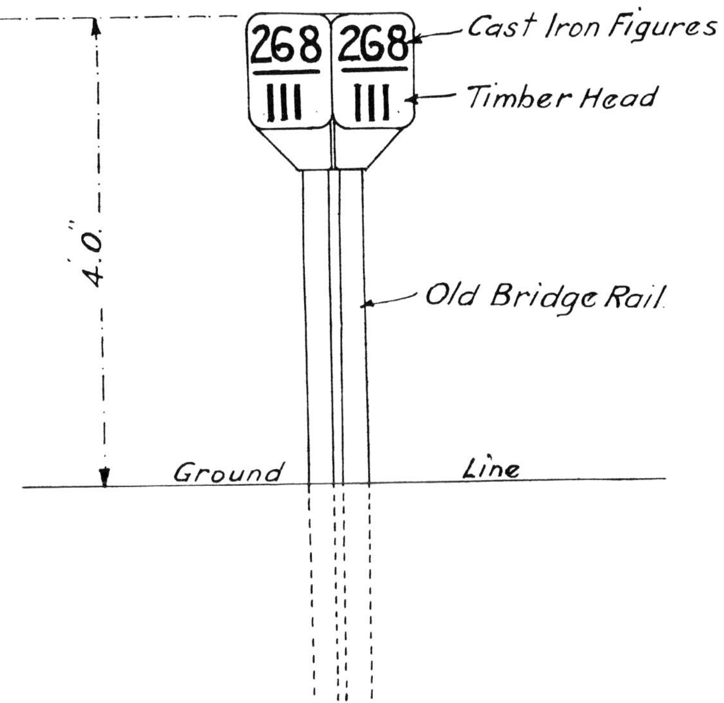

Plate 631
An official drawing of a mile post '268¾'. I have to thank my friend John Morris for driving to Pembrokeshire from Westbury to capture the matching photograph. 1974.

Plate 632
This is usually seen bolted to a sign as shown in *plate 628*. Note the hatched portion indicating the cross section.
British Rail

Plate 633
At Dulverton a hang board of G.W.R. origin.
Author 1957

(a)

(b)

(f)

(d)

(c)

(e)

(g)

(h)

(i)

(j)

Plate 634 Selection of signs.

(a) Hungerford 1950	*W.L. Kenning*
(b) Cholsey and Moulsford	*Author 1973*
(c) Appleford, Thames Bridge	*Author 1973*
(d) Badminton	*Author 1973*
(e) Box	*Author 1973*
(f) Bradford-on-Avon	*Author 1973*
(g) Pangbourne	*Author 1973*
(h) Frome	*Author 1973*
(i) Bradford-on-Avon	*Author 1973*
(j) Newbury	*Author 1973*

Plate 635
Signal box door sign at Hinksey South Box.
D. Chipcase 1973

Plate 636
Helpful wooden signs with iron letters and pointing hands, mounted on pieces of old rail at Frome.
Author 1973

Lineside Huts

Plate 637
These useful buildings were for the use of members of the Permanent Way department, to shelter from the weather, eat their meals, store their tools and congregate prior to moving off to some all night maintenance job at week-ends. This plate shows a hut made of Bath stone at the west end of Box tunnel.

Author 1973

Plate 638
What one might term the 'typical' hut for platelayers. It is built of old sleepers, the gaps between them being covered with strips of wood and made draught-proof from the inside by the simple expedient of stuffing old newspapers in the cracks. The roof is made of planks covered with roofing felt. The only brick work is the chimney stack. This hut was at Aynho.

Author 1974

Plate 639
An ambitious hut peculiar to its district. This is a well made, timber framed building with gables and rafters. The walls are made with the local stone, probably obtained from the sides of the cutting. With a good chimney and stove it makes a cosy shelter for meal breaks. Clink Road Junction.

Author 1974

Plate 640
A 'typical' lineside hut from the rear showing the chimney stack. Between the signal and the hut is the hand-turned grinding wheel for sharpening scythes and sickles. Bradford Junction 1974.
Author 1974

Plate 641 (*Top*)
An enlarged version of the 'typical' hut. The original building was at the far end, with the additional, 'clinker built' hut near the camera. Bradford-on-Avon.
Author 1974

Plate 642
The enlarged hut at Bradford-on-Avon from the original end.
Author 1974

Plate 643
View of Clink Road Junction's Permanent Way Department hut showing some details of roof construction.
Author 1974

G.W.R. STANDARD LAMP HUTS.

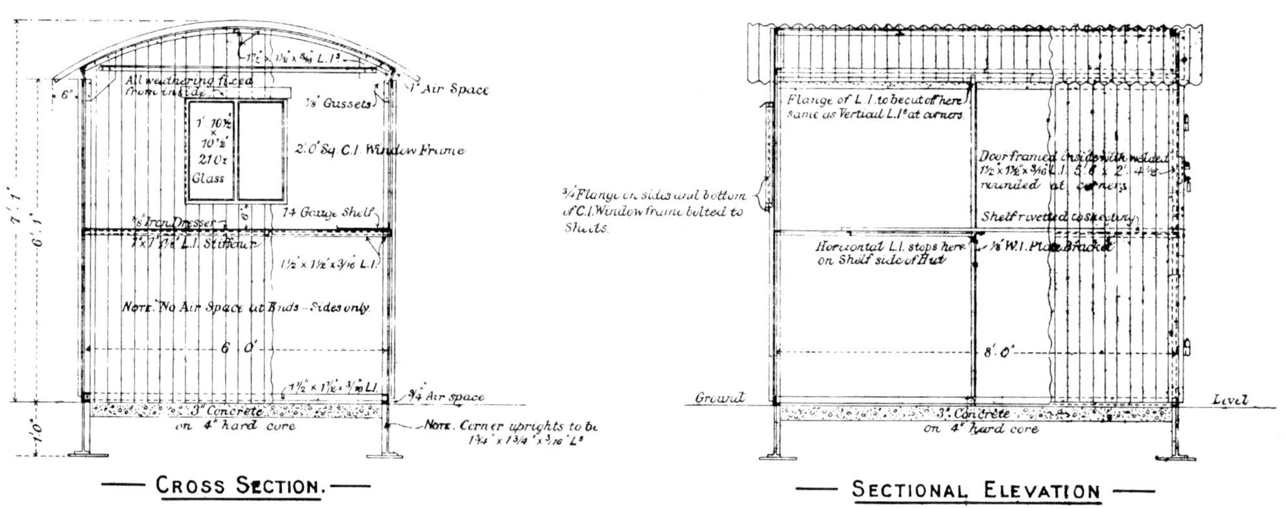

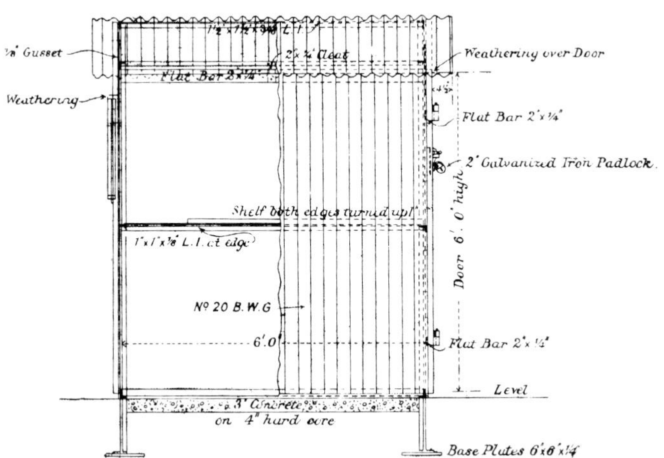

Plate 644
Official drawing and author's photographs of standard lamp hut and door latch.

G. W. R. STANDARD. CALVANIZED IRON, LOCK UP HUTS.

NOTE:—

1. Standard sizes of *Huts* are 14'·0" × 8'·0" and 20'·0" × 8'·0" the scantlings being the same in each case.
2. All the metal to be steel of British manufacture from material of British origin so far as is reasonably practicable, and of the quality known as B.S.S. "A" Steel.
3. The corrugated sheets to be coated with Zinc of such thickness that the flat sheet is increased in weight by ·15 lb. per sq. foot. The laps of the sheeting to be secured by ⅜" dia. rivets. The sheeting to be secured to framing by 5/16 dia. galvanized bolts. Rivets and bolts to sheeting to have all necessary washers and grummel washers. The framing to be secured by ⅜" dia. rivets.
4. All the framework to have one coat of Red lead oxide paint before leaving the makers works.
5. All fittings such as Locks, Bolts, Hinges &c. to be galvanized.
6. Special instructions will be given in the case of each Hut as to the number and position of Doors and Windows.

STANDARD DRAWING No 19/28

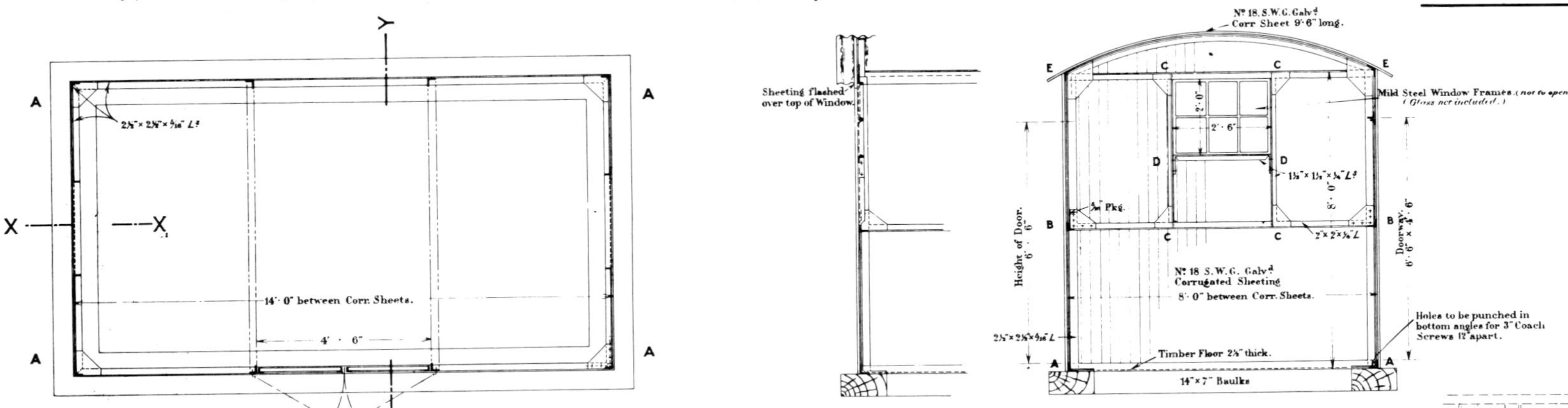

2½" × 2½" × 5/16" L^s

14'·0" between Corr. Sheets.

4'·6"

PLAN.

Sheeting flashed over top of Window.

SECTION X-X.

No 18. S.W.G. Galvd Corr. Sheet 9'·6" long.

Mild Steel Window Frames (not to open) (Glass not included.)

2'·0"

2'·6"

1½" × 1½" × ¼" L^s

¼" Pkg.

2" × 2" × ¼" L

Height of Door. 6'·6"

Doorway. 6'·6" × 4'·6"

No 18. S.W.G. Galvd Corrugated Sheeting 8'·0" between Corr. Sheets.

2½" × 2½" × 5/16" L

Holes to be punched in bottom angles for 3" Coach Screws 1'·apart.

Timber Floor 2½" thick.

14" × 7" Baulks

SECTION Y-Y.

SCALE:— ½ AN INCH TO A FOOT.

SCALE:— ONE INCH TO A FOOT.

Plate 645
Official drawing.

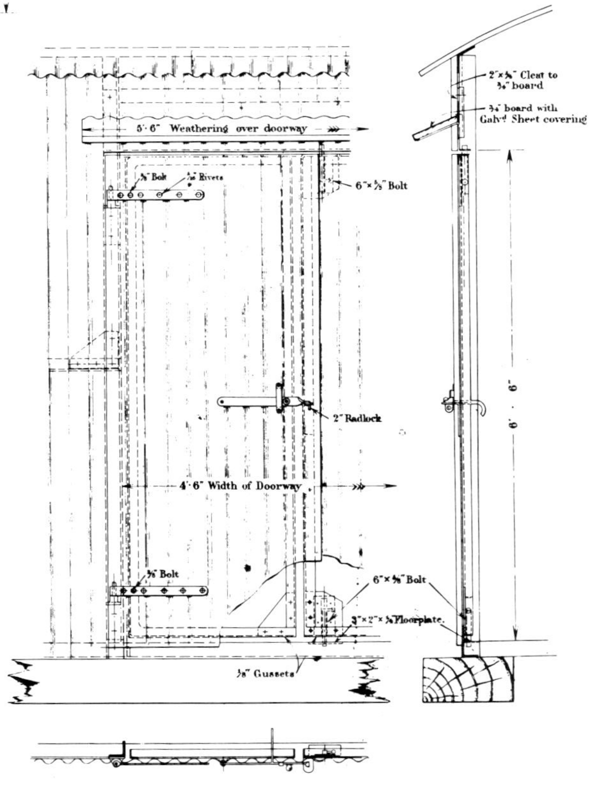

1½" × ¼" Flat bar

¼" × ¾" Keep

hole for 2" Padlock

1½" × ¼" Staple

⅝" dia.

6"

3"

1'·0"

Flat bar twisted & bent to suit.

DOOR LATCH.

½" dia.

1½" × ¼"

⅜" Bolt

1½" × ¼" Bar

⅜" Rivets

DOOR HINGE.

SCALE:— 3 INCHES TO A FOOT.

5'·6" Weathering over doorway

⅜" Bolt

⅜" Rivets

6" × ½" Bolt

2" Padlock

4'·6" Width of Doorway

6'·6"

6" × ⅜" Bolt

3" × 2" × ⅜" Floorplate.

⅜" Gussets

2" × ¾" Cleat to ¾" board

¾" board with Galvd Sheet covering

DOORS

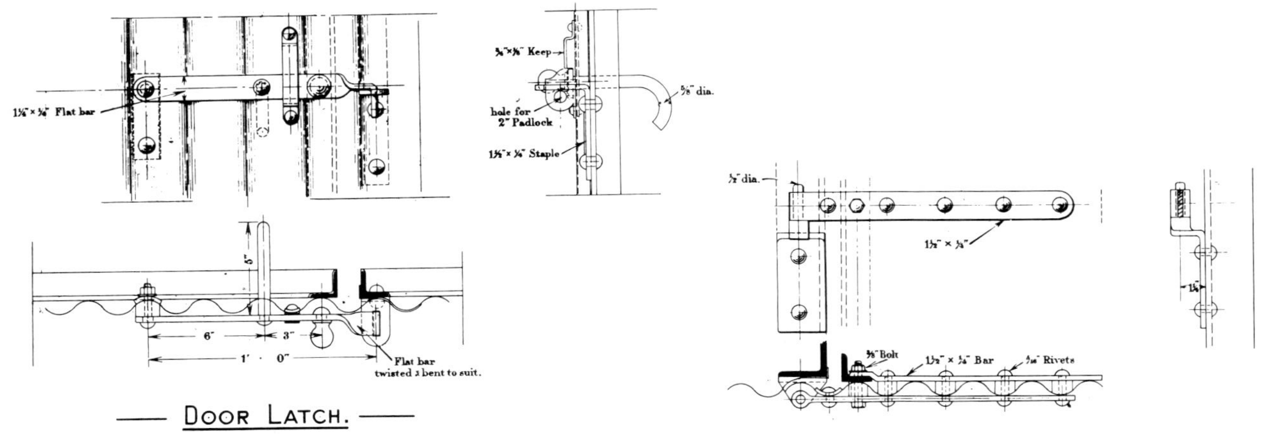

Plate 646

Extra large 'pagoda' shelter at Kelmscott and Langford station on the Fairford branch. Next to the 'pagoda' is an iron shed with sliding doors for storing bicycles.

Colin Judge

Plate 647

Just beyond the station buildings is yet another variation on the corrugated iron theme. It has swing doors and could be a store for station domestic materials.

British Rail

Station Nameboards

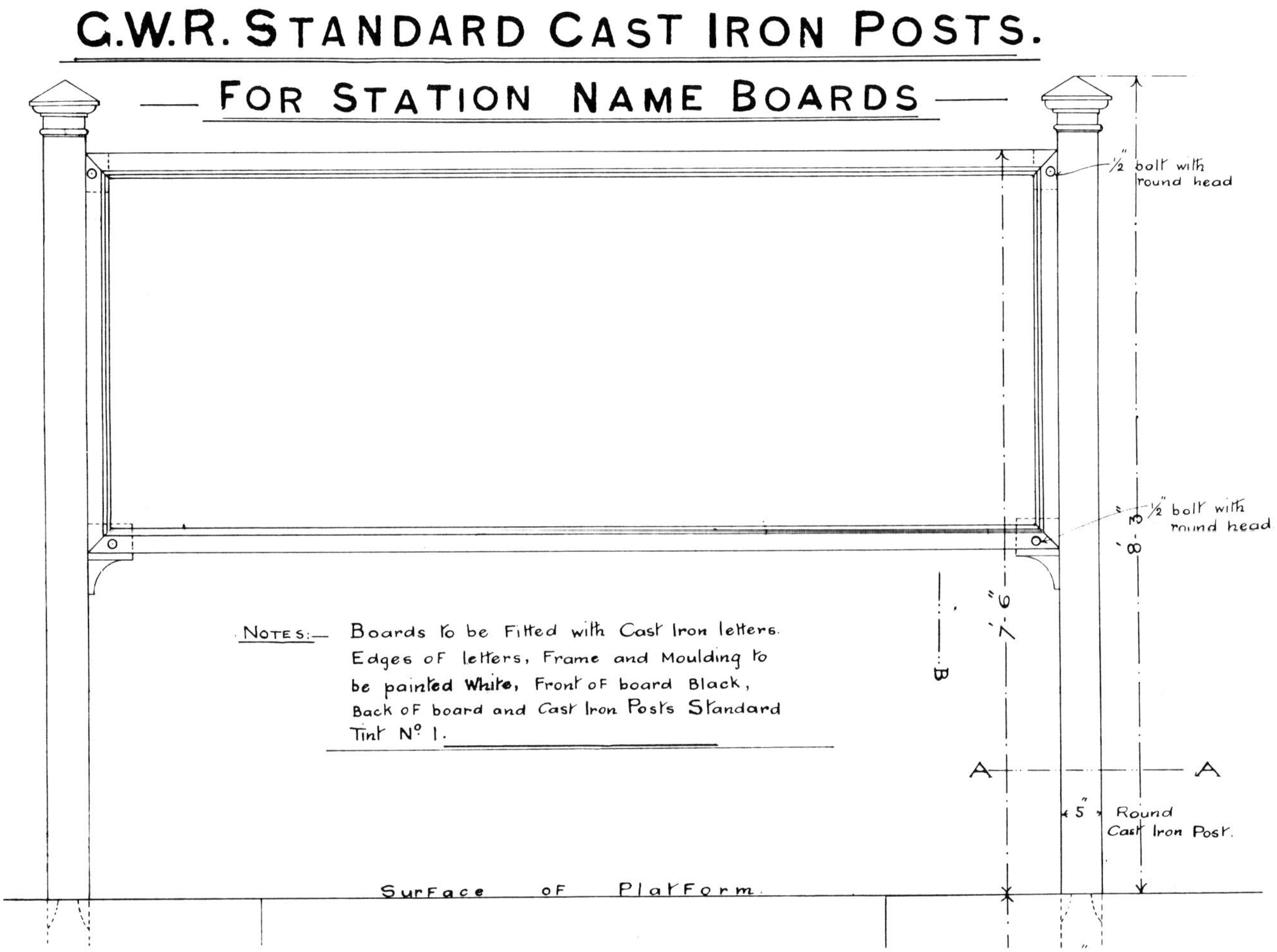

G.W.R. STANDARD CAST IRON POSTS.
FOR STATION NAME BOARDS
½" bolt with round head
½" bolt with round head
8'
7'-6"
B
NOTES:— Boards to be Fitted with Cast Iron letters. Edges of letters, Frame and Moulding to be painted White, Front of board Black, Back of board and Cast Iron Posts Standard Tint No 1.
A
A
5"
Round Cast Iron Post.
Surface of Platform.

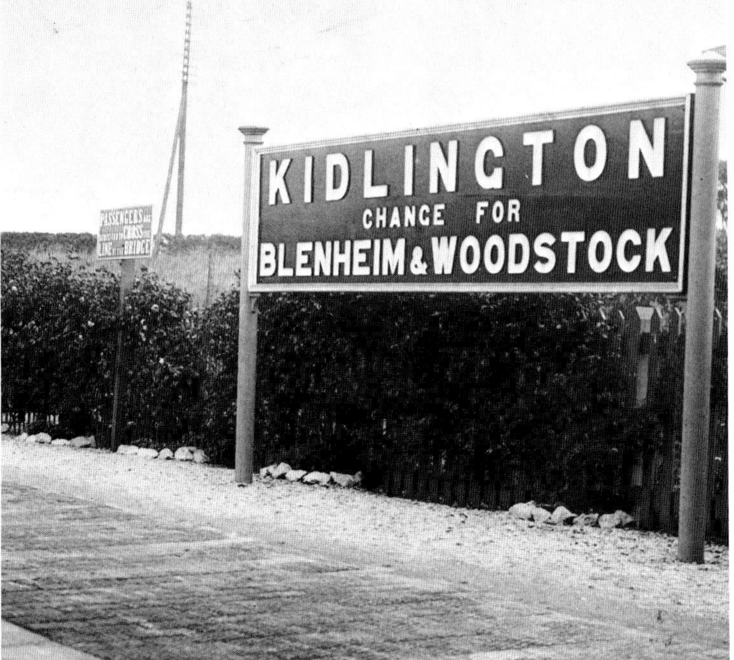

Plate 648a

This official drawing tells all there is to know – except the date. On the left is a fine example of this style of board in 'real life'.

KIDLINGTON
CHANGE FOR
BLENHEIM & WOODSTOCK

Colin Judge

APPLEFORD HALT

Plate 648b

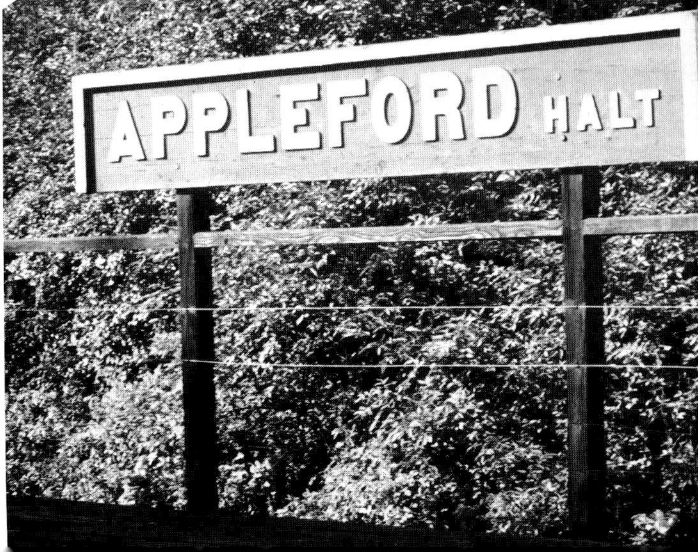

Plate 649
A variety of signs in a variety of styles. Notice the two methods of supporting the 'Taplow' nameboard, one with old rails and one with specially prepared wooden posts, probably the older method of the two.

Author 1974

Toilets

Plate 650
Cast iron sections bolt together to form this urinal screen built around 1887. Severn Tunnel Junction.
British Rail

Plate 651
Variation on the theme at Castle Cary. This is a smaller screen and has a nice cast pattern on the lower parts and lions' heads from the mouths of which rain water is supposed to issue forth through the guttering inside but which has long since blocked up.
Author 1973

Ornaments

Plate 652

This monogram is part of the railing type gates at the entrance to Windsor station.

Plate 653

Tablets on the wall of the Royal waiting rooms at Windsor station. On the right the crown and cypher of Queen Victoria and on the left that of Edward VII.

Plate 654

Plates 654/655
Gate posts in cast iron, dated 1902 in the casting, at Badminton station.
Author 1974

Plate 655

Plate 656
A fence post at the edge of the cattle pens, Castle Cary. The post is cast iron, square, with sunken panels and a ball top. Note how easy it is to remove the fence posts when a wagon needs loading or unloading.
Author 1973

Plate 657
A 'Brunelian' urn on a fine plinth on top of the retaining wall at Bradford-on-Avon.
Author 1974

Plate 658
The Royal Coat of Arms of Queen Victoria, carried on the engine or tender of the locomotive hauling the Royal Train. The Lion, Unicorn, shield and scroll work are so finely made that it is possible to pass a hand around their legs and bodies. The piece is made in brass and, I am reliably and emphatically assured, *is cast in one piece!* One would naturally assume that each beautiful component was cast separately and fixed onto the tableau later, but this is not the case. A foundryman at Swindon told me that in the factory today they cannot imagine how a sand mould could have been made to produce this masterpiece and he was quite sure that the work could never be repeated. The Coat of Arms hang in the lobby of the main entrance of the works of British Rail, Engineering Ltd., and I took this photograph by kind permission of the Works Manager, Mr. Roberts.
Author 1974

Show Stands

Plate 659

The Great Western Railway management understood the value of advertising and kept their line constantly in the public eye by this means. At the turn of the century to advertise could be seen as a vulgarity, hence those brief legends which appeared on stations for other products besides railway services; 'Pears Soap', 'Sutton's Seeds', 'Tangye Pumps'. Anything more, like . . . 'is the best you can buy' would have been not in the best taste so the more particular firms restrained themselves and hoped that their product and word-of-mouth recommendations would do the rest. The Great Western Railway posters were very beautifully designed and printed thus counteracting any accusations of bad taste that they might otherwise have suffered. These posters, showing elegant ladies leaning nonchalantly on trees or boulders looking pensively into the setting sun over some far western bay, or up to the blue mountain distance of Merionethshire remoteness are now sought-after collectors' items, gems of the Art Nouveau, yet in their day these were only advertising a day trip to Killarney or the pleasures of the Cornish Coast. Many books were issued by the Company to advertise the many interesting places served by the line. Perhaps the best of these were the trio, 'Abbeys', 'Cathedrals' and 'Castles'. These were expertly written and beautifully illustrated by the Staff Photographer. They were not mere pamphlets either but in hard covers, 100 to 150 pages of concentrated information by M.R. James, Litt.D., F.S.A.,F.B.A., Provost of Eton, and famous antiquarian. 'Castles' was by C. Oman, K.B.A., M.A., M.P. In the 20th century the Great Western Railway presented a very stylish face to the public, a great and dignified institution, so that when it became necessary to build a travelling booking and enquiry office for use at agricultural shows—the Great Western did a lot to encourage these—any such office had to be beautifully designed and constructed but suited to the holiday atmosphere of the event it was attending. This plate shows the tent-like octagon which was constructed as an enquiry/booking office in 1912. Its panels were painted in crimson lake with the Company's garter crest and bearers on alternate panels, and the roof, or spire, was white. Inside, the 20 square feet of space was presided over by a uniformed attendant who sold tickets, arranged for cattle trucks to be ready at the nearest station to remove purchases of livestock from the show, and generally made himself as useful as possible to the public, even perhaps going round the showground canvassing for traffic. This photograph was taken at the Bath and West show in 1915 and, as far as is known, the kiosk was last used at the Royal National Eisteddfod at Pontypool in 1924.

British Rail

Plate 660
Details of this stand are, unfortunately lacking. It reminds me of a double bed, or a four poster, but there is nothing sleepy about the attendant who is fixing a passer-by with his eagle eye as he advances upon him, leaflets at the ready.

British Rail

Plate 661

In most large towns the Great Western Railway had what it called 'Receiving Offices' where one could leave parcels and buy tickets. Often these were simply shops rented by the Company, there was one in the High Street in Oxford before 1939, but sometimes a special office was built by the Company. This cheerful little office was close to the Locking Road, Weston-super-Mare station.

British Rail

Plate 662

A specially built Receiving Office at James Street in Liverpool. The photograph was taken as the 'after' shot of a 'before and after' sequence. About the year 1910 the old 'R.O.' on this site was given a new front, all the original doors, windows and archways being retained and simply smartened up with this ornate brickwork. The fancy parapet with the aggressive emblazoning of the Company's Arms was new.

British Rail

DISTRICT OFFICES
GREAT WESTERN RAILWAY
MODERN
PASSENGERS OFFICE
PARCELS OFFICE
BAGGAGE INSURANCE
GREAT WESTERN
PASSENGERS
ENQUIRY OFFICE
GREAT WESTERN RAILWAY
PARCELS OFFICE
THE GREGG SCHOOL LTD
MODERN BUSINESS TRAINING
CHARLES BIRCHALL LIMITED PRINTERS ADVERTISING CONTRACTORS ETC.
The Journal of Commerce

Hostels

Plate 663

During the 1939-45 War locomotive men and other staff had to spend long periods away from home and it became very difficult for them to find lodgings for a night or day at locations unknown to them. It was not unknown for a man to leave home in the morning expecting to be home again by nightfall and not return home for three days, during which time he might have travelled from one end of the Great Western Railway to the other, and even onto other Companies' lines. So hostels for the men were built. The one in this plate at Didcot was a good one, specially built for the housing of men who needed a meal, bath and sleep. It was staffed continuously by cooks and others and enabled men to work through to destinations they would otherwise not have reached because they knew that they could get food and rest at journey's end.

British Rail

Plate 664

This is probably more typical of the sort of building which springs to mind if you were to say 'Wartime hostels' to long serving engine drivers. The old station at Newbury Racecourse was taken over and converted to accommodate enginemen's sleeping cubicles, rest rooms and canteens.

British Rail

Index

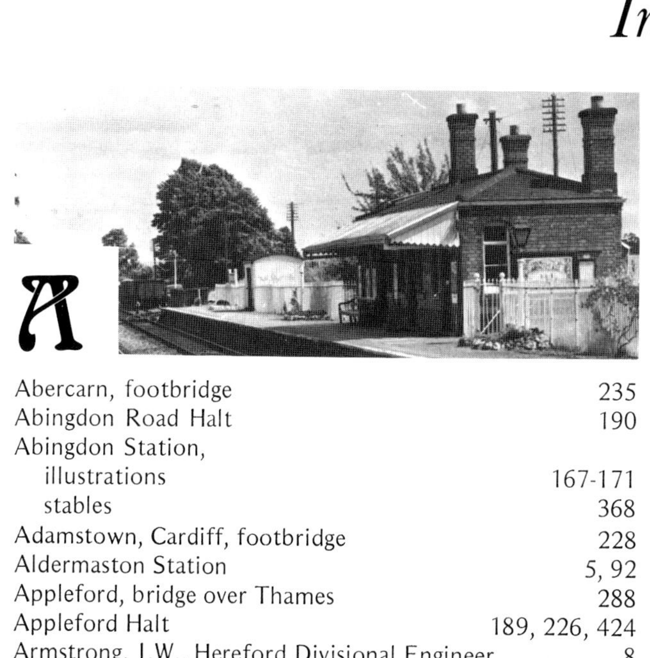

A

B

C

D

E

F

G

M

N

O

P

WAY OUT